CW01433567

WHAT MATTERS?

A COLUMBIA/SSRC BOOK

WHAT MATTERS?

Ethnographies of Value in a

Not So Secular Age

EDITED BY

COURTNEY BENDER

AND ANN TAVES

COLUMBIA UNIVERSITY PRESS   NEW YORK

COLUMBIA UNIVERSITY PRESS

Publishers Since 1893

New York   Chichester, West Sussex

Copyright © 2012 Columbia University Press

All rights reserved

Library of Congress Cataloging-in-Publication Data

What matters? ethnographies of value in a not so secular age /
edited by Courtney Bender and Ann Taves.

p. cm.

"A Columbia/SSRC book."

Includes bibliographical references and index.

ISBN 978-0-231-15684-4 (cloth: alk. paper) —
ISBN 978-0-231-15685-1 (pbk.: alk. paper)

1. Conduct of life. 2. Ethics. 3. Values. 4. Meaning (Philosophy).
5. Religion. I. Bender, Courtney. II. Taves, Ann, 1952–

BJ1531.W44   2012

204'.4—dc23   2011035955

∞

Columbia University Press books are printed on permanent
and durable acid-free paper.

Printed in the United States of America

c 10 9 8 7 6 5 4 3 2 1
p 10 9 8 7 6 5 4 3 2 1

References to Internet Web sites (URLs) were accurate at the
time of writing. Neither the author nor Columbia University Press
is responsible for URLs that may have expired or changed since the
manuscript was prepared.

CONTENTS

WHAT MATTERS?

INTRODUCTION

Things of Value

ANN TAVES AND COURTNEY BENDER

What does it mean to pursue, inhabit, or lead a valuable, ethical life in a secular age? This question has gained renewed attention, and importance, as scholars in the last decade have challenged the way that we think about *secularity* and what some have termed our secular age. Long gone are the days when social scientists regarded religion as an anachronism, fading into our collective past or remaining on the margins of culture as a side-show curiosity. Gone, too, are the days when scholars linked the language of spirits, haunting, and the spectral to investigations of the premodern and primitive: more and more frequently, enchanted language and ideas come alive in studies of modernity. The wholesale rethinking of *what the secular means* and how rethinking this category reframes our understanding of religion has been the driving engine of numerous recent investigations. At this point, however, we cannot help but notice that rethinking what the secular means opens up new ways of approaching the question, *what does it mean to be secular*? How do people in our secular (or not so secular) age decide what matters, what goals to pursue, and what things are of most value? When does the question of what matters come to be a question at all, and for whom?

This volume begins with two observations that orient its approach to these questions. First, we observe that processes of valuation and the making of meaning take place across a wide spectrum of settings, events, and organizations that could be considered religious, secular, or even spiritual. Second, we also observe that for many modern people the processes of experiencing things of value take shape in tandem with identifying their various projects and pursuits *as* secular, religious, or spiritual (or some combination thereof). Our first observation has led us to place an intentionally wide range of empirical studies into conversation with each other. Read individually, each essay presents a focused example of ways that modern people actively engage in something that matters to them, while drawing on (or confronting) a set of secular, religious, and spiritual frames to represent what they are doing. In considering disparate examples, such as transnational psytrance communities, Indian volunteer organizations, and American homeschooling settings, we find that that how people categorize their activity—whether as secular, religious, spiritual, or some variation thereof—is central to processes of valuation and meaning making. The question of what is religious, what is secular, and what is spiritual is not simply a matter for scholars. Although scholarly and "lay" engagements with these issues are not equivalent, we nonetheless find that paying close attention to processes of valuation adds a layer of analytical complexity to our understanding of modern life and heightens awareness of our own role as scholars in creating value.

Reading the chapters in this volume together highlights the extent to which modern processes of valuation take shape in tandem with practical and everyday actions that identify various institutions, ideas, or experiences as religious, secular, or spiritual. These determinations can take shape in various ways, but the chapters in this volume pay particular attention to the degree to which people reflexively consider the value of their activities and those of others. Thus, for example, we see that homeschooling parents seek to pursue or protect their children's "authentic childhoods" with secular and spiritual language, even though they note that their desire for their children's personal authenticity is a concept that also resonates within the neoliberal politics that homeschooling practices criticize. The language that parents use to work through these issues can be compared with that of volunteers in an Indian orphanage who value "experiences" of being present with children (in ways that echo earlier religious formulations) regardless of whether their actions successfully effect social change. When read together in this way, the chapters in *What Matters?* compel readers to consider the resonances between widely dispersed projects of valuation and appreciate the way people in practice complicate a simple "secular-religious" frame.

This introductory essay locates our focus on processes of valuation in relation to wider discussions of secularity, the secular-religious binary, and lived religion. We begin with a brief review of recent developments in the study of secularism, paying particular attention to the understanding of the secular and religious as co-constituted historical formations. Considering secularism and religion in this way provides scholars and laypeople alike with a different and arguably more empirically grounded view of the shape of religion. Yet as we also observe, the secular-religious binary has its limits. These limits are particularly evident if we consider how, in many secular spaces, terms and concepts (and experiences) people consider "spiritual" interact with and inflect either "religion" or "secularity." As we argue, thinking about "spirituality" and "spirits" both breaks up the limitations of the binary and puts renewed emphasis on the ways that these terms work dynamically as part of processes of valuation. Our interest is not in "the spiritual" or "spirits" per se, but in the way these and other related terms are at work in the world. We seek to understand the dynamic processes that connect or differentiate their uses and the powers each of these terms take on or dispense in the multiple settings where people in the modern world encounter or employ them. In order to map out this territory we suggest a methodological approach to processes of valuation that is attentive to the articulation of meaning within networks of social relationships. We conclude with a discussion of key terms—*spirituality, spirits, experience, authenticity,* and *authority*—to guide the reader through this volume and, perhaps toward future study.

FROM SECULARIZATION TO SECULARISM: THE SECULAR-RELIGION BINARY AND THE CHALLENGE OF SPIRITUALITY

The turn to secularism from secularization represents an important transformation in the ways that scholars understand religion in modern life. *Secularization,* in classical versions, narrates the decline of religious authority over all aspects of social life and its withdrawal into the space of private belief and private life.[1] Secularization denotes the consequences of intellectual developments such as the experimental scientific method and modern reason (the Enlightenment) and identifies social, political, and economic developments such as growing industrialization and urbanization as the engines of these changes. In these theories the rise of reason, science, and industrial society leads to religion's retreat. Secular society is what flourishes in the wake of this ceded territory. This robust narrative held sway in both the United States and Europe in the social sciences and in public understanding despite the fact that it did not fit the United States. Many sociologists noted the "problem" of American religious exceptionalism, but others in the discipline (and most outside it) continued to view the classical narrative as reflective of broad-scale social processes (Gorski and Altinordu 2009). In the late 1970s a number of world events (the public and powerful role of the Catholic Church in the Polish Solidarity movement, the political rise of the Moral Majority in the United States, and the Iranian revolution, among others) made clear that secularization theories provided little purchase on understanding religion in modern society, prompting scholarly rethinking of secularization *tout court*.

Key to this rethinking was a revived attention to the relational interactions between changing understandings of the religious and the secular, which invested new attention in the ways that particular actors and institutions framed these relations. Renewed attention to the historical and political dynamics in which such understandings took shape allowed scholars to observe that "secularism" was not merely an inert tabula rasa that emerged once the mystifications of religion were scrubbed away, but, rather, a formation in its own right that emerged and developed in response to, and in relation to, "the religious." Secularism, and secularity as well, did not emerge as religion retreated, but rather stands alongside it with projects, ideals, and goals of its own. As Talal Asad writes in his essays on the subject of "secular formations," the secular "is neither continuous with the religious that supposedly preceded it (that is, it is not the latest phase of a sacred origin) nor a simple break from it (that is, it is not the opposite, an essence that excludes the sacred)" (2003:25). It is instead an umbrella term that encompasses a range of formations that relate in various ways to diverse religious formations. Viewed in this way, we can identify multiple kinds of relations between religious and secular endeavors.

This is not the place to rehearse the full development of theories of secularism (which would be challenging given the number of disciplines now producing studies of "the secular"). Several elements of this turn are worth emphasizing, however, as they relate to our interests in this volume. First, this approach, which focuses on both religion and secularism as historical formations with content that takes shape in specific locations, draws scholarly attention to the question of how religion and secularism develop and interact rather than taking these interactions and their trajectories for granted. Secularism is viewed as an identifiable set of projects that takes place historically (and contemporarily) in relation to something called religion—a "something" that it has a large hand in defining and reframing "secularism." In other words, not only are these processes historically and empirically observable, but they also take shape in relation to different understandings of "religion" and its powers.

Second, by emphasizing that historically developing *secularism* has content that is shaped within empirically analyzable discourses, practices, and actions (such as changes in law, social interactions and arrangements, economic structures and demands) we can also consider in a more focused and relational way how concepts of religion have developed in tandem. We take both local and global processes and actors into account, and, insofar as global and national political and social movements are involved in shaping "religion" and "secularity" both in daily life and in scholarly discussion,[2] scholars can understand religion and secularity as dynamically related discursive and institutional processes.

Third, these calls for stronger analytical and empirical analyses of secularity in various contexts have taken shape in tandem with (and have often been informed by) theoretical frames that focus on practice. While much of the turn to "practice" in religious studies and in anthropology developed in ways that do not directly impinge upon discussions of the secular (Bourdieu 1990; Bell 1992), the turn to practice has directed scholarly attention to action, habit, discipline, and powers that arise in the context of embodied actions in a way that has been quite fruitful. For scholars of religion, emphasis on structures, habits, and disciplines encouraged studies investigating practices and institutions that shaped or reproduced both symbols and meaning.[3] In religious studies and sociology in particular, the turn to practice aligns the study of religion with other modes of cultural and social action.

These scholarly turns have had a profound effect on the questions asked by sociologists and scholars of religion while at the same time giving rise to new questions. To begin, we cannot help but notice that the studies of secularism and its related religious formations are frequently phrased in terms of a "secular-religious binary." This binary is conceptualized as a dynamic set of relations between religious and secular claims, interests, and concepts: they relate to each other in different ways, depending on the national, state, or transnational contexts observed. The focus on interactions (that are not assumed to be unidirectional) and of the powers shaping their forms, their historical development and change, all have much to recommend them. Yet this formation, as we have noted, has limits once we consider the relationship of spirituality (and spirits or the"the spiritual") to the binary.

At first blush, it would appear that spirituality and spirits would align unproblematically with the religious. Spirituality is after all a component of religion: we can speak of "spiritual traditions" within religious traditions and institutions; this has been the historical value and use of such terms. In this regard, spirituality is unambiguously a component of religion. Many who say that they are "spiritual not religious" within the United States and Europe, however, use spirituality to designate something that is not religious. Similarly, within a binary of religion-secular, scholars typically link "spirits" with a world of enchantment, distinct from the disenchanted space of the secular. Yet a closer look at the ways that people actually refer to spirits belies this easy distinction. Indeed, we observe that spirituality and spirits are often invoked as an aspect of secularity or are aligned with it. Insofar as people use these terms to describe experiences and denote positions and aspirations that are "more than" or "move beyond" either secularity or religion, it complicates a straightforward religious-secular binary. We offer a few examples to illustrate.

In some contexts spirituality denotes the underlying truths or *spirit* of religion. Popular literature directed to those people who are "spiritual not religious" describes the spiritual either as the truth of religion that is "beyond" the history of religious traditions (Bender 2010) or as the constant, ahistorical quality of human searching for the divine. Spirituality thus is a term that can be marshaled by atheists and secularists to mark their own pursuits and goals. Spirituality may, in other words, be compatible with secularism—and incompatible with religion. This is the argument made by many, including the critic of religion Sam Harris, who closes the *End of Faith* (2004)with a plea to his readers to develop their "spiritual intuitions." In Harris's view, spirituality *divorced* from religious fanaticism and irrationality is an important human pursuit. Spirituality is fully compatible with and indeed finds its ideal home within the secular.

Harris is not alone, nor is this view confined to the United States: the self-styled "faithful atheist" Andrew Comte-Sponville similarly notes, in *The Little Book of Atheist Spirituality* (2007), that people can do without religion and God, but they cannot do without spirituality. Harris, Comte-Sponville, and others, thus, rhetorically situate spirituality on the side of the secular, marshaling it against what they view as the fanaticism of religiosity. Spirituality, thus, is not a purely residual and ephemeral concept easily organized under the religious. It in fact is often used to critique religion. Historians of secularism and freethought will recognize this as a common refrain from the nineteenth century onward: nineteenth-century freethinkers argued for "pantheistic morality" and "spirituality," infusing their claims to universal reason and moral righteousness with language that would challenge the sectarianism and narrowness of religious morality.

What is spirituality doing in these secular places? We can ask this question not just of popular culture but also of scholarly work that invokes the spiritual in avowedly secular contexts. Thus, Charles Taylor (2007) invokes the "spiritual" (or "moral/spiritual") when he refers to various incommensurate projects of value and meaning that take place within what he calls the secular "immanent frame." William Connolly, another scholar committed to secular plurality (1999, 2005a), invokes the spiritual to discuss the "moods" and "dispositions" of various religious and nonreligious groups in ways that allow him to highlight the connections (or "resonances") between capitalist and evangelical "spiritual dispositions" and to raise questions about the emotional intensity of various "cultural" spiritualities (2005b). His invocation of the spiritual (unmarked or defined in any specific way) in his work on the evangelical capital "resonance machine" and on secularism provides another example of how spirituality is at work in scholarly discussions. In such contexts, it seems to mark relationships and dispositions for human action that lie outside of religious and secular formations. After linking spirituality to "disposition," Connolly, for example, counterposes it to things he considers "traditions." In so doing he precludes consideration of the kinds of traditions or trajectories in which spirituality develops.

We highlight this *use* of spirituality in scholarly work in order to note how, in such contexts, it is linked to religious-secular formations. In contrast to religion and secularism (both of which are frequently provided a history, a genealogy, or an indication of their historically changing uses and "politics"), spirituality typically receives little attention as a word with a history. Without a history or a tradition attached to it, it often enables scholars to gesture toward or indicate something that is "more than" or "underlying" the religious and secular. In this respect, the frequent invocation of spiritual and spirituality within both secular and religious contexts signals an interest in marking something as transcending the secular-religious binary. In this context, it is a discursive practice *that, in marking value, participates in its creation* and, at the same time, highlights the felt need of many—both scholars and nonscholars—to expand upon the secular-religious binary when seeking to designate what matters.

Of course, taking a longer view of the developments of religion within secularism (and secularism in relation to religion) over the last several centuries presents numerous examples of other "third terms" that took on new shape and power in relation to the secular-religious binary, often enabling actors to place themselves in enlivened (if not enchanted) relations with the social worlds they produced. Peter van der Veer notes, for example, how cosmopolitan imaginations in British Commonwealth countries were inflected by an "intricate interplay of rationalism and spirituality, universalism and nationalism, material science and spiritualism" that shaped the "engagement with the other in the colonial context" (van der Veer 2002; 2009). Moral and political reformers such as Swami Vivekananda and Annie Besant worked within these intricate contexts, transposing practices and traditions into religious or secular registers and reshaping others into "quasi-religion" or "nonreligion" or occult "magic" (Viswanathan 2008; Aravamudan 2006). As Pamela Klassen (2012) and Christopher White (2008) demonstrate, North American Protestant missionaries, healers, and scientists invested medical practices and modern technologies with divine forces and in so doing enchanted biomedical practices in ways they presumed were entirely consistent with the sciences in which they participated.

These processes are not confined to the past, of course. We can see, for example, that in *A Secular Age* Charles Taylor frequently invokes the term *spiritual* to evoke a variety of concepts surrounding things of value. For example, he notes that "the most important consequence of the shift to modern, secular life is the resituating of religion as one option among many, in other words, highlighting religious belief as a choice rather than something accepted or experienced: individuals experience religion as something external to their (bounded, "buffered") selves, which they can seek to incorporate or adopt if they wish." Secularity, as he puts it, "is a move from a society where belief in God is unchallenged . . . to one in which it is understood to be one option among others, and frequently not the easiest to embrace" (2007:3). Where Taylor suggests that, in earlier periods (and other places), *religion* was unreflexively absorbed and practiced, its authority taken for granted or presented in ways that make religious concepts and authorities the background frame on which life proceeds, modern Western *secularism* makes unreflexive religion impossible. As a consequence, people in the world confront a plural world of religious (and secular) possibilities, given that they are situated within a world where the background position (shaped in practices and institutions) makes religious choice possible and necessary. In short, secularity has transformed religion so that its practices and its beliefs take shape in a world where their unreflexive acceptance—as part of the field of social practices—is no longer possible. The same, presumably, can be said for secular forms of "belief." And it is at this juncture in his narrative, where belief in the traditional religious sense is no longer possible, that he invokes for the first time the "spiritual," and "spiritual life" and refers to the "spiritual/moral . . . condition" of life (2007:7–8, 11).

Investigating how scholars and philosophers employ the term *spiritual* thus presents opportunities to consider the shifts in concepts of meaning that take shape in relation to the dominant religion-secular binary frame. With this in mind, our interest in this volume is not to offer a better definition of spirituality or make a claim that it should be studied in some particular way. On the contrary, we do not view spirituality as having any more autonomy or value than religion or secularity; it has not, in our view, been "neglected" or "ignored." Rather, we are interested in how changing discourses around religion and secularity, and (increasingly) spirituality and other similar terms, create possibilities for marking, creating, and experiencing things of value, whether in our contemporary moment or in the past.

Our consideration of these issues has led us to focus our attention on the valuations that are made possible in and through these terms. Each of these terms and the discursive fields in which they resonate provide to their various users a sense of possibility and power, as well as limits, which are derived in part through their relations or comparisons with other terms. The chapters in this volume carefully consider how people (secular, religious, and otherwise) live within and through worlds they consider religious or secular and identify and/or create things of value in the process. In focusing on these processes, our aim is not to define or reinforce any particular set of relations between these forms but rather to observe what happens to processes of valuation in the context of historically developing secularisms. How do the historically contingent formulations of the religious and secular inform people's efforts to identify or create things of value, as well as their abilities to apprehend, experience, or create such things?

THINGS OF VALUE: PROCESSES AND RELATIONS

In different ways spirituality, religion, and secular become markers of value, as much or more so than they are containers of distinct kinds of actions or ideas. Positively, these terms may mark things, ideas, and practices as self-evidently meaningful or link them with "higher," more expansive aims. Negatively, as in the case of superstition, they mark something as over-valued or wrongly linked to higher aims. In this volume, anthropologists, religious studies scholars, sociologists, and historians explore the ways in which these terms are at work in a variety of settings, including international humanitarianism, psytrance festivals, the history of psychology and archaeology. Taken together, they provide a variety of sites and perspectives from which to consider what these terms make possible within the dynamics of modern secularity, while at the same time exposing the limits of current discussions that focus only on the religious-secular binary.

To advance our understanding of how people employ these markers to identify and/or create things of value, we suggest a focus on processes of valuation in the context of events and interactions (Taves 2011). By value, we simply mean the claims that people make regarding the importance of something (anything), regardless of whether the importance carries a positive or negative valence. Various academic disciplines, including ethics, law, linguistics, and economics, define and measure value in different ways. Anthropological theories of value understand the concept of value as a social-cultural construct closely tied to processes of meaning making (Graeber 2001; Werner and Bell 2003). In referring to "ethnographies of value," we signal our interest in the ways that people in various contexts *decide* (or *experience* or *identify*) what is of value as well as the processes that allow them (and us) to assign or apprehend such things. In considering value as ethnographically relevant, we thus focus on the processes through which people mark things as special or singular both through discourse and behaviors (Kopytoff 1986).

A focus on things people value highly enough to set them apart as special casts a wide net that captures most of what scholars have designated by terms such as *religious, spiritual, sacred, magical, superstitious,* and so on (Taves 2009). In contrast to a project such as Peter Van Ness's analysis of "secular spiritualities," which is premised on a scholarly definition of "spiritual significance" as "activities that bear *the special meaning* of relating their practitioners to the world as a cosmic whole and thereby transforming them in the direction of enhanced vitality" (Van Ness 1996:5; emphasis added), we are interested in the way that *subjects* identify things of value. By identifying that which interests us simply as things to which people grant special meaning, we are free to examine the ways people locate the things they most value in relation to various formations of the secular and religious as well as other "third terms," such as spirituality, that flourish in this web of meaning and practices.

We approach and query how things—actions, objects, experiences, institutions, rituals, and the like—acquire meaning in events and inter-actions. An understanding of processes of valuation requires that we pay close attention not only to events and interactions but also to the various resources, processes, and structures that enable the articulation of value. This enlarged focus allows us to examine the way people mobilize vari-ous terms (spiritual, religious, or secular) in specific contexts, as part of the process of marking things of particular value or coming to experience them as such.

The idea that things acquire value in the context of relationships, events, and interactions is consistent with relational theories that view "things" as the result of ongoing social processes rather than conceiving social processes as the outcome of "things" that act (Elias 1998; Emirbayer 1997). Emirbayer argues that "the very terms or units involved in a trans-action derive their meaning, significance and identity from the (changing) functional roles they play within that transaction." Transactions, under-stood as dynamic, unfolding processes built upon events, "become the primary unit of analysis rather than the constituent elements" (1997:287). To take up Ernest Cassirer's prose, things "are not assumed as indepen-dent existences present anterior to any relation. . . . Such 'things' are terms of relations, and as such can never be 'given' in isolation" (1953:36). Relationally developing "things" include not just categories or discourses but likewise the subject, the will, and the person (Bakhtin 1981; Lambek 2003). We also find that patterns in transactions, utterances, and prac-tices carry resonances of prior interactions, making possible certain types of actors, emotions, and relations. As a consequence, different questions about the role of histories, memory, translation, and transmission also come into focus.

Drawing upon processual and relational methods expands our inquiry beyond the boundaries that have, in prior generations, considered ques-tions of meaning and value within distinct "secular" and "religious" spheres. If nothing else, these theories allow us to recognize that the processes of distinguishing things, as distinct, as in relations of various kinds, is elemental: what appears to be naturally in one domain or another (or what appears to naturally span those domains) is better understood, for our purposes, as the result of processes in which people identify and mark things as valuable in identifiable and powerful ways. It is with these perspectives that we can ask a different kind of question about how things—secular things, religious things, spiritual things—*come to be* deemed as such (by scholars as well as nonscholars) and draw those processes into the center of our inquiry.

THE VALUE OF VALUING: PRACTICE AND BELIEF

The analytical questions we raise here share much with already well-established scholarly discussions and projects, including ethnographic and historical work undertaken under the rubric of "lived religion" (Hall 1997). Lived religion is a set of approaches and methods in the field of religious studies, with uncertain boundaries and much argumentation, which developed in the same time frame as the study of secular formations. This scholarly approach emphasizes practice as a key node through which to investigate the structuring force of religious traditions. It developed in response to scholarly practices that continued to distinguish between orthodox and heterodox religious forms and authorities without investigating the practices (scholarly and religious, among others) that shaped and formed those distinctions. Drawing from a variety of theoretical insights in anthropology, history, and literary studies, the key frame of "practice" took shape, understanding the power dynamics shaping religious forms without building in or "around a structure of opposition. Nor [does the study of lived religion] displace the institutional or normative perspectives on practice." A focus on practice helps us see that clergy were "complicitous in the ways of thinking and doing that [lived religious studies] map, complicitous because they, too, were caught up in the same dilemmas" (Hall 1997:ix). This means, as Robert Orsi argues, "Rethinking religion as a form of cultural work, the study of lived religion directs attention to institutions *and* persons, texts *and* rituals, practice *and* theology, things *and* ideas—all as media of making and unmaking worlds" (2003:172).

Rather than hold these elements "apart" or view them as differing instantiations of the same tradition (and with more or less authority and relevance), lived religion investigates their co-construction. Numerous studies have presented genealogies of religious practices, using the space of particular practices to investigate any number of issues: the intersecting relations and struggles of correct practice, orthodoxy, popular interpretation, the expression of religious agency and the disciplinary formation of various practices, the slip between "religious" and "secular" practice, and so on. As Orsi notes, the "cultural work" that takes place under the sign of religion includes scholarly disciplines and practices as well. "Practice approaches must always be informed by a clear and critical understanding of the political, social, and intellectual history of the discipline of religious studies so that those of us who do this kind of work can understand what we are setting ourselves against, what we are contending with in the nomenclature and theoretical apparatuses of the discipline, and what projects we are resisting" (2003:171–2).

Two elements of this approach are worth highlighting: first, the emphasis on practice as processes, where focus on a practice is not oriented toward isolating an object for study but rather calls attention to its embeddedness and relations within a range of settings and concepts. Attention to the emergence of meaning within a complex set of interactions and settings demonstrates a set of interests, where concepts of human agency and possibility of acting are being coordinated at the same time as the "objects" being acted upon (Bender 2012). This attention to practices means, more aptly put, a focus on *practicing* and the dynamic social processes wherein experience, authority, and creativity are reproduced in ritual, actions, strategies, and habits in both embodied and discursive senses.[4]

In addition, lived religion's emphasis on practice engages "religious" actions and activities that move well beyond the clearly marked "religious" contexts on which generations of scholars focused their attention. Studying practice has opened up a framework where scholars can observe the multisitedness of religious production including various "secular" or "nonreligious" institutions and settings. Thus, in the last decade, the study of American religion "outside" religious institutions has led to stronger and more focused analysis of how people in secular institutional contexts such as schools, voluntary organizations, courts, and prisons produce concepts and practices of religion (Sullivan 2007; Dubler forthcoming). Other studies have analyzed the generative and sometimes less obvious interactions among "secular" and "religious" bodily practices and cultural constructs and have done so with a close eye to the diachronic and historical trajectories of various "secular" and "religious" actions and identities (Griffith 2004; Lofton 2011; Klassen 2012; Goldschmidt 2006), further establishing and expanding the conceptual and methodological space wherein scholars of religion approach their topic.[5]

Lived religion's emphases on studying religion as practiced in multiple settings has clear connections and links with scholars who are interested in understanding the power and force of secular-religious relations taking shape in practice in modern societies. As a review essay notes, recent ethnographies of secularism focus primarily on postcolonial or colonial contexts (Keane 2007) or on Islam and the interaction between European "secularism" and Islam (Cannell 2010). Here, the question of the secular is intimately linked to the state and the construction of liberal selves. The issues of agency, practice, and structure also resonate clearly within these studies, however (see in particular Hirschkind 2009; Mittermaier 2010). While these two scholarly frames engage different subject matter, disciplines, and (frequently) levels or scales of research, both are, to a surprisingly similar degree, engaged in investigating the fields of religious and secular production through practice.

When we highlight these striking overlapping questions and issues, we can also see another shared theoretical and epistemological frame, namely, a set of studied moves away from focus on religious belief or even a focus on the "practice" of belief. The move away from belief as a central focus of investigation was prompted and reinforced by several intersecting views and evaluations. Primarily, religious studies and anthropology scholars both recognized the degree to which identification of belief (particularly, individual subjective belief) as the defining feature of religion is a reflection of a particular historical context, that of an Enlightenment-era infused with tacit Protestant presuppositions. The development of a universal definition of religion based on individual belief and (as many have since argued) the autonomous liberal subject who can have belief is, thus, a historically emergent one. Critical genealogies of commonplace definitions that frame religion as belief have prompted the turn to practice and, in some cases, a focus on religious practice as habit and discipline, as structure and power, that have little to say in return about the kinds of spaces in which "belief" actually takes shape.

Concurrently, sociologists of culture and others developed criticisms of social theories that framed culture broadly (and religion within it) as the beliefs, meaning systems, and worldviews held by individuals. Within these theories, issues of methodology and epistemology came to the fore, raising questions about the degree to which social "beliefs" were held individually outside of communicative, social settings. Scholars critical of the epistemologies underlying survey research and opinion polls (Wuthnow 1987), as well as ethnographic approaches that assumed there was little distinction between part and whole (Burawoy 1998), turned away from the question of "meaning" and "belief" to public, communicable cultural forms. Such agnosticism about the existence of "belief" as a unified individual program similarly led sociologists to investigate the cultural conditions in which the autonomous, individual believing subject could emerge (Somers 1994) and used narrative and practice approaches to address such issues from an empirical standpoint.

Taken together, these critiques have resulted in the decentering of questions of belief in our respective fields. One recent discussion even suggested that talk about belief is a "no fly zone," at least for scholars studying religion (Rutherford 2009). The value of this decentering is hard to overlook; the turn to embodiment, ritual, practices, and the like has been so fruitful for so many. Yet if it is true, as many note, that it is a "modern" self that can believe, then it remains likely that a range of practices shape that space of possibility in which beliefs take shape. We thus need to consider how practices give rise to belief (and vice versa) in a world where we can now consider the practices of belief (and, likewise, the processes of valuation) that take place across various fields and spaces. Viewed in this light, our interest in how things come to matter, and how processes of value take shape "within" the practiced settings of secular and religious life, take on more structure. Put another way, *What Matters?* attends to the question of how people come to believe in things that matter to them in this modern, contemporary context.

THE EMBRACE OF PARADOX: MODERN SPIRITS AND ENCHANTMENTS

By putting questions of value into the foreground and drawing on these approaches, we disrupt the classical and taken-for-granted distinction between belief and unbelief, religion and secularity. One of the central elements of secularization theories was the understanding that religious authority (irrational authority) would decline where rationality and scientific progress gained power. "Secularization" meant a trajectory from belief to nonbelief. For many generations scholars raised the question of how "modern" people could "still believe," generating a host of scholarly and theoretical views on how religious belief was reproduced or marshaled despite powerful processes that worked against it. Religious scholarship discussed, at great length, the cultural forms of a socially constructed world within which various objects, rituals, and experiences become marked as sacred, special, and uniquely able to transform humans into believing people. People's tendency to claim that the value of the things they valued was self-evident led scholars to focus on the particular social processes through which humans gave value to these things, while, at the same time, somehow obscuring (scholars assumed) their own role in the process. Belief then took shape in scholarly work as the set of internalized meaning structures that supported misrecognition. Much scholarship on religion in modernity has taken this social constructivist approach, seeking to identify the way in which the (human) processes of shaping things of value simultaneously "hide" or limit attention to their fundamental "constructed" qualities.

While in other contexts we have advocated a more nuanced social constructivist approach that takes seriously subjects' sense that some things surface to consciousness already laden with value and attempts to account for that sense in terms of unconscious cognitive processes (Taves 2009), the subjects depicted in these essays present a different sort of challenge. Thus, we note, in this volume, a striking *lack* of mystification surrounding people's claims to value, whether religious or otherwise. Although in some instances subjects clearly feel that things appear to them already laden with value, many of the subjects discussed in this volume recognize that what they value is shaped by social processes, acknowledge that they have played a role in shaping concepts that they value, and at times engage valued things as intrinsically so, while at the same time realizing they probably are not. Many of the actors depicted in this volume's essays, thus, exhibit varying degrees of reflexivity with respect to the things they value most. These reflexive actors self-consciously pursue, make, and engage things of value. They often do so pragmatically, in many cases maintaining the ability to question or doubt their choices while still insisting on their value. Tanya Luhrmann, drawing from her research on evangelical Christians in the U.S., has described such actors as "using a 'double epistemological register' in which God is described as very real— and as doubted, in some way." She refers to this "complex style as magically real or hyper-real . . . both more real than everyday reality and more fictional" (Luhrmann 2011; see also Smilde 2006). The actions of these reflexive actors, *both secular and religious*, suggest that misrecognition and mystification is not a necessary condition for holding something to be of value.

The possibility of both reflexive and ambivalent attachments to highly valued things, when coupled with the story of the secular-religious, allows us to consider social processes of articulating meaning that do not presuppose modern scholarly claims that religious belief necessarily involves irrationality and misrecognition. But in making this move, we advise caution in associating these features with particular historical processes. Narratives of modernity have argued that secularism brings with it an awareness of the constructed nature of human society and the things that we value: modernity in this view makes visible some of the work required to create structures, concepts, and processes that appear to be extrahuman, nonfinite, more than ourselves. In this narrative, ambivalence too is a modern process: it is the mark of the secular itself. The self-reflexive quality of modernity makes religion impossible (according to earlier secularization theses) or makes religion as belief a more difficult prospect than in earlier ages (as more recent theoretical iterations argue). The chapters in this volume, like Luhrmann's research, suggest that religious actors—even relatively conservative ones—can and do adopt a self-reflexive stance and thus can be as constitutive of religious forms as they have been of secular ones. To what extent this "double epistemological" style emerges as a distinctive feature of secular societies and is absent, as Luhrmann suggests, in "never secular" societies remains for us on open question. Similarly, the degree to which a "secular" stance can be shaped by mystifications and beliefs also remains for us an open question.

Leaving open the question of the historical conditions required to generate this self-reflexive style, we are nonetheless convinced that visions of secularity that link it with increasing demands for ambiguity and ambivalence unnecessarily hobble our inquiries into the ways that people incorporate ambivalence, doubt, and self-reflexivity into processes of valuation. Some self-defined religious or spiritual actors embrace and work through processes of value that are self-aware and/or ambivalent while, conversely, some secular or spiritual groups or actors seemingly do not.

Birgit Meyer's chapter on spirits in Ghana makes this argument, challenging Charles Taylor's vision of the "secular age" as providing only the possibility of disenchanted religion. Taylor argues that modern religion, like modern life, is largely disenchanted in the Weberian sense: the spirits have left or have been debunked. The "unbuffered self" of the premodern era (one who had close communion with spirit beings and spiritual forces) becomes "buffered." "Spirits" become "spirituality"—or become the "specters" or "spirits" of capitalism (or the ghosts in the machine). Spirit is transformed in an important way: it is a theoretical way of speaking of modern mystifications. These are not "real" bodies or spirits but rather ways of talking about secular, modern mystifications. In this way, then the language of spirit is contained yet transformed in modern religion and in modern secularism. Focusing on the place of spirits (rather than spirituality) in the context of the modern secular Ghanaian state, Meyer argues that the liberalization of the state-owned media in the early 1990s fostered the emergence of a heavily Pentecostalized public sphere. While spirits could be, and often are, viewed as signs of a traditional African past, Meyer views them as products of the interaction between African and Western missionary traditions. As evidenced in all kinds of public settings—from politics to entertainment—spirits resist confinement to a distinctively religious sphere. As framed by Ghanaian Pentecostal media and thus reproduced under modern conditions, the spirits illustrate one way in which notions of enchantment can play across an overt secular-religious divide.

Such phenomena are hardly limited to Ghana, to Africa, or to the "global South," nor are the preoccupations of spirits and spirit possession. Paul C. Johnson's genealogy of spirit possession (2011) provides further insight into the manner through which modern Western legal and philosophical concepts of property, ownership, and the capacity to be rationally "self-possessed" were shaped as antidotes or counterpoints to the "possessed" and possessable bodies that travelers, colonial agents and missionaries encountered. Thus, rather than marking the distinction of one from the other, Johnson calls attention to the ongoing if changing register of spirit possession in European contexts. "Not all spirits have retreated to metaphor, even in the very public sphere of the U.S.," he writes. Indeed, "a society purified of nonhuman agents becomes incomprehensible" (2011:393, 394; see also Latour 1993; Appadurai 2008; Modern 2010).

Jeffrey Kripal's contribution to this volume demonstrates just how central these preoccupations remain, by presenting the case of scientists' and scholars' efforts to consider ways of being in the world that do not depend on the thin ontologies of materialism yet take into account the criticisms and problematics of earlier attempts. Embracing alternative understandings of consciousness, and the deep ethnographic and narrative materials that attest to those forms, Kripal and those he studies challenge concepts of the disenchanted, self-possessed self. Kripal's interest in the continued efforts of scholars and scientists to move "behind the mirror" of materialism, or to engage the work of parapsychologists, physicists, and others in considering forms of consciousness, shows how "spirit" figures as a timeless present, one possible set of languages used to identify not individual spirits warring (in a disenchanted self) but rather a more pantheistic, limitless set of possibilities where consciousness is dispersed.

Attention to spirits, as the foregoing paragraphs suggest, destabilizes the neat distinctions between reflexive and nonreflexive "secularity" or "secular religious" and "religion." It highlights the difficulties inherent in scholarly characterizations of "what matters" to people as either secular or religious and points to beliefs that do not fit easily into given categories. It thus opens up promising new lines of inquiry, such as, for example, the question of how bodies are organized through varying capacities and claims to "believe" or to be "possessed."

KEY TERMS: EXPERIENCE, AUTHENTICITY, AUTHORITY

If spirits provide one illuminating window into what matters, *experience, authenticity,* and *authority* provide alternative vantage points to approach this question, and, likewise, different opportunities to highlight processes through which "religious" and "secular" distinctions come to matter. We close this introduction by highlighting these linked key terms, which resonate across papers that take on very disparate materials.

Experience

For many of the people and groups that populate this volume, experience is a key frame through which people encounter things of value and through which they consider the question of value altogether. We might ask why experience takes on so much focus, whether it is for doctors and volunteers who work through issues of immediacy of care for others or for the self, or for a global expatriate community seeking connection, as well as (in a different mode) scientists and scholars working through new and old ways to understand the "religious" or the "creative?"

Like *spirit, experience* is a term that crosses over various domains of secular and spiritual and religious, while carrying with it elements of its different uses in various institutional contexts and epistemological frames

(Bender 2010; Taves 1999, 2009). This volume provides some indication of these earlier crossings. Christopher White's contribution to this volume, for example, traces the development of concepts of "suggestibility" among psychologists grappling with the question of the unconscious, religion, and the problem of mob violence. While psychologists developed the term *suggestibility* as a way to explain and manage "religious experiences" in order to delimiting their authority and power, liberal Protestant believers found in the concept a new portal into understanding their tradition. Unable to understand or conform to their parents' evangelical Protestantism, they drew on psychological concepts to rethink the workings of the spiritual self. They did so with considerable ambivalence, aware as they were of the unpredictability and potentially explosive power of the unconscious. Tugged by various interests, they struggled, as White narrates, to find a way to spiritualize the unconscious—and its suggestibility—so that they could be both embraced and carefully measured. Such American believers ultimately found considerable value in the concept of unconscious suggestibility, using it both to explain excessively irrational practices *and* to call attention to a range of authentic and powerful spiritual forces in the self.

Experience—both the desire for significant experiences and questions regarding the significance of particular experiences—continues to be a fertile and contentious space in which processes of valuation and ways of apprehending what matters come into view. And, as the chapters in this volume make clear, the questions surrounding experience in the early twentieth century are far from settled. Jeffrey Kripal's participant-observation fieldwork with the Sursem group at Esalen presents the ways that contemporary scientists and scholars are pondering the "ambiguous signs" of experience that, he argues, continue to play a major role in the history of religions and demand a broadening of method to include both "experiment" and "experience" in considering topics such as reincarnation or transmigration. Kripal's work plays heavily with the ambiguities and occasionally ludic qualities of reincarnation experiences. When one of the Sursem members suggested that another member was the reincarnation of F. W. H. Myers, the nineteenth-century psychologist and psychic investigator, Kripal notes, "It was a joke, but also a quite accurate observation about intellectual resonances and spiritual lineages."

Kripal's essay explicitly approaches experience from multiple perspectives and challenges scholars who view it simply in terms of social construction or the psychological "unconscious" to consider data that continue to confound such approaches. In treating the idea of Myers's reincarnation both as a joke and a serious possibility, Kripal and other members of the Sursem group demonstrate both the reflexive self-awareness and the ability to hold doubt and possibility in tension that is characteristic of many of the subjects discussed in this volume.

Erica Bornstein's essay focuses on the emergence of "volunteer experience" as something of value in the Indian context. Her study of two Indian volunteer/humanitarian groups' calls attention to the centrality of the voluntary giver's "experience" in these two highly secularized organizations, both of which provide structured "volunteer experiences" and hold them up as recruitment tools. Volunteer experience becomes a goal in itself in these two philanthropic contexts, and both devote much of their time and resources to ensuring that the experiences have the desired form (as responses to the needs of others) and effect (as memorable opportunities for learning and personal growth).

As Bornstein notes, the effect of this focus on being in "the moment" deemphasizes the organizations' discussions of the outcomes of voluntary assistance for those who are in need, in ways reminiscent of the traditional religious concept of *dan* (giving). Experience (and the experience of the volunteer) in the Indian context thus resonates, interestingly, with White's early-twentieth-century liberal Protestants. Much as Protestants who could no longer "believe" in the theological tenets of their forebears might embrace religion (or spirituality) through a psychological understanding of "experience," modern volunteers in India, who may not be able to "believe" in the long-term efficacy of their actions, find in volunteering an emphasis on giving and being in the moment that recasts traditional religious motifs in a new secular form.

Experience, in these chapters, is thus both something that happens but also something that people shape, argue over, and strive to find. While the examples in Kripal's, White's, and to some degree Bornstein's paper all highlight the way that experience "bridges" or complicates the designations of secular, religious, and spiritual, Graham St John's paper on the international psytrance community brings these issues into clear focus. The topic of St John's paper, Portugal's Boom Festival, which regularly draws thousands of people from all over the world, expresses and articulates what St John calls an "experiential aesthetic" linked to a desire for transcendence and transformation albeit of the "secular spiritual" variety. "Indeed, transcendence is a critical motivation for enthusiasts as well as label managers, party collectives, and event organizers and is given expression across personal, social, and cultural vectors." (The question, for those who self-consciously construct the social arenas in which festivals take place, is how to make experience of this kind happen: how to make room for "transcendence" in a built environment—one that is, moreover, reliant on interactions with the "world music industry, growing technical bureaucracy, and compliance with state regulatory requirements." Boom participants, St John notes, are savvy enough modernists to recognize that their experiences emerge from within numerous social connections and cultural commitments and that they are in the process "manufacturing, selling, spending, and buying their own authenticity." As makers and marketers of an experience of transcendence they themselves value highly, psytrance festival organizers and participants epitomize the reflexive embrace of paradox that runs through this volume.

Authenticity

Boom Festival participants, Indian volunteers, and nineteenth- and twentieth-century researchers' valorization of *experience* highlights ongoing concerns about authenticity: How does one know that the experience "itself" is authentic or that the purported object of one's experience is "authentic" or "real"? In what ways do people question the authenticity of their experiences or leave their authenticity an open issue? The chapters in this volume provide a range of examples of how people respond to questions of authenticity, not only with regard to the quality of the experience but also to the processes of valuation themselves.

Here too the Boom Festival is illustrative. Challenged by those who question the legitimacy of appropriating the traditional practices of "native" or "world cultures," Boom Festival participants consciously embrace an identity as hybridizers and bricoleurs. Distancing themselves from new age practitioners and others who have been widely criticized, they intentionally forge a "syncretic cut-and-paste spirituality" that takes experiential form in the context of the Boom Festival. In self-consciously embracing a spirituality lived out experientially in the context of the Boom Festival, participants not only assert that the experiences they create are authentic but also challenge those who suggest that authentic experiences of transcendence are necessarily unmediated or unconstructed. In similar ways, Indian humanitarian groups assert the experience of volunteering is more authentic—more real—than ordinary experience and Sursem researchers argue research that takes difficult-to-explain experiences into account is more authentically scientific than research that does not.

If, as we have suggested, competing views—whatever their source—give rise to heightened reflexivity, then it is perhaps no surprise to see arguments for authenticity recast in ways that take these challenges into account. Experience, however, is not the only arena in which questions of authenticity arise. For various people discussed in this volume, other things matter more—childhood, human life, and our views of human nature. Given what matters most to them, they then make claims regarding authentic childhood, authentic life, and authentic human nature in ways that draw from concepts that are variously established as secular, religious, or spiritual.

The Family School participants discussed in Rebecca Allahyari's contribution to this volume are thus concerned chiefly with creating an environment in which they can provide their children with an "authentic childhood" through the recovery or recuperation of practices they view as threatened by neoliberal educational bureaucracies. Family School parents, as a result, invest a great deal of time both reflecting on what practices are most authentic and on practical questions of implementation. For most Family School parents "family time," whether focused on schooling or play, is the key to an authentic childhood. Yet, as Allahyari also makes clear, the quest for authenticity comes with costs: it is not only highly time consuming but also fraught with many of the same problems as the structures it attempts to overcome.

The shifting space of secular and religious claims to authentic living takes more ultimate form in contemporary secular humanitarian organizations such as Doctors Without Borders. In a paper comparing three twentieth-century humanitarian organizations with European roots—Albert Schweitzer's medical mission, the Red Cross, and Médecins Sans Frontières (MSF)—anthropologist Peter Redfield calls attention to subtle shifts in the rationales for valuing human life and thus what counts as authentic life. In Schweitzer's medical mission and in the Red Cross, Redfield finds that the value of human life is understood in religious terms against a backdrop of transcendent meaning. In contrast, MSF understands "life" itself as a non-negotiable value cast in "resolutely *human* rather than transcendent terms." In championing the value of life as non-negotiable, Redfield argues, MSF makes the historically remarkable claim that humans are not made to suffer in the name of future utopian ideals.

In this volume the role that ambiguous evidence can play in making an argument for authenticity is particularly clearly laid out in Silvia Tomášková's analysis of archeological debates over human evolution in postrevolutionary France. Excavations of prehistoric sites gave rise to heated discussions of skeletal remains and cave paintings that carried direct implications for thinking about what was most deeply (and, thus, authentically) human in human nature. Focusing on two key figures— Gabriel de Mortillet, the mid-nineteenth-century "father" of French prehistory, and Abbé Breuil, his most prominent twentieth-century successor—she argues that these debates were profoundly shaped by a distinctively French view of the religious-secular divide, which reflected the polarization of church-state relations.

Reflecting his strongly anticlerical views, the secularist de Mortillet insisted that the skeletal remains were not buried (at least not by Paleolithic humans) and provided no evidence of funerary rites or concern about death and that the cave paintings supplied no evidence of prehistoric religion. Ritual and religion, he argued, were later imports from elsewhere and not distinctively French at all. In the decades that followed, however, a new generation of archaeologists and scholars revised this secularist vision. Sidestepping the term *religion,* Abbé Breuil insisted that the cave paintings were prehistoric art. This evidence of prehistoric creativity was, by extension, evidence of prehistoric spiritual life. Magic, the desire to manipulate events, he argued, provided the spiritual motivation for artistic creativity.

Prehistoric art thus provided priest archeologists, such as Breuil, with a way to argue that proto-priests (shamans) and proto-religion (creative symbolic thought) were an integral part of human life from its early beginnings. In so doing, they framed humans as authentically "spiritual" prior to the historical existence of religious institutions, undercut the secular view of human nature advanced by de Mortillet and his followers, and avoided making direct claims about religion that might have jeopardized their standing within the Church. For Breuil, it was the development of the human spirit that mattered most, and in the prehistoric cave paintings he found evidence that he argued authenticated his view of the human spirit, transcending purely mundane "material" concerns.

Authority

Identifying things that matter is not an idle task and, ultimately, raises questions about the authorities people call upon to justify and defend their claims. What powers and forces compel individuals and groups to act? What brings thousands of people to the Portuguese Boom Festival to dance and commune, sends doctors into dangerous, challenging situations in order to save lives, compels parents to draw their children out of public schools and invest countless hours in their unschooling, or provokes scientists to reconsider and debate what archaeological data tells us about what it means to be human?

Our final keyword, *authority,* provides yet another approach to considering the resonances and questions raised by the chapters that follow. Authority is, of course, a central concern in both classical secularization theories and recent debates about secularism. Classical theorists argued that secularization diminished (or negated) not only the scope of religious authority but its transcendent qualities and force. As we have noted, these theories identified the isolation of religious authority into a differentiated domain as part of this diminishment. Yet, as many scholars have noted, this transformation had unintended consequences. Secular authority, bolstered or grounded by reason, rational governance, and scientific methods, seemingly lacked the grounding in tradition necessary to call those in power to obedience (or provide those who are not in power with alternative sources of authority). What was lacking, according to Hannah Arendt, was authority that "transcends power and those that are in power" (Arendt 1993:141). This absence led, as Jürgen Habermas cautioned, to modernity's "legitimation crisis" (Habermas 1975).

Theories of secularism, however, call these narratives of decline into question, and present other ways to consider issues of authority that take shape in secularism's wake. Our moment might then be viewed not as resulting from a simple decline in religious and traditional authority but rather from the recalibration of relations between competing forms of authority in which "secularities" are invested with their own theories, imaginations, and integrities. The latter approach draws attention to manifold ways secular political or cultural movements continue to draw legitimacy from religious or quasi-religious sources (Viswanathan 2008; Pecora 2006) and (often unwittingly) rely on particular conceptions of religious authority to determine who can make authoritative claims about value and meaning in public life (Fessenden 2007; Bender and Klassen 2010). In other words, in a secular age the question of authority is neither one that is wholly up for grabs nor a simply matter of individual taste— even if it appears that way sometimes. How, then, do processes of identifying (or "coming to recognize") certain objects, values, or concepts as "religious" or "secular" or "spiritual" influence their powers? Why, indeed, do people continue to concern themselves with the question of whether humanitarian actions are "religious" or "secular" (as is the case with MSF and with the French archaeologists in the late nineteenth century)?

One way to approach these questions is to consider how authorities of various kinds are located within distinct social and political settings. For example, in the American context "religion is not a subject for authority above the level of the individual—whether by the state or the church" (Sullivan 2009:1185). The source of religious authority, Sullivan argues, is ultimately understood as located in the individual: this "authority" involves not just the capacity for individuals to believe as they wish but likewise to determine what counts as religious—a fact Sullivan observes primarily within American legal contexts. The ability of Americans to locate and assert religious authority at this individual level (rather than at the state or even church-religious institution level) is shaped, she says, by "a convergence among a broad range of humanistic critiques of scientistic understandings of the person, social scientific and biological, social and political movements that originated in the mid-twentieth century," and so on (2009:1193). Nonetheless, many individuals are raised within traditions that do not locate religious authority in the individual and many choose to join such communities—that is clear. Thus, while the authority to decide what counts as religious may rest with the individual in the American context, many Americans cede that authority to others. And many Americans speak and act on behalf of religious or spiritual authorities they experience as external to themselves. The essays in this volume highlight the ways that groups and individuals in various contexts recalibrate and engage the relations between competing loci of authority, whether rooted in the individual, the group, or the state.

Thus, Rebecca Allahyari's homeschooling parents shift the authority for educating their children from the state educational system to families embedded in a homeschooling network. Drawing on their authority as parents and on spiritual and secular traditions that give them the authority to valorize their offsprings' natural enchantment, they strive to protect their families from the disenchanting effects of state education. These parents work to fashion their opposition to the state and the claims that it might make on their children as citizens-in-the-making yet, at the same time, hold up a utopian vision of an American public that draws selectively on neoliberal claims to self-reliance and self-empowerment.

Scientific authority, however, is tacitly presupposed in other essays in this volume. Christopher White's and Silvia Tomášková's papers—as well as Peter Redfield's—highlight this authority, making complex and at times unexpected connections between scientific claims for authority and processes of valuation. In White's and Tomášková's chapters, "science" is the site in which ultimate value and truth take shape. In White's chapter, psychologists' claims about the power of "suggestibility" to shape religious experiences are not disputed by liberal Christians. Rather, they reinterpret its meaning (and powers): the findings of "science" provide liberal Christians with scientific authority to claim that their religious practices are more reasonable and—to wit—more religious than the more expressive but less authentic religious enthusiasms of the masses. In a quite different way, Tomášková's chapter highlights the urgency and interest with which nineteenth-century French secularists argued that "early man" lived without art or spirituality, that humans are, at root, practical and utilitarian, not religious beings.

In a more recent turn, Peter Redfield's description of the challenges that Médecins Sans Frontières faces in establishing its secular humanitarian goals shows how a secular organization that develops genealogically from earlier, more "spiritualized" humanitarian organizations works to establish a new form of authority for its activities. Where earlier humanitarian organizations (and some contemporary ones) relied on transcendent claims to justify their efforts to ease the suffering of the dying, MSF rejects the view that there is any such thing as a "good death." As Redfield notes, "absent a soul or utopia, it is hard to transmute a stupid death into a good one." Having rejected a transcendent authority that exists beyond the pale of material and biological life, MSF draws on the authority of science and medicine to claim "life itself" as its goal.

The chapters by Kripal and Meyer point to the role of taken-for-granted cultural assumptions in authorizing what counts as legitimate in different contexts. Jeff Kripal reminds us of the unquestionable effects of the Cartesian frame that organizes most scholarly inquiry into human consciousness and limits time, attention, and investigation into "parapsychological" events and experiences. Authority, in this view, is not so much what is claimed as what is taken for granted. The effects of this epistemological (if not ontological) framework suffuse both secular and religious projects and prompt his subjects into deeper questioning of the limits of the scientific epistemologies that psychic researchers have themselves used to establish a position of exploration and critique.

Much as Kripal's chapter draws our attention to presuppositions that delegitimize the academic investigation of paranormal activities, Birgit

Meyer's chapter highlights the way in which presuppositions about spirits infuse and authorize claims regarding the actions of spiritual agents in the public sphere. Although the Ghanaian public sphere, which developed in the wake of colonial and missionary endeavors and subsequent independence, is secular by definition, it is, nonetheless, thoroughly "entangled" with various religious and spiritual authorities. As she writes, "what happens in the material world—from the level of a person's body to the nation and even the globe—is held to be backed by spiritual forces, which also is a way to say that there is need to be aware of what lies behind mere appearance, the surface of things" (Meyer, this volume).

The essays in this book thus highlight the elaborate convergences of institutions, meaning, and experience that shape the ways that modern people identify things of value and orient themselves and their lives in relation to them. As American Protestants invest psychology with their own enchantments, as volunteers in India purify "volunteer experience" as a source of power and change, they do so amidst a web of discourses and authorities that combine to simultaneously identify what matters and authorize that identification. They often do so self-consciously, such that the things they value appear to them as at once made and discovered, created and yet real.

৯৯

We began this introduction by asking the question: what does it mean to be secular? Our intention in highlighting this question is to attend to the issues of how people in our contemporary moment and the recent past confront the question of what it means to live in the world and how they do this. Secular, religious, and spiritual authorities, experiences, and beliefs jostle for attention, make different claims, mark different spatial and political territory. Such claims are not just limited to clear and obviously demarcated domains: the church, the state, science, popular culture, and so on.

Rather than try to answer the question of what matters, this volume presents a set of examples of how scholars from various fields might approach the question. Thus we have deliberately avoided adopting preconceived scholarly distinctions between religious, secular, and spiritual pursuits or authorities (or experiences) in order to focus on how actors make those distinctions in various contexts. We have, likewise, argued for closer attention to the question of belief, especially beliefs infused with a reflexive awareness of paradox and ambiguity, as a key aspect of the process of valuation. We have called attention to the ways various actors themselves consider vexing issues of authenticity and authority as well as the problematics of investing "experience" with value. And so, while this volume does not present a definitive answer to the question "what matters," it argues for and, we hope, demonstrates the importance of ethnographic and historical exploration of the question.

NOTES

1. Secularization theory has not been one, but many; its various iterations do not all suggest the decline of religion or its unidirectionality (Casanova 1994; Berger 1969).

2. Secularism thus emerged in new discourse as a "formation" that takes shape and structure in relation to ongoing interactions and dynamics with particular historical concepts of religion (Asad 2003): religion in modernity takes shape in relation to secular forms, in particular, specific settings. As a consequence, scholars consider secularisms in comparative perspective: secularism looks, feels, and acts quite differently in the United States, Turkey, and France or India (Hurd 2007; Jakobsen and Pellegrini 2008). As with any academic discourse, the study of secularism is not without its pitched debates: where some argue for comparison, others have identified secularism as an expansive yet singular political project with specifically European roots (Taylor 2007), one that expands as an organizational component of colonialism and empire (Anidjar 2006).

3. Saba Mahmood (2005). In a different context, Philip Gorski (2003) revisits Weber's classic thesis in *Protestant Ethic* in a way that connects various "disciplinary revolutions" to state-building enterprises in northern Europe. See also Hirschkind 2010.

4. In this respect, we wish to distinguish our interest in practices as processes from others' interests in religious specific practices such as prayer (Wuthnow 2008) or fly fishing (Snyder 2007).

5. And in this respect, studies of "lived religion" can be distinguished from studies of "domestic religion" or "everyday religion" that focus on the daily practices of domestic life without close attention to the structuring aspects of these various settings or the operations wherein various kinds of religious authorities are "produced" rather than merely "lived."

REFERENCES

Anidjar, Gil. 2006. "Secularism." *Critical Inquiry* 33:52–77.

Appadurai, Arjun. 2008. "The Magic Ballot." *The Immanent Frame.* http://blogs .ssrc.org/tif/2008/11/07/the-magic-ballot/ (accessed April 24, 2011).

Aravamudan, Srinivas. 2006. *Guru English: South Asian Religion in a Cosmopolitan Language.* Princeton: Princeton University Press.

Arendt, Hannah. 1993. *Between Past and Future: Eight Exercises in Political Thought.* New York: Penguin.

Asad, Talal. 1993. *Genealogies of Religion: Discipline and Reasons of Power in Christianity and Islam.* Baltimore: Johns Hopkins University Press.

——— 2003. *Formations of the Secular: Christianity, Islam, Modernity.* Stanford: Stanford University Press.

Bakhtin, Mikhail. 1981. *The Dialogic Imagination.* Austin: University of Texas Press.

Bell, Catherine. 1992. *Ritual Theory, Ritual Practice.* New York: Oxford University Press.

Bender, Courtney. 2010. *The New Metaphysicals: Spirituality and the American Religious Imagination.* Chicago: University of Chicago Press.

——— 2012. "Practicing Religion." In Robert Orsi, ed., *The Cambridge Companion to Religious Studies,* 273–95. New York: Cambridge University Press.

Bender, Courtney, and Pamela Klassen, eds. 2010. *After Pluralism: Reimagining Religious Engagement.* New York: Columbia University Press.

Berger, Peter. 1969. *The Sacred Canopy: Elements of a Sociological Theory of Religion.* Garden City, NY: Doubleday.

Bourdieu, Pierre. 1990. *The Logic of Practice.* Stanford: Stanford University Press.

Burawoy, Michael. 1998. "The Extended Case Method." *Sociological Theory* 16:4–33.

Cannell, Fenella. 2010. "The Anthropology of Secularism." *Annual Review of Anthropology* 39:85–100.

Casanova, Jose. 1994. *Public Religions in the Modern World.* Chicago: University of Chicago Press.

Cassirer, Ernst. 1953. *Substance and Function.* New York: Dover.

Comte-Sponville, Andre. 2007. *The Little Book of Atheist Spirituality.* New York: Viking.

Connolly, William. 1999. *Why I Am Not a Secularist.* Minneapolis: University of Minnesota Press.

——— 2005a. *Pluralism.* Durham, NC: Duke University Press.

——— 2005b. "The Evangelical-Capitalist Resonance Machine." *Political Theory* 33:869–86.

Dubler, Joshua. Forthcoming. *The Chapel.* New York: Farrar Straus Giroux.

Elias, Norbert. 1998. *The Norbert Elias Reader.* Oxford: Blackwell.

Emirbayer, Mustafa. 1997. "Manifesto for a Relational Sociology." *American Journal of Sociology* 103:281–317.

Fessenden, Tracy. 2007. *Culture and Redemption: Religion, the Secular, and American Literature*. Princeton: Princeton University Press.

Goldschmidt, Henry. 2006. *Race and Religion Among the Chosen People of Crown Heights*. New Brunswick, NJ: Rutgers University Press.

Gorski, Philip. 2003. *The Disciplinary Revolution: Calvinism and the Rise of the State in Early Modern Europe*. Chicago: University of Chicago Press.

Gorski, Philip, and Ates Altinordu. 2009. "After Secularization?" *Annual Review of Sociology* 34:55–85.

Graeber, David. 2001. *Toward an Anthropological Theory of Value: The False Coin of Our Own Dreams*. New York: Palgrave.

Griffith, R. Marie. 2004. *Born Again Bodies: Flesh and Spirit in American Christianity*. Berkeley: University of California Press.

Habermas, Jürgen. 1975. *Legitimation Crisis*. Boston: Beacon.

Hall, David, ed. 1997. *Lived Religion in America*. Princeton: Princeton University Press.

Harris, Sam. 2004. *The End of Faith: Religion, Terror and the Future of Reason*. New York: Norton.

Hirschkind, Charles. 2009. *The Ethical Soundscape: Cassette Sermons and Islamic Counterpublics*. New York: Columbia University Press.

—— 2010. "Is There a Secular Body?" *The Immanent Frame*. http://blogs.ssrc.org/tif/2010/11/15/secular-body/ (accessed April 27, 2011).

Hurd, Elizabeth Shakman. 2007. *The Politics of Secularism in International Relations*. Princeton: Princeton University Press.

Jakobsen, Janet, and Ann Pellegrini. 2008. *Secularisms*. Durham, NC: Duke University Press.

Johnson, Paul C. 2011. "An Atlantic Genealogy of 'Spirit Possession.'" *Comparative Studies in Society and History* 53:393–425.

Keane, Webb. 2007. *Christian Moderns: Freedom and Fetish in the Mission Encounter*. Berkeley: University of California Press.

Klassen, Pamela. 2012. *Spirits of Protestantism: Medicine, History, and Liberal Christianity*. Berkeley: University of California Press.

Kopytoff, Igor. 1986. "The Cultural Biography of Things: Commoditization as Process." In Arjun Appadurai, ed., *The Social Life of Things: Commodities in Cultural Perspective*, 64–91. Cambridge: Cambridge University Press.

Lambek, Michael. 2003. *The Weight of the Past: Living with History in Mahajanga, Madagascar*. Basingstoke: Palgrave.

Latour, Bruno. 1993. *We Have Never Been Modern*. Cambridge: Harvard University Press.

Lofton, Kathryn. 2011. *Oprah: The Gospel of an Icon*. Berkeley: University of California Press.

Luhrmann, Tanya M. 2012. "A Hyper-Real God and Modern Belief: Towards an Anthropological Theory of Mind." *Current Anthropology* 53.

Mahmood Saba. 2005. *Politics of Piety: the Islamic Revival and the Feminist Subject*. Princeton: Princeton University Press.

Mittermaier, Amira. 2010. *Dreams That Matter: Egyptian Landscapes of the Imagination*. Berkeley: University of California Press.

Modern, John Lardas. 2007. "The Ghosts of Sing Sing; Or, the Metaphysics of Secularism." *Journal of the American Academy of Religion* 75:615–50.

Orsi, Robert. 2003. "Is the Study of Lived Religion Relevant to the World We Live In?" *Journal for the Scientific Study of Religion* 42:169–74.

Pecora, Vincent. 2006. *Secularization and Cultural Criticism*. Chicago: University of Chicago Press.

Rutherford, Danilyn. 2009. "An Absence of Belief?" *The Immanent Frame*. http://blogs.ssrc.org/tif/2009/12/01/an-absence-of-belief/ (accessed May 3, 2011).

Sheehan, Jonathan. 2005. *The Enlightenment Bible: Translation, Scholarship, Culture*. Princeton: Princeton University Press.

Smilde, David. 2006. *Reason to Believe: Cultural Agency in Latin American Evangelicalism*. Berkeley: University of California Press.

Snyder, Samuel. 2007. "New Streams of Religion: Fly Fishing as a Lived, Religion of Nature." *Journal of the American Academy of Religion* 75:896–922.

Somers, Margaret. 1994. "The Narrative Constitution of Identity: A Relational and Network Approach." *Theory and Society* 23:605–49.

Sullivan, Winnifred Fallers. 2005. *The Impossibility of Religious Freedom*. Princeton: Princeton University Press.

——— 2007. *Prison Religion*. Princeton: Princeton University Press.

——— 2009. "We Are All Religious Now. Again." *Social Research* 76:1181–98.

Taves, Ann. 1999. *Fits, Trances, and Visions: Experiencing Religion and Explaining Experience from Wesley to James*. Princeton: Princeton University Press.

——— 2009. *Religious Experience Reconsidered: A Building-Block Approach to the Study of Religion and Other Special Things*. Princeton: Princeton University Press.

——— 2011. "2010 Presidential Address: 'Religion' in the Humanities and the Humanities in the University." *Journal of the American Academy of Religion* 79:287–314.

Taylor, Charles. 2007. *A Secular Age*. Cambridge: Harvard University Press.

Van der Veer, Peter. 2002. "Colonial Cosmopolitanism." In Robin Cohen and Steve Vertovec, ed., *Conceiving Cosmopolitanism*, 165–80. Oxford: Oxford University Press.

——— 2009. "Spirituality in Modern Society." *Social Research* 76:1097–120.

Van Ness, Peter H. 1996. *Spirituality and the Secular Quest.* New York: Crossroad.

Viswanathan, Gauri. 2008. "Secularism in the Framework of Heterodoxy." *PMLA* 123:466–76.

Werner, Cynthia, and Duran Bell, eds. 2003. *Values and Valuables: From the Sacred to the Symbolic.* Walnut Creek, CA: Altamira.

White, Christopher. 2008. *Unsettled Minds: Psychology and the American Search for Spiritual Assurance, 1830–1940.* Berkeley: University of California Press.

Wuthnow, Robert. 1987. *Meaning and Moral Order.* Berkeley: University of California Press.

—— 2008. "Culture, Cognition, and Prayer." *Poetics* 36:333–37.

FROM A MATERIALIST ETHIC
TO THE SPIRIT OF PREHISTORY

SILVIA TOMÁŠKOVÁ

Archaeology emerged as a recognizable scholarly discipline in Europe by
the late nineteenth century, focusing primarily on the rise of civilizations
and tracing the origins of the present. Deep prehistoric times in particular drew attention, as the emergence of humans from caves offered an
apt metaphor for modernist understandings of culture emerging from
nature. However, Darwin's evolutionary theory and historical materialism did not simply displace theology in theoretical discussions of "man's
place in nature." Relations between evolutionary theory, an essential
building block in prehistoric archaeology, and religious views and practices of scientists at the end of the nineteenth century and the early years
of the twentieth were far more complex and intertwined than most histories of archaeology reveal. The victory of reason and science over faith and
superstition may seem obvious from the perspective of the present. But
the role of priest scientists, especially Catholic priests in France, deserves
far more scrutiny and close attention. Discussions of the origins of art,
spirituality, religion, and social life provided a testing ground where one
could merge scientific and religious views and project them onto the past.
France was particularly fertile, since, unlike in the English- and German-
speaking worlds, Darwin's evolutionary theory met with a mixed reception there at best, including fierce competition from Lamarck's theory of
human development over time. Moreover, given the critical French role
in defining prehistory, it would be a mistake to position France simply as

an anomaly in the establishment of the study of human antiquity. Rather, French archaeology exemplifies a complex terrain in the early twentieth-century emergence of the science of prehistory, one that included local, regional, and international networks of scientists, amateurs, politicians, and religious figures.

I seek here to complicate the relationship between religion, science, and spirituality in the formation of archaeology at the end of the nineteenth and the beginning of the twentieth centuries. My focus will be on early scholarship and speculative analogy about prehistoric forms of religiosity, magic, and art. France presents a fascinating case, as the major periodizations of human prehistory became standardized here and, at the same time, Catholic priests played a significant role in the formation of scientific archaeology during a tumultuous period of social, cultural, and historical upheaval. In particular I examine two pivotal figures in a country that is arguably considered the birthplace of archaeology as a scientific discipline. On one side of the debate, firmly rooted in nineteenth-century discussions between science and religion, stands a French socialist free thinker, a rabid materialist, Gabriel de Mortillet, "father of French prehistory." Across the millennial boundary, at the beginning of the twentieth century, emerges the other "father of French prehistory," Catholic priest and prehistorian par excellence, Abbé Henri Breuil. These two men represent both the possible and the eventually established forms of the scientific discipline of archaeology, the blend of scientific foundation and religion-infused imaginings of the emergence of humans as spiritual, sentient beings. Gabriel de Mortillet laid the foundation of the earliest time divisions, and his chronology is still used today, albeit in a modified form (for a detailed history, see Blanckaert 2001; Chazan 1995; Coye 1997). Abbé Breuil, on the other hand, combined the evolutionary chronology with discussions of the emergence of higher thoughts expressed in art. Paleolithic art became a chronological marker of human capacity for religious ritual and thought. Although frequently presented as conflicting opposites, I argue that the relationship between these two men, de Mortillet and Breuil, actually represents something more than opposing contradictions of the new science of the past.

REMEMBRANCES AND GENEALOGIES

On June 9, 1900, Henri Edouard Prosper Breuil was ordained a priest in the Soissons diocese, in the Cathedral of St. Gervais et St. Protais. He was one

of several ordained priests that day, and there was nothing unusual about
the ceremony, a traditional Catholic ordination in a small French town at
the turn of the twentieth century. Abbé Breuil, as he came to be known in
his well-documented and productive life, is conspicuously absent from the
list of memorable, historically influential figures of the diocese. The list,
proudly posted by the official historian of the parish, is quite short and
would certainly benefit from a famous personage. Well known throughout
France, Europe, and as far as South Africa, Breuil's name would surely add
luster. And yet his renown echoes primarily through different circles than
those recognized and proudly displayed by a Catholic diocese: for scientists and lay readers alike, Abbé Breuil, is the acknowledged "father" of
French prehistoric archaeology in the twentieth century.

There is an obvious reason why the Catholic diocese of Soissons may
feel ambivalent about one of their own being the foremost prehistorian
of the country. Tensions and conflicts between religion and the science
of human evolution appeared throughout the mid-nineteenth century,
even before the introduction of Darwin's ideas, starting with Lamarck,
Geoffrey Saint-Hilaire, and their public arguments with Georges Cuvier
in the early decades of the century. Following the publication of Darwin's *Origin of Species* (1859) and its translation into numerous languages including French, the arguments acquired an international scale
and continued for decades. Yet the story of the relationship between
religion and science, particularly the science of human origins in France,
is far more complex and nuanced. It is not a simple story of the Church
opposing the teachings of human evolution, and a battle of two camps,
scientists and fathers of the Church, over the souls of ordinary people.
Numerous official members of the Church were dedicated and devout
scientists whose alliances were complicated and far from one-sided.
At the same time, many a scientist was not an atheist but rather an
ambivalent, often wavering agnostic or even a deist, expressing views
indirectly through research questions. The story of Abbé Breuil allows
us to examine how an ordained priest quietly managed not only to work
as a scientist of early human prehistory but also to become one of its
seminal figures. Was his position of a religious man in conflict with
his profession, and, if so, how did he solve such a seemingly obvious
dilemma? Without arguing for prehistoric religion, Breuil asserted his
views on spirituality through discussions of the emergence of art and
symbolism. I suggest that he, and many others who were receptive to
notions of religion as a universal phenomenon, got around an ostensibly

irreconcilable view of human nature by speaking about it indirectly and focusing on art and creativity.

In order to outline such a nonlinear history of French prehistory, it is essential to treat Breuil less as a singular figure worthy of hagiography—impressive and intriguing a prehistorian as he may have been—and more as a representative of a larger social historical position, that of religious scientists, who were common throughout France and much of Europe at the time. We thus have to situate his activities and views in their social context and examine them as a response to and part of a debate that already went on at the end of the previous century. To this end I will contrast Breuil's work and writing specifically with that of Gabriel de Mortillet, the mid-nineteenth-century "father of French prehistory." De Mortillet's adamant insistence on the nonexistence of prehistoric religion and his unwavering anticlericalism was the baseline from which every prehistorian in France operated at the end of the nineteenth century and the beginning of the twentieth. Abbé Breuil succeeded in shifting the conversation around this potential impasse, moving the science of prehistory in France forward by effectively sidestepping the question of religion altogether. Thus the modern scientific discipline of prehistory ultimately emerged in early twentieth-century France less in direct opposition to religion than along with its redefinition as a domain of human creativity and imagination.

RELIGIOUS SCIENTISTS

The fact that many priests, particularly Jesuits, have been involved in education and scientific research is hardly a subject of controversy. However, the involvement of Catholic priests in human origins research, particularly in France, has received little critical analysis (but see Grimoult 2003, 2008, Hurel 2003). Most archaeologists who work in Paleolithic Europe "know" that Henri Breuil was a priest, as he is referred to in all the literature as Abbé Breuil. Yet this aspect of his identity has received little attention in discussions of his work. If mentioned at all, his religious background is explained away in histories of archaeology by stating that he was a "nonpracticing" priest. For example, when writing about Breuil in 1964, the American physical anthropologist Carleton Coon stated adamantly: "He performed no parochial work at all, nor did he receive any pay. . . . Broderick reports two occasions only on which the Abbé said mass and one when he gave the last rites. The physician attending him at his death was a Muslim. Unlike his friend Teilhard de Chardin, Breuil had little to say about religion" (1964:948). Technically this is all true. Henri Breuil did not occupy a parish, did not serve any parishioners for pay, and did not attend services in an open, public fashion. Yet all the images and photographs of the Abbé routinely show him in a priestly outfit, overtly signaling his affiliation, making him instantly recognizable. Henri Breuil never severed his ties with the Catholic Church and in outward signs remained a celibate priest all his life. Furthermore, throughout his life Breuil moved in a wide network of priest scientists, starting with his seminary mentor Abbé Guibert and continuing with his many collaborators and companions such as the abbé brothers Bouyssonie or the Austrian priest and founder of Spanish prehistoric archaeology Hugo Obermaeir. He benefited from this circle tremendously in his personal and professional life. Rather than the facts of biography, it is the insistence of those who later wished to make him profoundly secular—and thus scientifically more credible—that suggests an inherently oppositional tension between science and religion in the history of archaeology.

Stories of priests walking the fields of their parish collecting archaeological materials during the nineteenth and twentieth centuries are well known throughout Europe. However, unlike most priests who were involved in prehistoric research at the time, Henri Breuil went through his ordination even as he became a respected prehistorian, the two transformations occurring simultaneously. Walking along parallel paths his entire life, Breuil described his vision in the following terms: "We must not confound religious truths with the symbolic forms by which they are passed on from generation to generation. These forms must be adapted and purified in accordance with the development of the human spirit. On the other hand, scientific truth founded on fact must not be confounded with provisional theories constituting working hypotheses" (Broderick 1963:141). The case of Henri Breuil thus offers something more than a biographical oddity, an interesting portrayal of an individual converting to critical reason through a possibly contradictory (or compartmentalized) life of religion and science. Rather it illustrates a generative moment in the institutionalization of European prehistory, where "the human spirit" might be another ground of truth, reducible neither to science nor to religion. By looking at early twentieth-century archaeology in relation to Breuil, we can see the conflicting social currents that surrounded it and suggest that at this particular juncture religion and science were actually co-constitutive in the formation of the new discipline.

THE BEGINNINGS OF ARCHAEOLOGY AND THE ORIGINS OF HUMANITY

France played a central role in the birth of European archaeology as a recognized science of the universal human past (Blanckaert 2001; Coye 1997; Trigger 2006). Some of the earliest formative statements about the stages of human evolution, the sequence of these stages, and the eponymic sites with archaeological remains illustrating the cultural sequence have their home in France. The earliest history of "anatomically modern" humans in particular, the Paleolithic period, can be traced by following the network of archaeological sites through central and southern France. This was also the location of some of the earliest examples of prehistoric art, cave paintings and portable carved objects. All these were a part of the general awareness of human antiquity by the turn of the twentieth century. However the place of tools, especially stone tools, was far more certain as the essential element of human progress than was any symbolic expression in the form of paintings or carved objects. The accepted range of human capabilities, cognitive wherewithal, and expression of symbolic needs was infinitely more contentious. An impassioned debate about the emergence of human spirituality raged relentlessly from the 1850s and continued well into the twentieth century. In early moments the discussion focused on mortuary practices, the presence (and even more the absence) of burials, and only later shifted to include the question of a broader range of symbolic abilities, such as art or human emotions like laughter (Sommer 2006). Thus in order to talk about Henri Breuil and the science of prehistory in the early twentieth century, we need to back up some fifty years and consider the milieu in which archaeology was transformed from a pleasurable outdoor activity for amateurs with time, income, and property to the serious pursuit of an educated elite with a specific social agenda.

French prehistory emerged as a scholarly field in a context framed by the dramatic relationship between church and state after the French Revolution. The fierce arguments between the clericals and anticlericals were by all accounts among the most significant political events of the last three decades of the nineteenth century prior to the 1905 official separation of church and state (see Zeldin 1970; McMillan 1985; Grimoult 2003; Hecht

2003). The rejection of the Church by members of the educated elite is frequently interpreted as a victory for science. In the case of research related to human antiquity, the eventual acceptance of Darwinian evolution usually represents the lasting legacy of the late nineteenth century. However, the path leading to this outcome was hardly as simple or straightforward as retrospective accounts suggest. To illustrate this I turn to the point when the radical feminist Clémence Royer, the first female member of the Society of Anthropology (Société d'Anthropologie), translated Darwin's *Origin of Species* (1859) into French, including her own strongly worded introduction with a Lamarckian twist. This was also the moment when a sometime socialist engineer named Gabriel de Mortillet returned from exile in Italy and embraced materialism as the definitive explanation of human progress from antiquity to his times.

POSITIVISM, MATERIALISM, AND THE SOUL IN ANCIENT TIMES

Gabriel de Mortillet's trajectory exemplifies the life of a man of science in the second half of the nineteenth century in that his political drive and belief in the possibility of a new kind of society deeply informed his practice of science. In the company of fellow freethinkers such as André Lefèvre, Eugene Veron, Charles Letourneau, Abel Hovelacque, and Henri Thulé, he actively promoted the political agenda of the materialist left through anthropology. A common perspective rather than occupation united the men; except for de Mortillet, who already worked at archaeology, all of them were lawyers, doctors, writers, or fellow travelers with independent means. In anthropology they found a science through which to express their views on the past, present, and future of human society. Using journals, laboratories, the museum, and the Société d'anthropologie to define a new science rooted in rationalism and allowing for social change, this group of "angry young men" worked at changing the empire.

Louis Laurent Gabriel de Mortillet was born in Meylan (Isere) in 1821 and educated at a Jesuit college in Chambery and a conservatoire in Paris, after which he became a geological engineer. Already as a student he got involved in radical politics and remained dedicated to socialism throughout his life. As a new owner of *La Revue Independent* (1847), and hence publisher of controversial pamphlets, he was quickly forced into exile in Italy after 1848. He settled into the life of an engineer and geologist in Savoy, returning to France only in 1864. While in exile, de Mortillet participated in several prehistoric projects, including the submerged Lake Varese dwellings in Italy, giving him a start on his interest in life in ancient times. Upon his return to France, de Mortillet settled in Paris and began the publication of a new journal, *Matériaux pour l'histoire positive et philosophique de l'homme*. It was in this journal that he laid out his views on the human path from antiquity to the present, tying every stage firmly to material evidence, representing the "history of labor and struggle for existence." The journal was the first ever to be devoted entirely to prehistory, but by all accounts it was "not so much a learned review as a combat journal" (Reinach 1899:75). De Mortillet waged this combat on two fronts simultaneously, opposing the Catholic Church in an attempt to confront its political and cultural influence, while also seeking to establish an evolutionary paradigm as the dominant scientific view.

In terms of simple primacy, Gabriel de Mortillet cannot be credited for the "invention of prehistory" in France, as he was not the first prehistorian in the country (Grayson 1983; Richard 1989, 2008). The antiquity of humans and their long history was of interest to a notable collection of scientists and thinkers since at least the end of the eighteenth century. The catastrophist Georges Cuvier, the customs officer (one of many memorable customs officers in French history) Boucher de Perthes, and the deist Geoffroy Saint-Hilaire were all instrumental in establishing the possibility and acceptance of human antiquity. By the time de Mortillet and his collective intervened in the debate in the 1860s, the main conceptual battle had been won—the "antediluvian" man of Boucher de Perthes was now referred to as a "prehistoric" ancestor, since the biblical flood no longer figured as a chronological marker of distant time. Rather, the past now revolved around geological markers and reference to natural events not mentioned in the Bible.

Nonetheless, while this linguistic turn was significant, prehistory only became a discipline in France when institutions, societies, and journals gave a tangible, material form to the discussion of human antiquity through collections, circulated publications, brick buildings, and a world exhibition. In this sense the institutional birth of prehistory in France occurred in the early 1860s, starting with the establishment of the Museum of National Antiquities in St. Germain-en-Laye in 1857 (inaugurated as an official museum ten years later in 1867). The publication of *Matériaux pour l'histoire positive et philosophique de l'homme* as a specialized publication devoted solely to prehistory followed in 1864. This journal eventually found an institutional base in the Ecole d'Anthropologie,

since the Muséum National d'Histoire Naturelle was closed to radical supporters of evolutionary theory. In 1867 Paris hosted a colossal Exposition Universelle on the Champs de Mars with over nine million visitors.
De Mortillet played a leading role, personally organizing and supervising
the Promenade Préhistorique at the exhibition, giving the newly emerging science of prehistory unprecedented public exposure and inspiring
long-lasting interest. The establishment of permanent university lectures at the Ecole d'Anthropologie in 1875 was the final building block.
Scientific materialists had succeeded in building an institutional home
for their prehistoric science, from which to influence science and society
through research, publications, and teaching. De Mortillet's small band
now claimed the human past.

CLASSIFICATION, CHRONOLOGY, AND STAGES OF PROGRESS

For prehistorians of de Mortillet's generation the main research question was to determine the process of cultural and physical development
by examining its prehistoric steps, thereby mapping a progressive path
that would be both comparative and universally applicable. Edouard Lartet, who excavated one of the first cave sites in France, the rock shelter
at Aurignac, drafted a tentative model in 1861 that claimed not only the
coexistence of ancient people and extinct mammals but also an evolutionary sequence. Lartet suggested a sequence that was based on the typology of animals that roamed the land with ancient humans, labeling the
periods as the Age of the Cave Bear (l'Age du Grand Ours), associated with
the Aurignac site, the Age of the Elephant and Rhinoceros, the Age of the
Reindeer, and the Age of the Auroch (Lartet 1864). The major innovation
and a historically significant turning point of Lartet's scheme was the
establishment of a contemporaneity between people and ancient mammals that no longer lived in Europe. Even more daring was the merging of
human and natural history, naming the periods not by the inhabitants of
ancient Gaul, or their suggested prehistoric cultural activities and technical prowess, but by the animals that they may have eaten (or were eaten
by). Following in Lartet's footsteps, de Mortillet took upon himself to
create a systematic linear developmental scheme, one that was based on
strictly materialist philosophy. Prehistoric physical and cultural developments were described as having gone through unwaveringly progressive
stages, gradual change and were assumed to have occurred universally.

Using French archaeological sites as eponyms, de Mortillet created a cultural and evolutionary sequence, describing the culture of the "Époque de Saint-Acheul," named after the stone tools found at the gravel site Saint-Acheul, near Paris, the Mousterian culture of the Ice Age, named after the site Le Moustier in the Dordogne valley, the Solutrean, named after the site of Solutré in the Loire valley, and finally the Magdalenian culture, named after La Madeleine in the Dordogne valley.

Using French archaeological sites, de Mortillet established the centrality of not just Western Europe but also France in the evolution of human culture. Large mammals may have roamed all over the continent but the juxtaposition of an evolutionary stage with stone tools from a location in France achieved several goals at once. De Mortillet asserted the materialist perspective as primary in the investigation of human antiquity, at the same time making labor and technology central to human progress. Locating this central argument geographically in France, he placed French prehistoric archaeology into the center and at the forefront of a new discipline. By taking this particular direction, de Mortillet was consciously speaking to multiple audiences. On the one hand was the international scientific community, since prehistoric research was also emerging as a vibrant and dominant field in Britain, Belgium, Germany, and Denmark. Furthermore, the older generation was deemed "excessive admirers" of Germany for their positivist philosophy (Hecht 2003:64). Making France the home base of scientific materialism not only established a new ground for the discipline of anthropology and prehistory but also gave the new philosophical approach a national genealogy. In 1879 André Lefèvre expressed sentiments felt by this anthropological community as follows: "When an independent group, unaided and committed to no sort of compromises, raised the banner of Free Thought towards the close of the empire, it did not walk in the footsteps of Virchow, Moleschott, Buchner, Vogt, though still encouraged by the alliance of such men; it resumed a possession of its own inheritance, which had well-nigh passed into the hands of strangers" (Lefèvre 1879:459).

Rejecting German genealogy, French philosophers were ready to take the stage. Equally central was de Mortillet's engagement with prehistorians and natural philosophers in the homeland. In the French context his new schema offered a radical contrast to anything preceding it, including the most popular version of transformative changes or revolutions of Georges Cuvier. A founder of vertebrate paleontology, Cuvier was a functionalist who believed that all similarity in form is the result of similar function, not

genealogy, and remained steadfast in his scientific opposition to evolutionary theory as well as his adherence to conservative politics. At stake was
a fundamental understanding of nature related to the central question of
evolution: can nature change without divine intervention? De Mortillet's
version of materialist philosophy tied human culture and its development
to the evolution of stone tools and technology (for a detailed discussion of
the issue, see Coye 1997:136–49). As a geologist, de Mortillet was well positioned to take a stand on stone tools as the connection between human
ancestors and the natural world. At the same time, the new classification
of stone tools and prehistoric cultures allowed for an eminently practical application of the scheme at an excavation in the field. Any practicing
prehistorian could now collect his archaeological materials and compare
them to the newly created scheme. The stone tool types were organized
in the display cases of the museum in St. Germain-en-Laye for everyone
to see, giving a visual guide to the philosophy that de Mortillet espoused.
By implication, human progress was not only possible and tangible but,
over the long run, inevitable, as reflected in the tools of labor left in the
archaeological record. Nature changed, de Mortillet asserted, through the
intervention of human labor and control of the natural environment.

This stress on the role of labor in the stages of human cultural development was most evident during the World Fair in 1867 that de Mortillet
organized. The "Promenade Préhistorique" comprised a major part of an
exhibit section entitled the Gallery of the Labor History.[1] The prehistoric
exhibit stressed that human beings are essentially productive, and must
fabricate their means of subsistence, in this case the prehistoric tools, in
order to satisfy their material needs. Material life determined, or at least
"conditioned" social life, and the primary direction of anthropological
explanation ran from material production to social form. This explanation was ideally suited for the prehistorians: it not only made their finds
in prehistoric technology central to a larger narrative of prehistory but
also allowed them to claim instrumental reason as the major force behind
human progress. Connecting technology to rationality at the onset of
human societies set up the stage for a denial of any need for religion or
superstition, as successful struggle for survival was the essence of what
it meant to be human. This claim cemented the extensive discussions in
journals and publications suggesting an absence of any spiritual or religious forms in the early stages of human societies.

The exhibition received favorable attention and positioned French
prehistorians prominently within natural history. Otis Mason, the first

full-time curator at the Smithsonian in Washington, DC, wrote ecstatically about the new discipline of anthropology in France, placing de Mortillet at the forefront of its accomplishments:

> The museums of human arts, however, are the crowning glory of Paris. In them may be traced the whole history of France from the first human action to the latest exposition. One should commence with the palace of St. Germain-en-Laye, 13 miles from Paris by rail, omnibus, or boat. This beautiful structure was erected by Francis I for a royal residence. Here were born Henry II, Charles IX, and Louis XIV, and here died Louis XIII. Surrounded by a park of ten thousand acres stands the building in which may be read the material record of France down to the beginning of the Middle Ages. In one of the upper halls, arranged in the most perfect order, is the story of the Stone period. Here in the upper left-hand corner, as on a printed page, you begin with the burned and wrought flints of the Abbe Bourgeois, to which archaeologists go for proof of the existence of man in early Tertiary. You will have no difficulty in finding your way around the hall, but the Congres d'Anthropologie were so fortunate as to have the venerable G. de Mortillet as guide, who organized and arranged the exhibits with his own hands.
>
> (Mason 1890:27)

With the establishment of an age-system defined through artifacts and a triumphant public display, the ascendancy of the materialist vision of prehistory seemed assured.

BRING OUT YOUR DEAD

Having established tool making and labor as the central forces of human evolution, de Mortillet and his supporters remained resolute about the absence of religion during the earliest period of antiquity. According to their interpretation of the archaeological evidence, relying on a distinctly materialist view of evolutionary theory, a daily struggle for food and shelter and animal-like life marked the beginning of human society. Only in much later stages, they asserted, did any sense of symbolic behavior and social life appear. This interpretation of the archaeological materials suggested that human spirituality was not a natural condition or an inevitable state of the human mind, but rather a secondary social development that played no role in the early emergence of human society. The satisfaction of basic needs may have later engendered new needs of both a material and social kind, given forms of society corresponded to the state of development of human productive forces. But, judging from stone tools, complex rituals or belief in an afterlife were unnecessary in the early stages of prehistory.

Since the archaeological record of the Quaternary period was rather sparse and consisted solely of tools used in the daily lives of the "troglodytes" (as their makers were then known), life itself seemed rather mundane. Hence death and possible attitudes toward death among ancient peoples attracted an inordinate amount of attention by anthropologists as well as philosophers, writers, even poets. The initial writings focused on the possibility of human burials and the rituals associated with them as a reflection of a belief system. The great majority of Paleolithic sites found at the time lacked any human remains. This is mostly due to the very poor preservation of skeletal materials, although archaeologists have also considered funerary alternatives to burials. In the absence of preserved human skeletons, any discussion of ancient burial practices remained purely a hypothetical argument driven mainly by imaginary, abstract views of prehistoric life. The standard image of the evolutionary path suggested prehistoric people emerged out of dark caves into the "light of history" (Richards 2002). According to the materialist, anticlerical view of anthropologists of the time, the darker portion of that path out of a cave resembled animal life, devoid of any spiritual capacity.

In discussions of the origin of funerary ritual, Clémence Royer was particularly adamant in denying any possible religious sentiments in the early stages of human evolution and describing attitudes toward death in as animalistic terms as possible. Now best remembered as the official translator of Darwin's work into French, Royer was perhaps better known at the time for her own evolutionary views presented in an unauthorized and spirited preface to the *Origin of Species*: "Yes, I believe in revelation, but a permanent revelation of man to himself and by himself, a rational revelation that is nothing but the result of the progress of science and of the contemporary conscience, a revelation that is always only partial and relative and that is effectuated by the acquisition of new truths and even more by the elimination of ancient errors" (Royer in Fraisse 1985:127).

Running a full thirty-seven pages, the preface presented a discourse on religion and science and a vigorous espousal of materialism as revelation. Although considered a philosopher and not a prehistorian, Royer frequently wrote on anthropological topics, particularly prehistory. Constructing her arguments on the basis of political adherence to anticlericalism, progressive politics, and conviction that evolutionary theory was the only possible path toward truth in science, she chose one aspect of religious life that remained a vexing issue even for the freethinkers—the question of death. For former Catholics among the anthropologists, the ritual of the funeral and thoughts of a life after seemed to have retained a strong grip on their imagination in the centrality of its denial. As Hecht (2003) showed in her study of the nineteenth-century Society of Mutual Autopsy (to which many of the anthropologists and prehistorians belonged), skulls lined the walls of the laboratories, museums, and offices. These fossils and skeletons evoked almost a religious fervor of denial of any possible burial rituals among prehistoric peoples. The prehistorians found the absence of human remains in the majority of Paleolithic sites to be expected rather than surprising, given that ancient people were simply "other animals," devoid of spiritual insights into death or afterlife.

> What is necessary to conclude from this, if not that the first feeling experienced by man at the sight of corpses of its own species was to move away, to flee, as it fled from all other corpses, and to give them up to natural causes of destruction, as all other animals do? One thus does not have to expect to meet the trace of funerary rites among the primitive human populations. Indeed, these traces seem absent during most of the quaternary time. The absence of given rites can only explain the scarcity of the human bones in the majority of the layers of this time.
>
> (Royer 1876:438, in Fraisse 1985)

Royer explained human behavior in the same way as animal behavior: a process of adaptation through progressive, evolutionary stages. She interpreted the absence of human remains as a clear indication of the absence of any spirituality and a sign that in Quaternary times humans had abandoned their dead, just as any animal would.

De Mortillet was just as certain of the absence of any funerary rites during the Paleolithic as Royer. However, unlike her, de Mortillet addressed the issue through a discussion of specific archaeological sites and their excavated materials. Convinced that ritual behavior (which he equated with religious sentiments) was not an innate human characteristic, he suggested that it had arrived late in Europe, only appearing with the invasion of Neolithic people from the East. The conflation of geographic location and human consciousness resulted in a claim that religion could not have possibly originated in France but had to be a foreign element brought from the outside. Paleolithic graves were assumed to have been nonexistent, and when human skeletons did appear in some caves, for example, in Aurignac, the dead were explained as invasive to the time period in question. Relying on his expertise as a geologist, de Mortillet accounted for skeletal materials in Paleolithic contexts as intrusive elements that most likely moved either through geological forces into lower layers or were directly buried by the more recent populations into greater depths. "During the Neolithic era the dead were very frequently buried in the caves and consequently placed very often in Paleolithic deposits. It is one of the great causes of error. It is thus necessary to be very circumspect in the determination of the age of the human bones" (de Mortillet 1910:311). Related discussions offered the possibility of the dead having been eaten by surviving group members as another explanation for the meager skeletal remains in the archaeological sites. While the anthropologists of this circle worked very hard to make every connection between the animal and human world, here they eventually balked. However, they rejected the cannibal hypothesis not by ascribing any moral sentiment to ancient populations but rather because they considered it to be a rare custom among closely related animals. De Mortillet's general conclusion remained that spirituality played no role in early prehistory: "Death was nothing for the man of these remote times. There was not thus belief in the existence of a spirit. There was not either belief in a god protector or one punishing his creatures. A concept of a spiritual being did not exist. Everything seems to indicate that the Paleolithic man was completely devoid of any feeling of religiosity" (de Mortillet 1910:336).[2]

ART, SYMBOLS, AND THE SPECTER OF RELIGION

In 1922 Marcellin Boule, professor at the Museum of Natural History and director of the Institute of Human Paleontology in Paris, delivered the Huxley Memorial Lecture at the Royal Anthropological Institute in London, the highest honor bestowed by the institute on an anthropologist. Boule dedicated his lecture on recent progress in "human paleontology" to Prince Albert I of Monaco, who had just passed away in 1922 and had been the founder and financial supporter of something known as L'Institut de

Paléontologie Humain. His presentation recognized a significant turn in the public face and presentation of prehistoric archaeology, a shift away from the materialist foundation set in the previous century and a public rejection of its founding father. Evoking many of the famous British geologists and prehistorians, Boule created a genealogy that differed strikingly from the French scientific materialism and evolutionary thought set as the dominant paradigm since the 1860s. After listing the numerous major contributions of Gabriel de Mortillet to prehistoric archaeology, Boule continued, "Gabriel de Mortillet rendered great service to prehistoric archaeology but he was frequently an obstacle to the progress of the same science due to his preconceived ideas and his anti-religious preoccupation" (154).

The issue at stake was the Grimaldi cave, discovered and excavated on the property of the Monaco royal family in the 1870s. The site contained prehistoric figurines as well as skeletal remains of some fifteen individuals, including several children who showed distinct signs of burial rather than abandonment. De Mortillet publicly attacked the scientific methods, questioned the stratigraphy of the caves, and suggested that the carved objects were obvious fakes (Bisson and Bolduc 1994). The dispute was one of many de Mortillet was involved in, which by the end of his life (1898) had become increasingly frequent. Not only was he opposed to any possible burials and funerary rites during the Paleolithic times, on the same grounds de Mortillet fought relentlessly against the idea of prehistoric art. Creativity was too close to spirituality and abstract thought, difficult to separate on the basis of evidence alone.

At the same time, this topic proved harder to explain away on theoretical grounds alone, as carved objects and later painted caves left a powerful impression and attracted many new scientists to prehistoric archaeology. When prehistoric archaeologists initially brought to light evidence of symbolic representation in prehistoric contexts, they encountered a standard denial and rejection of the evidence on the basis that religion and spirituality had been absent in the early stages of human evolution. The earliest finds of small carved mammoths on pieces of ivory at La Madeleine by Lartet and Christy in 1864 were used to prove a different point: the coexistence of ancient humans and large prehistoric mammals. The materialist prehistorians interpreted the depiction of animals as an adaptive response, an imitation of surrounding nature (the later basis for the "art for art's sake" explanation of prehistoric symbolic behavior). De Mortillet did not dispute the existence of carved objects, decorative pendants, and shells found at many sites in France. However, he insisted on treating them the same as all the objects of technology, the same as stone tools, items admired for their simplicity and adaptive value. Even when acknowledging the possibility of any symbolic status, he did so quite condescendingly: "cette enfance d'art était loin de l'art de l'enfant [this infancy of art was far from the art of a child]."

In 1870, however, the painted caves of Altamira were discovered in northern Spain by an amateur archaeologist, Marcelino Sanz de Sautuola. These new finds posed a dilemma of a different order than the portable carvings and objects recovered before then. The large, colorful, and skillfully executed paintings could not be dismissed as too simple or lacking in imagination. Instead their authenticity and age were called into question. De Mortillet and his colleague Emile Cartailhac were particularly adamant in rejecting the hypothesis of Sautuola that the paintings dated from the Paleolithic and loudly ridiculed even the suggestion at the 1880 Prehistoric Congress in Lisbon, stating (ironically, given earlier suggestions about Neolithic importation of religion) that art was solely a French domain (Moro Abadia and González Morales 2004). It was the lawyer Edouard Piette, not associated with the freethinkers and materialists of Paris, who took on the prehistoric art mission from the provinces of southern France and for decades fought de Mortillet. Only after de Mortillet's death did Emile Cartailhac publish a retraction of his position on Altamira in *L'Anthropologie* under the heading "La grotte d'Altamira, Espagne. Mea culpa d'un sceptique" (1902).[3] It was left to Abbé Breuil to turn the page on art in the new century and through it on the question of religion and spirituality in prehistoric times.

Reading the Boule speech in retrospect recalls a different speech in a different part of Europe on a different topic, yet similar in other respects: Khrushchev's speech in 1956 to the Twentieth Communist Party Congress. Here Khrushchev denounced the cult of personality surrounding Stalin, accusing him of having stifled progress and thinking about the present state of the world. Such a speech had to be given in a public space with numerous witnesses, had to have institutional support and protection—in Boule's case the Huxley Memorial Lecture in London. Boule was not saying anything new or revelatory. Rather he made public thoughts that had circulated privately for a number of years and, moreover, went abroad to say it. De Mortillet was a major figure who established prehistoric archaeology as a scientific discipline. Yet his strongly held anticlerical views led him to promote a certain theoretical approach in uncompromising terms and publicly scorn all dissent. As a consequence, he not only discouraged research into questions of prehistoric art, religion, and the origins of spirituality but actively suppressed and attacked it. He was a promoter of a particular doctrine, a founder of a new kind of church of materialism that in France picked up a devout following. The interesting point about the speech for us, then, is the extent to which de Mortillet had apparently succeeded in keeping a monolithic view of the past intact prior to Boule's open rejection.

By the late nineteenth century, cracks started appearing; Piette was relentless if isolated, and after de Mortillet's death the gates opened for art and religion to get a fresh new start. One of the most interesting twists of French prehistoric research at the beginning of the twentieth century is the activity of Catholic priest scientists who succeeded in advancing the goals of modernism. Through their very public clashes with the materialists, they were, in the end, the group that gave shape and direction to the research agenda of prehistory for the twentieth century. However, the struggle was not about the acceptance or rejection of Darwin's evolutionary theory, since each side had a mixed reaction to it. The conflict was about the role of art, imagination, and spirituality in the origins of human societies and ultimately about what it meant to be human—material existence or spirituality. Through their work, the religious scientists institutionalized and popularized prehistory as the new science of the past and identified the core of humanity in spirituality and art.

RELIGIOUS SCIENTISTS AND THE SCIENCE OF RELIGION

Connecting the provinces where fieldwork occurred with the center where knowledge was affirmed and reproduced through teaching and publications, the prehistorians of Breuil's circle gave a new direction to the emerging science of the past. A new institutional setting anchored their accomplishment: the L'Institute Paléontologie Humaine, established in Paris in 1910 with sufficient financial backing to permit independence from existing organizations and free its members to chart their own course. In due time Breuil and his collaborators occupied themselves with Quaternary art and wrote at length about art and magic, adroitly maneuvering between the edicts of religious doctrine and the dogma of materialist philosophy.

The list of priests active in prehistoric research in France is long and impressive. Here I will just mention three well-known and active

researchers to underline the depth of the field and the long scientific tradition within Catholic ranks in this country: Abbé Henri Bremond, the
literary scholar and author of many works on *sentiment religieux,* who
regularly engaged in polemics with prehistorians about the origin of said
sentiment; Abbé Antoine Ducrost, whose tombstone was decorated with
an allegorical statue of prehistory; the abbé brothers Amédée and Jean
Bouyssonie who discovered the Neandertal skeleton at La Chapelle-aux-
Saints. The biography and career of Abbé Breuil is thus representative of a
whole generation of priest scientists. Breuil received initial training in science and prehistory at the seminary Saint-Sulpice in Paris from his mentor Abbé Jean Guibert, a well-known natural science writer and author
of a lengthy 1896 study on human origins, the theory of evolution, and
the capacity for religion among the earliest humans entitled "Les origines:
Question d'apologétique." Since Breuil is mentioned in the acknowledg-
ments as one of the students with whom Guibert had extensive conversations about the subject matter, it is worth quoting its perspective directly,
as the text addresses several research questions of prehistorians of
the day:

> If religion has left no recognizable trace, there is also nothing to
> prove that the men of Chelles and of Saint Acheul therefore had
> none. The absence of all indications of religion is easily explained,
> but the absence of all religion in primitive man would be inexpli-
> cable. This short summary is sufficient to convince us that religion
> in the human races existed as far back as we can reach, not merely
> as recorded by history, but as known by legitimate induction. It is
> therefore natural to admit that primitive man was himself religious,
> or at least it would be very illogical to deny it.
>
> (Guibert 1896:367)

This premise, written by a Catholic science teacher at a seminary,
became the working hypothesis for a new generation of prehistorians,
which came in with the twentieth century, that came to be known as "the
clan Breuil," opposing "the clan Mortillet" (Hurel 2003). Yet this oppositional politics of the past in France at the turn of the twentieth century
does not map onto current contests between science and religion in any
simple fashion. The archaeologists did not see their place as prehistorians and as priests as contradictory but rather as complimentary. Similarly, the anticlericalism of de Mortillet and his supporters meant their

materialism derived from political rather than epistemological motivations; they opposed the Church more than they embraced evolution.

That said, within a broader European context, Breuil chose his intellectual path during rather tumultuous times. He was ordained a few years before the 1907 encyclical *Pascendi Dominici Gregis: On the Doctrine of the Modernists,* which extensively commented on the errors of modernity, and science in particular, with specific instructions for research in selected fields in higher education, including history and archaeology.[4]

Clerics and priests inscribed in a Catholic Institute or University must not in the future follow in civil Universities those courses for which there are chairs in the Catholic Institutes to which they belong. If this has been permitted anywhere in the past, We ordain that it be not allowed for the future.

(49)

Anybody who in any way is found to be imbued with Modernism is to be excluded without compunction from these offices, and those who already occupy them are to be withdrawn. The same policy is to be adopted towards those who favor Modernism either by extolling the Modernists or excusing their culpable conduct, by criticizing scholasticism, the Holy Father, or by refusing obedience to ecclesiastical authority in any of its depositaries; and towards those who show a love of novelty in history, archaeology, biblical exegesis, and finally towards those who neglect the sacred sciences or appear to prefer to them the profane.

(48)

Since Breuil did not serve a parish, he fell outside the obligatory anti-modernism rhetoric. Nonetheless, as an ambitious man and not a radical, he walked the path of science carefully, addressing in his research prehistoric skill and creativity rather than religion. The lack of an institutional home was a precarious position to occupy, and Breuil's work displayed diligence more than independence of mind or rebellious spirit. The young priest patiently studied prehistoric art, accumulating evidence and establishing a reputation as a skilled draftsman. Following in the wake of his mentor Piette, he was present in 1901 when images were discovered in caves at Les Combarelles and Font-de-Gaume. Although these finds met with skepticism, the following year a delegation of French archaeologists (including Breuil) visited the site of La Mouthe and recognized the images as authentic. He subsequently visited Altamira, measuring and sketching the paintings. The publication of these may have inspired Picasso, but it still encountered resistance. Although Gabriel de Mortillet was dead, his son carried on the fight, suggesting that Altamira had been painted "by Spanish Jesuits in order to discredit prehistory" (Broderick 1963:66; Moro Abadia and González Morales 2004). Breuil carried on, taking a position as a *privat-dozent* at the Catholic University of Fribourg in Switzerland, quietly following the papal encyclical, which discouraged instruction through secular higher education. However, his career and standing changed dramatically when he acquired the backing of an influential patron, Prince Albert I of Monaco, and through it a new institutional base.

In 1904 the royal from the tiny Mediterranean principality, known for his passion for natural sciences, received Breuil's reproductions of the cave paintings from Altamira, Font-de-Gaume, and Marsoulas. While he may have recognized their scientific value, Albert of Monaco was captivated first and foremost by the artistic representations and immediately committed to financing all of Breuil's research, reproductions, and publications (Breuil 1909; Capitan, Breuil, and Peyrony 1910; Hurel 2003). In one fell swoop, Breuil acquired full-time support for his prehistoric research throughout the Mediterranean region as well as a patron who regularly visited his excavations and accompanied him on numerous occasions in the field. However, the most lasting impact of Prince Albert's support was the establishment of L'Institut de Paléontologie Humaine in Paris in 1910. The new institute located Breuil's version of prehistory permanently on the map of scientific institutions, while permitting him to continue to amass evidence of prehistoric art.

Fieldwork was Breuil's trademark. Pictures of him in fields, caves, and rock shelters—inevitably equipped with hat and walking cane—accompanied many publications in scholarly and popular press. His collection of data was extensive, detailed, and not based in museum depositories. Unlike de Mortillet and the many gentlemen of science who resided in Paris and only occasionally made excursions to the countryside, Breuil was a passionate field archaeologist. Fieldwork gave him a certain monopoly on the view of the universe, a window allowing a glance that could not be replicated in a museum or a laboratory (Gieryn 2002). Breuil certainly capitalized on this aspect of the science, and he became a master of it. At the same time, his field focus left him with relatively attenuated means for the dispersal and circulation of the knowledge of the past that his work generated. His invited lectures, public discussions, even publications and printed exchanges were infrequent, and his network of fellow scientists consequently restricted, as the main circulation of knowledge was concentrated in a few Parisian institutions, not all receptive to his interests. The construction of a new building for the Institute of Human Paleontology, however, changed all that. Decorated with engravings of prehistoric scenes from selected archaeological sites that Breuil personally chose and commissioned, the institute provided prehistoric art with a new permanent and visible structure.

"What do buildings do?" a number of sociologists and historians of science ask (Forgan 2005; Forgan and Gooday 1996; Schroeder-Gudehus 1993). "Buildings stabilize social life. They give structure to social institutions, durability to social networks, persistence to behavior patterns. What we build solidifies society against time and its incessant forces for change" (Gieryn 2002:35). In the case of scientific institutions, buildings do all those things, *and* they provide an architectural statement about the epistemic truth produced among the walls. The 1910 Institute of Human Paleontology, an imposing structure taking up an entire city block, was built just around the corner from the venerable Museum of Natural History, until then one of the main spaces for the production of knowledge about prehistory. Yet this new institute was *not* a museum. It was a research laboratory, a new invention that combined fieldwork and laboratory space to encourage generation of new ideas. It presented knowledge about the past as actively scientific in contrast to the speculative and not demonstrative manner in which museums displayed their wares. Breuil and his collaborators gained a space and a place that allowed them to investigate the kind of past they considered central to human development by means of their choice. At the same time, Quaternary man and his artistic evolution could be studied without the interference of the Catholic Church. Thus Breuil's group could avoid the battles over materialism that embroiled de Mortillet and his supporters, either ignoring them or responding in their own terms through regular publications, lectures, and events hosted in the new edifice.

Henri Breuil was named a professor of "prehistoric ethnography" in the new institution, while Hugo Obermaier, an Austrian priest and prehistorian who was his inseparable companion, became "professor of geology and prehistory." The supporters of de Mortillet perceived this as an official endorsement of an antimaterialist line of research and direction for prehistory and thus denounced the new venture loudly and angrily. Writing in *La*

Grande Revue in 1911, Adrien Guébhard, the former president of the Prehistoric Society, labeled the newly established institute a modern "château des papes," a court reserved for "priest prehistorians," and accused the pope of having thus acquired a firm grip on the science of prehistory (Hurel 2003). Given the Catholic Church's opposition to prehistoric research within its own walls, the accusation held some irony. However, it reflected the deep conviction among de Mortillet's supporters that the clerical wing of archaeology and its interest in prehistoric art could only represent a cabal driven by religious sentiment. The political and intellectual reality was too complex to permit simple refutation. Breuil had to tread his path carefully, and by remaining beyond the bounds of the official priesthood he quietly avoided the religious question. The building that Albert of Monaco built, and the finances he provided, enabled Breuil and his generation of priest scientists to find a space between the polarized discussions for their work. Avoiding both the religious dogma of the Church and the embrace of devout materialism, they produced a new vision of prehistory focused on creativity and the human spirit they took it to embody.

Over the next three decades Breuil continued to pursue his vocation in ever-wider circles, expanding his involvement in prehistory to South Africa and China and authoring highly influential books. Throughout the Abbé's rise to prominence, his calling card remained prehistoric art. However, from his entrance into the setting of the Institute of Human Paleontology, he increasingly connected art to magic. Magic was the spiritual motivation, origin and force for art throughout time. Rather than entering debates over prehistoric religiosity directly, he focused on evidence of prehistoric creativity, and by extension spiritual life. His own public views on religion remained relatively muted, open and apparently untroubled. Breuil clearly regarded himself as a man of science, fully committed to the work of reason. At the same time his vision diverged sharply from de Mortillet's materialism: the true work of prehistory lay not in illustrating human progress through increasing stages of ingenious labor but rather ultimately in tracing "the development of the human spirit." For Breuil and his generation, art was the portal through which claims to spiritual life could reenter discussions of the human past. The process of doing so eventually reconfigured the Church, modernity, and materialism as well as the relations between them. For all that prehistoric archaeology remains firmed locked in an embrace with material analysis and evolutionary theory, it also carries with it a trace of something else: the images of ancient animals, once painted deep inside dark caves and then artfully reproduced by Henri Edouard Prosper Breuil.

Nineteenth-century materialism grounded the early twentieth-century discussions of early magic, spirit, and religion, providing the necessary scientific context for their study. Between them, de Mortillet and Breuil constructed an essential framework for archaeology as the new science of the past, one that we still recognize to this day. In doing so they redefined what it means to be human relative to deep history, describing the emergence of humans who were not only anatomically modern and sapient but also spiritual, religious, and artistic beings. Both religious and materialist claims to essential human qualities would now invoke prehistory, seeking origin amid the haunting traces such ancestors left behind.

NOTES

1. "Sous le rapport préhistorique, l'Exposition universelle de Paris est des plus intéressantes. La première galerie autour du jardin central, désignée sous le nom de Galerie de l'histoire du travail, est celle qui contient en majeure partie les richesses préhistoriques."
2. " Le mort n'était plus rien pour l'homme de ces temps lointains. Il n'y avait donc pas croyance a l'existence d'une âme. Il n'y avait pas non plus croyance en un dieu protègent ou punissant ses créatures. La conception d'un être spirituel n'existait pas. Tout semble indiquer que l'homme paléolithique était totalement dépourvu du sentiment de la religiosité."
3. With an appeal to the power of scientific fact, Cartailhac wrote: "C'était absolument nouveau et étrange. Il faut s'incliner devant la réalité d'un fait . . . Le monde est désormais sans mystère. . . . Notre science, comme les autres, écrit une histoire qui ne sera jamais terminée, mais dont l'intérêt augmente sans cesse (350). [It was absolutely new and strange. We must bow to the reality of a fact . . . The world is now without mystery. . . . Our science, like others, wrote a story that will never be complete, but whose value increases continuously.]
4. This encyclical was enforced until 1967. See http://www.papalencyclicals.net/Pius10/p10pasce.htm.

REFERENCES

Appel, T., 1987. *The Cuvier-Geoffroy Debate: French Biology in the Decades Before Darwin.* Oxford: Oxford University Press.

Artigas, M, T. F. Glick, and R. A. Martinez. 2006. *Negotiating Darwin: The Vatican Confronts Evolution, 1877–1902.* Baltimore: Johns Hopkins University Press.

Bisson, M., and P. Bolduc. 1994. "Previously Undescribed Figurines from the Grimaldi Caves." *Current Anthropology* 35:458–68.

Blanckaert, C., ed. 2001. *Les Politiques de l'anthropologie: discours et pratiques en France (1860–1940)*. Paris: L'Harmattan.

Bowler, P., 1974. *Fossils and Progress: Paleontology and the Idea of Progressive Evolution in the Nineteenth Century*. New York: Science History.

——— 1983. *The Eclipse of Darwinism: Anti-Darwinian Evolution Theories in the Decades Around 1900*. Baltimore: Johns Hopkins University Press.

——— 2003. *Evolution: The History of an Idea*. Baltimore: University of California Press.

Breuil, H. 1909. L'Evolution d'arts quartenaire. *Revue Archéologique* 13:378–411.

——— 1911. "L'Institut de paléontologie humaine (nouvelle fondation Albert-Ier)." *Revue Scientifique*, January 21, 1911.

——— 1952. *Four Hundred Centuries of Cave Art*. Montignac: Centre d'études et de documentation préhistoriques.

Broderick, A. H. 1963. *Father of Prehistory: The Abbe Henri Breuil, His Life and Times*. New York: William Morrow.

Capitan, L., H. Breuil, and D. Peyrony. 1910. *La caverne de Font-de-Gaume aux Eyzies (Dordogne)*. Monaco: Peintures et gravures murales des cavernes paléolithiques, publiées sous les auspices de S.A.S. le Prince Albert Ier de Monaco.

Cartailhac, E. 1902. "La grotte d'Altamira, Espagne: Mea culpa d'un sceptique." *L'Anthropologie* 13:348–54.

Chazan, M. 1995. "Conceptions of Time and the Development of Paleolithic Chronology." *American Anthropologist* 97:457–67.

Coon, C. 1964. "Father of Prehistory." *American Anthropologist* 66:647–48.

Corsi, P. 1988. *The Age of Lamarck: Evolutionary Theories in France, 1790–1830*. Berkeley: University of California Press.

——— 2001. *Lamarck: Genèse et enjeux du transformisme, 1770–1830*. Paris: CNRS.

Corsi, P., and P. Weindling. 1985. "Darwinism in Germany, France, and Italy." In D. Kohn, ed., *The Darwinian Heritage*, 683–729. Princeton: Princeton University Press.

Coye, N. 1997. *La préhistoire en parole et en acte: Méthodes et enjeux de la pratique archéologique (1830–1950)*. Paris: L'Harmattan.

Coye, N., ed. 2006. *Sur les chemins de la préhistoire: L'abbé Breuil du Périgord à l'Afrique du Sud*. Paris: Somogy.

Defrance-Jublot, F. 2005. "Question laïque et légitimité scientifique en préhistoire, la revue 'L'Anthropologie' (1890–1910). Vingtième Siècle." Special issue: Laïcité, séparation, sécularisation, 1905–2005. *Revue D'Histoire* 87:73–84.

Forgan, S. 2005. "Building the Museum: Knowledge, Conflict, and the Power of Place." *Isis* 96:572–85.

Forgan, S., and G. Gooday. 1996. "Constructing South Kensington: The Buildings and Politics of T. H. Huxley's Working Environments." *British Journal of the History of Science* 29:435–68.

Fraisse, G. 1985. *Clémence Royer, philosophe et femme de sciences*. Paris: La Decouverte.

Gaucher, G. 1993. "Henri Breuil, abbé." Special issue: Laïcité, séparation, sécularisation, 1905–2005. *Bulletin de la Société Préhistorique Française* 90:104–12.

Gieryn, T. 2002. "What Buildings Do." *Theory and Society* 31:35–74.

Grayson, D. 1983. *The Establishment of Human Antiquity*. New York: Academic.

Grimoult, C. 2003. *Histoire de l'historie des sciences: Historiographie de l'évolutionnisme dans le monde francophone*. Genève: Droz.

—— 2008. *Sciences et politique en France: De Descartes à la révolte des chercheurs*. Paris: Elipses.

Guibert, J. 1896. *Les origines: Questions d'apologétique*. Paris: Letouzey et Ané.

Hecht, J. M. 2003. *The End of the Soul: Scientific Modernity, Atheism, and Anthropology in France*. New York: Columbia University Press.

Hurel A. 2003. "Un prêtre, un savant dans la marche vers l'institutionnalisation de la préhistoire. L'abbé Henri Breuil (1877–1961)." *La Revue Pour L'Histoire du CNRS* 8:2–13.

—— 2004. "L'institutionnalisation de l'archéologie préhistorique en France métropolitaine (1852–1941) et l'Institut de paléontologie humaine." Ph.D. diss., L'Université Paris IV-Sorbonne.

—— 2007. *La France préhistorienne de 1789 à 1941*. Paris: CNRS.

Lartet, E. 1864. *L'Invention de la préhistoire. Anthologie*. London: Baillière.

Lefèvre, A. 1879. *Philosophy Historical and Critical*. London: Chapman and Hall.

McMillan, J. F. 1985. *Dreyfus to De Gaulle: Politics and Society in France, 1898–1969*. London: Arnold.

Mason, O. 1890. Anthropology in Paris During the Exposition of 1889. *American Anthropologist* 3:27–36.

Moro Abadia, O., and M. R. Gonzalez Morales. 2004. "Towards a Genealogy of the Concept of 'Paleolithic Mobiliary Art.'" *Journal of Anthropological Research* 60:321–39.

Mortillet, G. de. 1867. *Promenades préhistoriques a l'exposition universelle*. Paris: Reinwald.

—— 1910. *Le préhistoire: Origine et antiquité de l'homme*. Paris: Schleicher.

—— 1992 [1883]. "Le préhistorique." Reprinted in N. Richard, ed., *L'invention de la préhistoire: Une anthologie*, 288–98. London: Presse Pocket.

Reinach, S. 1899. "Gabriel de Mortillet." *Revue Historique* 1:67–95.

Richard, N. 1989. "La revue L'Homme de Gabriel de Mortillet—Anthropologie et politique au début de la troisième République." *Bulletin et Mémoire: Société D'Anthropologie de Paris* 1:234.

——— 2008. *Inventer la préhistoire: Débuts de l'archéologie préhistorique*. Paris: Vuibert.

Richards, R. 2002. *The Romantic Conception of Life: Science and Philosophy in the Age of Goethe*. Chicago: University of Chicago Press.

Royer, C. 1876. "Les rites funéraires aux époques préhistoriques et leur origines." *Revue D'Anthropologie* 3:437–78.

Rudwick, M. 1972. *The Meaning of Fossils*. New York: MacDonald.

——— 2005. *Bursting the Limits of Time*. Chicago: University of Chicago Press.

Schroeder-Gudehus, B. 1993. "Patrons and Publics: Museums as Historical Artefacts." *History and Technology* 10:1–3.

Sommer, M. 2006. "Mirror, Mirror on the Wall: Neanderthal as Image and 'Distortion' in Early Twentieth-Century French Science and Press." *Social Studies of Science* 36:207–40.

Spary, E. 2000. *Utopia's Garden: French Natural History from Old Regime to Revolution*. Chicago: University of Chicago Press.

Trigger, B. 2006. *A History of Archaeological Thought*. 2d ed. Cambridge: Cambridge University Press.

Zeldin, T., ed. 1970. *Conflicts in French Society: Anticlericalism, Education, and Morals in the Nineteenth Century; Essays*. London: Allen and Unwin.

CONQUERING RELIGIOUS CONTAGIONS AND CROWDS

Nineteenth-Century Psychologists and the Unfinished Subjugation of Superstition and Irrationality

CHRISTOPHER WHITE

The story of the conquest of a realm of fable by a campaign of enlightenment is always a tale of interest.

—Joseph Jastrow, *Fact and Fable in Psychology*

In older narratives about religion, science, and secularity in the modern West, the rise of science is seen as a crucial cause of religious decline. While scholars today are still debating the merits of this way of thinking, it was certainly the case that educated nineteenth- and twentieth-century Americans interpreted things this way. Science would triumph and rid the world of religion's unfounded superstitions, infantile illusions, and unsound explanations of the world. Among those mobilizing science in this way, no group was more ambitious or determined than American and European psychologists, including the prolific psychological popularizer and indefatigable opponent of irrationalism and belief in most of its forms Joseph Jastrow (1863–1944). Jastrow and other psychologists probed the religious dimensions of human personality, tried to understand its sources in the irrational parts of the self, and hoped that through more scientific forms of education people could control their irrational impulses.

But Jastrow's efforts, and the efforts of other psychologists studying religion, did not always produce the expected results. Psychological ways of analyzing religious experiences, and psychological techniques for measuring or controlling them, would be resisted in different ways, harmonized with religious practices, or even enlisted in the service of promoting faith or strengthening religious attitudes. In this chapter I examine these processes by looking at how one psychological category, suggestibility, a category that was originally fashioned to explain away religion or link it to pathological mental states, was reworked by religious Americans in an effort to reform religion and make belief possible again for themselves and others. Their successful efforts shows how scientific discourses sometimes associated with secularization actually were used to develop new ways of being religious. In this story at least, then, the result of the rise of science was neither secular triumph nor religious decline but a set of complicated exchanges in which religious positions were disciplined, reformed, and, in many cases, strengthened.

SUGGESTIBILITY AND EXPLANATIONS OF RELIGION

When the idea of the unconscious emerged as a way of thinking about memories and personality traits beyond the realm of conscious control, it was a deeply distressing moment for intellectuals hoping that a scientific account of human nature was within reach. The unconscious was a shadowy part of the self, a Pandora's box of irrational impulses, unseemly desires, and hidden cravings, including cravings for the supernatural. Could this part of the self be mapped out, examined, and controlled? Could its unpredictable passions and energies be tamed as a part of the effort to create a rational social order? Could unconscious strivings to transcend the human condition be transformed into conscious efforts to build a new, more thoroughly rational social order?

Psychologists at the turn of the twentieth century addressed themselves to these problems with determination, measuring unconscious drives, mapping out different elements in the human personality, and quantifying impulses that seemed to erupt out of deeper, unconscious places. They created one category of analysis, *suggestibility*, a synonym for how impressionable or credulous a person was, and attempted to measure this element in the general population. Typically this dimension of the personality was found in higher evidence in religious people—especially, at least in the American context, in American evangelicals. By studying evangelicals and other suggestive populations, psychologists believed they were discovering the mechanisms involved in being religious: People believed because certain religious ideas were "suggested" to them by others in the environment, and these suggested ideas implanted themselves in the impressionable unconscious.

Scientific discourses about *suggestibility,* then, were fundamentally discourses about mapping out and controlling human credulity. For example, social psychologists used suggestion to talk about the irrational tendencies of crowds and how to control them; child psychologists developed techniques and practices based on suggestion theory to manage unruly children; still other theorists thought these kinds of techniques could tame primitive peoples and races. One index of how pervasive this discourse became can be found in American advertising, an industry that at the turn of the century was exchanging older, more reasoned arguments for ads that stimulated irrational desires, instincts, and needs. Evidence, calm persuasion, carefully reasoned appeals—none of these worked as well as suggesting ways that products might meet irrational desires erupting from the unconscious. One of the most influential advertising scholars, and the first to import psychological insights into the field, Walter Dill Scott, thought the human animal was fundamentally irrational, a "creature of suggestion," unaware of the unconscious sources of cherished interests, beliefs, and choices. He spoke of advertising as a way of successfully manipulating the total environment of impressions so that consumers would be more "suggestible" when confronted with new products. He had in mind essentially a system of creating inner desires that could then be satisfied by consumer goods (Scott 1908:83, 216; Fox and Lears 1983:19–20).[1]

The group most responsible for popularizing the problem of the irrational and suggesting solutions to this problem was social psychologists. The modern social psychological tradition began with the popular French writer Gustave Le Bon and his classic *The Crowd* (1896), a book cited extensively by American psychologists, politicians, and even pastors worried about the irrational. Le Bon, a well-known French pundit who detested socialism and communism and wanted to find ways to renew French culture, worried about the riots and strikes that had troubled French history, from the French Revolution to left-wing demonstrations of the late nineteenth century. He also was aware of French clinical psychology and its concerns with hypnotism and dissociated states. His combination of interests produced a book that would be useful especially to leaders and society's experts; as Graham Richards has said, "understanding the 'laws' of crowd behaviour would enable national leaders to cultivate patriotic pride and self-confidence."

Le Bon believed that in crowds people reverted to a more primitive, irrational, and even hypnotic state, a state easily controlled by leaders who, in Le Bon's analogy, acted like mass hypnotists. Le Bon hoped this message would help leaders use the laws of hypnotism and suggestion to control the irrational energies of the crowd and, through ruthless discipline and manipulation, bend them to nationalist interests. His hopes were realized in unexpectedly dramatic ways. His views helped determine French military tactics in World War I and they shaped decisively the political and psychological strategies of Hitler, Stalin, and Mussolini, each of whom read Le Bon's work (Richards 1996:120–122). After Le Bon, psychologists tended to equate the unconscious with the masses.

In America as well, psychologists worried about the crowd and its uncontrollable impulses. One important group, a group of prominent Jewish American psychologists recently analyzed by Andrew Heinze, associated the unconscious with mass irrationalism, in part because of memories of European pogroms and anti-Semitism. (Non-Jewish religious liberals and American skeptics held similar views, though Heinze neglects this wider context.)[2] One important young Jewish psychologist named Boris Sidis, a graduate student of the Harvard philosopher and psychologist William James, borrowed some of Le Bon's insights and, like him, focused on the dangerous possibilities of crowd behavior. Sidis went to great lengths not just in describing how preachers and politicians implanted suggestions and produced automatic behaviors but also in showing how this process worked with page upon page of examples. American society was full of such examples, oscillating as it did, back and forth, between financial panics and "attacks of religious insanity," he wrote. "The clever stump orator, the politician, the preacher, fix the attention of their listeners on themselves, interesting them in the 'subject.' They as a rule distract the attention of the crowd by their stories, frequently giving the suggestion in some indirect and striking way, winding up the long yarn by a climax requiring the immediate execution of the suggested act" (Sidis 1898:297). The emotional crowd, the large assembly that, by its nature, inhibits individualism and instills conformity, the power of persuasive speeches and didactic commands and highly contagious religious emotions—all these made people suggestible, stripping them of their voluntary control mechanisms. All interfering impressions and contrary ideas were filtered out; all doubts and appetites for indecision were smothered by the stifling, contagious crowd. Everyone was entranced, hypnotized. Preachers suggested repentance and conversion; audience members, acting automatically, came forward.

Sidis even devised mathematical formulas to measure the economy of suggestive forces, adding long methodological appendixes and an accompanying diagram of "mob energy" to show how suggestion's powers might exponentially increase (figure 2.1). As suggestions cascaded down upon a passive mob, each individual absorbed ambient suggestions and increased

> the emotion of the mob in volume and intensity. Each new attack is followed by a more violent paroxysm of furious demoniac frenzy. The mob is like an avalanche: the more it rolls the more menacing and dangerous it grows. The suggestion given by the hero, by the ringleader, by the master of the moment, is taken up by the crowd and is reflected and reverberated from man to man, until every soul is dizzied and every person is stunned. In the entranced crowd, in the mob, everyone influences and is influenced in his turn; every one suggests and is suggested to, and the surging billow of suggestion swells and rises until it reaches a formidable height.

The total energy of this suggestive cascade could be calculated in the following way. The energy of the master, or hero, set arbitrarily at 50 units, awakens a half-measure (25 units) of energy in each of his 1,000 auditors. Each auditor in turn awakens a half-measure of energy (12.5) in all others. The total level of energy aroused by the master is therefore 25 times 1,000 (25,000); the total energy awakened by each individual in the crowd is 12.5 times 1,000 (12,500); and since each individual awakens 12,500 units of suggestive energy, and since there are 1,000 individuals, the total units of energy can rise to 12,525,000, which is the sum of the original energy generated by the master and the aggregate energy produced by auditors. Though these calculations strike us today as odd, they illustrate nicely the preoccupation of these psychologists. The cumulative forces of the unconscious were careening out of control—awakening, disinhibiting, inciting people to frenzy. Mob energy grew like wildfire. "Like a cannibal it feeds on human beings."[3]

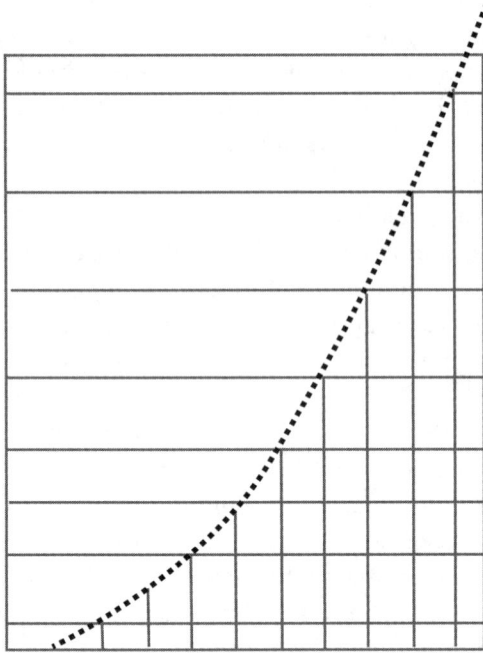

FIGURE 2.1

The category suggestion itself could cannibalize and feed on things around it, especially when it careened among ideas ripening in skeptical minds. Some embraced it as a way to explain all religious phenomena. Opponents of evangelical revivals in particular employed the notion ambidextrously to furnish natural or psychological explanations for supposedly supernatural happenings. Many borrowed from Sidis or Le Bon. "It is evident that no supernatural agency is necessary to explain the peculiar bodily exercises that attended the Great Revival in the western country," the historian Catharine Cleveland wrote in 1916, analyzing the great Kentucky revivals of 1800. "The individual, seized either at home or in public, had, previous to the seizure, received some suggestion through the sense of sight or hearing that resulted in bodily reaction." Some hint, image, or word had nestled in their unconscious and was waiting to emerge. Suggestion expanded in Cleveland's hands to encompass almost every supernatural marvel. What about believers who, when stricken by the spirit, suddenly expatiated in learned tones on the Bible or exhorted sinners? What about children of six or seven years who could "use language beyond their years" and speak convincingly from the Bible? "The cells which had stored up the impressions so received were discharged by the unwonted excitement which had affected the nervous system," Cleveland explained. Everyone in these settings "expressed themselves only in terms perfectly familiar to one acquainted with religious phraseology. The ideas were all suggested by, or taken directly from, the hymns, the Bible, and other books of a religious nature." It was even possible on such principles to account for the "'amazing language' of the scoffer or deist who caught the contagion." Could suggestion make a scoffer preach the Bible? This was a powerful notion indeed (Cleveland 1959 [1916]: 127, 122–23).[4]

While revived crowds and other mass behaviors became targets for many thinkers, any religious phenomena that dethroned reason could be subjected to these and related psychological discourses. Though some thought testing spiritualism, psychical phenomena, or other religious behaviors either beneath their dignity or beyond the scope of scientific psychology, many of the most prominent American psychologists could not resist attempting to prove such practices fraudulent.[5] Joseph Jastrow, for one, was certain that, according to Andrew Heinze, "the entire enterprise of popular psychology . . . depended on persuading Americans to abandon myth and superstition" (Heinze 2004:174, see also 110–13).

Suggestion was Jastrow's weapon. "Unconscious suggestion has been one of the most potent influences for the production of alleged marvels and pseudo-phenomena," he explained in *Fact and Fable in Psychology*, a book published the same year that Jastrow was president of the American Psychological Association (1900). "All the series of experiments brought forward at irregular intervals during the past century to establish supernormal sensibilities have depended for their apparent success (apart from trickery) upon unconscious suggestion of the operators, combined with the shrewd assimilation of the desired or expected result on the part of the subjects." Jastrow thought spiritualist performances, telepathic communications, trances, and visions could be explained by analogies to hypnotic and nonhypnotic suggestive processes. Performers could create suggestive environments, implant ideas in people's heads, and pressure and coax them into believing, acting, and thinking in certain ways. Jastrow led powerful campaigns against spiritualism and Christian Science in particular, no doubt because each threatened to collapse what to Jastrow were crucial distinctions between science and religion. Both spiritualism and Christian Science, Jastrow worried, "pertain to the domain over which medicine, physiology, and psychology hold sway." These systems were catching on rapidly, they were a "contagion" that played on people's emotions and fears. They were a "menace to rationality" (Jastrow 1971 [1990]:68–70, 27, 32, 39).

Jastrow's vehement pronouncements are tinged with their own kind of dogmatism and fear. *If ideas and spirits were powerful enough to shape matter or subvert what we knew of natural laws, what would happen to scientific pursuits?* "If spirits can lift tables and hold them suspended in the air in spite of the operation of gravity," James Angell, another psychologist worried, "then knowledge is at an end, the whole fabric of science deliquesces into a mere logomachy . . . and man himself becomes the plaything of every eddy that may happen to roil the waters of his ignorance" (Coon 1992:150). This kind of loss of control was the positivist scientist's greatest fear.

Healing techniques hawked by Christian Scientists or other metaphysical entrepreneurs also were explained with suggestive principles. "The belief in supernatural energies has cured diseases at all times and among all peoples," the Harvard experimental psychologist Hugo Munsterberg wrote. "Everywhere the patient sought help through the agents [i.e., priests] of higher forces and everywhere these agents themselves utilized their therapeutic success for strengthening the belief in their over-natural power." Reflecting on the credulous past, Munsterberg judged that the "psychologist would say that it was always the same story, the influence of suggestion on the imagination of those who suffer." There were complications to this one-size-fits-all explanation, different cultures with different metaphysical frameworks, but Munsterberg thought that the psychological mechanisms were the same. He chided modern Americans who, like savages in "darkest Africa" or Siberian shamans—"excitable persons with epileptic tendencies"—were tempted to ascribe divine origins to amazing healings (Munsterberg 1909:319–320). "We must not forget that it is not the solemn value of the religious revelation, nor the ethical and metaphysical bearing of its objects, which brings success, but solely the depth of the emotion," Munsterberg wrote in his immensely popular *Psychology and Life* (1899). Deep emotions, not divine beings, effectively suggested confidence, wholeness, and healing. It did not matter who or what power you evoked. "To murmur the Greek alphabet with the touching intonation and gesture of supplication is just as strengthening for the health as the sublimest prayer; and for the man who believes in the metaphysical cure, it may be quite unimportant whether the love curer at his bedside thinks of the psychical Absolute or of the spring hat she will buy with the fee for her metaphysical healing." Sudden healings and other miracles could be explained by using suggestive principles (Munsterberg 1899:245–48).

PSYCHOLOGICAL WAYS OF DISCIPLINING AND REFORMING RELIGION

This much, and much more, could be said about psychologists who developed categories to identify and discipline irrational, credulous, or superstitious parts of the self. They fashioned these categories with a sense of mission and an almost religious intensity. But the cultural history of the discourses these psychologists produced shows how hard they were to control. In churches, lyceums, and open-air lectures, popular pastors and other commentators changed the meaning of new scientific categories like suggestion to show that they explained not religious experience in general but only those religious experiences that were obviously excessive. In their hands, discourses about suggestion were a disciplining tool that helped believers cut away unseemly religious elements and preserve essential, spiritual ones.

Not all religious Americans were involved equally in this conversation; conservative evangelicals were more likely to ignore scientific interpretations of religion or religious experience and were thus less likely to speak out about these issues. Though evangelicals sometimes did borrow from or argue with psychologists, religious liberals, including liberal Protestant intellectuals and post-Protestant thinkers, were more involved in the arguments I'm narrating here. A wide range of religious liberals were interested in using both scientific and religious insights to understand how properly to be religious in the modern world. They were adept at using psychological insights and categories, and suggestion in particular, for their own purposes.

The first thing they had to do was show that human suggestibility could not explain everything about religious feelings, intuitions, or attitudes. Some pointed to obvious problems involved in reducing all religious phenomena to mental forces. If religious experience merely was the result of an economy of mental suggestions, couldn't all other things—all behaviors, all natural phenomena, all beliefs, all arguments for or against God—also be explained as products of mental suggestions? How far would such psychological reduction get us? The self-help writer and religious liberal Horatio Dresser thought escaping from this psychological reductionism meant holding onto a solid starting point, which to Dresser meant to "start with God and the spiritual world, and regard the human self as the recipient of life or power through the understanding and the will." Dresser used a kind of "common sense" argument to assert that things outside of the self existed, including God. This was a vehement assertion, however, or perhaps a plea for a more comforting personal philosophy, but it was not an argument.

But Dresser and others did have arguments. They argued that suggestive explanations accounted only for the mechanical dimensions involved in more complicated processes in the religious consciousness. Was religious change really as simple as suggesting religious ideas? Didn't real inspiration sweep more powerfully into the self, altering not just our thoughts but also our emotions, willpower, and actions? Mental healing through suggestion operated through thoughts, it was true, and it often worked; but spiritual change involved commitment, emotion, submission, love of God, and (ultimately) a new orientation to life. While skeptical psychologists might "see no difference between spiritual 'consciousness' and therapeutic 'suggestion,'" the difference, Dresser insisted, was empirical, and "the man who has not experienced the added value which religious belief implies is not expected to make the distinction." "To pass beyond the absorbing idea to vivid realization of the presence of God is to enter a superior region," he wrote, sounding a lot like his one-time mentor at Harvard, William James (Dresser 1910:111–12, 129, 160–62; Dresser received a Ph.D in philosophy from Harvard in 1907.)

Others agreed that religion had to be more than mere suggestion. Faith involved suggestive processes, but it also wrapped these processes in emotional urgency and attached to them a warm sense of certainty that prepared people to act. Faith brought "a strained expectancy which increases the circulation of the blood, the outlay of nervous force," and the convictions of certainty, the liberal Christian pastor and (later) dean of the Hartford School of Religious Education, Karl Stolz, wrote. In short, the religious consciousness provided a powerful set of subjective conditions in which healing or saving suggestions flourished (Stolz 1923:30–33). God's providential "means" of grace, like preaching and worship, represented the best environment for certain suggestions, for here the Bible's suggestions reinforced the preacher's suggestions and the worshipper's autosuggestions. These divinely designed settings produced powerful emotional expectations that also were more permanent than crowd behaviors or suggestions given in clinical or hypnotic settings.[6] In fact, many argued that the religious context was absolutely crucial in providing a healthy setting for suggested notions that moved in and out of the mind.

Samuel McComb, one of the founders of the influential Episcopal healing ministry called the Emmanuel Movement, warned that suggestive techniques practiced improperly could impair our self-control, create flimsy and uneducated beliefs, and erode our capacity for willed ethical behaviors. Suggestion alone could be dangerous, weakening the religious self. Real religious experiences, another religious liberal confirmed, "involves choice, the personal acceptance of value, the concealed and subliminal maturing of the principles of the good life, and the concrete expression of faith" (Clerical and Medical Committee of Inquiry into Spiritual, Faith, and Mental Healing 1914:43; also see Stolz 1943:142; Dougall 1923:136–137; Thouless 1928:35; Sadler 1920:491).

These arguments remind us that positions on suggestion and how it worked were enmeshed in normative discourses about the best types of religion. And in fact, even reductive uses of suggestion often were incorporated in discourses promoting liberal religious views. Most revival debunkers for instance were less interested in promoting atheism than they were in developing a faith purged of irrational elements. A liberal Protestant minister, psychologist, and university president, George Cutten, represented the majority view when he said that, while religion was "tangled with all forms of abnormal, and even insane, mental vagaries," the science of psychology would help believers "recognize laws of abnormality as we do of normal processes, and we may separate the dross from the metal." In his writings Cutten performed this remarkable act of reform with analyses of everything from speaking in tongues to witchcraft, stigmatization, and miracles. He employed suggestion as other liberals had, as a way to account for illegitimate forms of religiousness, and he pointed to the familiar set of particularly suggestible groups: women, children, southern "negroes," evangelicals.

Cutten's ideological project is quite clear. "The negro saw spirits in everything while in Africa, and if he kept on good terms with spirits his duty was done. He felt no obligation to his fellowmen, and religion had nothing to do with moral conduct." For people like this, Cutten thought, it was not inconsistent to be highly religious and highly immoral at the same time, and this was precisely the American negro's status. When, to their immoral character, negroes combined "dense ignorance and weak will with vivid imagination and volatile emotion," we had exactly the set of factors making a group highly suggestible and easily given to excessive forms of belief. Cutten's prescriptions for change can be summarized quite simply: be less emotional, practice self-control. Quoting other experts on mobs, he averred that religious contagions "are held in check only if there are a considerable number of individuals scattered through the population who are trained in the habit of control, who are accustomed to subordinate feeling to rational considerations," and who resist the "tide of imitation and emotion" (Cutten 1908:4, 171–73, 165).

Cutten was merely one example of a religious liberal using suggestion to forge a new normative religious discourse. Other psychologists of religion and believing social scientists also produced experimental results that either implicitly or explicitly authorized liberal positions. In the 1920s and 1930s the Quaker psychologist Edwin Starbuck and several students devised empirical studies of experience, religious temperaments, and suggestibility. In one set of such studies, performed by Starbuck's graduate students Thomas H. Howells and R. D. Sinclair, these students correlated personality traits with religious styles. Howells's study, published in 1930, divided his subjects into two groups, conservatives (i.e., those who want to preserve "ancient traditions") and radicals (i.e., those "restless minds who wish for freedom and the open road.") He surveyed 542 undergraduates at the University of Iowa and, based on their responses to a long questionnaire, identified 50 religious conservatives and 50 religious radicals. Howells then conducted a series of experimental tests on individuals in these two groups. The experimental tests were designed to test motor and sensory abilities, willpower, suggestibility, motivation, and general intelligence. A series of sensorimotor tests, involving auditory and sensory stimuli, electric shocks, coordination, muscle fatigue, and reaction time experiments, yielded few differences between the groups (Howells 1928:7, 13; figure 2.2).[7]

But the second and third battery of tests, on willpower, suggestibility, and general intelligence, revealed significant differences. The tests on willpower and suggestibility were used to discover if there was "something in the volitional make-up of the orthodox person which renders him more susceptible to intense stimulation or to social suggestion, and therefore more likely to conform to the doctrines and practices of an established faith." Howells used five suggestibility tests. In the first he showed subjects a picture of the British House of Parliament and then asked them to recall the picture's details, using questions that suggested the existence of

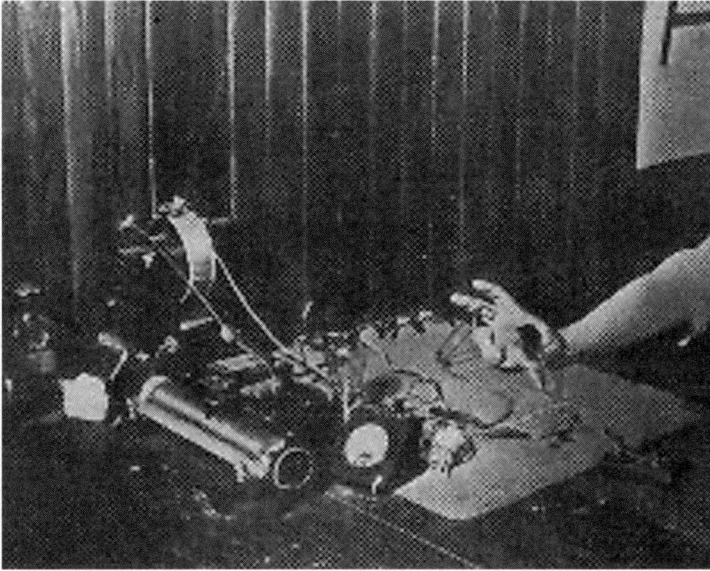

FIGURE 2.2

elements in the picture that were not there. In the second he assayed the effect of positive versus negative instructions on small coordination tests. In the third, fourth, and fifth tests he did electrical shock experiments. In test 3 he told subjects that gradually the electrical charge would increase and "that presently it would begin to be painful." For more suggestible subjects, this suggestion, and the fear and anticipation it elicited, heightened their experiences of pain and anxiety. In test 4 Howells applied a low-level current to the hands of his subjects and told them the current would slowly be increased, asking them to indicate when they detected a distinct increase in stimulation. In test 5 Howells showed subjects the rheostat, said they would experience sensations when it reached a certain level, secretly turned off the charge, and finally turned the rheostat gradually to that level and beyond, looking at the subject "with a serious and expectant mien."

When radicals and conservatives were scored on these measures, Howells saw a clear pattern emerge: There seems, he concluded, "complete agreement among all five of the suggestibility tests in indicating the greater suggestibility of the conservative." Moreover, in the face of suggested punishments or criticism, conservatives faltered. "He is more timid, or, in the common expression, has less 'grit' or 'nerve' than the radical." He also was more influenced by the experimenter. In short, he had less willpower and was "more influenced by the immediate situation." The conservatives—that is, the evangelicals—were more suggestible (Howells 1928:31, 33–39).

The third and last set of tests confirmed that evangelicals could not think for themselves. Their general intelligence, measured by scores in tests on memory, judgment, and problem solving, was noticeably lower than the intelligence of the average radical. The facts that "in most of the tests the differences are large enough practically to guarantee that similar tests of a large number of similarly selected sample groups would show differences of the same kind" and that "the different bits of evidence [from all the tests] are mutually supporting" led Howells to a fairly confident conclusion that conservatives were "relatively inferior in intellectual ability." Howells concluded his study by correlating questionnaire data on such measures as personality, health, church membership, and self-reported religious experiences with his two types, conservative and radical. Though differences were not always pronounced, he found that conservatives were more likely to go to church, be female, have had a conversion experience, and be older, more extroverted, more social, and more pessimistic (Howells 1928:47, 57).[8]

Howells's study is complemented by Robert Sinclair's, which used data from the same questionnaire but also hypothesized about differences between those who reported having a religious (conversion) experience and those who did not. Sinclair divided students into "positive" ("mystics") and "negative" ("nonmystics") groups. His mystics overlapped considerably with Howells's conservatives. Sinclair's information showed that mystics were more suggestible, less intelligent, less coordinated, and had slower reaction times. They were more likely to "see visions" and "hear voices." Though these results seemed to indicate nonmystical superiority, Sinclair left open the possibility that mystics might be differently organized psychologically and that their openness to mystical experience might lead to richer inner experiences, more energetic responses to life, and feelings of "adjustment and peace which enables the individuals to use more effectively the relatively inferior capacities which, according to the tests, they seem to have." These were backhanded compliments, to be sure (Sinclair 1930:54).

As my recent book has shown, these liberals wanted a touch of experience to dissolve hardened forms of rationality, but they clearly preferred what they thought of as sober and rational types of religious behaviors (White 2009). "A chief trouble with religion today is that it is borne down by the weight of an outmoded tradition and shackled with an unconscious pride of caste and authority," Howells wrote in a different, more reflective, study; today's church did not have "a monopoly of either virtue or spirituality," and it was clear that its creeds, enticements and superstitious religious behaviors appeared inadequate to the task of satisfying and motivating us. Howells had on his mind a typically liberal errand of religious reconstruction, one that began with differentiating the essential from the incidental and recasting those essentials in new forms. "The world needs to be persuaded to anticipate and even plan the occasional destruction of its little Buddhas, but always it should have courage to substitute more effective symbols" in their place. This was modern science as religious iconoclasm (Howells 1940:256, 276).

Here, psychological tools were used to critique evangelicals in particular; but in fact psychological tools were deployed ecumenically, and suggestion in particular was dispatched as a refining fire for a range of beliefs that seemed aberrant or excessive. Such was the case with liberals who argued against the strange revelations of spiritualist mediums, fortune tellers and psychic prognosticators. Combining in lecture demonstrations "the technic of a scientist" with the skills of an entertainer and "a speaker *par excellence*," the psychologist Howard Higgins toured Chautauqua circuits in the 1920s showing how the psychology of suggestion accounted for psychical phenomena. Higgins drew on psychologists of deception such as Jastrow. The first part of his program was a séance that incorporated features "from seances by leading mediums," "demonstrated spirit forces, spirit vision, writing by an invisible hand, spirit slate writing" and so on. Carefully, Higgins crafted a séance in which doctors, psychiatrists, Catholic priests and others in even "the most sophisticated audiences . . . are led to believe in the possibility of fortune-telling!"

"Dramatic, intensely interesting, educational and entertaining," the expose that followed was one "in which the technics [sic] used to establish belief in fortune-telling are exposed." Moreover, in exposing the principles underlying psychic phenomena Higgins engaged his audience in a "scientifically sound discussion of the psychology of suggestion—in an effort," Higgins thought, "to protect the public against fraud" (see figure 2.3). Higgins was interested in the psychology of public speaking and persuasion, and thus crucially interested in suggestion. "In order to influence people's beliefs it would seem wise to understand how they get their beliefs." Drawing on psychological studies, suggestion theory, advertising and psychology of religion texts, Higgins created a powerfully suggestive

FIGURE 2.3

environment: He invoked prestigious authorities, spoke with confidence, and repeated points hypnotically. Apparently, his lectures persuaded. Religious listeners in particular were convinced. One "not so easily pleased" seminary class from Concordia Seminary in St. Louis "commented again and again on [Higgins's] excellent program," while other Christians thought the show was "a real contribution to Christian thinking" or "a constructive piece of religious and education work."[9]

Other popular psychologists lectured on similar topics—and with similar results. One pastor of a Baptist church in Chicago thought another itinerant psychologist's explanation of spiritualism "clean, amusing, mystify-
ing, distinctly unique, and at the same time a telling blow against one of the
worst delusions and false religions of the day." This pastor was not against
belief in general, of course—just *this* kind of belief. Lecturers like these
were bringing their assaults on spiritualism and other illegitimate religions
to towns all over America. The credulous had to beware (Wilkins n.d.)!

SUGGESTIONS AS WAYS OF BUILDING FAITH

It is safe to say that religious Americans who used suggestion to reform
or purify religion put this category to uses unimagined by those positivist
scientists who originally fashioned it. But if using suggestion in this way
was unexpected, there was a still more surprising turn of events to come.
There were some, it turned out, who used the category of suggestion both
to understand better and *stir up* credulity in the deepest parts of the soul.
A range of religious liberals in particular used this category to help themselves overcome sin, imagine God's closeness, and assure themselves of
God's power and succor.

A number of people in this group were from the ranks of the New
Thought movement, which stressed the importance of immanent divine
energies in all things and techniques (such as meditation) that harmonized the self with these divine energies. The end result was psychological wellness and even physical healing. Henry Wood (1834–1908), who
encountered New Thought and was cured of nervousness and physical
ailments, turned his prodigious energies to producing popular self-help
books that combined insights from Christianity and psychology. To render the mind passive and receptive, Wood recommended retiring each
day, alone and silent, in a restful position. Breathing deeply for a few
minutes would relax the body and make the mind more open to "suggestions." Then Wood provided sets of suggestive phrases in bold, full-page
renderings as well as accompanying meditations on these phrases. Individuals were to read carefully the longer meditations first and then fas-
ten their eyes on the brief suggested phrase for ten to twenty minutes.
"Do not merely look upon it, but wholly GIVE YOURSELF UP TO IT, until
it fills and overflows the entire consciousness." Then close "the eyes for
twenty to thirty minutes more; behold it with the mind's eye, and let it

permeate the whole organism" and, later, call it to mind during wakeful hours of the night. Believers needed to inscribe those suggested phrases in their consciousness.

These phrases affirmed that God was immanent in the self and that human beings were receptive to divine impulses—"GOD IS HERE." "DIVINE LOVE FILLS ME." "I AM NOT BODY." Though confused, depressed, or afflicted believers might find these suggestions worthless at first, they should not despair. The spiritual growing that resulted would not be instantaneous. This was not superstition or magic, Wood wrote; it was a natural, and thus spiritually legitimate, process of growing. In other books he made this point more emphatically: "Absorb the ideals repeatedly until they *live* in and with you. They will increasingly become a spontaneous and well-defined feeling. . . . Ideals tend toward expression and actualization." Wood used suggestion to rebuild the self from the inside out: "You gradually create a new world for yourself" (Wood 1904:108–9; Wood 1908:19).

Of course Wood was not the only religious liberal to harmonize psychological advice and Christian categories. The pastor at the Washington Avenue Church in Brooklyn, Robert MacDonald, thanked God that the efficacious remedy for sin was finally at hand, bestowed providentially by psychologists, a remedy that was "so simple, so strong, so rich that its curative force is difficult to realize and incredible to believe." It was, of course, the power of suggestion, which MacDonald was certain "will pull down evil and build up good within the soul more speedily and surely than all the remedial punishments of earth." Though the unconscious was thick with "evil instincts, wrong habits, sickening realizations," biblical verses, when implanted properly there, "will spring up and choke out the weeds." The Bible was the "greatest source of powerful suggestions," and believers should whisper these powerful words to themselves at all times of day, remember them at bedtime and meditate on them daily. This same pastor liked Wood's strategy, though he had a slightly stronger biblical emphasis: Print out biblical suggestions in large letters, he instructed; "Place it on the wall of your silence chamber, or in some convenient place where you can sit, or lie in most easeful and relaxed position with the eye fixt upon it [sic]." Do not merely read it, or gaze at it; "yield yourself to it completely." A week's daily contemplation of "I have no fear. I am strong in the Lord" had cured a believer of morbid fears; a week's contemplation of "I am God's child. I am pure" cured another of lust (Brown 1910:136; MacDonald 1908:106, 107, 136–39). The science of suggestion was helping people believe.

Others thought that the science of suggestion proved the importance of older Christian "means of grace" and pointed to ways of improving them. The popular preacher and Chautauqua lecturer Elwin L. House (1861–1932), a Congregationalist who dealt "inspiringly and instructively with the fundamental facts of religion as interpreted by reverent modern psychology," insisted to grateful audiences that God's presence might be realized using different systems of suggestion, affirmation, and prayer (see figure 2.4, from House n.d.). He talked about suggestion as the mechanism that explained different kinds of influences on the self; suggestion was a part of advertising, healing, preaching, prayer, teaching, and child rearing. But the most potent suggestions came when using the means of grace Christ instituted for the church — praying, going to church, preaching. Preaching was the "very highest" form of suggestion. The preacher delivers God's authoritative word, the Holy Spirit creates an atmosphere "charged with inspiration and uplift," and parishioners, for their part, bring sensibilities of faith, which are always necessary for suggestion to work. Prayer and personal Bible study were highly suggestive environments as well. In these situations our worship "will thrill us and excite holy emotions," "rekindle old memories, awaken fresh sympathies, start new ideas," and "deepen mighty convictions." House offered specific texts believers might use in suggestive worship settings (House 1913:114–15, 140–50, 100, 115).

Liberal Christians worked out suggestive faith-building techniques in detail, producing new morphologies of conversion that rivaled in detail much earlier American Protestant models of salvation. In his outline of the four stages of suggestion, Karl Stolz began by saying that a "distinct effort of the will" usually was necessary to "lodge the requisite idea in the mind." Always there are ideas and emotions that competed with the faith-building suggestion. "Uncritical attitudes, ideas which are emotionally toned, instinctual drives and basic wishes are held in mental focus without conscious effort," Stolz wrote. In order for the proper suggestion to penetrate the self it "must be assented to as desirable or overpowering," and the will must force it to "dominate the personality." Once fixed in the self with willful attention, the believer must then faithfully expect automatic reactions—new convictions, new ideas, new actions. Finally, there followed moments of passivity when the suggested ideal ripened in the unconscious self. In general, though, the process was dependent on a strong will—the evangelical mistake was

FIGURE 2.4

precisely that they sacrificed a will-oriented religion for an emotional one. The will was essential. Other thinkers elaborated on this point at length (Stolz 1943:141–142; Sadler 1920:491; MacDonald 1908:111; for other examples, see Boyd 1909:115–118; Worcester 1933:106).

It was undoubtedly the case that psychologists who criticized credulous evangelicals and irrational revivalists helped shape new normative religious views on healthy and unhealthy forms of religion, as I suggested in the previous section of this chapter. Evangelical emphases on depravity and sin were among the first notions to be critiqued. Suggestions about avoiding evil or merely escaping divine punishment conjured all kinds of horrible mental images liberal Christians came to believe: "pictures of all that is terrible in unquenchable fire; the everlasting torment of gnawing worms; the bottomless pit and outer darkness." Concentrating on these images reinforced feelings of impotence. Many argued that the consciousness of hell, divine wrath, or the problem of sin, all frozen into the self with evangelical methods, might be replaced by more sanguine suggestions (House 1913:110, 231, 220; Lindsay 1922 [1907]:83; for another example, see MacDonald 1908:106–7, 131). Contrasting two worship styles, faith and fear, physician and Chautauqua lecturer William Sadler pointed out that the "prayer of faith is a source of favorable and powerful auto-suggestion to the mind of the one who prays; while the prayer of doubt and fear may become highly injurious because of its power of adverse suggestion." "Prayer," Sadler insisted, "may be so prostituted as to become a source of moral weakness and spiritual defeat." He knew this was true; he had seen the effects of this kind of religion in himself and in patients at his medical practice. He thought one could monitor the successes or failures of a belief system by seeing how it registered effects in the body. Was it producing calm states? Real faith, positive faith, produced characteristic heart rate patterns, affirmative postures of the head and body, and better nervous or digestive states (Sadler 1920:491). Positive suggestions led to strong faith and physiological health. Negative suggestions led to uncertain faith and physiological weakness.

ⲵⲵ

When the great debunker of spiritualism and psychic phenomena Hugo Munsterberg unexpectedly died in the winter of 1916, collapsing halfway through a psychology lecture to Radcliffe undergraduates, his religious opponents suddenly had an opportunity to utter the final word on psychological explanations of religion and religious experience. For years Munsterberg had studied and unmasked believers, psychics, and mediums, and he, like Jastrow, had used categories such as suggestion to account for all kinds of supposedly supernatural phenomena. But, just after the great psychologist died, a Boston medium contacted his disembodied spirit, reporting that the spiritual Munsterberg was now clearly seeing his mistakes. The account was in the *New York Times*. "When I was an inhabitant of the earth I did not then find any proofs that excarnate beings communicate with their earth friends," Munsterburg's spirit reported. "Although I have been in the spirit world but a brief time, I have received absolute proof that excarnate beings can and do communicate with their earth friends." This was an important message, Munsterberg continued. "Spirit return is a truth. I am Hugo Munsterberg" ("Word from Hugo Muensterberg" 1916:2; see Hale 1980:183).

Such examples of religious Americans attempting to undo the careful lifework of a scientist might strike us as perverse, but this is merely an extreme example of how many people reworked or resisted scientific discourses—especially when these discourses seemed hegemonic, simplistically reductive, or destructive of deeply held beliefs. And, as I have shown in this essay, religious liberals had less underhanded ways of turning scientific discourses to their advantage. The brief history of suggestion I have sketched here is one example of how categories originally fashioned to explain religiousness in secular terms also could be used to reform and, in many cases, promote belief.

NOTES

1. Other psychologists of advertising developed detailed taxonomies of suggestions and outlined how to use them. A. J. Snow's 1925 textbook is one example of many. Snow's book is adorned with sample advertisements that illustrate how suggestive techniques could be used. For background information I also used Wozniak's biography of Walter Dill Scott (1999:166–69).
2. Heinze ignores, for example, ways that religious liberals also recognized the problems of mob violence and demurred with popular Protestant mystical interpretations of the unconscious. See also Heinze 2001.
3. Sidis has a detailed set of mathematical calculations that accompany this graph (18 98:303–5).
4. Leigh Schmidt discusses these matters and broader enlightenment critiques of American revivals (Schmidt 2001 [1989]:xviii–xx).
5. They did so because the public was interested in such questions and because they were interested in carefully differentiating science from pseudoscience and religion. Many operated with a basic antimony: science, rationality, objectivity versus religion, irrationality, subjectivity, and feeling. On boundary disputes between psychologists and religious healers in this era, see Coon 1992; for broader issues related to how boundaries between science and nonscience are created, see Gieryn 1983.
6. Many liberal Christians made this argument; see, for example, House 1913:100.

7. For more on Starbuck, see White 2009.
8. The diagram is figure 6 in Sinclair 1930.
9. All quotations are from lecture promotional materials, "Among the Spirits" (Higgins n.d.), except Higgins's statement "In order to influence people's beliefs . . . " This statement is from *Influencing Behavior Through Speech* (Higgins 1930:9).

REFERENCES

Boyd, Thomas Parker. 1909. *The How and Why of the Emmanuel Movement: A Hand-Book on Psycho-Therapeutics.* San Francisco: Whitaker and Ray.

Brown, Charles Reynolds. 1910. *Faith and Health.* New York: Crowell.

Clerical and Medical Committee of Inquiry Into Spiritual, Faith, and Mental Healing. 1914. *Spiritual Healing: Report of a Clerical and Medical Committee of Inquiry into Spiritual, Faith, and Mental Healing.* New York: Macmillan.

Cleveland, Catharine. 1959 [1916]. *The Great Revival in the West, 1797–1805.* Chicago: University of Chicago Press, 1916. Reprint Gloucester, MA: Peter Smith.

Coon, Deborah J. 1992. "Testing the Limits of Sense and Science: American Experimental Psychologists Combat Spiritualism, 1880–1920." *American Psychologist* 47:143–51.

Cutten, George B. 1908. *The Psychological Phenomena of Christianity.* New York: Scribner's.

Dougall, Lily. 1923. *The Christian Doctrine of Health: A Handbook on the Relation of Bodily to Spiritual and Moral Health.* New York: Macmillan.

Dresser, Horatio. 1910. *A Message to the Well: And Other Essays and Letters on the Art of Health.* New York: Putnam's.

Fox, Richard Wightman, and T. J. Jackson Lears, eds. 1983. *The Culture of Consumption: Critical Essays in American History, 1880–1980.* New York: Pantheon.

Gieryn, Thomas F. 1983. "Boundary Work and the Demarcation of Science from Non-Science: Strains and Interests in Professional Ideologies of Scientists." *American Sociological Review* 48:781–95.

Hale, Matthew, Jr. 1980. *Human Science and the Social Order: Hugo Munsterberg and the Origins of Applied Psychology.* Philadelphia: Temple University Press.

Heinze, Andrew R. 2001. "Jews and American Popular Psychology: Reconsidering the Protestant Paradigm of Popular Thought." *Journal of American History* 88:950–78.

—— 2004. *Jews and the American Soul: Human Nature in the Twentieth Century.* Princeton: Princeton University Press.

Higgins, Howard. N.d. "Among the Spirits: Actual Demonstrations of Psychic Phenomena." Lecture promotional materials from Records of the Redpath Lyceum Bureau, Special Collections Department, University of Iowa Libraries.

—— 1930. *Influencing Behavior Through Speech*. Boston: Expression.

House, Elwin Lincoln. 1913. *The Psychology of Orthodoxy*. New York: Fleming H. Revell.

—— N.d. "The Psychology of Religion." Lecture promotional materials from Records of the Redpath Lyceum Bureau, Special Collections Department, University of Iowa Libraries.

Howells, Thomas H. 1928. "A Comparative Study of Those Who Accept as Against Those who Reject Religious Authority," *University of Iowa Studies in Character* 2:2.

—— 1940. *Hunger for Wholiness: Man's Universal Motive*. Denver: World.

Jastrow, Joseph. 1900. *Fact and Fable in Psychology*. Boston: Houghton Mifflin.

Lindsay, Arthur A. 1922 [1907]. *The New Psychology Complete: Mind the Builder and Scientific Man Building*. New York: Lindsay.

MacDonald, Robert. 1908. *Mind, Religion and Health: With an Appreciation of the Emmanuel Movement*. New York: Funk and Wagnalls.

Munsterberg, Hugo. 1899. *Psychology and Life*. Boston: Houghton, Mifflin.

—— 1909. *Psychotherapy*. New York: Moffat, Yard.

Richards, Graham. 1996. *Putting Psychology in Its Place: An Introduction from a Critical Historical Perspective*. London: Routledge.

Sadler, William. 1920. *The Physiology of Faith and Fear: Or the Mind in Health and Disease*. Chicago: A. C. McClurg.

Schmidt, Leigh Eric. 2001 [1989]. *Holy Fairs: Scotland and the Making of American Revivalism*. 2d ed. Princeton: Princeton University Press.

Scott, Walter Dill. 1908. *The Psychology of Advertising: A Simple Exposition of the Principles of Psychology in Their Relation to Successful Advertising*. Boston: Small, Maynard.

Sidis, Boris. 1898. *The Psychology of Suggestion: A Research into the Subconscious Nature of Man and* Society. Boston: Appleton.

Sinclair, Robert Daniel. 1930. "A Comparative Study of Those Who Report the Experience of the Divine Presence and Those Who Do Not." *University of Iowa Studies in Character* 2:3.

Snow, A. J. 1925. *Psychology in Business Relations*. Chicago: A. W. Shaw.

Stolz Karl R. 1923. *The Psychology of Prayer*. New York: Abingdon.

—— 1943. *The Church and Psychotherapy*. New York: Abingdon.

Thouless, Robert H. 1928. *The Control of the Mind: A Handbook of Applied Psychology for the Ordinary Man*. London: Hodder and Stoughton.

White, Christopher. 2009. *Unsettled Minds: Psychology and the American Search for Spiritual Assurance, 1830–1940*. Berkeley: University of California Press.

Wilkins, George L. N.d. "George Leo Wilkins: Incomparable Prestidigitator, In His Unique Lecture explaining the Psychical Phenomena of Spiritualism." Records of the Redpath Lyceum Bureau, Special Collections Department, University of Iowa Libraries.

Wood, Henry. 1904. *Ideal Suggestion Through Mental Photography*. Boston: Lee and Shepard.

—— 1908. *The New Old Healing*. Boston: Norwood.

Worcester, Ellwood. 1933. *Making Life Better*. New York: Scribner.

"Word from Hugo Muensterberg." 1916. *New York Times*, December 28, p. 2.

Wozniak, Robert. 1999. *Classics in Psychology, 1855–1914: Historical Essays*. Bristol: Thoemmes.

RELIGIOUS AND SECULAR, "SPIRITUAL" AND "PHYSICAL" IN GHANA

BIRGIT MEYER

Over the past decade, scholarly inquiry into contemporary religion has moved from an understanding of religion as waning in the face of ongoing secularization toward a focus on the mutual constitution and interaction of religious and secular that underpins both the ideology of secularism and modern religiosity (e.g., Asad 2003; Casanova 1994, 2008; De Vries 2008; Habermas 2005; Taylor 2007). This has produced pathbreaking research into the dynamics of religious transformation and generated deeper insights into the relation between religion and modernity. Importantly, these insights yield a new theoretical standpoint that transcends secularist ideologies according to which religion is bound to disappear—or at least to retreat into the private sphere—yet at the same time makes these ideologies subject to investigation. The fact that public debates about the so-called resurgence of religion often affirm the fault lines between "religious" and "secular" positions testifies to the fruitfulness of this new standpoint.

However, as outlined by Courtney Bender and Ann Taves in the introduction to this volume, framing our inquiries within the religious-secular binary may cause us to overlook ideas and practices that emerge in relation to this binary and yet are not fully contained by it. This volume calls for a broader framework through which these ideas and practices may come into view. Of key concern here is the puzzling field of spirits and spirituality. Placing emphasis on spirits or spirituality invokes quite different sets of practices and notions of personhood that each require detailed historical and ethnographic study. Still, it makes sense to bring spirits and spirituality together under the banner of the "spiritual," provided this is not taken as "a resting point" (or as a fixed "third category"), but rather as a "beginning place" for fresh inquiry into the paradoxes and contradictions of the religious-secular-spiritual nexus (see also Bender and Taves, introduction, this volume). Paying attention to the "spiritual," as the contributions to this volume show, challenges a view of modernity as disenchanted and thus as opposed to past or distant cultures that are "still" enchanted.

Such a view of enchantment as bound to erode with modernity underpins not only the by now much critiqued paradigm of secularization but is also lingering on, albeit less explicitly, in more recent studies. Charles Taylor's seminal work *A Secular Age* (2007), which has played a key role in reframing the contemporary study of religion, is a case in point. Taylor has noted that religion in modern societies is subject to transformation rather than simply "vanishing," or "returning" after a period of repression. In other words—and here Taylor's perspective resonates with Talal Asad's position outlined in *Formations of the Secular* (2003)—secularization and disenchantment transform modern religion instead of abolishing it.[1] Not only does Taylor use secularization and disenchantment interchangeably, thereby linking the privatization of religion to the decrease of spirits, he also suggests a development from belief in spirits, which he associates with premodern, enchanted societies, to a quest for spirituality in the secular, disenchanted age. My reason for invoking Taylor's work is that it explicates a quite widely shared, yet to some extent problematic, perspective. Seeking to unpack and rethink the relations between secular, religious, and spiritual—the central concern of this volume—this chapter will critically address the association of secularization and disenchantment, and the idea of a progressive transition from a concern with spirits to a concern with spirituality, by bringing in some complicating materials from my long-term anthropological research in Ghana.

In his introduction, Taylor quotes an example from my book *Translating the Devil* (1999:181–82): the case of Celestine who is accompanied by a stranger, who, it turns out, is only visible to her, not to her mother, and whom she later identifies as the Akan spirit Sowlui whose priestess she becomes. Taylor presents this case as a "contemporary example" (2007:11) that illustrates a condition of lived experience in which spirits are still an immediate reality—an experience that has eroded in our modern civilization. Taylor's interpretation of this case raises intriguing questions. While I certainly agree that in the setting I described the visible, material world is held to be linked with, and manipulated by, the invisible realm of spirits, I have difficulties with a view of contemporary Africa as bearing resemblance to the still enchanted prereformation period (that is, before 1500), for this implies a temporalization of other cultures and, as Johannes Fabian put it, a denial of coevalness (1983). That is why many anthropologists today feel uneasy about invoking contemporary cultural forms as "windows to the past." Certainly, in the case of Ghana, as will be pointed out in more detail below, we encounter a modern secular state that witnessed, after the turn to democracy and the liberalization and commercialization of the hitherto state-owned media in 1992, the emergence of a heavily pentecostalized public sphere in which much emphasis is placed on spirits. Spirits, it appears, elude confinement to the category of religion and appear in all kinds of settings, including politics, economics, and entertainment. Spirits, in other words, are not just there, as signs of a traditional past, but *reproduced* under modern conditions.

The point is that we have to explore, in a historical perspective, how African cosmologies of the relation between spirits and the physical world intersect, in complex ways, with the evangelizing work by Western mission societies, the introduction of the modern (colonial) and postcolonial state, and its transformation in our current age. In a somewhat later publication, Taylor himself questions his earlier perspective propounded in *A Secular Age* and makes some "hesitant comments about developments outside the West, or on a global scale," asking, "What is the West, after all? What are its limits?" (2008:228). Discussing the globalization of certain Western forms, such as missionary Christianity, he also refers to my historical-ethnographic exploration of missionary affirmations of the existence of a spirit world in *Translating the Devil* and submits that the Christian reenchantment of old gods may not be simply a "transition phenomenon" (2008:243), thus questioning his earlier suggestion of a linear move from ancient regime to modernity that entails secularization and disenchantment. He ends his piece with a pertinent question: "Are all regions of the world fated to head towards the predicament of Western modernity, with a disenchanted world, a strong sense of a self-sufficient immanent order, and a staunchly buffered identity?" (2008:243).

I think that recent anthropological work suggests that this question must be answered in the negative, while at the same time we need to take into account the actual spread and impact of Western forms in areas such as Ghana. The key question is how to develop a more encompassing framework for understanding the relation between secular and religious and, by implication, "public religion," that acknowledges historical and cultural specificity and difference yet, at the same time, accounts for actual Western influences, albeit by "provincializing Europe" (Chakrabarty 2001). This is the concern of this chapter. Instigated by Taylor's invocation of the case of Celestine as an instance of a still enchanted world—which he defines as "the world of spirits, demons, and moral forces which our ancestors lived in" (2007:26)—I will probe into the complicated relation between spirits, religion, and the secular. My aim is to show how in the Ghanaian setting we encounter a process that may well be described as secularization (provided we do not mean by this the vanishing of religion, but its reconfiguration in the setting of (post)colonial modernity, see also Larkin 2009) and the concomitant constitution of modern religion as a separate category, which, however, intersects with the category of "spirits" and "the spiritual," and hence enchantment, rather than disenchantment. As I will show, the category of spirits cannot be reduced to a timeless, primordial substratum in African cosmologies, but is subject to being framed and remediated by missions and contemporary Pentecostal media. On the whole, by calling attention to spirits I seek to call into question the association of secularization and disenchantment and to think through the implications of the resilience, and even proliferation, of spirits for our understanding of contemporary religion in a global perspective.

RELIGION, THE SECULAR, AND SPIRITS IN GHANA

Throughout British colonial Africa, the state administration did not only rely on the work of Catholic and Protestant missions in setting up educational structures, teaching civic virtues as part and parcel of "modern religion," but also affirmed chiefly authority and its backing in ancestral power—"traditional religion"—or supported, and subtly transformed, Islam as part and parcel of the policy of indirect rule. With regard to the Gold Coast (which later became Ghana), the colonial state acknowledged the relevance of both Christianity and local religious-cultural traditions for the purpose of governance, and this entailed a host of clashes and contradictions between them both. At the same time, those religious ideas and practices deemed detrimental to societal order were suppressed, if necessary by force. The colonial administration, in other words, distinguished not only between—and introduced the categories of—"modern" and "traditional" religion, but also "good" and "bad" religion.

The newly independent Ghanaian state faced and still faces the colonial legacy of these distinctions and the ambivalences and tensions that ensued. Under Ghana's first president, Kwame Nkrumah (1957–1966), the once church-run school system was nationalized,[2] although the obligation to attend Christian morning devotion—and for boarding school students the obligation to attend Sunday service—was retained, even if students were not Christian, but devoted to Islam or—far more rarely—traditional religion.[3] In particular in early post-Independence Ghana under Nkrumah and under the Rawlings regime (1981–1992), politicians espoused a markedly critical attitude toward Christianity, which was dismissed as the "white man's religion," colonizing Africans' minds. Instead they privileged indigenous culture, which served as a resource for performing the nation in state rituals and festivals. While this entailed frictions between the state and Christians, for instance, over the pouring of libation (which entails calling the spirits of the ancestors) at state functions, it is nonetheless important to realize that such acts were framed in terms of *cultural heritage* and not in terms of a national religion.[4]

Throughout the history of modern Ghana, the recourse to indigenous culture has been contested (Coe 2005). The state emphasis on national culture effected a folklorization of heritage, implying that traditional cultural and religious practices were not taken seriously in their own right. In other words, these practices were reframed as quite innocent national customs that had a high symbolic value—standing for the nation's heritage—but were, by the same token, placed outside the sphere of power. Nonetheless, both Christians and traditionalists questioned such state cultural policies. For many Christians, these policies did not merely retrieve a colorful national heritage. Resisting a reading of heritage in mere symbolic terms, they found such state policies implied an invocation of traditional spirits who, certainly from a Pentecostal perspective, were regarded as demons that led people into "backward" customs and brought them under satanic control. Cultural heritage, in this sense, was a "bad" religion in disguise, to be replaced by a "decent" religion as (Pentecostal) Christianity. Interestingly, this view of spirits as existing entities resonated with the attitudes of traditionalists for whom spirits were harbingers of power and value (Meyer 1999). In other words, the state attitude toward heritage was predicated on invoking a modern category of culture that thrived on folklorization, thus denying the power of spirits and effecting disenchantment. Though espousing opposed attitudes toward spirits, the reality of spirits and their being part of "traditional religion" was affirmed by a great many (Pentecostal) Christians and traditionalists alike.[5]

The notion of traditional religion itself had been developed in the context of the encounter between Christian missions and indigenous priests. The former framed the practices of the latter in terms of a primitive and indeed satanic form of religion that needed to be "left behind" through conversion to Christianity. Although traditional priests protested against the Christian attacks, they nevertheless adopted the Christian framing of their practices as "traditional religion," and this was reiterated by many scholars who invoked African Traditional Religion (ATR) as a common denominator for a diverse set of practices. In this sense, ATR is a modern category that is being called upon in "talking back" to Christian opponents, yet under a discursive framing not of traditionalists' own making (Meyer 2005a; see also Comaroff and Comaroff 1992). However, traditional religious practice did in many respects run counter to modern ideas about religion, especially because it was enmeshed with all aspects of life, from social relations to the market to politics.

Tellingly, under J.J. Rawlings a new initiative emerged that reframed African cultural and religious traditions in a format strikingly similar to that of Christianity. The Afrikania movement, founded by an ex-Catholic priest, sought to offer a real alternative to Christian churches that was both modern and African (Boogaard 1993).[6] Afrikania's modern religious format implied an authorized book similar to the Bible and Sunday services with a liturgy that resonated with the Catholic mass. In so doing, Afrikania moved beyond the folklorization of culture as heritage and reinstated ATR as a respectable, modern religion. Emphasizing the highly rational, intellectualist potential of modern traditional religion, spirits were virtually neglected. This, however, was and still is worlds apart from the religious practices of the priests whom the movement claimed to represent (De Witte 2005a, 2005b, 2008).

The new constitution, adopted in 1992, when, upon the instigation of the World Bank and the IMF, Ghana turned to "democracy," firmly asserts the secularity of the state. The constitution guarantees Ghanaian citizens the "freedom to practice any religion and to manifest such practice" (article 21c). The state does not privilege any of the many religions in the country (different brands of Christianity, Islam, indigenous religious traditions) and now obliges schools not to force religious minorities to attend Christian worship.[7] Religious institutions are required to register like NGOs—with the exception of traditional cults—and this allows them to be exempted from paying taxes.

Notwithstanding the formal secularity of the state, however, in the aftermath of democratization, Pentecostal-Charismatic Christianity has achieved a prominent public presence, yielding what I called a "pentecostalite public sphere" (Meyer 2004) characterized by the excessive presence and circulation of Christian cultural forms that openly challenge cultural heritage policies. These forms extend way beyond the sphere of churches themselves and reach into public culture. Shaped by the audiovisual technologies, program formats, and modalities of public exposure that became available with the deregulation and commercialization of media and the rise of new technological and religious infrastructures, these forms testify to Pentecostals' capacity to negotiate new media and adopt new modes of expression and address. Democratization offered unprecedented possibilities for the public articulation of religion, and this has been highly conducive to the rise of Pentecostal-Charismatic churches,[8] while African culture and religion are ever more attacked as devil worship (De Witte 2008; Gifford 2004; Meyer 2004). Recently, however, there are some instances of traditionalists talking back in new ways, as for example the Kumasi-based priest Kwaku Bonsam, who has publicly revealed that many Christian Pentecostal pastors rely on his spiritual power and who uses such new media as talkshows, crusades, and even a Web site to present himself in public—a point to which I will return.

In sum, Ghana witnessed the rise of the category of modern religion, which shaped not only Christianity but also to some extent traditional religion—most clearly in the case of Afrikania—and Islam, alongside with the interrelated categories of culture and heritage. The resistance and misgivings on the part of both Christians and traditionalists, albeit for different reasons, with regard to framing indigenous customs in terms of cultural heritage reveals a deep cleavage between a view of such customs in terms of really existing spirits, as claimed by the former, and a more or less disenchanted heritage, as posited by the state. The—admittedly brief—sketch presented in this section suggests the need to relate the constitution of the secular and the religious to another pair of terms: the relation between what is called "the spiritual" and "the physical."

SPIRITS AND "THE SPIRITUAL REALM"

As intimated already, in Ghana, as in many other African settings, the visible, material world is held to be linked with, and manipulated by, the invisible realm of spirits. While Africanists have long paid attention to the question of "spirits," the publication of Jean and John Comaroff's edited volume *Modernity and Its Malcontents* (1993) opened up a new field for conceptualizing spirits not merely as instances of traditional modes of thinking and living, but as being placed at the heart of modernity (e.g., Ashforth 2005; Comaroff and Comaroff 1999, 2000; Ellis and Ter Haar 2004; Ferme 2001; Geschiere 1997; Meyer 1999; West 2005; see also Thoden van Velzen and Van Wetering 1989). What is important for my discussion here is that spirits intersect with the religion-secular distinction in intriguing ways. As many scholars have shown, spirits are a category of beings that are held to impinge on the material world, or "the physical (realm)" from behind, yet only achieve visibility under certain conditions, for instance in dreams and daytime visions, or appear to people who have a "second pair of eyes," or in Pentecostal parlance, "the spirit of discernment."

The category of "spirit" as it features in Ghana today was shaped in the nineteenth-century encounter between local religious traditions and missionary Christianity. Let me explain this by briefly turning to my own research on the appropriation of missionary Protestantism by the Ewe in what is now Southeastern Ghana. In Ewe the term for spirit is *gbɔgbɔ*. As far as I could reconstruct, prior to the arrival of missionaries, who eagerly sought to convey Christianity in Ewe terms and who, at the same time, produced the first ethnographies of Ewe religion (Spieth 1906, 1911), the term *gbɔgbɔ* was employed to express "breath." With the formulation of a Christian vocabulary that also impacted on those who did not convert yet nonetheless reframed their traditional practices in new ways, the term *gbɔgbɔ* became more encompassing. It was now used to refer to a class of spiritual entities that had hitherto usually been referred to as *trɔ* (local gods). The Christians introduced not only a distinction between *gbɔgbɔ vɔ̃wo* (evil spirits) and *gbɔgbɔ kɔkɔe* (Holy Spirit) but also located *gbɔgbɔ* within the person. In so doing, they circumvented Ewe understandings of the human subject as constituted by *gbetsi* ("fate," e.g., recurring to a promise made by a person earlier in the realm where s/he dwelled before being born, about how [long] s/he would live in the world) and *luvɔ* ("soul" or "shadow"). The latter notion was retained and expresses the idea that a person's soul stays on after death, going to heaven or hell. However *gbɔgbɔ* became the central notion to express the idea of a personal spirit. According to the Christian view of the person, the personal *gbɔgbɔ* was not so much a separate spiritual entity, but more like an inner space—sometimes compared to a room or a house, that could not exist by itself (it would be empty) but was of necessity filled by either the Holy Spirit or by one or more "evil spirits," that is, local gods or witchcraft. In this sense the person's spirit is like a house *and* its occupants.[9]

The analogy of spirits and breath is intriguing here, as it suggests an understanding of being filled with a spiritual power as analogous to breathing, the continuous taking in and letting out of air, without which there is no life. The notion of spirit-as-breath suggests an understanding of air as thick with invisible, yet powerful substances that need to get into a person and that can also go out again (see De Abreu 2005, 2009 for a thorough analysis of breathing as a material, religious practice in the Catholic Charismatic renewal in Brazil). It is a force that is internalized and externalized in the rhythm of breathing.

This idea of the person as being subject to being inhabited—and thus "breathed," and kept alive—by different kinds of spirits points toward an understanding of the person as permeable and open, organically linked with the world around. As I have shown in quite some detail in *Translating the Devil*, one of the reasons why many Ewe found Christianity attractive was the fact that being "filled with the Holy Spirit" effected a kind of (albeit temporary) closure, turning the person's *gbɔgbɔ* into a bastion that could no more be taken by a *gbɔgbɔ võ* (see also Meyer 1998a). This is in certain respects quite close to Taylor's notion of the "buffered self." However, here the buffered self is in a constant need of being secured by powerful prayer and "vigilance." This testifies to an ambivalent understanding of persons as being embedded in and thus permeable to a wider social texture, in which kinship ties are of utmost importance, on the one hand, and as being severable from this texture by creating a kind of spiritual hedge, on the other. In this sense, the convergence of one's own *gbɔgbɔ* with the Holy Spirit is understood as an embodiment of power, through which "spiritual attacks" can be warded off and a person can be made inaccessible to potentially destructive ties (like witchcraft, inflicted upon by members of one's own family, or possession by family or village gods and other spirits). This occupation, in turn, materializes in tangible assets such as wealth and health.

The view of the relation between people and spirits at stake here can be illustrated by turning once again to the case of Celestine. What I found so intriguing when I interviewed her about her religious biography was that she not only described how she became a priestess after the stranger, who had been her invisible companion, slept with her (she felt him lean on her), but she was not quite happy with having to worship him. That is why she sent her children to school, hoping that they would become Christians (Christians were also called *sukutɔwo*—school people) and have nothing to do with *Sowlui,* whose worship was considered dirty and primitive from a Christian viewpoint. Actually, in Celestine's view it was due to the prayers of her daughter that she finally converted to Christianity. This conversion occurred after she received a visitor in her house who touched her and told her to throw away her *trɔ* things while her daughter was fasting on the prayer ground. She identified this stranger as Jesus, did as he told her, and became a church member.

Her account suggests a striking resemblance between her first encounter with *Sowlui* and the one with Jesus (in both cases Celestine is visited by a spirit, has a sensation of touch, and then devotes herself to worshipping the spirit). Traditional religion and Christianity operated and still operate on virtually the same plane, entailing an exchange of one spirit for another. However, while one occupant was exchanged for another, there was a deeper change implied in this shift toward Christianity: the valuation of spirits as "good" or "evil." While spirits traditionally were morally neutral, in that they were forces that could be called to do either good or harm, from a Christian perspective all traditional spirits are bad, involved in a struggle with the Holy Spirit. It is no coincidence that Celestine converted to a Pentecostal church (Agbelengor) in which spiritual power plays a far more central role than in the more Scripture-oriented mainline Protestant mission church, the E. P. Church, from which Agbelengor broke away. The Holy Spirit was called upon to occupy and protect her against certain dangerous forces from outside.[10]

What is so intriguing here is that Celestine's case (and many others) suggests that the idea about gbɔbgɔ, while certainly resonating with traditional notions, has been reconfigured into a Christian discourse that encompasses and at the same time claims to overpower traditional religion by placing it in a dualistic framework. This entails a process of devaluation and disempowerment of traditional forces, while reinstating a view of the world as enchanted. It is important to note here that throughout Africa Christianity, which was considered the religion that "opened people's eyes" and brought "civilization" and "progress," played a central role in keeping the world *enchanted.* Invoking a dualistic opposition between evil spirits and the spirit of God, who was held to be able to overcome the former, missions developed their own modes of enchantment. Currently, Pentecostals are much engaged in talking about spirits. Next to the old gods, ancestors, family spirits, and witchcraft, also poverty, despair, adultery, and so on are understood as evil spirits that try to get hold of people and are to be cast out by filling the person with the Holy Spirit. Whatever happens to a person has a spiritual dimension. This points toward a considerable cleavage between Max Weber's view of Protestantism, on the one hand, and missionary Christianity and the appropriations it produced, on the other. Whereas, in the former case, Protestantism effected disenchantment, in the latter it engaged with an enchanted world by affirming the reality of spirits and articulating its power therein. It needs to be noted, though, that the Western missionaries themselves were somewhat hesitant to fully immerse themselves in the narrative of the Holy Spirit fighting evil spirits. The Holy Spirit and spirits appear to be difficult to control (Kirsch 2008). By contrast, emphasis on the power of the Holy Spirit became the distinctive feature of African Independent and, later, Pentecostal-Charismatic churches. The fact that the latter operate on a global scale, yielding networks of "born again" Christians who share a concern with the evil machination of Satan and view the world as a stage for spiritual warfare, shows that a concern with spirits is not confined to Africans but integral to global Pentecostalism, which is often represented as a global religion par excellence.

Gbɔgbɔ not only entails a particular positioning of a person in the world, suggesting a conflation of one's spirit with forces from outside, but also is at the center of the realm of "the spiritual" (in Ewe: *le gbɔgbɔme*) that underlies "the physical realm" (in Ewe: *le nutilame*). It is interesting to note here that *nuti* means body, implying a view of spirit and body as entangled and dependent on each other. None exists in a separate, pure form.[11] Just as a person's gbɔgbɔ is invisible, and its occupant can only be discerned on the basis of concrete material signs, the physical world, too, is held to be dependent on spiritual powers that remain invisible as such to the naked eye, yet affect everyday life and can be seen under special conditions. People also account for visits to the spirit world. While such ventures are part of the work of traditional priests who may move into "the bush" to invoke spiritual powers, many Pentecostal preachers claim that prior to their conversion they also had regular encounters with the "underworld"—an experience that authenticates their authority in dealing with "spiritual warfare" and "deliverance." They describe this underworld as a kind of parallel world located at the bottom of the ocean that is highly developed and full of riches—a kind of America that is, however, governed by the devil (Meyer 1998b; Ellis and Ter Haar 2004). This realm of the powers of darkness has been emphasized in the Christian imaginary, which thus attributes much power to forces that are simultaneously despised. While people sense being under attack by demonic forces, they also place these forces in a spiritual war with the Holy Spirit who will ultimately be victorious (Meyer 2006).[12]

The point here is that "the spiritual" is not a separate realm into which people may strive to move (as may be the case in Western searches for spirituality, which is usually understood as opposed to matter or at least as an escape from prosaic materialism, as several contributions to this volume also show). The spiritual is inextricably entangled with the physical or material realm or, as Mariane Ferme put it, the "underneath of things" (2001). What happens in the material world—from the level of a person's body to the nation and even the globe—is held to be backed by spiritual forces, which also is a way to say that there is need to be aware of what lies behind mere appearance, the surface of things. While people talk about spiritual forces as behind or underneath, it is nonetheless important to realize that "the spiritual" and "the physical" are completely entangled and that, in a sense, spirits and the spiritual are within, in the midst of, "the physical." In many respects, the spiritual and spirits are the powers that shape the course of things and make people act and think in the way they do. As Ellis and Ter Haar aptly put it, "spirituality is not an abstraction, of interest only to theologians and philosophers, but becomes a power within the reach of all" (2004:52).[13]

This brief analysis of the discourse woven around spirits and the spiritual thus suggests that Christianity, via strategies of diabolization and an overall dualistic perspective, engaged in keeping enchanted the lifeworld into which the Christian message was preached. This entailed 1. the introduction of a broad notion of spirit that refers to both an inner space and an occupying, "breathing" force from outside that fills the self; 2. the launching of the notion of a spiritual war according to which traditional spirits are demonized, which informs what happens to persons and the world as a whole; 3. tying into local views of spirits and the spiritual as not opposed to but materializing in matter; and 4. the presence of spirits in all spheres of life, be it the market, politics, family relations, or religion.

SPIRITS ON STAGE

With the institutionalization of democracy and the liberalization and commercialization of the media, a new public sphere emerged, in which spirits shifted from being framed as forces operating in secret, below and behind the surface of appearance, to becoming subject to vision and visibility. When I did research in Ghana in 1996, I was amazed by the difference between the ways in which spirits featured in public debate at that time and during my earlier fieldwork period between 1988 and 1992. Whereas in the late 1980s and early 1990s spirits were talked about in a more or less secretive manner, often using the semipublic registers of gossip and rumors through which "public secrets" (Taussig 2003) circulated, now the revelation of alleged links between people and spirits was the order of the day. Talk about spirits was all over the place—even reaching into the sphere of politics. I still remember a much discussed incident when President J. J. Rawlings slapped his vice president Arkaah for stating in a cabinet meeting that Rawlings owed his power to having swallowed a live frog in his home area in the Southern Volta Region, which was known and feared for its powerful *dzo* (magic; Akyeampong 1996:163; Meyer 1998c). While rumors about Rawlings's links with a powerful Ewe shrine had been all over the place before—perhaps not even to his dismay, as this asserted his power—the articulation of spirit affairs in an official public setting such as a cabinet meeting was new.[14]

Concomitantly, in the wake of the 1996 elections, I noted a strong inclination on the part of politicians to stress that they were "born again" and to assault other politicians as being in league with demonic spirits. In many ways, the sphere of politics was recast as one of the fields in which the war between demonic spirits and the Holy Spirit became tangible, turning the nation into a prime arena of this war. This implied that the attempt to reveal and, if possible, give a visible proof of a person's ties with spirits became an important aspect of the project of politics—a view that immediately invokes parallels with the situation in the USA in which politicians, too, feel pressed to tap into religious-spiritual registers, notwithstanding the formal secularity of the state (a point I will briefly touch upon in the conclusion). Also, in the time leading up the recent elections in Ghana (in December 2008), suspicions and revelations about politicians' involvement with spiritual forces were a central issue. Before returning to this in more detail, let me briefly explain the key role of Pentecostal-Charismatic churches and media in this process.

PENTECOSTALS AND MEDIA

After 1992, the Pentecostals were the first to profit from the new possibility to buy airtime and express their views on radio and television (De Witte 2010). Next to forming megachurches that address masses of believers—and believers as a mass—many Pentecostal-Charismatic churches also organize large-scale public events such as "Crusades" and "All-night prayers," often broadcast on radio and TV. Pentecostal TV programs popularize a particular Pentecostal mode of worship with its own speech genres, music and dance, style of dres, and way of comporting oneself—in short, a new religious aesthetic—that contrasts significantly with the much more sober and less exuberant way of being a believer in Catholic, Methodist, Presbyterian, or Anglican churches. Announced in a self-assured manner as "break through" events, pastors engage in the production of miracles. Preaching styles, dramatization, and spectacularization are mobilized so as to affirm the power of the pastor to invoke the Holy Spirit and perform miracles (Asamoah-Gyadu 2005; Gifford 2004).

This is paralleled by Ghanaian and Nigerian video movies that often surf along with the popularity of Pentecostalism. Claiming to visualize the spectacular fight between Satan and the Holy Spirit, skillful use is made of special effects (Meyer 2005b, 2006). In Nigeria there are a number of Pentecostal churches that produce their own miracle films, thereby seeking to support their accounts of the normally invisible spiritual realm with evidence (Haynes 2002; see also Pype 2008). While traditionalists and intellectuals who are in favor of tradition and cultural heritage critique these movies for misrepresenting traditional powers, people often refer to them so as to vest claims about the existence and action of spirits with truth ("I saw it in that film . . . "). Such movies, people, say, are able to show "what is there."

Media are far more than just instruments. They are substantial ingredients through which the power of God is made tangible. For instance, when I attended a prayer service—*Jericho Hour*—organized by Action Faith Chapel in Accra in January 2008, and the electricity supply broke down, I realized the importance of microphones. Everything came to a standstill, and prayers could only continue when the generator was switched on. Loudness—to such an extent that participants' bodies vibrate from the excess of sound—and also pastors' use of microphones in rhythmic sayings—ah-oh-ah-oh—contribute to inducing a certain trancelike atmosphere that conveys a sense of an extraordinary encounter with a divine force that can be made to enter by opening up and stretching one's arms. This is not to say that media are just used instrumentally to make up—not to say fake—the presence of the Holy Spirit, but to indicate the inextricable entanglement of media in religious communication (Meyer 2005b). Similarly, media such as the microphone, radio, television, or books are being sanctified as suitable harbingers of divine power—a sine qua non, as it were, for the transmission and presence of God. Divine power must be expressed—and from a more distant perspective we might say is produced—via forms of worship utilizing certain media that have been authenticated as suitable.

What I find fascinating here is the way in which faith, seeing, and audiovisual media are brought together. While faith offers spiritual vision—"faith is your spiritual eye!"—visibility is also mobilized as evidence to persuade followers and potential believers of the pastor's power to perform miracles by calling upon God. What looks to be a miracle to an outsider is actually achieved by a powerful intervention in "the spiritual." During a visit to Ghana in 2003, for instance, I encountered much talk about a certain videotape, circulated by a Nigerian Pentecostal church, in which the pastor T. B. Joshua was shown to make a dead person, who had been brought to church in a coffin, rise again. This video has been subject to as much admiration as critique (Moyet n.d.). In April 2004 the Nigerian Broadcasting Corporation (NBC) banned these kinds of miracles on TV and radio because, as it was put, the pastors were unable to verify them. Reactions on the part of those defending the broadcasting of these miracles were very interesting. As expected, it was argued that faith exceeds reason, but also that the NBC itself failed to offer scientific standards for providing evidence. Perhaps most interestingly, it was claimed that the ban violated the constitutional right of freedom of religious expression. The popularity of such programs shows—albeit in extreme form—how Pentecostals engage in different audiovisual techniques of make-believe in order to feature as successful and convince others.

Here we can note Pentecostals' world-embracing attitude: new technologies are taken up and incorporated in such a way that they become vehicles of the Holy Spirit and the project of outreach. What we find, in other words, is a congruence of media technologies and the transcendental they claim to mediate. God is located in the medium, and the drive to use these media in the religious project of reaching out makes Pentecostalism a public religion par excellence. By employing modern audiovisual technologies to convey the performance of miracles, religion and technology thus come to be entangled in a striking way. As Derrida put it provocatively in his discussion of the nexus of television and the religious: "There is no need any more to believe, one can see. But seeing is always organized by a technical structure that supposes the appeal to faith" (2001:63). Far from occupying different provinces, religion and technology, miracle and special effects, as Hent de Vries (2001) also argued, are not ontologically different but mixed (see also Stolow 2005, 2008). By calling upon audiovisual technologies to visualize spiritual forces and making belief dependent on visibility, Pentecostal-Charismatic churches are prime examples of this process. Gradually this adoption of audiovisual technologies is also adopted by Catholics, Presbyterians, and Anglicans, because it is realized that resistance to this process will entail a loss of members, certainly among the youth. Muslims, too, have now started to adopt new media. And, as we shall see in the next section, there is even some positive appreciation of audiovisual media on the part of the traditionalists.

A TRADITIONALIST IS STRIKING BACK

For quite some time it looked as if the visualization of spirits (and the working of the Holy Spirit) was a privilege of Pentecostals, while the traditionalists whom they despised remained outside of the limelight of publicity. Many traditional priests felt, and still feel, uncomfortable with adopting Pentecostal modes of representation, as, in their view, spiritual power demands some degree of secrecy. As Marleen de Witte explained in her comparison of a Pentecostal-Charismatic church (the International Central Gospel Church headed by Mensa Otabil) and the already mentioned Afrikania movement (2008), the latter faced many difficulties correcting the negative image of traditional Pentecostal practices and convincing the priests to allow cameras into the shrines. Traditional people would claim, in one way or another, that cameras could not be used during the ceremonies of calling the gods (see also Meyer 2005a; Spyer 2001).

On the other hand, as a host of photographs and films of, for instance, Ghanaian possession ceremonies shows, this should not be a generic problem.[15] The point is that in the aftermath of Christianization the traditional practices of invoking spirits were more and more pushed into the secret sphere. While the Ewe saying *Mawu vide, trɔ vide* (a bit of God and a bit of spirits) suggests that converts to Christianity also kept on consulting traditional gods, it needs to be noted that they did not come out for this openly, as it was considered detrimental to their reputation. A successful, modern person had to present him/herself as Christian. At the same time, however, the most publicly respected forms of Christianity, as epitomized in the mission churches, were experienced as little suited to bring people in touch with the Holy Spirit. Paradoxically, missionary Christianity had unleashed a systematic discourse on spirits, yet could not provide actual spiritual empowerment (at least this was claimed by many converts). This is what motivated converts to still consult traditional spirits, albeit in the middle of the night. Interestingly, while African Independent and Pentecostal-Charismatic churches claimed to make up for this lack and offer immediate access to the Holy Spirit, there have always been rumors that pastors themselves also consult the spirits in secret.

In recent years, also stimulated by Nigerian and Ghanaian movies about "fake pastors," there is a host of suspicions about powerful charismatic pastors who allegedly owe their power not to God but to a spiritualist in the countryside. In many respects it seems that the realm of African spirits is impossible to conquer, notwithstanding Christian rhetoric of "spiritual war." Indeed, Christianity, it appears, needs to reproduce the realm of spirits as a condition for its own appeal yet is, at the same time, haunted by the power of the very spirits it invokes. This came out clearly in May 2008, when the *Daily Guide* reported on the traditionalist Kwaku Bonsam, who had stormed into the Vision Charismatic Chapel in Kato (Brong Ahafo region) and publicly called upon its pastor Agyei Yeboah to pay for the juju (e.g., magic) he had done for him or return it.[16] Bonsam claimed that his own gods had pushed him into this public act, as they had threatened to kill him if he would not force the pastor to pay his debts to the spirits. He also revealed that there were over one thousand pastors who relied on his spiritual powers and threatened to reveal their names. One Pentecostal man of God, Reverend Adarkwa Yiadom, founder and leader of the Ebenezer Miracle Worship Centre in Kumasi, took up the challenge and agreed to participate in a public contestation over spiritual power. However, due to some alleged misunderstandings, Reverend Adarkwa failed to show up in Kumasi Jubilee Park, while Kwaku Bonsam, "to the amazement of the crowd," set up a spectacular show, in the course of which he miraculously produced bank notes (*Daily Guide*, May

16, 2008). Meanwhile, Kwaku Bonsam has become a national celebrity, celebrated by some and despised as an embodiment of Satan by others (it may be no coincidence that *bonsam* means devil in Twi). He appeared on TV talkshows (TV3), runs his own Web site, and organizes public all-night prayer services devoted to praying for peaceful elections, just as many Pentecostals do.

The coming out of Kwaku Bonsam is, of course, exceptional. Because of his background (allegedly he had been a Christian before) and his spectacular performance (which distinguished him from more ordinary traditionalists), he is regarded as not a "100 percent" traditional priest (personal communication, Kwadwo Adusei). Even though it may be too early to interpret Kwaku Bonsam's forceful move into the limelight of audiovisual media as indicative of a new trend, the event itself, and the attention it received, is remarkable and telling. It signals that the longstanding opposition, as it emerged in the course of colonialism, between traditionalists thriving in secret and Christianity featuring as the respectable religion of modernity is eroding. Kwaku Bonsam's actions openly challenge Pentecostalism's superiority claims and dismissal of traditional religion as satanic. Revealing Pentecostal pastors' secret spiritual resources (thereby affirming widespread rumors) and adopting formats and modes of representation that are similar to those employed by Pentecostals, he challenges the view that Pentecostalism and traditional religion are fundamentally different. While his reconfiguration of tradition diverts from Afrikania,[17] it is still the case that Kwaku Bonsam embraces Christian forms.[18] Opposition to Christianity is expressed through resemblance on the level of performance, using audiovisual media, and is geared toward staging spectacular effects that make spiritual power visible, amazing the audiences.

SPIRITS IN POLITICS

In an article in *Ghana News* of September 6, 2008, journalist Kofi Akosah-Sarpong takes issue with the entanglement of spirits and politics. He starts by praising the virtues of democracy over one-party systems. However, as he explains:

> Despite how democracy brings light and opens up the development process, somehow in Ghana, which has been struggling to consolidate democracy for the past 16 years, certain dark cultural

practices have been inhibiting it. True to the fact that all democra-
cies are eventually influenced by its environment, in Ghana, proph-
ets, traditional priests, juju-marabout mediums and other spiritualists, as part of the Ghanaian milieu, are swinging on the democratic
scene big time, especially as the December 2008 general elections
approaches. As Jean-Francois Bayart would say in *The State in Africa:
The Politics of the Belly,* this is the "cocoa season" for spiritualists of
all spectrums to make dough from the emotionally helpless politicians who consistently find it difficult to minimize such irrational
image [*sic*] and project higher rationalization of Ghana's development reality and challenges. It is in this atmosphere that the Accra-
based *Ghanaian Observer* reports that "Barely three months into the
December 2008 elections, finite mortals are taking a peep into the
unseen world of spirituality and fathoming the mind of the Divine.
Most politicians, now admitting their finiteness, are therefore relying on God for answers—some through fasting and prayers and others through sacrifices to witchdoctors and other mediums."

Having thus set the scene, calling upon the work of the French political
scientist Bayart (1993), Akosah-Sarpong presents a harsh critique of spiritualists, who "have become political and partisan, confusing the superstitious and the gullible," predicting "different victories for different parties,
most times based on money offered than genuine divination." His point
is, however,

> not to degrade the spiritualists, the trouble is how their amazingly
> excessive influence on the Ghanaian life weakens rationalization
> and reality of the development issues, so much so that even elites,
> like Edward Mahama, Paa Kwesi Nduom, John Atta-Mills and Nana
> Akufo-Addo, who are expected to radiate higher reasoning to illu-
> minate the development path, are under the heavy sway of the
> prophets, Voodoo priests, Malams, juju-marabout mediums, witch-
> doctors, Shamans and other spiritualists to the injury of Ghana's
> larger progress. The December 2008 general elections should do less
> with the spiritualists and more with issues/reality on the ground,
> hard work, strategy, long-term planning, commitment, steadfast-
> ness, and struggles, and not any unseen forces manipulating Gha-
> naians to vote for John Atta-Mills, Edward Mahama, Paa Kwesi
> Nduom or Nana Akufo-Addo simply because a God told a prophet.

This is an intriguing article that well illustrates the intersection of spirits with formally secular politics. It needs to be noted that the public invocation of spirits as powerful forces behind the democratic elections is not new. Ever since the first elections after the return to democracy in 1996, Pentecostal-Charismatic churches have organized prayer services for national peace.[19] Politicians consulted pastors for spiritual help— Rawlings, for instance, was said to get the support of Duncan Williams of Action Faith Chapel—and made public statements about their faith in church. In this sense, the spiritual dimension—in this case the Holy Spirit—has been central to the election period ever since the inauguration of democracy. What is new is the self-assurance of spiritualists from the traditionalist camp (e.g., "voodoo-priests," "malams," etc.). Of course, the popularity of these spiritualists triggers a massive opposition on the part of Pentecostals, many of whom, however, retort by declaring a "spiritual war" (as the already mentioned Reverend Adarkwa Yiadom).

Particularly interesting in Akosah-Sarpong's analysis is his claim that democracy in Ghana is "inhibited by dark cultural practices," and his critique that spiritualists' "amazingly excessive influence" works against rationalization and development. Putting traditional and Christian spiritualists together as a challenge for rationalization, he clearly favors the disenchantment of politics as an ideal, in the light of which the Ghanaian version of democracy leaves much to be desired. His view typifies a rationalistic, "enlightened" attitude toward politics that is adopted by (part of) the intellectual elite. My concern here is, of course, not to echo Akosah-Sarpong's view of the (then still upcoming) elections as mobilizing superstitious beliefs and attributing too much power to spiritualists, but to grasp how spirits and politics come together in the popular imagination and are increasingly mobilized openly in the political sphere. I have already explained how the category of spirits and "the spiritual" was framed in the context of the encounter with Christian missionaries, and how, in the wake of democratization and liberalization, spirits gained ever more visibility and publicity. Here it is important to note that the democratic system itself seems to ensure insecurities that make proponents turn to powerful spiritual support. This expresses a "quest for spiritual security" (Ashforth 2005) on the part of those who wield political power. At the same time, the very mastery of spiritual forces, as claimed by both traditionalists and pastors, should be understood as a language of power that not only speaks about powers, but is powerful in itself (see also West 2005), as evidenced by the fact that politicians go for it and people flock to prayer services to pray for victory or the peace of the nation.

Many of my Ghanaian friends pointed out to me that in the aftermath of the elections, which brought the formerly oppositional NDC party back to power after eight years, the mixing of spirits and politics is even increasing. The elected president of Ghana, John Evans Atta Mills, openly thanked the Nigerian Pentecostal preacher TB Joshua, founder of the Synagogue Church of All Nations, for his spiritual support. TB Joshua, whose advice is sought by many African leaders, apparently prophesied the victory of Atta Mills and now attends to the president's spiritual needs.[20] Exactly because spirits and "the spiritual" intersect with all dimensions of life, their importance cannot easily be denied, most certainly not in a sphere that, notwithstanding the ideal of democracy as transparent, is difficult to grasp and penetrate. As the nation has become cast as the site of the "spiritual war" between God and Satan, the public display of spiritual power has become ever more important. If, in earlier years, traditional priests would offer their service discreetly and in secret because their clients were eager not to be found out, nowadays staged and mediated events have become ever more valued. It is as intriguing as frightening to see how the domain of spirits is redeployed so that showing off spiritual power has become ever more important. In this way, Ghana's new public sphere has transformed itself into a stage on which not only the spiritual war between God and Satan but also between Christian and traditional models of spiritual power are fought in public, where pastors and spiritualists run the show while those in political office are reduced to their clients, who cannot do without spiritual support from one side or the other (see also Sánchez 2008).

৩৯ ৩৯

As pointed out in the beginning, it was my concern to explore unexpected intersections of spirits, religion, and the secular. The Ghanaian state, certainly after adopting a democratic constitution, can well be described as secular, in that the state does not endorse and privilege a state religion (tradition being a matter of cultural heritage), rather guaranteeing religious freedom. It is intriguing to see that, contrary to what one might have expected from a liberal perspective, democracy was favorable to the rise of public religion, implying the mediated staging of spiritual power. While the state is formally (constitutionally) secular, Ghanaian society and politics are heavily inflected with religion and a concern with spirits. If for some years Pentecostals appeared to run the show, more recently traditionalists have given signs of retaliation. This points to the deep entanglement of Pentecostalism and traditional religion, which both invoke spirits—the former to fight them in the name of God, the latter to stress the superior power of traditional spirits. The notion of the omnipresence of spirits, and the ever more public talk about them, exceeds the sphere of religion and questions the modern understanding of religion as bound to a separate sphere. Pastors and traditional priests alike share an understanding of spirits and "the spiritual" as being deeply enmeshed with the world, thus affecting, indeed, empowering, all spheres of life, from the private realm to politics, and turning those who allegedly access spiritual power into prime movers.

While the category of the secular has been subject to considerable scholarly reflexion, spirits are often invoked as if it were clear what they are. In embedding the notion of spirits in a specific cultural setting, and tracing the constitution of an encompassing view of "spirits" and "the spiritual," I sought to show that spirits are not so much entities in which people believe and whom they worship, and thus belong to the sphere of (African) religion. In this setting, they should rather be understood as powers that generate power (see also Akyeampong 1996). Talk about spirits offers a statement about what "powers" the world. While Spirit and Matter are often opposed in Western thought, in the world explored here they require each other—much like breath and body. The fact that the notion of spirit is often used as a general category, without reflecting on how spirits are understood in the specific context of study,[21] may partly be due to a still lingering—and in fact old-fashioned—idea according to which (belief in) spirits belongs to an earlier period or a cultural elsewhere, prior to the enlightenment, as also suggested by Taylor. In modern settings, by contrast, spirits in the plural have given way to Spirit as an abstraction, as in Weber's Spirit of capitalism, Herder's *Volksgeist*, or Hegel's Spirit of History, and a playful engagement with spirits under the banner of "suspension of disbelief" (During 2004).[22] In this chapter I hope to have shown that this view of enchantment as a marker of premodern societies and cultures that "still" believe in spirits is problematic because it posits a too general idea of spirits and frames their presence as foreign to—or even inhibiting, as journalist Akosah-Sarpong put it—modernity and democracy. If spirits are encountered in such a setting, this is seen as a sign of superstition. This is of little help in reflecting on contemporary settings in which spirits feature strongly, as, for instance, in Ghana, but certainly not only there.

This view of spirits as located in past or faraway cultures may well be indebted to Max Weber's genealogy of modernity. Weber himself barely used the term *secularization*, and his prime concern was not the decline of religion (or its retreat into the private domain) but the productive role of Protestantism in the rise of capitalism.[23] Importantly, Weber's use of disenchantment places his reflections on the role of religion in modern societies in a frame other than the paradigm of secularization that emerged much later. Protestantism offered a new kind of religiosity that thrived on disenchantment and entailed a new kind of subjective experience Weber found to be distinctive of modern capitalism, which instigated rationalization and intellectualization. Weber invoked disenchantment to describe a process set in motion by the Reformation, thus arguing that the rise of a modern religion as Protestantism and disenchantment may well go together, albeit for some time. Disenchantment denied people the possibility of using magical and other means to influence God, and this was constitutive of the rise of the spirit of capitalism, which, however, could eventually do without its Protestant underpinnings, leaving modern people in the "casing of steel."

It seems to me that the material explored in this chapter calls on us to probe into the relation between secularization and disenchantment. The fact that both terms are often used interchangeably is not only problematic because they belong to different theoretical traditions but also because their conflation makes it difficult to acknowledge that one may occur *without* the other. As this chapter shows, a society may well witness a process of secularization without, however, being disenchanted. Indeed, as I have argued, Protestant missions set in motion the articulation of a new category of spirits and produced new modes of enchantment in an enchanted world. These forms of enchantment are now mobilized in the setting of democracy, which offers unprecedented technological possibilities and grants the freedom to put spirits right on stage, so much so that the nation is cast as the prime arena of a spiritual war in which politicians, like ordinary people, are in need of accessing resources of power.

In my view, the case of Ghana not only shows that, to invoke Taylor again, not all countries need to "head towards the predicament of Western modernity, with a disenchanted world, a strong sense of a self-sufficient immanent order, and a staunchly buffered identity." It also evokes striking parallels with, for example, the United States. Tellingly, in the wake of the deep financial crisis, just weeks before the end of his presidency in the fall of 2008, President Bush called upon citizens to have faith in country and market, and, in the election debates going on at the time, the linkage of politicians with the Holy Spirit was a matter of national concern.[24] While it may be true that Americans, like Ghanaians, have the freedom to chose the religion they want to adopt, as a liberal secular state ensures, it is, all the same, clear that this does not necessarily yield the process of disenchantment Weber had in mind. Not only is religion increasingly going public, getting enmeshed with and spreading via electronic media (Hoover 2006; Meyer and Moors 2006; Meyer 2009a), but all domains of life, including politics and the market, are affected by new modes of enchantment, as the celebration of Obama as the savior of the nation around the time of he election, if not the world, also shows. What enchantment actually implies is subject to concrete exploration, as I also tried to propose in this chapter. Only in this way will we get further than understanding enchantment as what was simply prior to disenchantment—a matter of the past—moving toward an approach to enchantment as intrinsic to modern projects (Meyer and Pels 2003). The world as we encounter it suggests that spirits, the spiritual—and even Spirit—mess up modern categories of analysis. This calls for a new space of inquiry in which we allow "spirits" and "spirituality" to generate exciting empirical research and theoretical debates.

NOTES

I would like to thank Courtney Bender, Ann Taves, and Jonathan van Antwerpen for inviting me to the SSRC conference in October 2008 on which this volume is based. Asking to pay attention to spirits and spirituality in relation to the opposition of secular and religious, they have stimulated me to have a fresh look at my own research materials. My thinking about this issue has also benefited from the discussions during the conference; particular thanks go the discussants Tanya Luhrman and Gauri Visvanathan. I would also like to thank Kwadwo Adusei, Kodjo Senah, Marleen de Witte, and Jojada Verrips for helpful, informative, and stimulating comments and criticisms on earlier versions of this chapter.

1. His work has instigated an intellectually exciting, critical debate about the transformation—and, indeed, intensification—of religion in our time, as the many contributions to the online SSRC discussion board *The Immanent Frame* also testify. We witness the rise of a new multidisciplinary zone for debate that

involves philosophy, history, sociology, political sciences, psychology, cultural studies, religious studies, and anthropology. However, the debates stimulated by *A Secular Age*, appear to be quite biased toward Western settings and tend to privilege a Western understanding of modernity, albeit implicitly. *A Secular Age*, as has been pointed out by Tomoko Masuzawa in her contribution to *The Immanent Frame* (2008), is predicated upon the Great Divide between the West and the Rest. This raises not only the question of how far a historical analysis of what Taylor calls Latin Christendom can be confined to the Western world (and thus be uncoupled from Europe's sphere of expansion), but also the question of how to address the phenomena we seek to capture with a term such as *public religion* in, for instance, African settings (my own field of research).

2. The British colonial authorities espoused an ambivalent attitude toward Christianity. On the one hand, also in line with the policy of indirect rule, the importance of traditional customs (insofar that they did not violate certain civilizational standards) for sustaining traditional authorities, and thus law and order, was emphasized. On the other hand, in the project of "civilizing" and "uplifting" native culture, the colonial administration relied heavily on Catholic and Protestant missions, which had the school system almost entirely in their hands. This ambivalence—respecting traditional culture and values and promoting education provided by mission schools—has been lingering on until the present.

3. In fact, traditional religion came to be regarded as "uncivilized," and Christianity as a religion of progress, modernity and civilization, that had "opened people's eyes" (Meyer 1999). This did not at all imply that Christian converts would no longer consult traditional priests. The dismissal and primitivization of traditional religion pushed it into the sphere of secrecy, to the "underneath of things" that many hold to be more powerful than the more public performance of Christianity.

4. I am currently involved in a research program that investigates the Ghanaian state project of cultural heritage that evolved around the Akan symbol of *Sankofa* (depicting a bird looking back, meaning "Go back and take it"). This research is conducted by Marleen de Witte and myself and is part of a research program, sponsored by the Netherlands Foundation for Scientific Research (NWO) and directed by Mattijs van de Port, Herman Roodenburg, and myself, titled Heritage Dynamics. Aesthetics of Persuasion and Politics of Authentication in Brazil, Ghana, South Africa, and the Netherlands.

5. As I have shown (Meyer 1999), Pentecostals build upon and incorporate earlier grassroots understandings of Christianity that evolve around the demonization of traditional religion and that may well be called Africanization from

below. The struggle for political independence also generated debates about a specific African Christianity among Christians that would allow room for a positive appropriation of local culture and religion. However, this positive appropriation is subject to heavy contestation, as especially Pentecostals advocate an uncompromising stance according to which the positive incorporation of traditional forms boils down to inviting the devil into the church.

6. In the field of Islam, the Ahmadiyya movement did something similar, in that it sought to develop a modern version of Islam, with a Western-oriented school system, that resonates with the modern understanding of religion as espoused by churches. The Ahmadiyya movement is quite strong in Ghana yet heavily contested among Muslims.

7. To get reliable figures is not easy. The Ghana Religious Freedom Report, published by the U.S. State Department, states, based on the Household Census conducted in 2000: "According to the 2000 government census, approximately 69 percent of the country's population is Christian, 16 percent is Muslim, and 9 percent adheres to traditional indigenous religions or other religions. The Muslim community has protested these figures, asserting that the Muslim population is closer to 30 percent" (http://atheism.about.com/library/irf/ irf03/blirf_ghana.htm). Despite their numerical strength, in Ghana Muslims have far less impact on shaping the public sphere than Christians. This may also have to do with the fact that, traditionally, the South, where the capital is located, is populated by ethnic groups that became predominantly Christian. The Muslims present in the South mainly consist of migrants from northern areas and have less easy access to state positions, media, etc. However, more research is needed to investigate (the transformation of) the relation between Christianity, Islam, and local religious traditions in Ghana.

8. The simultaneous emphasis on heritage and tradition as resources of national pride and the right of religious freedom is echoed by tensions in society. Pentecostal-Charismatic churches, especially, espouse an uncompromising attitude toward certain kinds of heritage, and this creates conflicts over and over again.

9. In Akan, a similar idea of spirit exists. There are two Akan terms for spirit: *sunsum* and *hɔnhɔn*. *Sunsum* denotes not only shadow but also refers to a spiritual substance that links a child to his father, while descent and heritage are counted in the matriline, e.g., to the mother's brother. In the course of Christianization a similar idea of the relation between a person's spirit— understood as a container—and its occupants emerged. While both *sunsum* and *hɔnhɔn* are used for spirit, the term preferred by Pentecostals to refer to the Holy Spirit is not so much *sunsum krɔnkrɔn*, but *hɔnhɔn krɔnkrɔn*, as opposed to *hɔnhɔn bɔne* (evil spirit). The latter are also referred to as *sunsum bɔne*. (Kwadwo Adusei and Marleen de Witte, personal communication).

10. This idea is not confined to Ewe people alone. For instance, when I had a conversation with the well-know Nigerian actress Joke Silva in November 2008, she told me that whenever she had to play an evil character in a film, she would pray and use Jesus as her "hedge."

11. This questions Western ideas about Spirit and Matter as opposed and suggests that both spirit and matter imply the other on all levels, from the personal to cosmology.

12. As my student Kwadwo Adusei, who originates from Ghana, asserted when I discussed the question of spirit with him: "there can be no neutrality," as a person is always inhabited by one or the other spirit.

13. Exactly for this reason I cannot follow these authors in locating spirits in the sphere of African religion (see also Ter Haar and Ellis 2009). In my view, the power attributed to spirits to emerge in all spheres of life questions the understanding of religion as a separate category and challenges us to develop alternative conceptualizations (Meyer 2009b).

14. The association of the head of state with occult powers also pertained to Nkrumah, who was rumored to be protected by spiritual forces that made him immune to several assassination attempts. He was often seen with a white handkerchief that allegedly linked him to his spiritual protector (Kodjo Senah, personal communication).

15. The film *Demons of Ghana* (Linus Mork and Rine Hjarno Rasmussen, Denmark 2007) is an intriguing example. It shows how possession by spirits, such as the mermaid at the bottom of the sea, Mami Water, and deliverance in Pentecostal churches, where people are exorcised, are two sides of the same coin. The film shows impressive scenes at, for instance, the Larteh Shrine. However, the makers told me that they were heavily critiqued by the traditional priests for the film title, as it seemed to endorse the Christian view of spirits as demons. The question of filming acts involving spirits that are held to operate in secret is complicated. In his work on Candomblé, Mattijs van de Port (2006) argues that priestesses engage in what he calls the public staging of secrecy; at the same time, cult members like to get televised accounts of their initiation into shrines. This raises many questions about the relation between audiovisual technologies of revelation and the power of secrecy.

16. I would like to thank Marleen de Witte for sharing with me her clippings, collected via the Internet, that relate to this much-discussed case.

17. In contrast to Pentecostal churches, Afrikania has great difficulty in accessing spiritual power; as its concern is to make African religion respectable, possession is downplayed at the expense of an intellectual attitude. For a brilliant analysis of this paradox, see de Witte 2008.

18. Kwaku Bonsam asserts that he has been educated as a Christian yet called back into the worship of spirits. He does not at all conform to the stereotypic image of the traditional priest as being in need of hearing the Gospel so as to convert.

19. The very first elections took place in 1992, making the transition from a one-party regime to a democratic system. In preparing for these elections, the freedom of press was still quite limited.

20. In a comment on an earlier version of this chapter, Kwadwo Adusei wrote the following: "I watched a clip that showed Atta Mills giving thanks in TB Joshua's church in January this year. Atta Mills claimed that TB Joshua saw the 2008 elections will go for a third round—which actually happened. TB Joshua also asked his church to pray for Atta Mill to finish his term of office. This has been interpreted to mean Atta Mills might die before his term of office ends in 2012, hence Rawling's readiness to take over. Apart from healing Atta Mills of the eye problem, gossip has it that TB Joshua keeps coming to the Castle to anoint and pray for him. When this became public, Atta Mills remarked in a newspaper that he wished Ghana were a prayer camp and he sees pastors as allies. I have a copy of the *Times* publication" (e-mail communication, April 14, 2009).

21. Even in the work of many Africanists working on spirits, one finds little attempt to unpack this notion. What spirits are, and do tend to be, taken for granted. See Lambek 2008 for a sophisticated discussion on how to translate spirit and the question of deixis.

22. The need to think through implications of this invocation of spirits by major social thinkers has been pointed out elaborately by Pels 2003.

23. Importantly, as the German Weber expert Wolfgang Schluchter suggests, Weber's account of the rise of modern capitalism attributes utmost attention to Protestantism and can thus differ from a simplistic take on secularization.

24. See Arjun Appadurai's, evocative statement made in *The Immanent Frame*, where he argues that as scholars we have tended to overlook the deep concern with faith and trust in the market that underlies neoliberal capitalism. His proposition that anthropologists do have a sense of this is much to the point. In the anthropological study of the spread of modernity, and the way in which globalization reconfigures local cultures, many anthropologists (e.g., Michael Taussig, the Comaroffs, Filip de Boeck, Peter Geschiere, Todd Sanders and Henrietta Moore, Bonno Thoden van Velzen, Robert Weller, and also myself) have pointed out how the ways in which people in the South expressing their anxieties about their incorporation into global capitalism through the registers of the fantastic may actually be read as a telling analysis of this economy. Somehow these explorations are easily prone to invoking a contrast between

people suffering from spiritual insecurity and reflecting about the opportunities and dangers of occult economies, on the one hand, and rational Westerners, on the other. This idea has always been false, as the rational Westerner is just an ideal (Verrips 2001), but current developments make this ever more clear as parallels are unsettlingly obvious.

REFERENCES

Akyeampong, Emmanuel. 1996. *Drink, Power, and Cultural Change: A Social History of Alcohol in Ghana, c. 1800 to Recent Times*. Portsmouth: Heineman.

Appadurai, Arjun. 2008. Welcome to the Faith-Based Economy. *The Immanent Frame*. SSRC Blog, posted Oct. 14.

Asad, Talal. 2003. *Formations of the Secular: Christianity, Islam, Modernity*. Stanford: Stanford University Press.

Asamoah-Gyadu, Kwabena. 2005. "Anointing Through the Screen. Neo-Pentecostalism and Televised Christianity in Ghana." *Studies in World Christianity* 11:10–28.

Ashforth, Adam. 2005. *Witchcraft, Violence, and Democracy in South Africa*. Chicago: University of Chicago Press.

Bayart, Jean-François. 1993. *The State in Africa: The Politics of the Belly*. New York: Longman.

Boogaard, Paulien. 1993. "Afrikania traditionele religie. Een politiek-religieuze beweging in Ghana." Master's thesis, University of Amsterdam.

Casanova, José. 1994. *Public Religions in the Modern World*. Chicago: University of Chicago Press.

—— 2008. "Public Religions Revisited." In Hent de Vries, ed., *Religion: Beyond a Concept*, 111–19. New York: Fordham University Press.

Chakrabarty, Dipesh. 2001. *Provincializing Europe: Postcolonial Thought and Historical Difference*. Princeton: Princeton University Press.

Coe, Cati. 2005. *Dilemmas of Culture in African Schools: Youth, Nationalism, and the Transformation of Knowledge*. Chicago: Chicago University Press.

Comaroff, Jean, and John Comaroff. 1992. *Ethnography and the Historical Imagination*. Boulder: Westview.

—— 1999. "Occult Economies and the Violence of Abstraction: Notes from the South African Postcolony." *American Ethnologist* 26, no. 3 (August): 279–301.

——, eds. 1993. *Modernity and Its Malcontents: Ritual and Power in Africa*. Chicago: University of Chicago Press.

——, eds. 2000. "Millenial Capitalism and the Culture of Neo-liberalism." Special issue of *Public Culture* 12, no. 2.

De Abreu, Maria José Alves. 2005. "Breathing Into the Heart of the Matter: Why Padre Marcelo Needs No Wings." *Postscripts* 1, nos. 2/3: 325–49.

—— 2009. "In Midair—Breath, Media, Body, Space: A Study of the Catholic Charismatic Renewal Movement in Brazil." PhD diss., University of Amsterdam.

Derrida, Jacques. 2001. "Above All, No Journalists!" In Hent de Vries and Samuel Weber, ed., *Religion and Media*, 56–93. Stanford: Stanford University Press.

De Vries, Hent. 2001. "In Media Res. Global Religion, Public Spheres, and the Task of Contemporary Comparative Religious Studies." In Hent de Vries and Samuel Weber, eds., *Religion and Media*, 3–42. Stanford: Stanford University Press.

——, ed. 2008. *Religion: Beyond a Concept*. New York: Fordham University Press.

De Witte, Marleen. 2003. "Altar Media's *Living Word*: Televised Charismatic Christianity in Ghana." *Journal of Religion in Africa* 33, no. 2: 172–202.

—— 2005a. "'Insight, Secrecy, Beasts, and Beauty: Struggles Over the Making of a Ghanaian Documentary on African Traditional Religion.'" *Postscripts* 1, nos. 2/3: 277–300.

—— 2005b. "The Spectacular and the Spirits: Charismatics and Neo-Traditionalists on Ghanaian Television." *Material Religion* 1, no. 3 (November): 314–35.

—— 2008. "Spirit Media: Charismatics, Traditionalists, and Mediation Practices in Ghana." PhD diss., University of Amsterdam.

—— 2010. "Religious Media, Mobile Spirits: Publicity and Secrecy in Ghanaian Pentecostalism and Traditional Religion." In Gertrud Hüwelmeier and Kristine Krause, eds., *Traveling Spirits: Migrants, Markets, and Mobilities*, 83–100. New York: Routledge.

During, Simon. 2004. *Modern Enchantments: The Cultural and Secular Power of Magic*. Boston: Harvard University Press.

Ellis, Stephen, and Gerrie ter Haar. 2004. *Worlds of Power: Religious Thought and Political Practice in Africa*. London: Hurst.

Fabian, Johannes. 1983. *Time and the Other. How Anthropology Makes Its Object*. New York: Columbia University Press.

Ferme, Mariane. 2001. *The Underneath of Things: Violence, History, and the Everyday in Sierra Leone*. Berkeley: University of California Press.

Geschiere, Peter. 1997. *The Modernity of Witchcraft*. Charlottesville: Virginia University Press.

Gifford, Paul. 2004. *Ghana's New Christianity: Pentecostalism in a Globalising African Economy*. London: Hurst.

Habermas, Jürgen. 1989. *The Structural Transformation of the Public Sphere: Inquiring Into a Category of Bourgeois Society*. Boston: MIT Press.

—— 2005. "On the Relation Between the Secular Liberal State and Religion." In Eduardo Mendieta, ed., *The Frankfurt School on Religion: Key Writings By the Major Thinkers*, 327–38. New York: Routledge.

Haynes, Jonathan, ed. 2002. *Nigerian Video Films*. Ohio: Ohio University Press.

Hirschkind, Charles. 2001. "The Ethics of Listening: Cassette-Sermon Audition-ing in Contemporary Egypt." *American Ethnologist* 28, no. 3(August): 623–49.

—— 2006. *The Ethical Soundscape: Cassette Sermons and the Islamic Counter Public*. New York: Columbia University Press.

Hoover, Stewart M. 2006. *Religion in the Media Age*. New York: Routledge.

Kirsch, Thomas G. 2008. *Spirits and Letters: Reading, Writing, and Charisma in African Christianity*. Oxford: Berghahn.

Lambek, Michael. 2008. "Provincializing God? Provocations from an Anthropology of Religion." In Hent de Vries, ed., *Religion: Beyond a Concept*, 120–39. New York: Fordham University Press.

Larkin, Brian. 2009. "Modern Religions, Modern Media: Islamic Renewal in Northern Nigeria." In Birgit Meyer, ed., *Aesthetic Formations: Media, Religion, and the Senses in the Making of Communities*, 117–34. New York: Palgrave.

Masuzawa, Tomoko. 2008. "The Burden of the Great Divide." *The Immanent Frame*. http://blogs.ssrc.org/tif/2008/01/30/the-burden-of-the-great-divide/.

Meyer, Birgit. 1998a. "'Make a Complete Break with the Past': Memory and Post-colonial Modernity in Ghanaian Pentecostalist Discourse." *Journal of Religion in Africa* 27, no. 3: 316–49.

—— 1998b. "Commodities and the Power of Prayer: Pentecostalist Attitudes Towards Consumption in Contemporary Ghana." In Birgit Meyer and Peter Geschiere, eds., *Globalization and Identity: Dialectics of Flow and Closure*, *Development and Change* 29, no. 4 (October): 751–77.

—— 1998c. "The Power of Money: Politics, Sorcery, and Pentecostalism in Ghana." *African Studies Review* 41, 3 (December): 15–38.

—— 1999. *Translating the Devil: Religion and Modernity Among the Ewe in Ghana*. Edinburgh: Edinburgh University Press.

—— 2004. "Praise the Lord: Popular Cinema and the Pentecostalite Style in Ghana's New Public Sphere." *American Ethnologist* 31, no. 1 (October): 92–110.

—— 2005a. "Mediating Tradition: Pentecostal Pastors, African Priests, and Chiefs in Ghanaian Popular Films." In T. Falola, ed., *Christianity and Social Change in Africa: Essays in Honor of J. D. Y. Peel*, 275–306. Durham: Carolina Academic.

—— 2005b. "Religious Remediations: Pentecostal Views in Ghanaian Video-Movies." *Postscripts* 1, nos. 2/3: 155–81.

—— 2006. "Religious Revelation, Secrecy, and the Limits of Visual Representation." *Anthropological Theory* 6, no. 4 (December): 431–53.

——, ed. 2009a. *Aesthetic Formations: Media, Religion, and the Senses*. New York: Palgrave.

—— 2009b. "Comment on Ranger and Ter Haar and Ellis." *Africa* 79, 3: 413–15.

Meyer, Birgit, and Annelies Moors, eds. 2006a. *Religion, Media, and the Public Sphere*. Bloomington: Indiana University Press.

—— 2006b. "Introduction." In Birgit Meyer and Annelies Moors, eds., *Religion, Media, and the Public Sphere*, 1–25. Bloomington: Indiana University Press.

Meyer, Birgit, and Jojada Verrips. 2008. "Aesthetics." In David Morgan, ed., *Key Words in Religion, Media, and Culture*, 20–30. New York: Routledge.

Meyer, Birgit, and Peter Pels, eds. 2003. *Magic and Modernity: Interfaces of Revelation and Concealment*. Stanford: Stanford University Press.

Moyet, Xavier. N.d. "The 'Pastor's War': An Appraisal of Entanglement Between Pentecostalism and the Popular Press in Contemporary Nigeria." Unpublished MS.

Pels, Peter. 2003. "Introduction." In Birgit Meyer and Peter Pels, eds., *Magic and Modernity: Interfaces of Revelation and Concealment*, 1–38. Stanford: Stanford University Press.

Pype, Katrien. 2008. *The Pentecostal Melodrama: The Making of Visions of Youth, Gender, and Religion in Kinshasa's Media World*. PhD diss., Leuven University.

Sánchez, Rafael. 2008. "Seized by the Spirit." *Public Culture* 20, 2 (Spring): 267–305.

Spieth, Jacob. 1906. *Die Ewe Stämme*. Berlin.

—— 1911. *Die Religion der Eweer in Südtogo*. Berlin.

Spyer, Patricia. 2001. "The Cassowary Will Not Be Photographed." In Hent de Vries and Samuel Weber, eds., *Religion and Media*, 304–20. Stanford: Stanford University Press.

Stolow, Jeremy. 2005. "Religion and/as Media." *Theory, Culture, and Society* 22, no. 4 (August): 119–45.

—— 2008. "Salvation by Electricity." In Hent de Vries, ed., *Religion: Beyond a Concept*, 668–86. New York: Fordham University Press.

Taussig, Michael. 2003. "Viscerality, Faith, and Skepticism: Another Theory of Magic." In Birgit Meyer and Peter Pels, eds., *Magic and Modernity: Interfaces of Revelation and Concealment*, 272–306. Stanford: Stanford University Press.

Taylor, Charles. 2007. *A Secular Age*. Cambridge: Belknap.

—— 2008. "The Future of the Religious Past." In Hent de Vries, ed., *Religion: Beyond a Concept*. New York: Fordham University Press.

Ter Haar, Gerrie, and Stephen Ellis. 2009. "The Occult Does Not Exist: A Response to Terence Ranger." *Africa* 79, no. 3: 399–412.

Thoden van Velzen, H. U. E., and W. van Wetering. 1989. "De Betovering van het Moderne Leven." *Sociologische Gids* 36:155–186.

Van de Port, Mattijs. 2005. "Priests and Stars: Candomblé, Celebrity Postscripts: Discourses, and the Authentication of Religious Authority in Bahia's Public Sphere." *Postscripts: The Journal of Sacred Texts and Contemporary Worlds* 1, no. 2–3: 301–24.

—— 2006. "Visualizing the Sacred. Video Technology, 'Televisual Style,' and the Religious Imagination in Bahian Candomblé." *American Ethnologist* 33, no. 3 (August): 444–61.

Verrips, Jojada. 2001. "*The Golden Bough* and *Apocalypse Now:* An-other Fantasy." *Postcolonial Studies* 4, no. 3: 335–51.

West, Harry. 2005. *Kupilikula: Governance and the Invisible Realm in Mozambique.* Chicago: University of Chicago Press.

VOLUNTEER EXPERIENCE

ERICA BORNSTEIN

Volunteering differs from other forms of humanitarian practice such as financial donation and professional aid work. Undertaken as a leisure activity, it contrasts the productive realm of wage work and, as such, it is a particularly powerful phenomenon that is gaining global currency. Some people seek out volunteer experiences, while others try to encourage people to volunteer. The bounded experience of volunteering brings the volunteer closer to the afflicted, the poor, the suffering, and the needy, if only for a short time. The attraction of volunteering lies in its promise of a transformative experience—one that may seem structurally similar to a religious experience; yet it differs from spiritual transformation in its categorization as a secular practice. It is to these transformative social experiences that I turn in this essay.

As volunteering exceeds the realm of routine everyday requirements, it enters into an arena of free action that is uncoerced and selfless and thus allows itself to be constituted as an "experience." By experience, I refer to Victor Turner's (1986:37) reassertion of Dilthey's view that "experience urges toward expression, or communication with others." Emerging from Turner's concept of a "social drama," narratives of experience mark rites of passage. Thus they refer to situations that are formative—not simply "experience" but "an experience."[1] Turner notes that such experiences "erupt from or disrupt routinized, repetitive behavior" and "begin with shocks of pain or pleasure." He also notes that etymologically, in Greek and Latin "experience is linked with peril, pirate, and experiment." Narratives of experience can be compared with narratives of sacrifice and religious transformation as in mysticism and conversion (James 1982 [1902]). In the Indian context these narratives also reference the possibility of worldly renunciation and spiritual freedom. Volunteering, as Derrida (1992) has pointed out, is the ultimate gift: the gift of time, and giving in India is associated with renunciation, sacrifice, and service. It contrasts Mauss's conception of the obligated gift (1990 [1950]) since it does not require a return (see Bornstein 2012 for giving and humanitarianism in contemporary New Delhi; Heim 2004 and Nath 1987 for ancient practice; Laidlaw 1995, 2000; Parry 1986, 1994; and Raheja 1988 for religious and rural contexts of dān/donation practice).

In our contemporary world, voluntarism has come to stand in for a more general global good. As much as volunteer activities are sought after by high school students looking to apply to college, universities such as the one where I teach require global studies majors to conduct an international internship as part of their course of study. The particular form of secular, liberal voluntarism that is advocated by university settings may be unique to our contemporary age, where we assume that to create world citizens we must engage through service in the world. These narratives are enforced by books and articles in the popular press that advocate individual action toward changing the world such as Kristoff and WuDunn's best-selling book, *Half the Sky* (2009), which narrates stories of life-changing and world-changing social action and lists Web sites and organizations that encourage voluntarism. The book is filled with humanitarian responses to social atrocities, mostly suffered by women: genocide, mass rape, gendered economic exclusion, sexual slavery and trafficking, maternal mortality, religious misogyny, and female infanticide. Each chapter contains a story of a woman who managed to turn her life around and then help others. As a manifesto for global engagement, it is a forceful call to action empowering women. Chapter 14, titled "What You Can Do," is followed by a chapter titled "What You Can Do in the Next Ten Minutes" and an appendix listing the Web sites of organizations for which one can volunteer. Having recently taught this book in a "Humanitarianism in Global Perspective" course, I was surprised to find that half of my forty students found the text inspirational, while half found it naive and unrealistic. Volunteering is an inspirational model for social engagement, yet it is not an easy endeavor. The unease of the experience of volunteering is central to its transformative potential as a rite of passage. Some have argued that volunteer tourism is a type of pilgrimage (Mustonen 2005), others (Kristoff 2010; Kristoff and WuDunn 2009) consider it a viable form of social engagement that transforms both volunteers and the world. Volunteering represents a particular form of liberal cosmopolitanism. Calhoun (2003) has critiqued extreme liberal cosmopolitanism for its inherent assumption that world citizenship is morally superior to local solidarities, particularly when the worldly belonging of liberal cosmopolitanism is made to contrast supposedly illiberal local affinities. The assumption of a liberal, global universal good is evident in voluntarism as well as in the affective and universalist aspects of humanitarian efforts geared toward specific populations such as children (as in Malkki 2010).

Here, I look at the emotional crisis that volunteering has the potential to produce and examine how this experience gains currency— specifically, how some people seek out this dramatic experience and then try to encourage others to volunteer. I compare two groups attempting to organize volunteers in New Delhi in 2004–5, including: a pilot program recruiting students from Delhi's top universities to volunteer over the summer with NGOs in rural India and expatriates volunteering at Mother Teresa's Missionaries of Charity welfare home for children. While these two groups may differ structurally and contextually (one is comprised of Indians volunteering in rural India, the other of expatriates in urban New Delhi), in their experience of volunteering the role and value of "experience" is central.

I explore how the experience of volunteering becomes one that is sought after, an experience of value, and how seeking out and empathizing with persons or social contexts radically different from one's own becomes desirable. Bypassing strictly psychological analyses, I favor an approach that integrates a political economy of sensibilities. The feelings encountered in volunteering are structured, not solely "personal" and "private," hence my theoretical distancing from psychology and its more atomized understanding of emotion. William James (1982 [1902]), for example, has written about experience, particularly religious experience as individual, inner, and personal. Emile Durkheim in *The Elementary Forms of Religious Life* (1995 [1912]) subsequently built upon and revised James's pragmatic conception of religious experience, articulating it as eminently social, mediated by institutions. Whereas James emphasized religious feelings and impulses and their practical use in daily life, Durkheim focused on how social representation made experience possible by linking it to group

membership.[2] Only through social institutions could experience be articulated to others. As an anthropologist, I am drawn to Durkheim rather
than James, particularly to his emphasis on the collective and how social
institutions facilitate and mediate experience. All experience, for Durkheim, is mediated by social groups. In the case of voluntarism, the experience is mediated by particular NGOs that facilitate its activity as a social
form. By focusing on the social and institutional forms of experience, we
can see how volunteering has both the potential to enhance distinctions
between groups and to surpass them. Through volunteering, categories of
"the other" such as foreigners/Indians; wealthy/poor; internationalists/
nationalists; able-bodied/disabled—are reified in the attempts to overcome them. Volunteering asserts distinction—I am not this—and strives
to efface these divides through the potential of empathic experience.[3]

A VOLUNTEER REVOLUTION

Volunteering as organized philanthropic practice is relatively new to India,
in contrast to service to society (*samaj seva*)[4] and donation (*dān*),[5] which,
along with the work of charitable organizations, have long histories in
India (see Sen 1992, 1999; Tandon 2002, 2003). India has been known by
many outside its borders as a nation requiring international aid—for poverty reduction, economic development, and disaster relief. More recently,
however, India has aimed to position itself as a global power and a benefac-
tor of aid. Immediately following the tsunami that hit the Indian Ocean in
December 2004, Prime Minister Manmohan Singh refused aid for disaster
relief from the United States government (Nagi 2005), as it lobbied for a
seat on the UN Security Council. The liberalization of the Indian economy since the early 1990s has seen an increase in wealth alongside poverty, which both nongovernmental organizations (NGOs) and the Indian
state have sought to address, often in collaboration. Some scholars have
traced the history of NGOs and their service to society (*samaj seva*) to the
Gandhian period of nation building directly following independence, during which many NGOs emerged in partnership with the state (Gupta and
Sharma 2006; Sen 1992, 1999; Tandon 2002, 2003). The nationalist project of institutionalized service emerged in a historically internationalist
moment marked by independence from colonial rule.

Despite this historical precedent for voluntarism in India, in 2004–
2005, when I conducted my research in New Delhi, the civic discourse of

voluntarism was notably absent in the Indian press, especially as contrasted to similar efforts in the U.S. (cf. Wuthnow 1991 and Allahyari
2000). Originally, I hoped to volunteer as an ethnographic exercise, but
I soon found myself interested in understanding the process of organizing volunteers itself. I encountered an NGO that I will call *Volunteer Now*
through the Web site for Give India.[6] The NGO was starting a new program geared toward encouraging civic responsibility in urban youth, called
National Fellow. Before I knew it, I was involved with the program. After
meeting with the National Fellow coordinator, I found myself enmeshed
in the selection process.

I received a letter from the director of Volunteer Now requesting money
to support an National Fellow. I had been involved with the program in
Delhi and supported his fund-raising marathon when I returned the previous year, but this year his plea was to "Sponsor a fellow" in the model of
sponsoring a child. I found this an interesting strategy. It was something
we had discussed when I was in Delhi as a possible way to support the program. Attached to his plea was a narrative about the National Fellow "experience." Volunteer Now was trying to start a "volunteer revolution," and
one of its vehicles was this pilot program, supported by the Sir Ratan Tata
Trust called National Fellow. Its aim was to give urban, educated youth
the "experience" of rural India (70 percent of India is rural) with the hope
that if and when these youth entered positions of power in the nation that
they would remember the six-week internship in rural development and
the "experience" would carry into national development policy. Many of
the urban college students in Delhi, for example, had never been to a rural
area—and this was the "experience" National Fellow was aiming to give.
The following letter is a fund-raising plea to support the program. The first
year the program was run out of the Delhi office exclusively. The aim was to
branch out and make it a national program and a volunteer revolution. The
brochure for the program in 2005 began with the provocative slogan "Volunteer Now, If you mean it, Do it!" and continued with a description that
linked development with civic responsibility, voluntarism, and revolution:

> The desire to change lives of the less privileged around us lies at the
> back of most [of] our minds. Often we make donations of money,
> medicines, food or clothing. We at times sponsor a child's educa-
> tion or just adopt an animal. These are indeed commendable work
> but wouldn't it be wonderful that we help them to help themselves.
> Share our skills to prepare them to face life more courageously?

The best way is to get actively involved with them and their work by Volunteering. By spending some valuable time helping them and in return experience an enriching adventure that would leave its impact all through your life.

History has proven that any major change in society has always been made possible by youths only. The indomitable spirit of the young people had always propelled the revolutions, be it French or Russian. Students' determinations to make a drastic change in the community is what we at Volunteer Now are aspiring. To curb the rampant insensitivity of the masses towards the development sector, today India is looking at You—the YOUTH of India. Be a leader of the movement called social evolution, be the pioneers of this adventurous journey to the rural India—the real India.

Reach out to the millions who are not as fortunate as you are. Many have never seen a school or are those who are braving cancer, AIDS. Or someone just looking for a buddy in you. Come get involved to spread the spirit of comradeship. Join the cadre of National Fellows!

To promote the spirit of volunteerism Volunteer Now in partnership with SRTT has introduced an internship program called National Fellows.

The idea is to create a "cadre" of volunteers like the Peace Corps of USA and Millennium Volunteers of UK, to serve our country for a cause by living and working in the community. This would not only bring in a sense of pride among the youths but would also sensitise them about the problems these communities and the NGOs face in their operations. When they are back after the completion of their 6 weeks internships, they would have imbibed the notion of "social responsibility" and would be more vigilant of this aspect when taking decisions as a CEO or MD in future.

National Fellow was structured on the model of exchange—the volunteer gave time in exchange for experience and exposure. "What do you hope to learn?" was juxtaposed with "what can you give?" Of the 230 student applicants recruited to apply from Delhi's top universities, 161 were short listed for interviews. Out of those short-listed, 18 were disqualified because they did not show up for the interview, 36 were rejected, 40 were selected, and 23 were wait-listed. There were 20 slots available at 10 NGOs. The program coordinator had also scouted, interviewed and selected the

NGOs from a list of those funded by Sir Ratan Tata Trust. It was a match-making endeavor for the coordinator, based on the needs and desires of the NGOs and the volunteers.

The challenge of placing National Fellows with NGOs involved practical problems. For example: one NGO wanted a Muslim girl to do interviews and data collection with women's self-help groups focusing on young girls in the Muslim community. But Volunteer Now had no Muslim girls in Delhi who would venture out into a rural village. There was only one Muslim girl, but she specified she would not live in a village. The project coordinator asserted, despite fears of sexual harassment, that "people in villages are so scared—they are so remote and so scared" and the possibility of harassment was slim. Another NGO was charging too much for food (4,500 rupees, with the entire stipend 3,500 rupees). The NGO was in Himachal Pradesh and used to hosting foreign volunteers; they said the rate of 4,500 rupees was the concession rate for an Indian student, but it was too high for Volunteer Now. Two of the other NGOs specified they wanted male volunteers.

The funder, Sir Ratan Tata Trust, was trying to mainstream Indian youth into the NGO sector. It wanted to reach a large group of people and, eventually, to nationalize the program. The trust found that bright students were not going into the development sector—hence the national program on the scale of the U.S. Peace Corps or the UK Millennium Volunteers. The immediate goal of the program was to keep the volunteer at the center and to focus on his/her *experiences*. The long-term goal of the program was to recruit one thousasnd students from one hundred universities in India. If the present project was only a pilot, the anticipated scale of the program was large. However, volunteering, for Indians, was not a common social form. It had to be encouraged and taught. While giving, *dān*, and other forms of philanthropy have long histories in South Asia (see Heim 2004; Nath 1987), this was a relatively new institutionalized endeavor.

The application for National Fellow asked the question: "Why are you interested in National Fellows Program? How do you think it will benefit you?" The applicant responses (n = 179) fell into six basic categories: 1.39 percent responded "to help others"; 2.38 percent answered "for a new experience"; 3.30 percent were seeking to prepare for a career in social work or development; 4.29 percent said for society (which included: to serve country/be a responsible citizen of India); 5.26 percent responded "for personal growth"; and 6.6 percent said they wanted to do something worthwhile on their summer vacation. The ideal National Fellow had never been to a rural area, and those with extensive experience in rural areas were disqualified (with the logic, why give such and "experience" to someone who already had it?).

What was Volunteer Now looking for in its applicants? First, it was a particular age group: between sixteen and twenty-five years. Those too old were disqualified. Those who answered narrative questions on the application form with stereotypical answers were also disqualified. Answers that "came from the heart" or gave an insight into the person's mind or heart were considered good answers. Those without any functional skills, such as cooking, were also not interviewed. One question asked: "Have you been to a rural area?" Those who said yes were considered to have already made up their mind, which was negative. The program sought people with an open mind, those who had not had too much experience. Since the idea of the program was to "sensitize urban youth to rural issues," if someone had too much experience it was thought best to give the opportunity to another candidate.

I was brought in on the team of Volunteer Now interviewers and participated in the selection of potential fellows. "Real India still lives in villages; you can contribute to the development of India" the applicants were told. In a warm-up session each applicant was asked to describe themselves: where they came from and two things about that place. That interview day, all of the applicants were women—six were from Delhi University. In the recruitment effort for the 20 volunteer positions, 650 forms had been distributed at universities. Tremendous effort was expended to initiate this volunteer revolution. The candidates were shown pictures and asked to write a paragraph or two about one of them in fifteen minutes. One photo was an image of the face of an old man, smiling, weathered, with wrinkles and one tooth. Another photo featured a dilapidated boat, another a group hiking on a mountain peak; in another a young boy walked barefoot on railroad tracks. Each picture was provocative in its own way, with stories yet to be told. The small group was then given a narrative of a village social drama to read and asked to discuss it. It was a story filled with morals and no correct answer. I filmed the discussions, which generated heated arguments. The candidates forgot the selection process and lost themselves in the drama.[7]

After these exercises the candidates were interviewed by two members of Volunteer Now (one interviewing, one observing and taking notes); their expectations of the program were fascinating. About being a National

Fellow, one girl said, "It will help me—it will make me a more responsible citizen." When asked what she expected to get out of it, she replied: "I'll learn from them. I'll try to understand their life. I've never seen a rural person—I've never been in contact with such a person. I'll extract things out of them." What will you give back? we asked, and she answered, "Whatever I have, happiness, maybe a feeling of strength." Another candidate, when asked what they would bring back from the National Fellow internship, replied, "Fond memories and new friendships. I will also have acquired a greater respect for life and to not take for granted what I have, for example, electricity and lights." The candidates were asked how they demonstrated concern for others as well as to give an example of a difficult situation they had faced. We were searching for compassionate, creative, thoughtful young people. One of the staff members interviewing with me explained to a candidate: "We at Volunteer Now are trying to create a revolution in terms of volunteering. You will be our ambassadors." What were the qualities of a good ambassador? "Flexibility and adaptability, sensitivity to the needs of others, practical problem-solving ability, and a commitment to learning." Most of all, we were looking for a certain spark that was hard to describe.

Those who were selected as National Fellows received an extensive two-day workshop/orientation session, which I attended and filmed for the NGO. The turnout for the orientation was disappointing to the coordinator and the director of Volunteer Now. She expected thirty-four volunteers, but, at the last minute, people were calling to back out. Only eighteen volunteers attended the orientation. "It is hard to get commitments from people" she explained. "Some are saying if they don't get posted in Uttaranchal, they won't go!" The summer in rural Rajasthan (a desert region) did not appear to be an appealing adventure after all, for many potential volunteers, and people dropped out when they saw where they were placed. The coordinator had, just that morning, fought with the father of a volunteer who had been selected—he was demanding that his daughter go to Uttaranchal (instead of Rajasthan). Another girl's parents had decided they would not let her go. She came to the second day of the orientation in order for the coordinator to save face. One problem was that girls could not be placed alone—it was dangerous and not socially appropriate, hence the pairing of volunteers. The next day there was an orientation for the NGOs, and thirteen NGO were scheduled to attend the workshop. The coordinator was concerned that there were not enough volunteers to match with the NGOs in pairs. "We'll see who actually goes" she said, "who gets on a bus and goes. A lot can still happen and people can back out." Another staff member was trying to find some foreign volunteers to go in the place of the National Fellows, if they fell short. There was a group of six from the UK, but they wanted to be posted together: another matching challenge. While Indian volunteers had to be convinced and encouraged to take up a post in rural India, foreign volunteers paid two hundred British pounds for the opportunity. Volunteer Now boasted that they provided the lowest fee and the most services when compared to competitors such as Cross-cultural Solutions, Goabroad.com, and Volunteeringabroad.com.

Many of the students at the orientation were frightened of the prospect of living in a rural area for six weeks, and the anticipation of the cultural adventure needed institutional translation. There was also parent resistance in addition to student fear. The orientation was meant to allay fears and concerns. There was a session on health, led by a doctor, and one on safety for women, led by a women's activist. The search for experience and adventure held within it a threat: the very difference that attracted had the potential to become a horror. There were inspirational as well as informational speakers, and exercises for the fellows to participate in. One speaker asked the volunteers why their world of materialism and air conditioning was more "real" than the world of the rural villagers they would soon come to know. In the conversations that ensued, the volunteers expressed their excitement and nervousness.

Despite the orientation, preparation, and signing of a contract, one student came back to Delhi early. I sat with him and the project coordinator for the program and listened to his complaints. The student was frustrated and a bit defensive—his experience had not been good in rural Rajasthan. He said the NGO he was placed with was not prepared for a volunteer. For three days there was no place for him to sleep, and there was no work for him. The NGO didn't know what to do with a volunteer. The program coordinator described how she had visited the NGO earlier to make sure they were prepared to accept a National Fellow. The student repeatedly mentioned that his parents had said he shouldn't have gone. He sat from 9 AM to 6 or 7 in the evening with nothing to do. The reporting officer didn't know why he was there. He waited an entire week and had finished three novels. Between Monday and Saturday, Friday was the only day he had worked. On Sunday he left. He wondered: "Why am I here? Why can't I read novels at home?" His health was in jeopardy; he had lost weight. He didn't like the food. He didn't eat much. He said, as a volunteer, "you don't know how to handle the situation. When you see they themselves are doing it and you see you have come as a volunteer to help them and not be a burden. It was very hard for me." He was used to respecting elders, so he felt he could not rebel, and it was hard for him to refuse the food. He couldn't say no to the food and he couldn't eat. When asked why, he explained that "the chapatis were four times as thick" as he was used to. The culture shock was also the reality of his independence. Wealthy and middle-class students in urban India are sheltered from the world by their families, and this is exactly why the National Fellow program was initiated—to give such urban, educated students exposure and experience. But this experience was not always positive and sometimes came as a shock.

The project coordinator was frustrated. She later told me there was a discrepancy between the "NGO version" and the "student version" of the story of why he left. During her visit to the NGO, she had been shown the room the student would stay in. But the student said he was not given a room. The director of the NGO told him, "You are a burden for me for 40 days. I don't know what to do with you." Volunteer Now had sent out a mailing to the NGOs funded by the Sir Ratan Tata Trust. Because the request to host a volunteer came from one of the NGO's financial supporters, perhaps it felt it could not refuse the volunteer. Most of the students had been in placements with another student, but this volunteer had been placed alone. There was a discussion about how Volunteer Now should not "have sent a person alone to an NGO where there is no one from the city." There was too much culture shock for the volunteer to handle alone—too much difference. Indeed, the apprehension of embarking on such a volunteer experience as National Fellow was not held by the students alone. One or two days before the orientation for the selected fellows, quite a few had called to back out. Others did not show without any warning. Surprisingly, for the project coordinator, it was not the girls who were having a problem with placement. The boys needed more hand-holding than the girls. Urban middle and upper class Indian children were protected from the world. When thrust into a situation without guidance, they were at sea. While used to studies, they were less adept without directions to follow.

There was a tension in the volunteering endeavor of National Fellow between the families of the volunteers and the open vista of voluntarism that revolved around the question of "independence." In college, middle-class Indian children were not considered independent. It was not until a child was married (for a girl) or started a career (for a girl or boy) that the mark of independence was made. There was no reason why parents should trust a rural NGO to care for their child. The goal of "experience," while novel for building a nation of civic-minded leaders, was not foremost in the minds of parents or the potential volunteers themselves. In fact, parental consent was such an important factor in the program that the application process included signed consent forms for both parents of the applicant as well as a question about how their parents viewed the program in the interview process.

Not all responses to the program were negative—far from it. The narratives sent back to Volunteer Now (self-reports, or testimonials, which are part of a wider genre) were filled with stories of transformation, surviving a trial and experiencing a classic rite of passage. For example, one National Fellow wrote about his apprehension before going to rural Maharashtra to help children in a village for an entire summer. It was his "first tryst with rural India," and he was anxious about the "searing heat in this village." "I couldn't shake the one question that continually haunted me all through the signing of the contract at the orientation and on the day I left: Was six weeks too much?" He arrived in the village after a "grueling fifteen-hour journey." Yet he was surprised by what he encountered:

We got to work soon after, and, with my first few interactions with students, both dropouts and school going, I was amazed at their humility. Every house that I entered with the lady social worker, they offered us *nimbu pani* [lemon water] and snacks. They earned the most meager wages, and yet they would offer us so much. I wondered why. In the end, I was a total alien, looked it with my yet-to-be-tanned-to-an-appropriate-village-tone skin. Drinking water with Chloriwat [water purifier] wouldn't really champion my cause either. The weather was stifling though. The temperatures were touching 45c [113 F]. The highest I had encountered in Mumbai was a paltry 40c [104 F]. Add 50 percent of humidity and I thought I would die. I suddenly wanted out. In three days. So much for willpower. I would try to sleep under a fan, and my bedsheet would be soaked with sweat in twenty minutes flat. But when the good Lord decides to hurt you, he doesn't stop there. Just when I thought it was cooling off in the night, two words would come back to haunt me: load shedding. For six hours everyday. Life didn't have to be this tough, I thought to myself. But then, I've always believed in signs.

And I found mine . . . It was past six in the evening. I had gone to his house. It began to rain. The first real respite from the heat. And then he stood in front of me. Less than three feet tall, a twisted foot, and an asthma patient. I could hear the wheezing every time he breathed in and out. Just then the lights went out. My conscience hit me. Hit me hard. I cried. I felt so utterly shallow, it was ridiculous. To return home now seemed like a farce and if I weaseled out, I wouldn't be able to forgive myself for a WHILE. That much I was sure of. So I stayed. The next day was 45c again. My bedsheet was soaked again in my sweat, the lights went out again, but it was a small price to pay, I swear. I took a new interest in my work and blocked Mumbai out for the time being. Before I knew it, I had survived ten days in the wilderness. We took a timely few days off and went to Hyderabad to reward ourselves. The time spent in Hyderabad was good, but in the matter of two days I yearned to get back to Sagroli and continue work. Quite the transformation, if I may say so myself. After we returned, I enjoyed my work a lot more, and there was a sense of purpose to what I was doing.

The volunteer's visit to (or, experience of) poverty included doing things he never thought he would, like traveling in a crowed auto packed with twelve other people and sleeping on a *khatiya* (string bed) for the first time in his life.

Another National Fellow wrote a testimonial titled "The National Fellow Experience" in which she described her motivation for volunteering as "yearning to be a part of something new, different and challenging from the routine of my normal, mundane life. Something that would really compel me to step out of my comfort zone, of my perfectly organized and structured world." Also placed in Maharashtra for the summer, although in a different village, she described the experience as one of empathy: "The time spent with the people in the various villages also brought in a fresh perspective to life. I tried to see the world from their perspective, tried to analyze their problems and worries. . . . There are so many things I suddenly became aware of and began to feel for, I was sensitized to so many issue I initially used to turned [sic] a blind eye on." She describes the experience as an enlightenment, as being "a complete one" in which she tested herself and grew: "the experience really shaped my thinking and outlook towards life a great deal. The leap I took in the dark at the beginning brought a whole new light in my perception and attitude."

Other fellows wrote narratives that followed the same structure: apprehension, anxiety before the adventure, a loss of self and transformation in the rural environment, and a return to their former life with a new perspective and appreciation for their structural position in the world. Volunteers were encouraged and instructed to keep a diary of their experiences, and many of their reports contained excerpts or summaries of their writing in the field. One National Fellow who had been placed in Uttaranchal in 2006 wrote: "Where the people are all about generosity and modesty . . . and where the nature is all about peace and tranquility . . . a heaven where one can experience eternal happiness . . . just by diving deep into its realm . . . what we term as 'the other' or the rural . . . is actually a home away from home . . . another world . . . not as alien as it seems . . . but familiar and intimate . . . welcoming, forthcoming and friendly . . . an accommodating territory." While Volunteer Now was working hard to give Indian youth a chance to "experience" the "other" India, some expatriates who found themselves in New Delhi were also seeking this experience on their own.

A CIRCLE OF CARE

The Circle of Care was an informal group of expatriates who volunteered at three orphanages in New Delhi: St. Michael's, Holy Cross, and Nirmal Hriday (run by the Sisters of Charity, started by Mother Teresa).[8] I encountered this group through a membership organization for expatriates, mostly wives of businessmen and embassy workers stationed in India's capital, called Delhi Network, and its smaller member group, the American Women's Association. The Circle of Care was notably comprised of women. It was not a registered NGO and therefore did not keep receipts or confer tax advantages on its members. One of its foci was to give medical care for orphans at the homes—often arranging it at no cost or well below cost. The Circle of Care took children who were unadoptable in the Indian context and made them desirable for potential adoptive parents abroad, for whom physical disabilities, especially when corrected, were less stigmatized. For example, the Circle of Care recently fixed the cleft palates, clubfeet, and heart defects of orphans and helped arrange for their adoption abroad. One boy had just had open-heart surgery. Four places needed to be repaired, and the doctor had only charged the Circle of Care 100,000 rupees (roughly $2,200). The women in the group had taken the boy into their homes and cared for him after the operation. In addition to organizing medical assistance, volunteers met and visited the children in the orphanage regularly to hold them, to give them love and physical attention, often without the ability to speak with them in Hindi.

The goal of the Circle of Care was "to make a difference" in the lives they touched, often literally. Volunteers spent most of their time picking up children and holding them. What was this difference, and was the difference one also made in the lives of the volunteers? Some of the volunteers I spoke with were frustrated by the conditions of the orphanage and by their inability to "do anything in the nursery." One volunteer was a neonatal nurse, and the orphanage did not allow her to practice medicine with the children, some of whom had serious health problems. In one room, there were twenty-one iron cribs lined up like animal cages in three rows of seven cribs. Those children who could stand were standing in their cribs; some were rocking themselves. Others lay sleeping or were unresponsive. One child had a severe case of hydrocephalus. I was informed she was later moved to the Mother Teresa's Jeevan Jyoti (Light of Life) Home for Disabled Children in New Delhi. The girl had an extremely large head and skinny limbs and lay surrounded by mosquito netting on her back; her prognosis was not good. She was not adoptable, and it was not likely she would survive long with her condition. My heart broke as I walked past her crib. One volunteer, an American nurse, said, "I don't know what will happen to her." That the future was unresolved made the moment all the more salient. Three of the girls were likely mentally disabled, and no one wanted them. These children were the excluded, the abandoned. As we left the home, a volunteer noted that she "forgot how hard it is to go there sometimes."

The volunteers saw themselves as giving the children love, something that was not being done for them in the institution. A few of them had medical qualifications—such as an Italian doctor who found herself for the first time abroad without a contract to practice medicine so she volunteered her time. One of the American volunteers said, "Our work is mostly for us. I think we get more out of it than anyone else. Mostly we're in the way." It was true. The critique leveled at the orphanage from members of the Circle of Care was one Mother Teresa's home in Kolkatta had received, most publicly by Christopher Hitchens in his book *The Missionary Position* (1995).[9] Hitchens criticized the Sisters of Charity for giving love *instead* of medical attention to the terminally sick and dying and for not attempting to overcome the structural inequality that perpetuated the ailments of the poor. While these criticisms are justified, they discount, in prescriptive terms, the actions of groups such as the Sisters of Charity and the Circle of Care as ineffective. These groups are, however, doing something. In addition to surgeries, they offered humanitarianism, in the form of experience, for the volunteers.

The allure of this type of work was a form of service with missionary zeal. In the context of Nirmal Hriday, the issue of conversion did come up: the sisters, though all foreigners, were Christian, one volunteer explained, and they were happier to have their children adopted by a Christian family. The experience of volunteering, in this context, was one of transcending boundaries of culture, class, language, and history to one of bare, at times poignant, humanity. The accomplishment, an instrumental task, varied from acquiring donations and arranging for a successful surgery to advocating for, and providing, clean diapers at the orphanage.

There were some attempts to institutionalize change in the orphanage although they were not successful due to cultural misunderstandings. For example, in India children are toilet trained at an early age, often as early as six months, and diapers are considered dirty and expensive, thus not commonly used with older children. The American volunteers in the Circle of Care were horrified by the "unsanitary" conditions and convinced they knew how to care better. The director of the Circle of Care was critical of the insufficient attention paid to the orphans. They brought toys for the children, but they would come and find them broken. There was almost a complete lack of cross-cultural communication about the value of objects as well as the representation of love.

The director of the Circle of Care knew before she arrived in Delhi that she planned on working with Mother Teresa's orphanage. She had always wanted to, but the other posts her husband had been on, in Pakistan and Turkey, as a Drug Enforcement Agency employee did not offer such opportunities. She had adopted her fourth child in Pakistan—her husband was Pakistani American—and had been involved with foster care in the U.S. for many years, having fostered children of her own. When she first got to Delhi, she put up signs at the embassy that said "Huggers Needed." Thirty volunteers signed up immediately. They were going to the orphanage four to five days a week in different groups. She talked to the women the first time they went about the "dos and don'ts" of volunteering at the orphanage. She encouraged them to be sensitive to the "culture":

Don't criticize. Be accepting of things we cannot change. You can't change things. Everything is so culturally ingrained here. The kids don't need to be picked up, the kids don't need toys. Their basic needs are met. [I ask why] I think a lot of it is Indian. If you see kids in—not an upper-class home but if you see kids in a middle-class to a lower-class home, they don't have a lot of toys. They're not held a lot. They're carried only to transport them . . . They're not coddled a lot. . . . A lot of it is Mother Teresa's [home]. We've been to many orphanages that have brought their own cultures with them wherever they have come from, their own plans to meet their children's needs . . . When Mother Teresa came here she said we will become just like the culture where we are. We're not going to come in to be a separate entity.

She advised volunteers at the Delhi orphanage not to cry and to try to save their emotions:

It is depressing, but we ask (the ladies) that you not cry there. It upsets the kids and it upsets the sisters. The sisters don't see anything wrong. The kids are better off than they are in the streets, etcetera, etcetera. But we've had a couple of women just get hysterical, and I've said please try to save your emotion till you get out. A lot of times we'll go out to lunch [after], just so everyone can vent and get it out of their system. And they say we need to do this and we need to do this. And I say OK, we tried this, and this is what happened. Everything you can imagine wanting to change or do to better their lives we've tried. Some of it's worked. Some of it hasn't.

The first thing the Circle of Care did when they first started volunteering at the orphanage was to cuddle and hold the children. Then they began trying to make changes:

[We] rediapered the place. We went out and bought 80,000 rupees worth of diapers and diaper covers and washcloths and bibs. We rediapered, bibbed, and washclothed the whole place. And then we saw the need for floor coverings. When we arrived, there was nothing on the floor but just the cement, and kids were falling and hitting their heads, and it was really just tragic. And then we were thinking, what about winter? So we went and designed these mat covers (all made locally) like you would see in a gymnastics place in the States. . . . Then the surgeries came around.

The baby she held the first day had clubfeet, and she wanted to fix them. When she discussed the possibility of having his feet surgically repaired with the sisters, they said OK, but let us show you some of the other children who need help as well. They were introduced to a child who was born without a rectum, a child with a heart defect, and one with a cleft palate. They soon prioritized the children in terms of those that most urgently needed surgical attention and arranged for the surgeries at one of Delhi's top hospitals, Apollo Hospital. The director and her best girlfriend—who was also the Circle of Care cofounder—started by funding the surgeries themselves on their credit cards. Then they went to the American Women's Association, which paid for the floor pads. Then they went to the community. A lot of women at the meetings said, here's 500 rupees, here's this. "People were so overwhelmed with what they see, but don't know where to begin" (referring to the poverty in India). In two years of doing this work, the Circle of Care had arranged for five successful surgeries to be completed.

Volunteer work was not just time consuming, it was emotionally consuming. The director said, "You either get in there and you love it so much you want to be there every day. Or you get in there and it's so emotional you can't ever do it again." Some volunteers can't handle the orphanage so they do other work such as letter writing, purchasing, and fund-raising. I asked her how she prepared volunteers for the taxing work at the orphanage, and she advised them not to think too much about the past or the future, but to be in the moment with the children:

We tell them some of the kids are very sick, some might have disfigurements that can be a little appalling. The place is not clean. The place is very run down. The toys are very dirty and gross and disgusting. The food is awful. But go in and do what you can do. What your job is, is to go in and hold that baby, sing songs to that baby. Take that baby out for a walk. Take that kid out for a walk. We have the older kids age group that we take in playdough and finger paints and all that kind of stuff if you're not into the baby scene. You're there to make a difference during that 1–2 hours that we're there.

And that's all you have to think about. You can't think about what's going to happen after you leave. You can't think about what happened before you arrived and you can't think about what's going to happen tomorrow. You can make a difference in those 2 hours, and that's all that you need to focus on.

The volunteers were encouraged to focus on the experience of the moment, not the historical or political economy that created the moment. Part of this was the practical reality of being expatriates, strangers in the Indian cultural context. The hardest part of this was, for her, a factor of this cultural divide:

Having every resource to change these children's live and not being able to. Not being able to get your point across that it is very important that a child is stimulated. That it is very important that a child has a balanced diet. It is very important if a child is on an antibiotic that you refrigerate it. And that if you do refrigerate it, you don't wait 2 hours to bring it to room temperature to give it to them. If a medicine says 10 days you give it to him for 10 days. If a child is in pain and discomfort you need to react, and take care of it.

The best part was "making a difference. I love it. I don't see how anyone could come here and not try to do something. Even if it is going to a *jugghi* [slum] and reading to kids. If it's buying medicine for a hospital. You can't come here and not do anything. We have so much. We have been so blessed. You have to come here and you have to do something."

Thus even while denying the political economy in the moment of the experience of voluntary action, she had an understanding of inequality that left her "blessed" and others in need. The Circle of Care worked exclusively with expatriates, except for the doctors, who were Indians. The Indians she encountered could not understand why she did her volunteer work: "Most Indians are like: what are you doing? Why are you out taking care of these babies? Why? Why do you do this? You have four kids, you have a husband, you have a nice house. Go to lunch, shop, go get your hair done. Why do you need to be out there—putting yourself not in danger but putting yourself in situations that you don't need to be in?" I wondered why, culturally, people were saying this to her, and she replied: "It's people who would be like at our level as far as the caste [also class] system is concerned. They just don't see why you'd want to do it, if you don't have to." If Indians did not understand the work of the Circle of Care, Missionaries of Charity was famous for welcoming foreign volunteers. Around the world, Missionaries of Charity was used to having volunteers come in, but they were not used to volunteer groups: "People come to India just to go there. And they will go for one day or two days or they'll go to the Dying and Destitute [home in Calcutta] for 6 months, you know, they're used to having people in and out. They're not used to having people come and stay as long as we have." She was critical of the attitude of the sisters at the Delhi orphanage. The "kids deserve to have more than the basic needs met if you can do it. And they can, they just choose not to do it." Why, I asked? And she replied with another story of cultural confusion, this time over the use of toys:

> I have no idea. We have put so many toys out there you cannot imagine. We have invested so much money in toys. Fisher Price stuff, manipulatives. They had two blind babies. We went and got—we went and purchased blocks that were textured blocks so that the blind babies would have something to play with, that was just for them. We've organized it and watched it and you go back and it's just a disaster. What they do have is usually put up [out of reach of the children]. If you go to Mother Teresa's here, they have the toys and stuff, but they are always put up or destroyed. They don't ever teach a child how to play with a toy. They never sit down and play with a child with a toy. One of the funniest stories we—we were here I think almost a year and the British High Commission outreach had wanted to sponsor a reading center. This was one of the things on our wish list. And we had it down to the books we wanted to get and puzzles and we wanted to put it in a cabinet and we wanted to have a *dhuri* for them to sit on.

The sisters wanted to lock up the books and puzzles. Two days later everything was put on top of the shelf so the children couldn't reach it. Then they were gone, put away. She had organized two toy drives—Toyota Qualises full of toys. The toys got locked up in cabinets. The sisters "don't want kids to play with them. They want to save them. I think that's a very Indian thing." At "Mother Teresa's [the sisters] put a lot of the toys away. They don't want the kids to ruin it. You'll see them hanging from wires or from off the ceilings or you'll see them up in glass shelves not to be played with." Regarding the *ayas* (maids/nannies) that came to live at their homes when the children were recovering or preparing for surgeries, the disjuncture was both a cultural and a class division. The ayas were trying to preserve the toys: "The minute we walk away the toys are put away in the nice little basket and they are sitting there staring at the baby. And I have to take all the toys out, whichever baby we have, and press the little buttons and talk to him, and as soon as I leave the room, all the toys are put away again because everything has to be clean" (we laugh). "It's mind boggling." The children were abandoned by the world and then abandoned (in the eye of the volunteers) by the people who were supposed to be looking after them. This double abandonment was filled with horror for the volunteers of the Circle of Care. Yet amidst attempts to hug an orphan, to exist in the moment with a representative of "bare humanity,"[10] fissures of culture became more noticeable. These unbearable distinctions were transcended only through the prospect of surgeries and adoptions, which permanently transformed orphans into potentially adoptable kin.

≈≈

The portraits of these two groups have contributed to our understanding of how volunteering gains value through the concept of experience. The examples acknowledge the context of the moment and encourage attention to what "the moment" means for people involved. In this form of humanitarian effort, exemplified by the groups I have mentioned— National Fellow through Volunteer Now and the Circle of Care at Mother Teresa's orphanage—emphasis is on actions instead of a strict teleology of outcomes. For the sake of my argument, what is important is not what the act of assistance does but what it means to the people who assist. One could even venture to say that voluntarism in the humanitarian context offers the gift of experience from the recipient to the donor.[11] The religious tone of this awareness spans across faiths. Many religions posit a notion of poverty in relation to the spiritual, with some articulating other people's poverty as a condition of one's own spiritual liberty. In the secular context, the transformative liberty is one of experience.

When one looks at the act of volunteering—of giving time (Derrida 1992) in New Delhi—one could interpret volunteering through the lens of Indian ideas of *dān*, of religious donation and renunciation (Bornstein 2009), or through ideas of service (*seva*). With this perspective, the lack of emphasis on outcomes, effects, and teleologies makes logical sense. With dān, which is a sacred act of giving, the inequality of the giver and recipient are understood and expected. That dān reinforces the hierarchy and inequality between donor and recipient does not negate its significance. The worthiness of the recipient—and here I mean in terms of merit or moral worthiness of the gift (Parry 1994)—reflects back upon the donor. It is not an exchange between equals and it is not reciprocal in the way that Mauss (1990 [1950]) might have identified. It is, however, transformative as change is inhabited, if only for a moment. The experience of this moment—sought after and reflected upon—is how humanitarianism is, as Volunteer Now described it, "being change" and "practical dreaming," echoing Mahatma Gandhi's directive to "be the change you want to see in the world."

NOTES

This chapter is based on research (2004–5) made possible by a grant from the National Endowment for the Humanities and the American Institute of Indian Studies. I am grateful to the Social Science Research Council for funding a resident fellowship at the School for Advanced Research in Santa Fe, NM (2006–7), which afforded precious time to think and write. This chapter is part of a larger ethnographic project on humanitarianism in New Delhi (see Bornstein 2012).

1. Turner (1986:35), again referring to Wilhelm Dilthey.
2. For comparison of Durkheim and James, see Jones (2003).
3. Joan Scott (1991) has written about the use of experience as evidence and the dangers of its uncritical use. Instead of assuming that experience is an essential and uncontested truth (connected to particular identities and groups), I follow Durkheim (1995 [1912]) to emphasize how it is mediate by institutions. Experience is always represented socially, and its representation reifies collective identities. As Scott notes, "It is not individuals who have experience but subjects who are constituted through experience" (1991:779).
4. See Watt (2005), also Tandon (2003) on background of Gandhian ideas of service in the non-profit sector in India.
5. Dān is a particular form of giving in Hinduism without the expectation of a return. See Bornstein (2006, 2009, and 2012) for relation of dān to philanthropy. For scriptural accounts of dān, see Heim (2004) and Nath (1987). For anthropological accounts, see Parry (1986, 1989, 1994) on dān in the context of Banaras funeral priests and Raheja (1988) for dān in context of rural village prestation and the reassertion of caste privilege.

6. Give India is a Web portal for philanthropy.
7. Cf. Turner (1986) on the relationship between experience and social drama.
8. This name is a pseudonym.
9. Also see Prashad 1997, Redfield and Bornstein (2011), and Farmer (2003) for the social justice critique more broadly.
10. Cf. Redfield's (2005) use of Agamben's concept of "bare" life as a form of naked existence—particularly in relation to humanitarian action.
11. This stance is most likely to be controversial in circles of humanitarian practitioners. See the excellent collection by Barnett and Weiss (2008) on this topic, and Reiff (2002) and Calhoun (2008) on the distinction between value rationality and instrumental rationality in humanitarianism.

REFERENCES

Allahyari, Rebecca. 2000. *Visions of Charity: Volunteer Workers and Moral Community*. Berkeley: University of California Press.

Barnett, Michael, and Thomas Weiss, eds. 2008. *Humanitarianism in Question: Politics, Power, Ethics*. Ithaca: Cornell University Press.

Bornstein, Erica. 2005. *The Spirit of Development: Protestant NGOs, Morality, and Economics in Zimbabwe*. Palo Alto: Stanford University Press.

—— 2006. "No Return": A Brief Typology of Philanthropy and the Sacred in New Delhi" In *The Politics of Altruism: Caring and Religion in a Global Perspective*, ed. Keishin Inaba and Ruben Habito, 165–79. Cambridge: Cambridge Scholars.

—— 2009. "The Impulse of Philanthropy." *Cultural Anthropology* 24, no. 4 (November): 622–51.

—— 2012. *Disquieting Gifts: Humanitarianism in New Delhi*. Palo Alto: Stanford University Press.

Calhoun, Craig. 2003. "'Belonging' in the Cosmopolitan Imaginary." *Ethnicities* 3, no. 4 (December): 531–68.

—— 2008. "The Imperative to Reduce Suffering: Charity, Progress, and Emergencies in the Field of Humanitarian Action" In Michael Barnett and Thomas G. Weiss, eds., *Humanitarianism in Question: Politics, Power, Ethics*, 73–97. Ithaca: Cornell University Press.

Derrida, Jacques. 1992. *Given Time: I. Counterfeit Money*. Trans. Peggy Kamuf. Chicago: University of Chicago Press.

Durkheim, Emile. 1995 [1912]. *The Elementary Forms of Religious Life*. Translated by Karen E. Fields. New York: Free Press.

Farmer, Paul. 2003. *Pathologies of Power: Health, Human Rights, and the New War on the Poor*. Berkeley: University of California Press.

Gupta, Akhil, and Aradhana Sharma. 2006. "Globalization and Postcolonial States." *Current Anthropology* 47, no. 2 (April): 277–93.

Heim, Maria. 2004. *Theories of the Gift in South Asia: Hindu, Buddhist, and Jain Reflections on Dāna.* New York: Routledge.

Hitchens, Christopher. 1995. *The Missionary Position: Mother Teresa in Theory and Practice.* London: Verso.

James, William. 1982 [1902]. *Varieties of Religious Experience.* New York: Modern Library.

Jones, Sue Steadman. 2003. "From Varieties to Elementary Forms: William James and Emile Durkheim on Religious Life." *Journal of Classical Sociology* 3, no. 2 (July): 99–121.

Kristoff, Nicholas D. 2010. "The D.I.Y. Foreign Aid Revolution" *New York Times,* October 20, 2010. http://www.nytimes.com/2010/10/24/magazine/24volunteerism-t.html (accessed October 21, 2010).

Kristoff, Nicholas D., and Sheryl WuDunn. 2009. *Half the Sky: Turning Oppression Into Opportunity for Women Worldwide.* New York: Vintage.

Laidlaw, James. 1995. *Riches and Renunciation: Religion, Economy, and Society Among the Jains.* Oxford: Clarendon.

—— 2000. "A Free Gift Makes No Friends (Anthropological Analysis of the "Pure" or "Free" Gift)." *Journal of the Royal Anthropological Institute* 6, no. 4 (December): 617.

Malkki, Liisa. 2010. "Children, Humanity, and the Infantilization of Peace." In Ilana Feldman and Miriam Ticktin, eds., *In the Name of Humanity: the Government of Threat and Care.* Durham: Duke University Press.

Mauss, Marcel. 1990 [1950]. *The Gift.* New York: Norton.

Mustsonen, Pekka. 2005. "Volunteer Tourism: Postmodern Pilgrimage?" *Journal of Tourism and Cultural Change* 3, no. 3: 160–77.

Nagi, Saroj. 2005. "Why India Refused Global Aid." *Hindustan Times,* January 4, p. 4.

Nath, Vijay. 1987. *Dana Gift System in Ancient India: A Socio-economic Perspective (c. 600 BC–c. AD. 300).* New Delhi: Manoharlal.

Parry, Jonathan. 1986. "The Gift, the Indian Gift, and the 'Indian Gift.'" *Man* (n.s.) 21:453–73.

—— 1989. "On the Moral Perils of Exchange." In J. Parry and M. Bloch, eds., *Money and the Morality of Exchange,* pp. 64–93. New York: Cambridge University Press.

—— 1994. *Death in Banaras.* Cambridge: Cambridge University Press.

Prashad, Vijay. 1997. "Mother Teresa as the Mirror of Bourgeois Guilt." *Economic and Political Weekly* 32, nos. 44-45: 2856-2858.

Raheja, Gloria Goodwin. 1988. *The Poison in the Gift: Ritual, Prestation, and the Dominant Caste in a North Indian Village.* Chicago: University of Chicago Press.

Redfield, Peter. 2005. "Doctors, Borders, and Life in Crisis." *Cultural Anthropology* 20, no. 3 (August): 328–61.

Redfield, Peter, and Erica Bornstein. 2011. "An Introduction to the Anthropology of Humanitarianism." In *Forces of Compassion: Humanitarianism Between Ethics and Politics,* pp. 3–30. Santa Fe: School for Advanced Research.

Rieff, David. 2002. *A Bed for the Night: Humanitarianism in Crisis.* New York: Simon and Schuster.

Scott, Joan. 1991. "The Evidence of Experience." *Critical Inquiry* 17 (Summer): 773–97.

Sen, Siddhartha. 1992. "Non-profit Organizations in India: Historical Development and Common Patterns." *Voluntas* 3, no. 2 (November): 175–93.

—— 1999. "Globalization and the Status of Current Research on the Indian Nonprofit Sector." *Voluntas* 10, no. 2 (June): 113–30.

Sharma, Aradhana. 2006. "Crossbreeding Institutions, Breeding Struggle: Women's Empowerment, Neoliberal Governmentality, and State (Re)Formation in India." *Cultural Anthropology* 21, no. 1 (February): 60–95.

Sooryamoorthy, R., and K. D. Gangrade. 2001. *"NGOs in India: A Cross-Sectional Study."* Westport, CT: Greenwood.

Tandon, Rajesh. 2002. *Voluntary Action, Civil Society, and the State.* New Delhi: Mosaic.

—— 2003. "Overview of the Non-governmental Sector in India." In C. India, ed., *Working with the Non-Profit Sector in India,* pp. 23–33. New Delhi: Charities Aid Foundation

Turner, Victor W. 1986. "Dewey, Dilthey, and Drama: An Essay in the Anthropology of Experience" In Victor W. Turner and Edward M. Brunner, eds., *The Anthropology of Experience,* 33–44. Urbana: University of Illinois Press.

Turner, Victor W., and Edward M. Bruner, eds. 1986. *The Anthropology of Experience.* Urbana: University of Illinois Press.

Watt, Carey Anthony. 2005. *Serving the Nation: Cultures of Service, Association, and Citizenship.* New York: Oxford University Press.

Wuthnow, Robert. 1991. *Acts of Compassion: Caring for Others and Helping Ourselves.* Princeton: Princeton University Press.

SECULAR HUMANITARIANISM AND THE VALUE OF LIFE

PETER REDFIELD

> For what matters today is not the immortality of life, but that life is the
> highest good.
>
> —Hannah Arendt, *The Human Condition*

What claim to value might reside in the entreaty—ubiquitous in contemporary humanitarian settings—to "save lives"? How might it fit historically with earlier concerns for human welfare and salvation, particularly the legacy of Christian charitable action? Lines of superficial connection are obvious amid international relief efforts, which frequently indulge in the language of deliverance. Like colonial missionaries before them, aid workers have fanned out through the world to pursue good works, if not quite to save souls. Although many organizations and individual actors remain motivated by overtly religious precepts, the general frame of international aid is formally secular, its relative success measured in calories, bodies, and legal statutes rather than spiritual redemption. Nonetheless, the missionary comparison remains an uneasy subtext in discussions of humanitarianism, human rights, and international development, rarely embraced, but never quite exorcised by its denial.

This chapter considers the degree to which an avowedly secular organization might find something like a sacred purpose through seeking to preserve human existence. My key example for this endeavor will be the independent humanitarian association Médecins Sans Frontières (otherwise known as Doctors Without Borders or, in the aid world, MSF). Beyond regularly deploying calls to "save lives," the group offers the nominal advantage of combining an assertive faith in medical care with global

ambition. Founded four decades ago in a French effort to create an independent alternative to the Red Cross, MSF has since grown into a mul-
tinational fixture of health crises worldwide. Its militant appeal to life
entails action and extends, in a potentially limitless way, from emergency
response to the provision of AIDS drugs. Médecins Sans Frontières is also
a secular organization, one that operates with no mandate other than
its charter, a document proclaiming its members will "maintain complete
independence from all political, economic, or religious powers."[1] Loosely
framed by the longer sweep of French Republican universalism, this particular iteration of secular sensibility also emerged among other influences; key figures involved in the group's formation had associations with
Judaism and Catholicism as well as militant politics and labored under
the moral shadow of the Holocaust (Fox 1995; Taithe 2004). The adherents of MSF found their common ethical calling as doctors, however, and
by expressing medical concern in the face of suffering they asserted the
primary value of human life.

My approach will be to examine one end of the historical analogy
between aid workers and missionaries, outlining the story of MSF's vision
in relation to two canonical antecedents: the founding inspiration of the
Red Cross and the long labors of Albert Schweitzer. Less a genealogy than
a sketch of relevant landmarks, the goal is to distinguish MSF's particular attachment to life from other relevant points of possibility. Positioning the group's trajectory against these two alternative figures, I suggest,
highlights both an emerging focus on the delivery of medical care and
a shifting sensibility about life related to biological existence. In crude
terms, as the agent of care grew more medically defined, the aid offered
increasingly emphasized the value of living. Through this modest illustration, I seek to provide greater content to the "secular" dimension of
contemporary humanitarian feeling and practice, understood in human
and historical rather than categorical terms. As medical care increasingly
framed secular humanitarian sentiment, it has provided a ready measure—easily quantified and statistically represented—for asserting and
contesting international moral claims. In this sense it constitutes both a
figure of legitimacy and something like a sacred value, particularly apparent in moments of exceptional duress.

Before beginning two more theoretical caveats: by referring to this
contemporary secular value as effectively sacred, I do not mean to suggest either simple continuity with the past or the substitution of Christian theology by faith in humanity. As outlined in this chapter, MSF's

humanitarian vision deviates significantly from the response of religious traditions to suffering and concentrates on action rather than contemplation. Thus I would prefer Hans Blumenberg's emphasis on reoccupation rather than transposition for comparing this contemporary secular form with its antecedents (Blumenberg 1983). What, exactly, is worth saving? In response to this functional question of intervention, MSF finds an actionable answer in human life—understood to be mortal, finite, and available to biomedical care. The value of this life, however, remains particularized and nonfungible; one life cannot substitute for another, anymore than could an immortal soul. It is in this sense that it recalls the sacred.

Likewise, when considered from this perspective, MSF's secular concern for life is not simply an expression of "biopolitics" in the vein of Michel Foucault's biopower, transposed to nonstate actors (Foucault 2003; Rabinow and Rose 2006; Fassin 2009). The organization certainly reflects a biopolitical expectation that states *should* attend to the health of their populations. It also practices a minimalist, mobile version of such care for those it perceives to be in danger (Redfield 2005). However, the vision exceeds questions of governance when framing the good; in moral terms MSF's populations represent a collective of specific individuals whose clinical status will always outweigh their collective regulation. The vision thus effectively reverses the emphasis between life and power. Whereas a state might display the capacity to "make live" or "let die" (as opposed to the sovereign right to kill), a humanitarian in MSF's vein can never legitimately reject a suffering other. Here, then, I will cast this resolutely pastoral conscience as a form of "biomorality" or, more precisely, a biomoral claim on ethical action, practiced amid what Didier Fassin calls the "politics of life" in an unequal world (Fassin 2007, 2009; Foucault 2000 [1979]). I mean this term to highlight the increasing centrality of life— and the corresponding diminution of death—within this secular strand of humanitarian morality.

"A BEING NOT MADE TO SUFFER"

By way of introduction I turn to one of MSF's innumerable fund-raising brochures. Like most, it features bold graphics of red and white and the commanding catchphrase "You can help save a life." In this particular instance the exhortation appears above an itemized list equating donations with material effects. The reader learns that a modest $35 contribution will provide "all the medical and logistical supplies to supply 40 people a day with clean water," while a more generous $500 translates into a "medical kit containing basic drugs, supplies, equipment and dressings to treat 1500 patients for three months." An impassioned quotation from an MSF volunteer attests to the number of "tiny" children overwhelming a therapeutic feeding center in Darfur, and, in a small image next to the group's logo, a white-shirted caregiver leans over a bundled infant, two additional indications that need is real and action possible. The insert is hardly unique in either form or theme; I present it here merely as a particular illustration of a larger genre.[2] Even a cursory examination of humanitarian fund-raising materials reveals the extent to which they target human feeling and seek to transmute it into revenue. Here a piteously distorted lip of a child, there a harrowing description of a refugee's flight—instance after instance suggests a need to loosen purse strings or risk appearing callous and inhuman. By foregrounding the sorrows of others, especially in their particular and personalized form, organizations expect to evoke moral sentiment.[3] With a few terse lines and figures, MSF seeks to turn that feeling to the medical task of saving lives "around the world."

Tying sentiment to claims on universal humanity has a distinguished pedigree. In 1759 the philosopher Adam Smith famously included a propensity for sympathy near the heart of human nature. "That we often derive sorrow from the sorrow of others, is a matter of fact too obvious to require any instances to prove it," he wrote, "for this sentiment, like all the other original passions of human nature, is by no means confined to the virtuous and humane, though they perhaps may feel it with the most exquisite sensibility" (Smith 1976 [1759]). After all, even "the greatest ruffian" could be prone to pity and compassion in moments of weakness. At the same time, Smith recognized that sympathy varied in accordance with the attachment of a spectator to a scene. Only by knowing about and identifying with suffering could one react with feeling. Moral sentiment involves affective imagination, a fact several commentators have astutely noted in examining the vital role that visual media play in the dynamics of contemporary aid (Benthall 1993; Boltanski 1999; Ignatieff 1984). Once one could see through distance, however, suffering strangers might also evoke sympathy if properly presented. The alchemy of contemporary fund-raising lies in transmuting such sentiment into structured social action, connecting a more general philanthropic impulse to specific instrumental goals like the brochure's call to supply "40 people a day with clean water" (Bornstein 2009).

Although MSF's worldwide scope may be newly expansive, its appeals for assistance also resonate with longer traditions of charity. Indeed, acts of mercy may represent something of a panhuman heritage, inasmuch as major religions feature prescribe sanctioned forms of generosity, ranging from Buddhist compassion, Christian alms, and Islamic *zakat* to Hindu *dān* (Isaac 1993; Bornstein and Redfield 2011). Although differing significantly in form, conceptions of charity recognize suffering and suggest that a proper response to it constitutes an essential, and regular part of religious practice. At the same time, however, it is also important to note two things relative to MSF's solicitation. First, charitable traditions have frequently designated preferred recipients for aid by social criteria as much as bodily state. Although suffering might describe a common condition, then, historically its alleviation operated under other principles than humanity equality. Second, they weighed agony on a scale extending beyond material well-being; indeed, physical pain and torment might serve a greater purpose when suggesting purification or sacrifice (Asad 2003). Living was not simply an end in itself.

By contrast, in the mid-1990s Rony Brauman, the influential former head of MSF's French section, could define the human as "a being who is not made to suffer (Brauman 1996:7)." Such a statement—clearly intended as a provocation—is far more historically remarkable, and a significant departure from most religious cosmologies. Although few other humanitarian organizations would state their rationale in Brauman's stark terms, their very framework for delivery of such aid itself presupposes both that any measurable human suffering requires response and that the response to it should take the form of material care. Rather than seeking justification for suffering through appeal to other ends, such as religious value, social cohesion, or political gain, humanitarians meet human misery with attempts at direct assistance. In a more radical inflection, the sort favored by MSF, such assistance opposes any established order that would justify suffering or sacrifice people's well-being for power (Bradol 2004). As significant as the negative framing of the claim is its moral injunction: if humans are not meant to suffer then they should not. Humanitarians thus find moral certainty in alleviating anguish and protecting life. Medical care offers a direct means to render this moral vision immanent. The perspective embodied by MSF, then, both formalizes Smith's situational sentiment of compassion into a moral principle and reverses its terms. Sympathy not only indicates a human propensity; its active form defines the humane human.

Moreover, the medical variant of humanitarian action approaches suffering emphatically in the name of life itself. Mercy here does not imply euthanasia, or any other easing of pain beyond health; whether or not the being "not made to suffer" might find release in death, moral value here accrues from preserving existence, from "saving a life." To illustrate this last point through contrast, and better situate this contemporary vision of the aid doctor, I turn to the first of two well-known precursors to MSF: the concerned Christian gentleman converted to battlefield nurse.

DUNANT'S PASSION ON THE BATTLEFIELD

A century after Adam Smith contemplated moral sentiment, a form of it flared in the wake of war waged with modern weaponry by national armies. Unlike most individual gestures of compassion, this inspired an influential movement and an enduring complex of institutions known colloquially as the Red Cross.[4] However worn through repetition in canonical accounts of humanitarianism, the story still merits close attention. The combination of mechanized weaponry, conscript citizen armies, war correspondence, and photography suggests a dramatic new template for regarding "the pain of others" well before the advent of television (Sontag 2003). Moreover, the fact that war is the classic edge of law, the moment in which norms can be altered or suspended, underscores the extent to which this central humanitarian lineage rests on claims of exception.[5] Here, however, I wish to concentrate on details that might distinguish this visionary moment from present norms, not suggest familiar lines of connection. In particular, I emphasize the degree to which this formative concern for suffering soldiers related to death as well as life and included care not directed at survival.

On the evening of June 24, 1859, a Swiss civilian named Henry Dunant stumbled onto the battlefield of Solferino. The pious son of a Genevan family of means, he had pursued the French emperor to Italy in order to lobby for his business interests in Algeria and had little experience to prepare him for what he saw. Following a heavy day of fighting, the wreckage of both French and Austrian armies littered the field. Wounded men groaned miserably, a combination of hot weather and poor provisioning adding thirst to their shared torment. A nearby church received some of the wounded, and it was there that Dunant made his way, spontaneously offering what assistance he could. Although a stranger to military combat, he was no newcomer to charitable endeavors; active in a movement to unite Christians and Jews, he had also played a prominent role in organizing the first world conference of the YMCA in Paris in 1855. But the plight of these suffering soldiers touched a new chord of feeling. He threw himself fervently into the work and for several days labored alongside women from the town and assorted travelers he managed to press into service.

The shock of the experience marked Dunant, and he composed and published a short memoir describing what he had seen. The book, titled *Un souvenir de Solferino* (A Memory of Solferino), would prove widely influential. Its author launched a crusade to improve care for wounded soldiers and quickly received invitations to capitals all over Europe. He imagined a relief effort of committees led by well-born volunteers, who, motivated solely by noble sentiments, would prove more reliable than paid help. Military professionals were alternately intrigued and skeptical of Dunant's proposals—even his counterpart Florence Nightingale would doubt their suitability, arguing that, since this was the proper responsibility of governments, substituting for them might make war too easy (Moorehead 1998). Nonetheless, Dunant's plan found fertile ground in his own city. A wealthy and philanthropically inclined lawyer named Gustave Moynier took up the cause and began the practical steps to realize its organization, along with a retired Swiss war hero and two doctors. In 1863 the first of a series of international conventions met in Geneva. It established a set of resolutions to authorize committees that would assist with the care of the wounded in the time of war, and a uniform sign—a red cross against a white background—that would render their members distinctive.[6]

Although Henry Dunant was but one of a wave of reformers horrified by the effects of modern warfare, it was his legacy that defined a key kernel of the eventual international system advocating humanitarian care. The Red Cross eventually expanded into an array of organizations undertaking a variety of missions.[7] Told as a triumph of human spirit over barbarity, Dunant's story features prominently in progressive accounts of the aid world. Given that the Red Cross is a defining component of the aid apparatus (as well as a direct ancestor of Médecins Sans Frontières), and the Geneva Conventions a landmark series in international humanitarian law, such attention is only due. When considered relative to the present and later concerns for life, however, Dunant's moment on the battlefield exhibits some crucial differences from present appeals. In the first place,

Dunant's inspiration derived more from heartfelt faith than from secular reason or medical sensibility. A deeply religious man, he appealed openly to Christian sentiment in his effort to "civilize" warfare. The men who joined him in Geneva were not only prominent citizens of the city but also devout, and, while emerging from a Protestant milieu, they framed their appeal as an ecumenical concern. The very symbol used by the organization carried religious connotations, a fact that would prove a source of lasting controversy when the Red Cross expanded beyond Europe.[8] At the same time, the group initially imagined war in terms of formal engagements between national armies on a clear battlefield. The impetus for its origin derived in no small part from recent innovations in combat, both the heightened destructive force of weaponry and the use of conscript citizen armies rather than mercenaries. And, finally, although the initial vision of the Red Cross came from ordinary citizens offering battlefield care, it focused on easing death alongside saving life.

This last point merits particular amplification. Dunant's short book includes a good deal of impassioned description, combining romantic visions of battlefield heroism by dashing, aristocratic officers with heartrending accounts of the agonies of wounded common soldiers.[9] Some have faces "black with flies," and others are "no more than a worm-ridden, inextricable compound of coat and shirt and flesh and blood." Here a swollen tongue hangs from a broken jaw, there a skull gaps open, there again a back quivers red, furrowed by buckshot (Dunant 1986 [1862]:61–62, 66–67). Faced with this suffering, Dunant and his companions offer cool bandages, sponges, warm compresses, a drink of water, or—once his driver forages supplies—lemonade. At times, however, their primary gift is companionship, offering a hand to grip, a prayer or reassurance. "I spoke to him," Dunant wrote of one stricken soldier who raged against his cruel fate, "and he listened. He allowed himself to be soothed, comforted and consoled, to die at last with the straightforward simplicity of a child" (Dunant 1986 [1862]:66). In Dunant's rendering, the suffering of the dying at Solferino was not only a physical matter. Many soldiers, realizing they would expire, begged for a letter that might inform their families of their fate and ease their mothers' distress with the certainty of mourning. Death here was not simply an individual concern but also a social fact, an event that demanded appropriate recognition. In response, Dunant's small band of volunteers offered the comfort of communication, whether in the form of a farewell letter or simply a promise to convey the sad news of an individual's demise.

Dunant famously made no distinctions on the basis of nationality, and the women with him proclaimed a brotherhood among the wounded. Nonetheless, their work held its own anxieties, even when sustained by religious fervor as well as faith in common humanity. The little group faced decisions, confronting an overwhelming scene of need with few resources. In a particularly striking passage, Dunant reflects on the horrifying experience of his own predicament, caught between emotional appeal and the need to act:

> The feeling of one's own utter inadequacy in such extraordinary and solemn circumstances is unspeakable. It is indeed, excessively distressing to realize that you can never do more than help those who are just before you. . . . Then you find yourself asking: "why go to the right, when there are all these men on the left who will die without a word of kindness or comfort, without so much as a glass of water to quench their burning thirst?"
>
> The moral sense of all the importance of human life; the humane desire to lighten a little the torments of all these poor wretches, or restore their shattered courage; the furious and relentless activity which a man summons up at such moments: all these create a kind of energy which gives one a positive craving to relieve as many as one can. There is no more grieving at the multiple scenes of this fearful and solemn tragedy. There is indifference as one passes even before the most frightfully disfigured corpses. There is something akin to cold calculation, in the face of horrors yet more ghastly than those here described, and which the pen absolutely declines to set down.
>
> (Dunant 1986 [1862]:73–74)

What constitutes action in this context? Amid the sea of needs and requests, the Genevan businessman improvises frantically and feels the weight of his own limits. He recognizes he can only aid those directly before him, but that doing so would condemn others to a lonely death without human comfort, or even "a glass of water to quench their burning thirst." A "moral sense of the importance of human life" drives him, but it finds expression in simple gestures. It also inspires a frenzied mix of relentless activity, cold calculation, and sudden heartbreak at an unexpected detail that "strikes closer to the soul" (Dunant 1986 [1862]:73–74). Although much of his turmoil echoes through contemporary humanitarianism, Dunant's mission is ultimately one of mercy more than medicine.

Washing wounds and whispering comfort, he prefigures later Christian icons such as Mother Theresa as much as Doctors Without Borders. Dunant acts in the name of life, but it is the life of a larger person whose demise extends beyond a particular body. The work of compassion here includes ensuring dignity in death.

The movement constructed by others around Duant's vision certainly addressed itself to physical suffering, helping equate the symbol of a red cross with medical care in many parts of the world.[10] Nonetheless, the core organization in Geneva retained an attachment to the wider narrative sense of life by involving itself in such activities as registering prisoners and tracing missing persons. It played a significant role in nascent international law and strove to achieve a variety of internationalism constructed around political neutrality and the possibility of appeals for decency across religious and cultural difference (Ignatieff 1997). On the basis of these accomplishments, Dunant shared the first Nobel Peace Prize in 1901. However, neither the Red Cross nor the Geneva Conventions initially encompassed the colonized world. Only later in the twentieth century—particularly after decolonization—did this less "civilized" terrain emerge as a central focus of humanitarian concern associated with warfare and emergency.[11]

SCHWEITZER'S MEDICAL MISSION

When the Red Cross did gingerly extend beyond Europe, it encountered another form of humanitarianism. Medicine played an increasing part in the colonial drama during the nineteenth century, both as a "tool of empire" and as an arm of colonial service and authority (Headrick 1981; Hardiman 2006). The specifics varied by region, empire, and period. But during the emergence of germ theory and the advent of modern research-oriented medical practice—what anthropologists term "biomedicine"— work on diseases endemic in the tropics offered one potential path to scientific glory. Such work was also a matter of practical concern for European military forces and colonial administrators. Charged with governing mobile forces and increasingly interconnected populations, they faced a constant threat of epidemics. After a long era of astonishing death rates, the health of European troops in tropical postings improved dramatically by the early twentieth century. The well-being of colonial populations, however, remained a continuing and vexing problem. Diseases like sleeping sickness inspired determined health campaigns, involving medical officers even in the most remote regions and connecting the project of empire directly to a microscope (Lyons 1992; Vaughn 1991). Such efforts were clearly political in the large sense of the term. They derived from grand schemes and affected myriad local interests. They incorporated the lives and welfare of remote peoples into the calculations of government and the apparatus of rule, albeit perhaps more as objects than as subjects. The motivations behind them, however, were often complex, mingling altruistic sentiment with desires for profit and control.

In Africa missionaries played a significant role offering medical care, particularly in the British case. From David Livingstone on, the image of a heroic white doctor toiling in darkest Africa struck a romantic chord for Europeans. Although the increasing focus on physical health alongside spiritual states generated some tension, a larger story of salvation remained intact. Missionary work appeared a noble and self-sacrificing form of altruism. Hospitals, moreover, provided a ready venue for proselytization, in which the labors of a worldly healer might suggest the value of a more glorious physician and a "Great Dispensary in the Sky" (Vaughn 1991:56–57). Missionary medicine walked a line between sacred and secular care, removing tumors and cataracts in a public flourish, mixing treatment with prayer, and constructing and staffing clinics and hospitals, many of which remain in use. Even as Africans encountered Christianity through health care, the European reading public encountered Africa through reports of suffering on the "sick continent." In materials from early in the twentieth century we find common tropes of contemporary aid brochures, such as calls to "adopt" a patient or an appeal to send funds for doctors because "Congo boys and girls are dying" (Vaughn 1991:62–63). Yet the focus on life remains within a religious and distinctly Christian frame.

Here I will focus on an exceptional figure from the middle part of the century, one who came to exemplify the medical mission as a moral calling. Born in Alsace, Albert Schweitzer was first a theologian and subsequently a doctor. He was inspired to study medicine after reading an appeal from the French Protestant Missionary Society in Paris at the age of twenty-nine, returned to school, and eventually devoted much of his life to running a hospital in what was then French West Africa. Rather than talking about the gospel of love, he would "put it into practice." And, in return, Africa would give Schweitzer his signature understanding of purpose. As the official presentation of his 1952 Nobel Peace Prize recounted: "One day in 1915—he was forty years old at the time—while traveling on a river in Africa, he saw the rays of the sun shimmering on the water, the tropical forest all around, and a herd of hippopotamuses basking on the banks of the river. At that moment there came to him, as if by revelation, the phrase which precisely expressed his thought: Reverence for life."[12] This "reverence for life," together with its expression through efforts on behalf of suffering Africans, provided a moral exemplar for the waning days of European rule. Aspects of Schweitzer's mission continue to resonate in secular humanitarian projects, particularly his pragmatic focus and emphasis on protecting life. However, the "reverence" in his case was literal, and the impulse fully sacred. Even after becoming a doctor, Schweitzer remained in essence a theologian.

The new doctor's turn to missionary medicine, however, occurred prior to his moment of vision. Unlike Henri Dunant, unexpectedly hurrying about a battlefield, Schweitzer prepared himself professionally before embarking on treating the afflicted. Health care, he felt, would provide him with a broad passport into utility, deeply purposeful and mobile. "I wanted to be a doctor that I might be able to work without having to talk. . . . Medical knowledge made it possible for me to carry out my intention in the best and most complete way, wherever the path of service might lead me" (Schweitzer 2009 [1933]:92). His conception of this "path of service" was deeply humanist, if never quite secular. As he wrote in a sermon titled "The Call to Mission" in 1905: "For me, missionary work in itself is not primarily a religious matter. Far from it. It is first and foremost a duty of humanity never realized or acted upon by our states and nations. Only religious people, only simple souls have undertaken it in the name of Jesus. . . . Why? Because to be a disciple of Jesus is the only culture in which a human being is always a human being, always someone who has a right to the assistance and sacrifice of his fellow men" (Schweitzer 2005:75–76). With Schweitzer, then, medical care was not simply a tool for conversion in the narrow sense. Rather, it was the means to realize the humanistic promise of Christianity and in doing so offer a measure of redemption for the failures and sins civilized rule.

Schweitzer rooted his thought through meditation on experience, not rational exposition alone. He cast his reverence for life quite broadly, feeling concern for the well-being of nonhuman animals and even plants. It was an attitude, not a specific creed, focused primarily on awareness (Brabazon 2000). He had few illusions about a natural basis for mercy: "When one has seen whole populations annihilated by sleeping sickness, as I have, one ceases to imagine that human life is nature's goal" (Schweitzer 2005:151). The duty of humanity was not a given; rather it derived from the challenge of dedicated spiritual work and difficult practice. This practice was a daily and ordinary endeavor, not only a response to exceptional circumstances like battlefield slaughter. In this sense his project had as much in common with later attempts to foster development and improve public health as with the initial efforts of the Red Cross. In a modest way, the theological doctor sought to change the world by emphasizing matters of the heart. He could kill if necessary to end suffering or to serve a greater good, but only with awareness of his actions. Even the death of a mosquito or harmful microbe proved a matter of contemplation, likewise the rescue of a young pelican that would demand fish (Brabazon 2000:282–83). Although human patients came first in the doctor's duty of humanity, they were never the limit of his vision.

At the same time, Schweitzer's relations with African collaborators proved complex. He asked his workers to move heavy palm trees to spare them from cutting—a philosophy that struck them as "perverted"—while maintaining rigid divisions between Europeans and Africans. It appeared to many that he only fully accepted the latter as patients, sick and needy (Mazrui 1991:98–101). He did, however, care for their souls as well as their bodies, preaching every Sunday morning in his hospital, hoping they would carry his gospel far and wide.[13] In later years his project received increasing criticism, not only for its paternalism and social remove but also for its resistance to change. When it came to questions of both political and medical progress, the hospital struck a distinctly cautious note. Even while emphasizing the survival of his patients and his forest hospital, the good doctor still kept one ear cocked for "the sound of bells in a Christian country" (Fernandez 1964:537).

Schweitzer's vision, like Dunant's, positioned moral sentiment about humanity beyond politics. A Protestant from Alsace with a Prussian wife, he had to tread carefully in a French colony, promising to remain "mute as a carp" on religious matters and paying his expenses through private fund-raising.[14] Under surveillance by French authorities, he also maintained an uneasy relationship with the colonial medical service, whose local resources he soon outstripped. Schweitzer was cooperative but stubbornly independent. Unlike the Red Cross, which worked through states, the missionary doctor did not expect states and nations to take up the "duty of humanity" as an official policy; instead he relied on religious congregations and individual charity, those who properly understood

Christianity as a culture "in which a human being is always a human being." Moreover, the Schweitzer's project differed in the slower pace of its peacetime setting and in its broader emphasis on life. As on Dunant's battlefield, a better death might arrive through care, the soul's passage accompanied by the relief of prayers as well as physical comfort in the mission hospital. However the force of *reverence* lay with the living and the recognition that life came "each day as a gift." To take up this path fully required more than a willingness to engage in acts of mercy or even medical training: ultimately one needed a properly contemplative world-view. "There are no heroes of action," Schweitzer maintained, "only heroes of renunciation and suffering" (Schweitzer 2009 [1933]:88–89). One could only approach life with proper respect if fully aware of death: "It is the number one question about life: where do you stand with regard to death? If in our thoughts we are comfortable with death, then we accept each week, each day as a gift, and only when we allow life to be given to us in such a way, bit by bit, does it become truly precious" (Schweitzer 2005:165–66). In this respect, for Schweitzer reverence took precedence over physical salvation. Life was the essential ground for sacred under-standing and hence not simply an end in itself.

JACOBINS WITHOUT THE GUILLOTINE

In 1971, more than a century after Dunant's battlefield, and long after Schweitzer's conversion to medicine, a small group of French doctors and journalists created something they ambitiously named Médecins Sans Frontières. The appearance of the organization quickly acquired a reassur-ing shroud of myth, dissolving any longer horizon into a gauzy moment of generational conscience and French national pride. Before recount-ing a version of it, therefore, several points require emphasis. The first is that the movement—like the Red Cross before it—quickly grew into a complex organization, with multiple national sections beneath its inter-nationalism, not always in alignment. The particularities of MSF emer-gence, then, cannot simply explain the extent of its subsequent appeal, which rapidly extended beyond France. Secondly, the forms MSF drew on were likewise not simply French, but rather part of a longer history of European internationalism, charity, and advocacy as well as the interwo-ven tangle of rival colonial empires. Finally, the sense of national identity involved refracted back through moments of international encounter, most ironically illustrated, perhaps, by the French embrace of the English designation of "French Doctors" for MSF and similar organizations.[15] Although located in France, then, this story is not simply French, but part of Europe's wider encounter with the world.

Such points aside, MSF's national heritage still merits attention, for it illustrates the degree to which a medically framed concern for life could simultaneously recall and resolve long-standing political tensions. As Renée Fox notes, the dominant ethos of the French doctor movement recalls a long oppositional lineage framed by postwar concerns, assuming the mantle of the Rights of Man as a birthright, if not necessarily an ideological claim (Fox 1995). Steeped in the romance of resisting fascism, on the one hand, and militantly opposed to the practice of genocide, on the other, key actors combined a revolutionary sensibility with a revulsion for mass violence. Although largely incubated in the hothouse of the French political left, they lost faith in its abstract utopianism, while also finding inspiration in the concrete legacy of Catholic charity. The result, Bertrand Taithe observes, united Republican ideals with those of the Catholic Church, reversing two centuries of bitter opposition (Taithe 2004). The fact that the Jewish Holocaust loomed large in the background only underscores the sense of historical resolution; a common front against suffering effectively banished the ghost of Dreyfus. At the same time, MSF's perspective offered a new moral legitimacy for international intervention, countering the bitter memory of Indochina and Algeria with that of colonial doctors such as Eugène Jamot, who had pioneered an impatient, frontier style at odds with both bureaucracy and the ponderous approach of missionaries like Schweitzer (Lachenal and Taithe 2009). For oppositional intellectuals growing disillusioned with Communism, such a vision offered not only an alternative form of moral indignation but also an unexpected point of common ground with a French state struggling to maintain a place on the world stage. As France reluctantly retreated from empire, it could reunite around medical humanitarianism.

To provide a greater sense of the particularities leading into MSF, I will chronicle its early history in some detail, highlighting a few of its most influential members. Like the Red Cross, the group appeared in response to moments of exceptional suffering, namely, concern for starving civilians in a breakaway province of Biafra during the Nigerian civil war, on the one hand, and the painful birth of Bangladesh out of East Pakistan, on the other. The Red Cross was a literal as well figurative ancestor: of the group of thirteen men who founded Médecins Sans Frontières, five had been Red Cross volunteers in Biafra. One of these, Bernard Kouchner, was destined to become a charismatic force in international humanitarianism and French political life. Passionate and telegenic, he had already emerged as a something of a public figure at the time. In the mythic version of the group's birth, it came into being through Kouchner's rejection of Red Cross silence. The large arc of the story rings true, as MSF came to embody an alternative Red Cross, filtered through youthful rebellion and a media age. The historical record, however, offers more qualifications and details. The break with traditional discretion actually occurred over a period of years, and the initial impetus for the group's founding came from several directions, including the vision of a pair of restless journalists and the hunger of suburban French doctors for charitable adventures. Even among the Biafran veterans Kouchner was hardly alone. Several of his colleagues were older hands at aid work and played a prominent role at the outset.[16] And several of his younger successors were actually closer to the generational moment and would do far more to realize the organization's practical potential. But it was Kouchner who spoke the initial vision most grandly and left an abiding mark. Decades after angrily parting ways with the organization, his name has remained attached to it, much to the frustration of his successors when their positions diverge.[17]

The child of a Jewish doctor and a Catholic nurse, Bernard Kouchner entered the world during the uncertain lull at the onset of the Second World War. He grew up in a France shadowed by that conflict and infused with the cult of the Resistance. Haunted by the Holocaust, particularly after learning of the death of his own grandparents, Kouchner easily gravitated into leftist politics and joined the Communist student union in 1959. He opposed the Algerian War and defined himself around antifascism. Although studying medicine, he also nursed journalistic aspirations and wrote for the student union's publication. He visited Yugoslavia and Cuba and even met with Castro. In the middle of the decade, however, the party tightened its control over the student group, excluding Kouchner and his associates. Some went on to form small Maoist and Trotskyite collectives. For his part, Kouchner helped edit another leftist publication and finally finished his studies in gastroenterology in May 1968. That very month the Latin Quarter in Paris erupted in a student revolt. Although later identified with this historical moment, Kouchner was actually nearing thirty at the time and had already passed through one political baptism and disillusionment. Amid the tumult in the streets he heard a different call to arms and departed for Biafra.

Between September 1968 and January 1970 some fifty French volunteers made their way to a hospital in Biafra for varying stints of medical duty.[18] Kouchner would ultimately go three times, growing increasingly passionate. When back in Paris he agitated for the Biafran cause, and he and other colleagues signed an open letter to diplomats attesting to the suffering they had seen. On October 23, 1968, together with a senior colleague, Kouchner published a testimonial in the French newspaper *Le Monde*, the first of a series of such efforts by members of the team. Although a departure from Red Cross discretion, this publication remained a modest one. As Anne Vallaeys notes, it focused on medical issues and, far from denouncing the Red Cross, actually exhorts would-be humanitarians to join the mission (Vallaeys 2004:61, 75). Nonetheless, it demonstrates a point of continuity in Kouchner's own trajectory: the medical student had become a journalist, and the journalist found new voice as a doctor.

After the fall of Biafra, the mission's veterans started a group that might serve as a sort of medical expeditionary brigade for the Red Cross.[19] When a hurricane struck East Pakistan, they waited vainly for a call. The situation spiraled into secession and civil war, and as neither Pakistan nor India showed much willingness to cooperate with foreign relief efforts, the Red Cross did not send them. Nonetheless, they saw an appeal for volunteers to form an emergency group in a medical journal called *Tonus* and decided to respond. Sponsored by a pharmaceutical company and directed toward suburban general practitioners, *Tonus* was hardly a radical publication. Its editor Raymond Borel, however, had broader horizons. The author of several novels, he had lived in Brazil and spent time in Hollywood as an aspiring scriptwriter and, as East Pakistan disintegrated into disaster, he published a call to arms for French doctors to aid the victims. It featured a physician who, witnessing scenes of chaos and bureaucratic impasse following a recent earthquake in Yugoslavia, imagined a medical strike force that could mobilize quickly and freely to save lives. His French colleagues, he was sure, were not "mercenaries," but rather implicitly ascribed to such higher values.[20]

A few stylistic differences aside (Kouchner apparently did announce himself "a mercenary"—albeit of emergency medicine), the Biafrans quickly found common ground with the *Tonus* initiative (Vallaeys 2004:116). Realizing that their initial name, Secours Medical Français (French Medical Aid) might have an unfortunate ring in former colonies, the editors eventually came up with another permutation of the same initials: Médecins

Sans Frontières. On a gray December night, the collective assembled to establish a legal association and settle on a charter. A humanitarian alliance between journalism and medicine was now official.[21]

A more mythic synopsis of MSF's birth would quickly brand it as an updated, outspoken Red Cross realizing the mobile allure of its name. The phrase *sans frontières* resonated widely, first through France, where it described a whole genre of organizations—*sans frontièrisme*—and subsequently worldwide when the English equivalent, "without borders" became a hallmark of global sensibility. Whether or not the shift from SFM to MSF eased the burden of colonial history, it clearly opened a new rhetorical horizon.[22] The choice of an emblem proved less sure, but was in its own way revealing; MSF first adopted a variant of the cross in red and white tilted against a red swatch.[23] It would retain this insignia until the mid-1990s, when—facing legal action by the Red Cross—it switched to a stylized "running man" in red and white. Like its name, the evolution of the group's symbol is to some degree instructive of its larger trajectory. Where the roots of Dunant's organization were clearly Christian, those of MSF also filtered through a figure of humanity. Founded as a "free association" under the relevant law of 1901, part of the secular legacy of French Republicanism, MSF acquired no official status and presented itself without reference to religious tradition. At the same time, it absorbed the influence of religious as well as political opposition movements, offering a point of convergence around a common concern for life.[24]

The early years of MSF's existence were filled with enthusiastic dreams and heated discussions, but relatively few effective missions. Even as the group solidified and grew, however, it also gained a new generation of younger adherents. Having come of age politically during May 1968, many shared a history of leftist orientations, skepticism, and confrontational style, and several had gone to medical school together at Cochin in Paris. They also shared the common experience of encountering MSF as an existing entity and approaching it from the perspective of field missions. One leading member of this generation was Claude Malhuret, who would also later become a French minister, and mayor of Vichy. As a student he matched his medical education with socialist politics and *tiersmondiste* ("third worldist") sympathies. In 1974 he first heard of MSF and was struck by the name, which reminded him of the May rebellion (Vallaeys 2004:233). He eventually went to work for nearly a year in a refugee camps in Thailand, where he grew disillusioned with leftist accounts of

Cambodia, and, witnessing vast and pressing medical need, increasingly frustrated with MSF's inability to provide much support.

Another key figure in this second wave was Rony Brauman, who became a long-serving president for MSF's original French section and remained leading intellectual light well beyond his term in office. Born in Jerusalem as the son of Polish Jews, Brauman's childhood bore a deep imprint of the Holocaust, and as a student he gravitated toward anarchism and then Maoism, spending a period as an activist. Further to the left of Malhuret, he responded more skeptically when first hearing of MSF, suspecting it of bourgeois tendencies.[25] He went instead to a rural hospital in Benin with a Catholic organization, and later to an urban hospital in Djibouti. These experiences only deepened his humanitarian convictions, though, as he told me later, he still sought a group "that wouldn't have religious discourse, even if activist." Joining MSF at last he also went to a camp in Thailand. Like Malhuret, the Khmer Rouge debacle in Cambodia brought Brauman to a final break with Communist ideology. Henceforth his considerable intellectual energy would focus on more immediate and specific conceptions of human suffering.

Viewed at a distance, key early figures of MSF—including Kouchner, Malhuret, and Brauman—exhibit considerable similarities.[26] While elements of biography, approach, and style varied, all found their deepest engagement with the world through a secular faith in medical care. Their interest in politics shifted form and tense: rather than a utopian future, they concentrated on suffering in the present. Unlike Schweitzer, they were restless, mobile, and combative. Life was a crucial value, but the spirit of engaging it now more radical than reverent. They also had a larger horizon than a single hospital: as Kouchner once infamously put it on a television show discussing May '68, his generation belatedly "discovered" the third world and its misery (Ross 2002:156–57). Responding in 1978 to an interviewer's question as to whether he was not tempted stay put like Schweitzer, Kouchner replied: "It's a respectable image, but one that belongs to the domain of charity rather than that of medicine. However, if a *médecin sans frontières* looks into the essence of himself, he will certainly encounter the secret desire to be the Good Samaritan. Jesus Christ, perhaps" (Vallaeys 2004:254–55). Malhuret and Brauman shared Kouchner's ambivalent view of charity, but desired a more comprehensive and instrumentally effective organization: a lighter and more activist Red Cross. In keeping with Kouchner's distinction, their model of MSF's engagement would remain resolutely "medical." The refugee camp, however, rather than the battlefield or hospital, would prove the group's defining terrain.

The subsequent trajectory of MSF only deepened its focus on the moral significance of saving lives, even as its protagonists fought over how best to achieve this end. In 1979 Bernard Kouchner departed following a bitter schism to found a rival organization, Médecins du Monde (Doctors of the World). The precipitating event came when Malaysia denied entry to a boatload of Vietnamese refugees in full view of the media. The image of thousands suffering aboard inspired a project to create and equip a "Boat for Vietnam" to demonstrate solidarity with the refugees. This appeal engendered a remarkable display of solidarity across France's own political divides: most notably long-time opponents Jean-Paul Sartre and Raymond Aron both signed on, joined by a host of other intellectual luminaries such as Roland Barthes, Simone de Beauvoir, and Michel Foucault. Kouchner naturally championed the venture. Malhuret and others who had spent time working in camps in Thailand were skeptical, seeing the mission as more of a publicity stunt than an effective aid project, and tension between factions only grew. In the event, the boat—christened *L'Île de Lumière* (The Isle of Light) no less—sailed without MSF's official sanction, but with Kouchner and associates on board. Rather than rescuing refugees, it became a hospital ship, anchoring off an island and offering medical services. At a stormy board meeting later in 1979, Malhuret called for a more professional and less spectacular organization, including compensation for volunteers, as "the time of Doctor Schweitzer is over." Kouchner countered that MSF was effectively dead, killed by "technocrats of assistance" (Vallaeys 2004:299). He then walked out, followed by his allies.

It is easy to read this split retroactively as the ascendance of pragmatism and medical professionalism within MSF, in keeping with most internal accounts from that side (with Kouchner emphasizing purity of principle). The schism did allow a largely younger generation to seize control of the organization, reforming and expanding it rapidly over the ensuing decade. They would also take a more strictly humanitarian line, whereas Kouchner's smaller faction embraced human rights rhetoric more directly, remaining a step closer to journalistic sensibilities. However, it would be a mistake to overstate the differences between MSF and its new rival. Despite personal animosities on the part of some protagonists, and shifting emphases, the two groups would undergo a largely parallel evolution in their prioritization of suffering over other moral and political considerations. Shortly after the schism, both famously intervened in Afghanistan's civil war, riding mountain trails with the muhajideen. Amid the romance of running clandestine missions, any pretense of strict adherence to principles of neutrality and discretion was quickly lost. "Like our forerunners in Biafra," Rony Brauman would later write, "we had implicitly picked our side" (Groenewold and Porter 1997:xxii). Legitimacy derived not from international law or political allegiance but from the moral worth of providing services where there were none, in a war where "a million died." Amid subsequent crises both groups would adopt a variety of positions through similarly complex political settings, at times in parallel and at times angrily opposed. However, their common moral loadstone remained the claim of human suffering.

In 1982 Brauman became president of MSF, a post he was to hold for the next dozen years. An ally of Malhuret, he would oversee the remarkable expansion of the organization during the 1980s. The budget increased exponentially, as did the number of volunteers and missions. Médecins Sans Frontières adopted increasingly sophisticated fund-raising techniques to target individual donors, some self-consciously borrowed from the United States (Vallaeys 2004:372). It established administrative and logistic structures to manage both people and supplies. Although still very much an informal and sometimes haphazard affair, it began to exhibit greater professional expectations and developed an array of equipment dedicated to ensuring short-term human survival. In the space of just a few decades, MSF grew to match its global name, its flag fluttering in all manner of remote outposts.

Not all of the growth emanated from Paris. Even in the 1970s, MSF had begun to explore the possibility of internationalization, so obviously implicit in its self-designation. The group's actual expansion was neither smooth nor wholly planned, and the 1980s saw acrid feuds between factions, echoing the schism of the previous decade.[27] Nonetheless, a new international structure gradually took shape. There would be five largely autonomous "operational" sections of MSF sponsoring missions: France, Belgium, Holland, Switzerland, and Spain. Around them the first and largest three would assemble "partner" sections in still other countries to provide assistance with finances and human resources. This particular humanitarian vision was now pan-European, with tendrils stretching beyond.

Following the dissolution of the Soviet Union and the unraveling of cold war geopolitics, a new international complex of aid agencies came into its own during the 1990s: UN peacekeeping and relief missions increased, and NGOs propagated exponentially. For its part, the MSF collective continued to grow, stumbling from one catastrophe to another. Following another bitter period of turmoil in Rwanda, relations between the sections generally improved, and the scope of the group's projects expanded beyond emergency care. In 1999, the year it won its Nobel Prize, MSF decided to launch an ambitious advocacy campaign, seeking greater pharmaceutical equity worldwide, and soon began a massive program to provide antiretroviral medications to AIDS patients in poor countries. Both these ventures entailed significant organizational shifts and realignments. At the same time, the ensemble continued to mount seventy to eighty field missions a year, with ever-increasing personnel and resources. It was by now a large, complex transnational federation, with a combined budget of hundreds of millions of dollars. In addition to sponsoring several thousand international "volunteers," the group engaged ten times as many local staff and had begun to recognize uneasily that their different status might mirror older colonial divides, even as it worried yet again about devolving into a business.[28] To fuel its many operations, the group regularly sent out appeals—such as the letter previously cited—requesting potential donors to help "save a life."

DOCTORS WITHOUT BORDERS AND PREVENTABLE DEATHS

What then distinguishes this secular humanitarian concern for life? In comparison with Dunant's ministrations to wounded soldiers, groups like MSF give relatively little attention to the needs of the dead and dying or the larger social world they represent. In practice its focus rests firmly on clinical bodies and the populations they comprise.[29] Unlike Schweitzer, MSF has spent little time elaborating a philosophy of life as such. This is hardly due to an absence of reflection in general; the group has devoted an impressive measure of reflective attention to other abstract concepts— for example, "humanitarian space" (the constitution of proper conditions for humanitarian action) or *témoignage* (a variety of witnessing as ethical advocacy). Life, however, is simply to be saved. A humanitarian cannot legitimately exchange one human existence for others or sacrifice it to a greater good (Fassin 2007; Redfield 2008). In this sense, Brauman's radical definition of the human as "a being who is not made to suffer" provides an accurate categorical touchstone. The humanitarian response to suffering frames itself as action, not contemplation. At the same time, MSF remains a deeply realist organization, fully committed to responding to the shortcomings of an actually existing world. The point in "saving" life thus lies not in denying death per se, but rather in opposing *preventable* deaths, the view that—in one telling phrase I have often encountered—"people shouldn't die of stupid things" (see also Farmer 2003:144). The list of such stupid things is both varied and long, including conflict, disasters, and a range of epidemic and chronic diseases, all of which might be averted with sufficient political will.

MSF's attention centers on what the group describes as "populations in danger" or "populations in distress." This root concern for the world's wounded parallels that of the battlefield instantiation of the Red Cross, if focused on civilians and cast at a grander, global scale. All those who suffer deserve care, regardless of social background, political position, or prior actions; only medical criteria should determine their relative priority.[30] In contrast to Dunant, however, MSF seeks to offer the best biomedical treatment possible under given conditions, not just acts of human mercy. It does so defiantly, as a form of opposition to the situation that created suffering in the first place. Although sharing the Red Cross hope that political powers might learn to act more humanely, MSF's adherents remain generally less sanguine about the prospects and less formal in their methods. The group also operates without a specific mandate, other than its collective conscience, and strives to remain largely independent from state support, relying instead on its own ability to raise funds from supporters. In this respect it is a true "nongovernmental organization," parallel to the missionary tradition. As its name implies, MSF also views itself as a fundamentally medical organization, if not simply a collectivity of doctors. Its faith, so to speak, rests with the possibility of medical intervention as a form of moral action.

When preventable deaths do occur, MSF frames its action in terms of witnessing and advocacy. Although témoignage does not always take the form of "speaking out" or open denunciation, such moments have deeply defined the group's mythic self-conception as well as its broader reputation. Beyond distinguishing it from the Red Cross tradition of discretion, these moments of public speech also indicate the fundamental attachment of MSF's ethical views to the domain of secular politics. For there is no direct redemption for lives lost rather than saved in this vision, no afterlife or martyrdom that would render them immortal. The sacredness of their being stems from the fact of their existence—from life itself.[31]

Once extinguished, meaning can only come from memory, appeals to their legacy, and admonitions that such unhappy fate should never occur again. Absent a soul or utopia, it is hard to transmute a stupid death into a good one.

All that escapes or exceeds medicine falls under the supplemental good of human "dignity," a category shared more widely with human rights discourse. Since MSF itself favors the present and builds few memorials, its version of history remains largely undefined and only thinly enacted at the level of material practice. While the group's tradition of speaking out may spring from the same source as testimony in war crimes tribunals or truth and reconciliation commissions, it is even less clear what audience or conception of posterity might be involved. Médecins Sans Frontières recognizes that speaking out is no magic formula, only a moral imperative.[32] Its hopes for justice ultimately rest with other, more directly political, actors. As a bitter, memorable press release put it at the height of Rwanda's agony in 1994, "You can't stop genocide with doctors."[33]

The degree to which the group identifies with both the possibilities and limits of the medical profession becomes clear in such moments of témoignage, neither fully religious nor juridical. As a prominent figure within the French section of the organization suggested to me, medical personnel can claim a privileged perspective when it comes to facts of life:

> Doctors can diagnose causes and states. They are the ones who can measure. In Rwanda it was clear we couldn't protect population during genocide. We were told at checkpoint you can fetch the wounded and we'll kill them here. But afterwards, in prisons, life expectancy was six months, while the wait for trial something like ten years. So you had death before trial. Now who can get in to prisons? Those who work there and those who work in health. So medical personnel can perform a diagnostic of a situation. It's a different angle than that of "they're all *génocidaires*" (which many were, of course). We can view each of them as individuals, talk of people and their life chances, pathologies, etc. It's a way of medically objectifying the political situation of why people are not living. It's about human facts, and not questions of philosophy, law, etc. The doctor can speak of the sick, of a precise person and not in generalities. It's always individual—not talk of [abstract] desirable things, but of life and death. Doctors can talk in mortality rates.[34]

Although not a doctor by training herself, this member of MSF saw that professional legacy playing a central role in the group's collective persona, particularly the clinical tradition of focusing on specific cases and the precision of health measures. Claiming medical authority permitted not only access but also a mode of speaking that could redefine a situation by objectifying it. The resulting facts promised to shift ethical focus away from generalized assumptions of guilt and return it to considerations of individual existence. In this indirect manner, attention to life might sometimes lead to justice.

SECULAR HUMANITARIANISM AND SACRED LIFE

Although MSF and its offshoots may struggle fiercely over the terms of their engagement, they have remained in agreement about the value of human life and a concomitant refusal to justify present suffering in the name of future utopian ideals. Rather than approaching crisis from the long-term perspective of some unfolding history or libratory struggle, they perceived it in relation to the immediate needs of an affected population, understood in medical terms. Moreover they reinforced this fundamental consensus most powerfully in their very operations. During the 1970s and 1980s, the variety of suffering found in refugee camps offered MSF's humanitarians moral clarity at the level of practice. Instead of political abstractions, their action would focus on particular bodies suffering in particular times and places; in response to violations they could both speak out and actively intervene at the level of health. Thus MSF focused its energies on a direct response to inhuman conditions, wherever they might be found and whatever their origin. By the early 1990s the group had a global logistics system in place and had become more technically proficient, part of a growing trend of nonprofit professionalization (Redfield 2011). Even if emergency conditions rarely resolved cleanly, they did lend themselves to clear technical response alongside moral denunciation. Biomedicine could contain an outbreak disease or offer short-term alleviation from disaster. Undertaking such action could also represent a deeper moral rejection of the situation itself, an "ethic of refusal" as MSF's Nobel acceptance speech would put it.[35] Amid the compressed time of crisis, humanitarians found moral clarity in action.

How to account for the relative sacredness of human existence? Writing a half-century ago in *The Human Condition*, Hannah Arendt offered a suggestive synopsis of how life might have emerged as the "the highest good" for modern Europe. The existence of ordinary, individual humans, she observed, became sacred when Christianity reversed the order of classical antiquity, replacing the immortal cosmos with "the most mortal thing, human life" (Arendt 1998 [1958]:314). Only through passing through a mortal coil on Earth could one achieve the everlasting; in this sense immortality became a personal affair. When the modern world reversed Christian doctrine through secularization and returned individual life to mortality, it retained attachment to life as the highest value: "The only thing that could now be potentially immortal, as immortal as the body politic in antiquity and as individual life in the Middle Ages, was life itself, that is, the possibly everlasting life process of the species mankind" (Arendt 1998 [1958]:321; see also Brient 2000). If Arendt's general diagnosis holds, it provides a background against which "saving lives" might emerge as a moral exhortation. It likewise suggests how, by touching directly on "life itself," medical action might acquire particular moral standing.

How then might secular humanitarian medicine compare to earlier antecedents and the work of missionaries? Here I have traced one lineage of medical intervention inspired by human suffering. Aspects of MSF's labors resemble those of both the early Red Cross battlefield and Schweitzer's tropical hospital. All share a concern for the suffering patient and define their action through medical practice. Like Dunant and the early Red Cross, the humanitarian doctors focus on exceptional states, finding human feeling most easily in moments of urgent rupture. Like Schweitzer they primarily toil amid the larger shadow of colonial legacies. But, in contrast to both, they place little value on easing death or expressing reverence for life in general or finding redemption through prayer. If not fully political in form, their version of witness nonetheless emerged from a political conception of the value of speech and retains a this-worldly ethos. Any transcendence it might claim would remain temporal and essentially attached to the figure of the human. Although at times their efforts might suggest something like a sacred value to life, the terms of evaluation are intrinsically medical: the relative health of bodies and well-being of minds remain unquestionably paramount, the only legitimate measures for relative "success" or "failure."

In its secular medical version, then, humanitarianism has increasingly concentrated on a distinctly material project of salvation. As well as a biological matter of existence, and a political object of concern, life emerges as a key moral value (Collier and Lakoff 2005). The "life" at the center of humanitarian concern appears as a common quality, shared by all humans. However, it is also nonfungible and so eludes legitimate exchange or sacrifice for future utopian visions. In lieu of a soul or a larger field of reverence, focus rests on actions to maintain existence and enhance prospects for survival. Humanitarian medicine, after all, by itself offers little redemption from death, the inevitable long-term outcome of any individual clinical case. The bulk of humanitarian efforts respond to preventable disorders with familiar remedies, not experimental procedures that might at least hold out the hope of enhanced care for future patients. Lives lost thus yield little prospect of future scientific gain. Instead, appeals to human dignity or historical witness suggest something approximating sacred value, now located in material experience. By signaling humanity, the universal subject of secular reason, the suffering body defines and reveals a moral threshold (Feldman and Ticktin 2010). As a matter of practical morality, then, the worth of this form of life derives precisely from saving it.

NOTES

1. For the full text see http://doctorswithoutboders.org/aboutus/charter.cfm (accessed November 18, 2009).
2. I received this particular solicitation in 2008. For parallel slogans, see "There are many ways to rescue a life" (International Rescue Committee); "Have you saved someone's life lately?" (Smile Train); "Saving lives one drop at a time" (UNICEF for a vaccination campaign); "Survive to 5" (Save the Children—a venerable charity known in aid world shorthand as Save). Such solicitations distinguish a distinctly "humanitarian" aesthetic of appeal; fund-raising for "development" projects commonly deploy themes of work, education, and a bright future. For more on the shifting sense of humanitarianism and its use in the contemporary aid world, see Bornstein and Redfield 2011 and Calhoun 2008.
3. Both humanitarian experience and psychological studies suggest that donors respond more readily to natural disasters than to structural inequities and to stories of individuals than to those of any mass (Slovic 2007; Wilson and Brown 2009; MSF-F and Factanova 2002).
4. The focus here is on the International Committee of the Red Cross, based in Geneva, rather than national Red Cross and Red Crescent societies or the

International Federation of Red Cross and Red Crescent Societies. For more background, see Moorehead 1998; Hutchinson 1996; and Forsythe 2005.

5. Agamben 2005. As Calhoun (2008) notes, the history of the term far exceeds the Red Cross legacy.

6. Hutchinson (1996) notes that the documentary record fails to clarify the precise rationale for the selection of this emblem, only later suggesting it to be a reversal of the Swiss emblem. Whatever the precise origins of the Red Cross symbol, its subsequent connotations were clear and twofold, recalling both Christianity and the Swiss national flag. Thus, while the movement was international from the start, the terms of its engagement remained historically circumscribed at the level of its very symbol.

7. In addition to separate national societies, a league emerged to coordinate their greater union. At the same time, the International Committee of the Red Cross (ICRC) continued its own path in Geneva, becoming a fixture of international law by virtue of overseeing the Geneva Conventions. The collective purview of these entities grew to include far more than the care of wounded soldiers, gradually encompassing sailors, prisoners, and civilians as well as responses to natural disasters.

8. The Christian legacy in particular produced an early and lasting problem once the movement reached cultural frontiers. Although the Ottoman Empire had agreed to the initial Geneva proposal, from an Islamic point of view the cross symbol evoked bitter memories of the Crusades. During its war with Russia in 1876, the Ottoman government announced it would modify the official insignia, substituting a red crescent for a cross. Despite Russian objections, and their own desire for a single emblem, the International Committee eventually agreed. At the same time, they sought to limit the range of possible alternatives and continued to insist that the cross was simply a geometric figure rather than a religious endorsement (Benthall 1997). Tensions have continued over the appropriate primary symbol for aid until the present, particularly in the case of Israel, with the inclusion of a new "Red Crystal" in 2006.

9. See (Hutchinson 1996:14–18) on the class assumptions structuring Dunant's account.

10. Dunant was ultimately a visionary more than a true founder in the organizational sense; the scandal of business failure forced him to resign from the fledgling Red Cross in 1867. Only very late in his life would he enjoy rehabilitation and regain renown.

11. The exceptions to this rule involved settings at the threshold of European recognition, e.g., the Ottoman Empire. See Sven Lindqvist's unconventional work *A History of Bombing* for one account of colonial experiments in violence,

amid the larger historical complex of military and humanitarian intervention (Fassin and Pandolfi 2010).

12. Nobel Peace Prize Presentation Speech, 1952. At http://nobelprize.org/nobel_prizes/peace/laureates/1952/press.html#not_7 (accessed May 1, 2008).

13. Schweitzer's initial self-presentation in 1913 to his flock in Gabon was more overtly religious. In that sermon he has the people of his home city instructing him: "And if you care for their bodies, tell them that their souls are well rather than sick and that the soul is more precious than the body, as the Lord Jesus has said. And though there are many good medicines for the body, there is only one thing—only one—for the cure of the soul. This medicine is the gospel that was preached to them for many years and that many have rejected and no longer listen to" (Schweitzer 2003:3–4).

14. Quoted in Headrick 1994:258–70. Headrick underscores the extent to which Schweitzer's appeal resonated far more strongly in English- and German-speaking countries than in France. See also Lachenal and Taithe 2009.

15. The expression, applied by American media to teams from Médecins Sans Frontières and Médecins du Monde working alongside the mujahideen in Afghanistan during the bloody 1980s, appears in every French work about the organization that I have read.

16. Max Récamier and Pascal Grellety-Bosviel, who both oversaw the Biafran team, were older than Kouchner. They already had extensive experience and had come of age amid a milieu of third world solidarity that largely involved religious organizations. Récamier's humanitarian convictions derived primarily from Christian charity, not the revolutionary tradition that had shaped Kouchner. Nonetheless, the two could come together in the face of what they thought to be genocide, foreshadowing later humanitarian alliances (Vallaeys 2004).

17. Although consistently popular with the French public, Kouchner has long been a controversial figure, even before becoming France's foreign minister. For a caustic assessment of his trajectory as a generational icon see Ross 2002:147–69. See also Taithe 2004:147–58 and Guillemoles 2002. Within MSF his public legacy has proved a source of continued frustration, such as when the organization won the Nobel Peace prize in 1999 and found itself misidentified in the press with his positions (Vallaeys 2004:749–50).

18. From the perspective of humanitarian organizations, the Biafran conflict served as something of a watershed. Many of the elements involved—including the manipulation of civilians and aid—were not entirely new. Nonetheless, they came together in a newly evocative and disturbing way. As the Nigerian army slowly strangled the rebellion over the next three years, the new wonders of satellite transmission conveyed images of starving children

to televisions in European living rooms. At the same time, improvements in air transport diminished the distance involved, and the standardization of emergency medicine fostered a new sense of the possible when it came to intervention. The actual geopolitical alignments surrounding the conflict were complex; France, Portugal, South Africa, and Israel supported the rebels, whereas Britain, the United States, and even the Soviet Union backed the Nigerian regime. Furthermore, the conflict carried religious undertones, since the majority of the afflicted civilians came from the largely Christian Ibo, and Catholic missionaries played a significant role in advocating for attention and shaping media coverage. Media accounts, however, emphasized civilian suffering and the threat to innocent life. The separatist government mounted a highly effective and emotional public relations campaign, warning loudly of genocide (Waters 2004).

19. In addition to Kouchner and friends, its associates included Xavier Emmanuelli, another former Communist and future politician, who had worked as a doctor in the merchant marine and following an accident nursed a vision of rapid intervention. See Emmanuelli 1991.

20. Vallaeys 2004:107–26); Bernier 1970.

21. The Biafran precedent notwithstanding, the new association's charter included the Red Cross principle of neutrality, and adhered to the tradition of medical confidentiality and public silence (Vallaeys 2004:121–22).

22. The expression may have appeared a few times before—in a youth travel agency called Jeunes sans frontières and in a renamed European game show, *Jeux sans frontières*, both dating to the late 1960s. But MSF popularized it. Moreover, it established a new form, serving as a prototype organization that adopted a borderless sense of space together with an ethos of direct intervention and media involvement. Alongside Doctors, the world has gained Reporters, Pharmacists, Engineers, Animals, Sociologists, Magicians, Knitters, and even Clowns Sans Frontières. The translation of *frontières* into "borders" would remain a point of slight contention. To adherents of MSF, the name more often denotes a willingness to expand and overcome barriers than any statement about national borders. Even when yielding to the international dominance of English as the language of world governance, and expanding far beyond its French origins, the movement would retain its original acronym. Nonetheless, "without borders" has made up for any lack of proper *élan* with epochal ambition. Henceforth, doctors would go anywhere.

23. According to early bulletins, the organization considered several symbols, including a flying bird, which would mark Kouchner's later group, *Médecins du Monde*. Jean-Paul Ryst, "L'oiseau blanc et rouge," *Bulletin Médecins Sans Frontières*, no. 3 (April–July 1975): 14–15.

24. The law of 1901 appeared amid the struggle between church and state in the French Third Republic, extending state sanction over free associations and limiting the autonomy of religious congregations (Archambault 1997). At the same time, it is important to note that MSF's secularism was far from anti-Catholic. Brauman and Kouchner both cite the inspiration of Abbé Pierre, who turned from politics to address poverty, and Emmanuelli would eventually announce his own religiosity (Taithe 2004; Emmanuelli 1991:249–50).

25. Moreover, on his initial approaches Brauman ironically was turned away (Brauman 2006:51).

26. For a less abbreviated cast of characters and greater social analysis of their context see Dauvin and Siméant 2002.

27. For an early vision of expansion, see *Bulletin Médecins Sans Frontières* 3 (April-July 1975): 33. Real internationalization proved less harmonious; at one point the French group even sued their Belgian counterparts over the use of their common name. The suit stemmed partly from the French establishment of a think tank called Liberté Sans Frontières that took a public stand against the leftist tradition of *tiers-mondisme*, accusing it of romantic misrepresentation of the true causes of misery. The Belgians saw this as an unwelcome injection of reactionary politics. By the time I interviewed him in 2003, Brauman could describe the feud as something of a youthful folly stoked by rival ambitions, albeit one with significant bearing on the very goal of humanitarianism. In his interpretation, whereas the French operation was far more centralized and deeply imbued with the "Jacobin spirit of France," the Belgians had a different understanding of the state and resented the imperious attitude of their colleagues. See Vallaeys 2004:461–509.

28. The status of local staff was a topic of debate at the 2005 La Mancha assembly of MSF sections, and the fear of institutionalized charity endemic to the organization, Kouchner on.

29. In exceptional circumstances, individuals endeavor to recognize the needs of the dead bodies; see, e.g., the account of the Rwandan genocide in Orbinski 2008.

30. See the statement in 2009 of the president of MSF's international council advocating that resources for a potential flu pandemic be according to need, not wealth, on both medical and ethical grounds. http://www .msf.org/msfinternational/invoke.cfm?objectid=DF6C28EF-15C5-F00A-25F6853731E2D809&component=toolkit.article&method=full_html (accessed November 12, 2009).

31. Fassin (2009:47–48) proposes using the phrase "life as such" for human existence at the level of a particular body inserted into history, the ultimate object of concern for groups like MSF. Since, in this chapter, I wish to stress a biological quality of being, however, I retain "life itself," which better conveys

the urgency of a fund-raising brochure. See also Benjamin 1978:299; Collier and Lakoff 2005.

32. Rackley 2001. The French section of the organization has produced a series of casebooks of MSF's most controversial moments under the collective title *Prises de Parol Publiques de MSF/MSF Speaking Out*. Tellingly they retain sufficient controversy to remain partly internal documents rather than serving as a more public history. See Soussan 2008 for a more detailed account of MSF's evolving practice of témoignage.

33. MSF-France press release dated June 17, 1994. For more commentary on témoignage, see Redfield 2006.

34. From the author's fieldnotes, Paris, June 2003.

35. http://nobelpeaceprize.org/en_GB/laureates/laureates-1999/msf-lecture/ (accessed November 12, 2009).

REFERENCES

Agamben, Giorgio. 2005. *State of Exception*. Chicago: University of Chicago Press.

Archambault, E. 1997. *The Nonprofit Sector in France*. Manchester: Manchester University Press.

Arendt, Hannah. 1998 [1958]. *The Human Condition*. 2d ed. Chicago: University of Chicago Press.

Asad, Talal. 2003. *Formations of the Secular: Christianity, Islam, Modernity*. Stanford: Stanford University Press.

Barbazon, James. 2000. *Albert Schweitzer: A Biography*. Syracuse: Syracuse University Press.

Benjamin, Walter. 1978. *Reflections: Essays, Aphorisms, Autobiographical Writings*. Ed. Peter Demetz. Trans. Edmund Jephcott. New York: Schocken.

Benthall, Jonathan. 1993. *Disasters, Relief, and the Media*. London: I. B. Tauris.

—— 1997. "The Red Cross and Red Crescent Movement and Islamic Societies, with Special Reference to Jordan." *British Journal of Middle Eastern Studies* 22, no. 2 (November): 157–77.

Bernier, Philippe. 1970. "Sommes-nous des mercenaires?" *Tonus* 442, no. 23 (November 23): 1, 6.

Blumenberg, Hans. 1983. *The Legitimacy of the Modern Age*. Trans. Robert Wallace. Cambridge: MIT.

Boltanski, Luc. 1999. *Distant Suffering: Morality, Media and Politics*. Cambridge: Cambridge University Press.

Bornstein, Erica. 2009. "The Impulse of Philanthropy." *Cultural Anthropology* 24, no. 4 (November): 622–51.

Bornstein, Erica, and Peter Redfield, eds. 2011. *Forces of Compassion: Humanitarianism Between Ethics and Politics*. Santa Fe: School of Advanced Research.

Brabazon, James. 2000. *Albert Schweitzer: A Biography*. 2d ed. Syracuse: Syracuse University Press.

Bradol, Jean-Hervé. 2004. "The Sacrificial International Order and Humanitarian Action." In F. Weissman, ed., *In the Shadow of 'Just Wars': Violence, Politics, and Humanitarian Action*, 1–22. Ithaca: Cornell University Press.

Brauman, Rony. 1996. *Humanitaire, le dilemme*. Paris: Textuel.

—— 2006. *Penser dans l'urgence: Parcours critique d'un humanitaire*. Paris: Seuil.

Brient, Elizabeth. 2000. "Hans Blumenberg and Hannah Arendt on the 'Unworldly Worldliness' of the Modern Age." *Journal of the History of Ideas* 61, no. 3 (July): 513–30.

Calhoun, Craig. 2008. "The Imperative to Reduce Suffering: Charity, Progress, and Emergencies in the Field of Humanitarian Action." In Michael Barnett and Thomas Weiss, eds., *Humanitarianism in Question: Power, Politics, Ethics*, 73–97. Ithaca: Cornell University Press.

Collier, Stephen J., and Andrew Lakoff. 2005. "On Regimes of Living." In Aihwa Ong and Stephen Collier, eds., *Global Assemblages: Technology, Politics, and Ethics as Anthropological Problems*, 22–39. Malden, MA: Blackwell.

Dauvin, Pascal, and Johanna Siméant. 2002. *Le travail humanitaire: Les acteurs des ONG, du siege au terrain*. Paris: Sciences Po.

Dunant, Henry. 1986 [1862]. *A Memory of Solferino*. Trans. American Red Cross. 1939. Geneva: International Committee of the Red Cross.

Emmanuelli, Xavier. 1991. *Les prédateurs de l'action humanitaire*. Paris: Albin Michel.

Farmer, Paul. 2003. *Pathologies of Power: Health, Human Rights, and the New War on the Poor*. Berkeley: University of California Press.

Fassin, Didier. 2007. "Humanitarianism as a Politics of Life." *Public Culture* 19, no. 3 (Fall): 499–520.

—— 2009. "Another Politics of Life Is Possible." *Theory, Culture, and Society* 26, no. 5 (September): 44–60.

Fassin, Didier, and Mariella Pandolfi, eds. 2010. *Contemporary States of Emergency: The Politics of Military and Humanitarian Interventions*. New York: Zone.

Feldman, Ilana, and Miriam Ticktin, eds. 2010. *In the Name of Humanity: The Government of Threat and Care*. Durham: Duke University Press.

Fernandez, James W. 1964. "The Sound of Bells in a Christian Country—In Search of the Historical Schweitzer." *Massachusetts Review* 5, no. 3 (Spring): 537–62.

Forsythe, David P. 2005. *The Humanitarians: The International Committee of the Red Cross*. New York: Cambridge University Press.

Foucault, Michel. 2000 [1979]. "'Omnes et Singulatim': Toward a Critique of Political Reason." In *Essential Works of Foucault, 1954–1984*, vol. 3: *Power*, 298–325. Ed. James Faubion. New York: New Press.

—— 2003. *"Society Must Be Defended": Lectures at the Collège de France, 1975–1976*. Ed. Mauro Bertani and Alessandro Fontana. New York: Picador.

Fox, Renée C. 1995. "Medical Humanitarianism and Human Rights: Reflections on Doctors Without Borders and Doctors of the World." *Social Science and Medicine* 41, no. 12 (December): 1607–26.

Groenewold, Julia, and Eve Porter. 1997. *World in Crisis: The Politics of Survival at the End of the Twentieth Century*. London: Routledge.

Guillemoles, Alain. 2002. *Bernard Kouchner: La biographie*. Paris: Bayard.

Hardiman, David, ed. 2006. *Healing Bodies, Saving Souls: Medical Missions in Asia and Africa*, Amsterdam: Rodopi.

Headrick, Daniel. 1981. *The Tools of Empire: Technology and European Imperialism in the Nineteenth Century*. Oxford: Oxford University Press.

Headrick, Rita. 1994. *Colonialism, Health, and Illness in French Equatorial Africa, 1885–1935*. Ed. Daniel Headrick. Atlanta: African Studies Association Press.

Hutchinson, John F. 1996. *Champions of Charity: War and the Rise of the Red Cross*. Boulder: Westview.

International Committee of the Red Cross. 2000. *International Red Cross and Red Crescent Museum*. Geneva: ICRC.

Ignatieff, Michael. 1984. *The Needs of Strangers*. London: Chatto and Windus.

—— 1997. *The Warrior's Honor: Ethnic War and the Modern Conscience*. New York: Holt.

Isaac, Ephraim. 1993. "Humanitarianism Across Religions and Cultures." In Thomas Weiss. and Larry Minear, eds., *Humanitarianism Across Borders: Sustaining Civilians in Times of War*, 13–22. Boulder: Lynne Rienner.

Lachenal, Guillaume, and Bertrand Taithe. 2009. "Une généalogie missionnaire et coloniale de l'humanitaire: le cas Aujoulat au Cameroun, 1935–1973." *Le Mouvement Social*, no. 227 (April-June): 45–63.

Lyons, Maryinez. 1992. *The Colonial Disease: A Social History of Sleeping Sickness in Northern Zaire, 1900–1940*. Cambridge: Cambridge University Press.

Mazrui, Ali A. 1991. "Dr. Schweitzer's Racism." *Transition*, no. 53: 96–102.

Moorehead, Caroline. 1998. *Dunant's Dream: War, Switzerland, and the History of the Red Cross*. London: HarperCollins.

MSF–F (Médecins Sans Frontières–France) and Factanova. 2002. "Resultats etude qualitative phase entretiens donateurs." Paris: Médecins Sans Frontières–France.

Orbinski, James. 2008. *An Imperfect Offering: Humanitarian Action for the Twenty-First Century*. New York: Walker.

Rabinow, Paul, and Nikolas Rose. 2006. "Biopower Today." *BioSocieties* 1:195–217.

Rackley, Edward B. 2001. *Bearing Witness: Strategies and Risks, a Reference Tool for MSF Field Workers*. Brussels: Centre de Recherche, MSF Belgium.

Redfield, Peter. 2005. "Doctors, Borders, and Life in Crisis." *Cultural Anthropology* 20, no. 3 (August): 328–61.

—— 2006. "A Less Modest Witness: Collective Advocacy and Motivated Truth in a Medical Humanitarian Movement." *American Ethnologist* 33, no. 1 (February): 3–26.

—— 2008. "Sacrifice, Triage, and Global Humanitarianism." In Michael Barnett and Thomas Weiss, eds., *Humanitarianism in Question: Politics, Power, Ethics*, 196–214. Ithaca: Cornell University Press.

—— 2011. "Cleaning Up the Cold War: Global Humanitarianism and the Infrastructure of Crisis Response." In Gabrielle Hecht, ed., *Entangled Geographies: Empire and Technopolitics in the Global Cold War*. pp. 267–91. Cambridge: MIT Press.

Rieff, David. 2002. *A Bed for the Night: Humanitarianism in Crisis*. New York: Simon and Schuster.

Ross, Kristin. 2002. *May '68 and Its Afterlives*. Chicago: University of Chicago Press.

Schweitzer, Albert. 2003. *The African Sermons*. Ed. Steven Melamed. Syracuse: Syracuse University Press.

—— 2005. *Essential Writings*. Ed. James Brabazon. Maryknoll, NY: Orbis.

—— 2009 [1933]. *Out of My Life and Thought*. Baltimore: Johns Hopkins University Press.

Slovic, Paul. 2007. "'If I Look at the Mass I Will Never Act': Psychic Numbing and Genocide." *Judgment and Decision Making* 2, no. 2 (April): 79–95.

Smith, Adam. 1976 [1759]. *The Theory of Moral Sentiments*. Oxford: Claredon.

Sontag, Susan. 2003. *Regarding the Pain of Others*. New York: Picador.

Soussan, Judith. 2008. MSF and Protection: Pending or Closed? Foundation Médecins Sans Frontières report. Les Cahiers du CRASH, June. http://www.msf-crash.org/en/publications/?section=2

Taithe, Bernard. 2004. "Reinventing (French) Universalism: Religion, Humanitarianism, and the 'French Doctors'." *Modern and Contemporary France* 12, no. 2 (May): 147–58.

Vallaeys, Anne. 2004. *Médecins sans frontières: La biographie*. Paris: Fayard.

Vaughn, Megan. 1991. *Curing Their Ills: Colonial Power and African Illness*. Stanford: Stanford University Press.

Waters, Ken. 2004. "Influencing the Message: The Role of Catholic Missionaries in Media Coverage of the Nigerian Civil War." *Catholic Historical Review* 90, no. 4 (October): 697–718.

Wilson, Richard, and Richard Brown, eds. 2009. *Humanitarianism and Suffering: The Mobilization of Empathy*. Cambridge: Cambridge University Press.

HOMESCHOOLING THE ENCHANTED CHILD

Ambivalent Attachments in the Domestic Southwest

REBECCA A. ALLAHYARI

Stories of homeschooling reveal questing for enchantment within the family. While marrying and having children often predicate increased church attendance, not all spiritual searching takes place in religious congregations. Early parenting is a flashpoint in the quest for domestic meaningfulness. One mother telling me why she appreciated her children attended the half-day Family School program told me, *We play games in front of our fireplace every night when it's too cold or too dark, or whatever, in the winter, it's just so much fun to be with the family*. Were her children to have two hours of homework to begin after dinner, she explained, they would miss out on that *quality family time* that she loves. Rather than let school structure their time, and hence familial interactions, homeschooling parents spoke of time with their children as a gift. Another mother told that before homeschooling, when her young son was in school, she dreaded time at home, since they wrestled over how he would finish his homework. But, with homeschooling, she said, *now, I really want to be at home. . . . It's so incredible to watch the evolution of the relationship*. Parents who left traditional schools for homeschooling, or who enrolled in the half-day Family School program, spoke often of the joy they encountered in their time with their children. Entrance into school had seemingly stolen this playfulness not only from the child, but from the family.

For parents who experience the social world as stiflingly bureaucratized and rationalized, children embody the potential for an encounter with awe and enchantment. Young children are, to many parents, not yet fully of the rationalized—and hence disenchanted. The social presence of a child opens a more wondrous world for parents. Historian Gary Cross argues that, for many Americans, babies no longer represent the fall from grace but rather embody a spirited purity and innocence. In his words, "Childhood has become a time to cherish and to protect from the modern Fall of growing up" (2004:5).[1]

Yet, growing up is often imagined of as a process of disenchantment. For those who experience the growing-up process as a disenchanting of the family, probably the most significant event in this process is the entrance of the child into school. If, in the Weberian sense, "the evocative term *enchantment* neatly captures the sense of the magical, the numinous, and a state of mind seemingly at odds with the modern outlook" (Owen 2004:12)[2] then growing up, with its conventional immersion in schooling, is often understood as disenchanting. Think of Huck Finn rafting down the Mississippi and Heidi frolicking in the Swiss Alps as culturally resonant stories of children partaking in enchanted childhoods in which they resist the disenchanting confines of schooling, with its temporal and bodily disciplining. To grow up is to leave that wondrous desire behind in childhood. While parents do not use this particular language in describing children's lives, their stories resound with joyful experiences of enchantment outside school and crushing experiences of disenchantment within school. For some parents, childhood is such a special time that they expend great effort and many hours seeking an educational path that nurtures their child's wondrous spirit rather than dampening it.[3]

Parents' work to sort through decisions of "school choice" may assume the tenor of religious seeking. Writing of "The American Experience," religious studies scholar Nancy Frankenberry describes an ongoing dialectic between self and community that is infused with religious emotions, even in seemingly secular realms: "The American secular quest pivots aesthetically around the relational interplay between the one and the many, the individual and the community, and the self and the cosmic whole." Considering those she calls the American pragmatic naturalists, such as William James and John Dewey, she identifies these religious inclinations as being about the desire to "*increase* in the depth, range, harmony, and vividness of felt qualities," especially as related to personal and community transformation. In families, parents seek this depth of feeling in selves and communities that nurture children in the process of becoming. If such "spirit bloweth where it will" (Frankenberry 1996:106, 106–7, 108), devotional parenting opens up a spiritual deepening of parenting.

Americans have long sought transcendence in places outside of churches (see Partridge 2004 for a consideration of alternative spiritualities). While perhaps a nation of *Restless Souls*,[4] our "American utopian method" to borrow from sociologist Lewis Mumford has inclined us to familial experimentations. Writing in the early twentieth century, Mumford cautioned that for many "that small, private Utopia is the only one for which they feel a perpetual, warm interest" (Mumford 1962 [1922]:5, 19). Although many have debunked Christopher Lasch's 1979 characterization of the home as a "haven in a heartless world," utopian dreaming still propels visions of family life. Many hope not only to enchant the family, but fiercely desire to build a rich spiritual community. In considering the value of children in contemporary U.S. society, sociologist Suzanne Shanahan writes, "The child is a buffer against the profound loneliness of modernity" (2007:415). Parents experience their children through this haze of emotional investment and a nostalgia for childhood (both real and idealized), further obscured by their aspirations.

Parents tinker with their family lives in the practice of *devotional parenting*.[5] Homeschooling appeals to those intent on resisting the institutional demands of schooling in favor of enchanted childhoods. Parents reveal spiritual or religious identities in which they creatively meld expert discourses from religious, educational, and parenting authorities with the particularities of their families' lifestyle. Yet not all parents seeking enchanted childhoods shun formal education. Parents remain troubled by the conviction that the experts may know something important and not easily replicated without formal training. Parents often begin their search by choosing a school that promises flexibility and autonomy.

Homeschooling charter schools—a burgeoning and hybrid form of education—appeal to families seeking escape from a social world experienced as stiflingly bureaucratized yet uncertain of their capacity to homeschool without guidance. For many such families, transcendent moments in educating the child hold the potential for an encounter with awe and enchantment. Many of these parents, often mothers, fear too what they imagine to be the isolation of homeschooling. Enrollment at the Family School in Albuquerque provides a spiritual way station for families questing for meaningful childhoods. Exemplifying American utopianism in education, charter schools promise a public education seemingly

loosened from the shackles of bureaucratic disenchantment. Often organized around ideological commitments to community, equality, or experimental pedagogy, charter schools promise both heightened flexibility and
autonomy for the child and the family with dense social bonds as volunteerism is oft mandatory. Rather than seek a new congregation or a traditionally religious education, families, sometimes deeply religious, may
choose an educational path that might enchant the family.

FAMILY SCHOOL: A SPIRITUAL WAY STATION

Accountings of who homeschools and why grew increasingly sophisticated
by the turn of the millennium. Kurt J. Bauman of the U.S. Census Bureau
estimated that "the number of home schooled children was well under
1 million in 1999, and the growth rate from 1996 to 1999 was unlikely to
have exceeded 15 percent per year." Despite his relatively conservative
evaluation, Bauman noted homeschoolers outnumbered those involved in
voucher programs (only a few thousand in a few cities) and those involved
in charter schools (estimated to be just over five hundred thousand in
2000). Bauman found that homeschoolers were slightly more likely to
be girls than boys and that "home schooled children are more likely to
be non-Hispanic White, they are likely to live in households headed by
a married couple with moderate to high levels of education and income.
They are more likely to live in households with three or more children and
they are likely to live in a household with an adult not in the labor force."
Homeschooling families were typically "of middle income—neither rich
nor poor." And, at least in 1994 and 1996, "Hispanics were less likely to
be home schooled and Blacks were much less likely to be home schooled."
Bauman argued that, even if homeschooling were to remain limited to
families with one parent at home, "the number of home schooled children
could grow from 790,000 to over 30 million without exhausting this core
constituency" (Bauman 2002).

The National Center for Education Statistics—under the auspices of
the U.S. Department of Education—estimated that approximately one in
five homeschoolers were enrolled in private or public schooling less than
twenty-five hours per week. This study did not find differences in place or
urban and rural distinctions. Nearly 50 percent cited concerns for quality of education as motivating homeschooling, and just under 40 percent
cited religious motivations. Because respondents could offer more than

one motivation, an explanatory distillation into pedagogy versus ideology as motivations for homeschooling was less likely. In 2003, further analysis showed that the homeschooling population had increased from about 1.7 percent of the school-age population to 2.2 percent, or about 1.1 million students in 2003 (a 29 percent rate of increase in the homeschooling population over the four-year period). However, at both points in time approximately one out of five of these students participated part-time in organized schooling.[6]

Potential homeschooling mothers often express great ambivalence about the trade-offs between schooling and homeschooling.[7] While desirous of the independence of home education, the legitimacy of age-graded schooling, with its assurance of professional oversight, offers a powerful lure. A public yet self-determining charter school for homeschooling that promises flexibility and innovation seemingly offers the best of both worlds: enchantment and joy in home-based learning coupled with the guidance of professional teachers. Neoliberal educational reform is perhaps at its most avant-garde in the charter school movement. With localism, resistance to bureaucracy, and critique of standardization, charter schools provide what one theorist has called "enclaves of experimentation" (see Wells et al. 1999 for an incisive analysis).

Albuquerque teacher Gael Keyes founded the Family School in 1991 with the ostensibly secular intent to provide homeschoolers a half-day of classroom experience and to offer their parents instruction in how to teach their children. Although Family School students have received some of the highest standardized scores of students in the Albuquerque Public School district, Gael Keyes reports that parents thank her not for the high test scores but for the *care and interest in our families*. Keyes serves as both principal and teacher as well as director of the math program and assistant in the parent instruction. On Fridays children do not attend school, but teachers meet for further professional training. Keyes imagined the Family School as a way to retain homeschooled children in the district (with their funding) while assisting their parents in better educating their children. In the words of one parent, *it's the best of both worlds home and public school. We need each other. I'd be fearful to take it on by myself.*[8] Mothers I talked with explained earnestly that while they often talk of themselves as homeschooling in order to complete their fifteen hours of work outside of school, Gael describes them as *family schooling*, not *homeschooling*.

On the Web site greatschools.net, one parent wrote of Family School that, although his or her children were learning a tremendous amount, *I have, at times, felt it was not the best fit our family because of the huge expectation they put on our kids to excel.* Another parent, writing of the exceptional curriculum and the heavy commitment from families to fulfill the home-based education, explained, *it also produces children that take responsibility for their own education and a community that is involved not only with their kids, but also with each other.* What emerges is the sense that Family School demands a tremendous amount from its families in order to produce achieving students.

Portraits of familial questing reveal how parents desired to live in the world with their children. Although much media and casual discussion of homeschooling focuses on *why* families homeschool, I found the concerns at play in *when* and *how* families homeschool more telling. Narratives, or life stories, may be understood as opening a window onto peoples' efforts to make sense of their life experiences.[9] Sociologist Anita Ilta Garey advocates that researchers "start with the whole" rather than "the artificiality" of the "one-point-in-time approach" to understand how women weave together paid work and motherhood. Garey's interpretive strategy focuses on women's "strategies of being" with attention to "doing motherhood." This approach shares with life course studies the interpretive reminder that decisions arise out of a demographic context—such as becoming a parent of an infant and then of a school-age child. In Garey's attention to doing motherhood, decisions about whether and how to work reflect strategies often constrained by financial demands and the marketplace to control how one wants *to be* a mother (Garey 1999:164, 18, 9, 23, 26). Similarly, decisions to homeschool involved strategies of identity construction for the family. Parents—and often particularly mothers—contemplated how they wanted *to be* as a family. Families tinkered with homeschooling identities as children grew older.

My intent is that the four portraits offered here lay bare fears and hopes that underlay the mundane work of educating and raising children in a charter school that caters to homeschoolers. While not intended to be celebratory, they do bring to the fore utopian desires. Sociologist Sara Lawrence-Lightfoot argues for the importance of studying that which is resilient and hopeful in education: "I was concerned, for example, about the general tendency of social scientists to focus their investigations on pathology and disease rather than on health and resilience. This general propensity is magnified in the research on education and schooling, where investigators have been much more vigilant in documenting failure than they have been in describing examples of success" (Lawrence-Lightfoot and Davis 1997:8). Hence Lawrence-Lightfoot's book, *The Good High School*, offers portraits that combine a commitment to aesthetics and the scientific observation to provide for a "methodological stance that might record the complex evidence of goodness," but which do not overlook the dangers, paradoxes, or unintended consequences of a particular case (Lawrence-Lightfoot and Davis 1997; Lawrence-Lightfoot 1983).[10]

Considering four families and their devotional parenting allows for an exploration of the ambivalent attachment to the Family School. Does family schooling, with its promise of flexible guidance into a practice of innovative school and home-based learning, enchant the family? Or, is it the tie binds? Perhaps, for families seeking a top-notch research-informed education for their children, Family School fully satisfies. But, for those questing for transcendence through the life of the child, the rigors of the educational demands appear to stifle enchantment.

STORIES FROM THE FAMILY SCHOOL

> Education is not after all to either teacher or child the fine careless rapture we appear to have figured it. We who teach and they who learn are alike constrained; there is always effort to be made in certain directions; yet we face our tasks from a new point of view. We need not labour to get our children to learn their lessons; that, if we would believe it, is a matter which nature takes care of. Let the lessons be of the right sort and children will learn them with delight. . . . The intellectual habits of the good life form themselves in the following out of the due curriculum in the right away.
>
> Charlotte Mason, *A Philosophy of Education* (1989 [1925])

I open with a portrait of a family that homeschooled in pursuit of the best education available for their son. A child-centered family with a working mother who herself taught, the Carlsons dedicated themselves to their son's education and a life of meaning that revolved around responsibility, family, and healthy pursuits. They typified a family for whom Family School met their ideals. They sought not enchantment through schooling but elevation through concerted cultivation of skills and healthy development of the child.[11]

When I met Kim Carlson, she staffed the literacy program at an Albuquerque Elementary School. Prior to that she taught for five years at the

Family School while her son Mark attended Family School. I met Kim in the literacy program room at the end of her school year in May of 2003. The room—bright and cheery with comfortable reading areas—housed a wonderful collection of multicultural books at different reading levels. The children, who came and went as we spoke, greeted Kim warmly, and she knew most by name. Her diction was clear without being stern and she wore a matching cotton top and pants with a beaded necklace, her blonde hair and bangs loose.

Kim became interested in teaching after Mark's birth in 1987. She came from a family of educators—grandmothers, aunts, and a mother who in earlier years homeschooled and then taught in public schools in upstate New York—and was motivated herself *to know what my son should be learning*. Kim began to work in the preschool of a friend of hers in Stockton, California. As Mark grew up, Kim *followed him up*, working with increasingly older children, until Mark entered high school and Kim returned to work as a reading specialist with elementary-age children.

Kim attributed her teaching success to her *music and art background* and her commitment to doing *cultural* projects that *incorporated social studies and science and math and language arts*. Such projects not only engaged children of diverse backgrounds but also provided a way *to get families in the classroom. You have to put things in the classroom, in the curriculum that they understand*. Kim believed that all this stood her in good stead with the Family School when her family moved to New Mexico for a work opportunity for her husband, Eric, a geologist turned project manager at a national laboratory. Kim believed that public education in New Mexico appeared doomed to repeat some of California's worst *failed experiments*. Because of this, and her belief that Mark was gifted, she explored alternative education.

Kim discovered the Family School as Mark finished first grade and thought it would be ideal for her son. Kim thought it even better than homeschooling and noted that her husband, being *very traditional*, would have had a *hard time* with homeschooling. Eric *wanted Mark to have all the advantages of public school, like being able to be on a sports team. Homeschooling it's really hard to find those kinds of things*. Nonetheless, when at Family School, Mark did miss out on *regular public school sports because of the hours*. Yet Kim felt Family School offered a top-notch education with some of the other advantages of a school. *I wanted him to have the social aspect of being with other kids, but I really felt as though we could move at our own pace and by that time I was a trained teacher.*

Despite this conscious turn from a pure homeschooling path, Kim iden-tified the family as homeschooling. For example, in explaining their Chris-tian identity as a private matter, Kim told me, *He is very active in his Sunday School and we're not ever, we've not ever been homeschoolers for religious rea-sons. We are religious, but we're quite private about it. It's never been, um, part of the education thing for me, particularly.* When I noted how she talked of herself as a homeschooler, she responded, *Yeah, because I was homeschool-ing. And I read a lot of homeschooling literature; I followed Charlotte Mason, I dearly loved her.* Although I don't know if the school founder was influenced by Charlotte Mason's philosophies—gentle Christian thematic studies with an emphasis on the natural world and observational methods—the Family School certainly resonated with such an approach. Kim explained how, even though the Family School followed a *really specialized curriculum,* she perused homeschooling resources for teaching ideas. *I always loved the things that I read in the lesson plan books that people had thought to do.* So, even though it wasn't wholly relevant, *I leaned to really appreciate home-schooling.* A local homeschooling group, as well as a bookstore catering to homeschoolers, provided inspiration for her teaching. *That's one of the best things about homeschooling for me was it gave me so many resources.*

When I met Mark shortly after my first interview with Kim, he was in the summer before his junior year in high school, long finished with his upper elementary years at Family School. An articulate and self-confident young adult with a quietly wry presence, he flourished in his local public high school. Mark didn't identify himself as having homeschooled until his mother talked with me about our upcoming interview. He recounted telling Kim, *When we did all this stuff, that was homeschooling? Ah, it was! Oh, I see. So I just figured it out now! We were just doing all these fun things and learning about them, I didn't really see them as homeschooling.*

As a teacher at Family School, Kim created numerous opportunities for parent volunteers in education. In addition to encouraging involve-ment in learning projects in the classroom, Kim directed parents to take responsibility for reinforcing basic skills such as phonics and mathemati-cal computation at home. Kim felt *what worked the best* was if the students *would do skill drills at home.* Such an approach accounted for the very dif-ferent skill levels of a first through sixth grade class. *What I expected from families in the Family School was, depending on the age and the interest of the student, that they would supplement our theme to some extent, but also that they would fill in the parts that really were impossible for us to do in the classroom.* For instance, P.E., art, and music were taught to some extent in the classroom, but with a *flexibility of schedule* families could do far more hours of them outside of school. With frequent meetings, Family School teachers monitored the home-based work of her families. *They turned in their lesson plans every week, and we went over them.* Gael, the director of the school, created *a checklist* that standardized the lesson plans to facilitate the teachers' review of the plans. Kim explained, *I figured there should be an hour of math everyday . . . and there should be an hour of language arts everyday. And then they had all day Friday besides.*

Kim taught half-time at Family School for five years. Mark was in her classroom for second through fourth grades, but in fifth grade, when he got a *little rebellious*, she *put him in a regular classroom for one year*, then Mark returned to Family School for sixth grade, but not in Kim's classroom. Kim noted that her experience being employed in a classroom half-time four days a week and homeschooling Mark differed starkly from that of most of the other parents. When Mark entered seventh grade, Kim took a year off from work. *I was tired. Family School is wonderful, but, man, it is just exhausting. I, I suppose some teachers are better at balancing it than I, but I really would work every night until one or two in the morning.* Kim explained, *It was a huge amount of planning.* Not only did Kim have work related to her teaching but also *dinner, sports, family time* in addition to Mark's academic work. Although Mark, like the other students, did not have class on Fridays, Kim had teacher meetings for one to three hours three out of four Fridays a month. During these meetings, the teachers worked on curriculum development. And meetings with the students' parents to introduce upcoming projects often took place in the evenings.

Kim and her husband Eric diligently researched different high schools for Mark. Although accepted to an Albuquerque prep school, Mark chose to enroll at the local well-regarded public school. Kim made a point of meeting all Mark's teachers ahead of time and explaining his educational background. She recounted she told each teacher, *I'm not here to see what kind of a teacher you are* but because Mark had been *homeschooled and family schooled for years and years now, and this is a big adjustment for him.* She checked his homework each night and maintained close communication with his teachers for the first few months.

As he approached his junior year of high school, Mark excelled in his classes and extracurriculars. Because he had the *shocking* experience of earning his first B in his sophomore year, the pressure of *trying to go for valedictorian* was removed. His boy choir planned a trip to Australia and he worked to finish his Eagle Scout project and continued to compete in track and cross-country. He began lessons in more advanced painting but at his mother's insistence dropped it. He explained, *it's good to be done with some of these things and not spread myself so thin.* Mark imagined that he would probably go directly to college, perhaps the University of New Mexico, and become an engineer. *That may change, I'm still thinking about architecture. That would be cool too. But I may want to be an engineer and come to work at Sandia Labs and make a lot of money and get a lot of pension . . . and do like cutting-edge research, which would be really cool.* I was impressed not only with his paintings and computerized architectural drafting but even more with his focus, composure, and wit.

Kim reflected that, even with Mark in high school, *our family still to this day revolves around Mark's activities.* Kim doubted that *I'll ever go back to a regular classroom.* Instead, after Family School, she worked on a master's degree in elementary ed at UNM intending to earn a reading endorsement for the state. She explained her commitment to half-time work: *You know, Mark has still got so many involvements that I can't really work full-time now. . . . Although I know that half-time is much more work, it still gives me flexibility.* Kim practiced her advice for other parents: *I would tell any parent that was looking for what they should do for schooling for their kids, put your kids somewhere where parent involvement is allowed and plan to be a very involved parent.*

෯෯

> Breastfeeding, with its many important physical and psychological advantages, is best for baby and mother and is the ideal way to initiate good parent-child relationships. The loving help and support of the father enables the mother to focus on mothering so that together the parents develop close relationships which strengthen the family and thus the whole fabric of society. And, LLL [La Leche League] further believes that mothering through breastfeeding deepens a mother's understanding and acceptance of the responsibilities and rewards of her special role in the family. As a woman grows in mothering she grows as a human being, and every other role she may fill in her lifetime is enriched by the insights and humanity she brings to it from her experiences as a mother.
>
> La Leche League Website (2003)

Sandra Garcia, Pueblo Indian on her father's side and European on her mother's side, married her high school sweetheart, Don, a Mexican

American from her hometown of Bernalillo, at age eighteen. Two years after they married, while still in college, the young couple had the first of three children. When I met Sandra and the children in January of 2003, the oldest, Joseph, and the middle child, Tara, attended the Family School in grades seven and four respectively, while the youngest, Stéfan, remained home with Sandra rather than enrolled in kindergarten at the Family School. When I arrived to interview Sandra, she and her children were in the kitchen doing a science experiment oft repeated in the house to explore what happens when combining oil, water, and cocoa.

The family had moved recently into a home on a small cul-de-sac off a busy thoroughfare on the west side of Albuquerque beneath the Sandia Mountains. The modest house, reddish brown wood with a decorative fence surrounding river rocks, was immaculate inside. Sandra's husband worked initially for an engineering company and then a bank, but after being laid off he worked for Sandra's parents' construction company. Sandra explained their satisfaction with his most recent and foreseeably permanent employment, *We talked . . . and decided that the whole fast-track life wasn't for us. And he traveled around. It was incredible. Incredible effort. Hardly ever home. We looked at the quality of life.* Gesturing uphill toward the Sandia Mountains, where the neighborhoods consisted of suburbs of large new homes interspersed with older established neighborhoods, Sandra acknowledged, *The houses are incredible, but there's no one home. I mean, who wouldn't want more money? But we are happy here. I get to be home.* Sandra worked mostly at night when Don could watch the children. *Several nights a week I teach at UNM. I teach child development. It's early childhood multicultural education, so it's actually the College of Ed. . . . And then I do, um, consultant work for an agency and I do workshops, basically targeted to early childhood professionals, about all different kinds of things.*

The Garcias chose this home, nestled in among mostly retired residents, not only because it didn't tax them financially but also because it distanced them from the drugs present in their previous neighborhood and put them just a few minutes from the Catholic church that her in-laws attended, where the children made their first communion. Joe attended a youth group at the church once a week. Of living in Albuquerque, Sandra explained, *I've been here my whole life, and my family is here, and my husband is one of eight, and they all have kids, and it's a huge, extended family.* When we spoke of church, Sandra quickly clarified, *We really didn't homeschool for religious reasons. . . . We don't go regularly. We go occasionally.* Rather, the spirit of La Leche League with its emphasis on attachment parenting inspired Sandra to homeschool.

Sandra's approach to homeschooling flowed seamlessly from her commitment to breastfeeding and volunteer work for La Leche League and on the board of directors for the International Board of Certified Lactation Consultations. Sandra explained, *It has really become a gift to our life, really.* Sandra began her mothering with a hospital birth yet chose a homebirth with her youngest, refused most vaccinations in recent years, and endorsed a family bed where children sleep with parents. She spoke frequently of *attachment parenting* in our interviews, alongside her commitment to multiculturalism in education and family life. While her friends and homeschooling community were ethnically and economically diverse, her work at La Leche League often found her one of a very few women of color. Sandra welcomed the phone counseling offered by La Leche League, for in this context she talked with mothers of greater racial and ethnic diversity than at the meetings themselves, which tended to be gatherings of Anglo women whom Sandra called, fondly, *career mothers.*

When Sandra began to homeschool, she schooled at home, essentially. *I was very regimented; I had a calendar; I had a schedule I followed.* Then, as she *left that behind,* they *would have days when we would just read or days when we would study geography or we would study history.* Sandra continued homeschooling her children up until Joe would have been in fifth grade. Then, because Joe *really wanted to go to the local elementary school,* despite Sandra's second thoughts, she permitted him to attend school after spring break that year. Joe enjoyed participation in the play and the history of the Civil War and World Wars I and II, but *he also got stuck with busy work that was so redundant.* The teacher yelled at the classroom everyday, and Sandra knew he wouldn't return to that school. Through friends from La Leche League, Sandra knew of the Family School. Participation at Family School—while a break from homeschooling—provided continuity with the La Leche League community. *And some of my best friends are in La Leche League. A lot of them in our group, their kids go to Family School, also. So, it is an amazing support group and it is good to be a part of.*

A half-year into the school year at the Family School, and Sandra recounted, *I love it.* Parent involvement seemed *so critical to its success.* Sandra talked about the required meetings without much ado, but spoke glowingly of the small classes, ranging from fourteen to sixteen students, and how there was always a parent volunteer in each class. The school had just finished a landscaping project in which the parents donated what

Sandra estimated to be about five thousand dollars worth of plants and supplies and all the labor. Sandra believed that, for families intimidated by the idea of homeschooling, Family School *fills that need for parents who might otherwise think I can't possibly do that that. . . . There's going to be gaps. Or parents who have that socialization concern. Or parents who are intimidated about teaching an eighth grader calculus or geometry.* In Tara's class, of about thirteen children, Sandra believed everyone had been homeschooled prior to enrollment at the Family School.

When she homeschooled the older children, Sandra admitted she did worry if there were *any gaps in their education.* Sandra had not tested Joe and Tara when homeschooling, but at the Family School they took the Terra Nova, and Joe *did very well.* Sandra acknowledged that it was very *reassuring* but then launched into a critique of the ethnocentricism of national testing, asserting, *There's no reliability. There's no validity. I mean, what are you comparing it to? You compare them to a kid in Michigan. What does that tell you? This is New Mexico. There's not any cultural issues. I mean, it's interesting how your kids end up in relation to the rest of the country, but if you have a good teacher, they can tell. These tests don't predict future performance. We are such a standardized country.* In contrast to what Sandra argued was the narrow window into education framed by standardized testing, the curriculum at Family School opened up her children's worldview.

Sandra acknowledged that planning for Joe's high school program was *something we think about a lot.* Sandra and Don thought they might apply for a scholarship for Joe to attend a private prep school. But she worried about the pressures. *The kids are so stressed. . . . I mean, he can handle it, I know he could, and I mean, if he really wants to go, and he wants to take the entrance exams, then he'll go.* Speaking of Albuquerque's two most elite private high schools, Sandra criticized the lack of diversity because *that is not true of our state or our world.* With certainty, Sandra explained, *we definitely encourage him to go to college.*

In January of 2003 the Garcia children appeared firmly on a school-based education track. But, when I talked with Sandra six months later, I was surprised to learn that they had left the Family School and returned to family-based homeschooling. A knot of concerns lay at the center of the decision to leave Family School. One unfolding school policy Sandra said they found alienating mandated that there be *"no celebration or no acknowledgment" of any kind of special occasion or holiday* at the school. An experienced proponent of multicultural education, Sandra suggested that the school acknowledge many different holidays and religious practices. *I've sent some letters and I have some stuff from a circuit court, from district court saying that if we teach about, for example, the winter holidays—if you teach about winter solstice, and Christmas and Kwanza and Ramadan and Hanukah and everything—then that's part of the curriculum. But there were a few kids from the school that did not acknowledge any holidays or any celebrations and were prohibited from saying happy birthday or anything. And I don't understand that.* Sandra concluded, powerfully, *Thereby, I think we were forced to practice their religion, by not acknowledging our beliefs. . . . We were forced, in effect, de facto, to practice their religion and we didn't think that was OK.* Sandra acknowledged that school did have to exercise some limits but argued that had the school been more inclusive of diverse religious holidays it could have effectively broadened the study of world geography and cultures.

But more difficult to assess, and particularly troubling for Joe, was what Sandra characterized as a *difference of opinion about the philosophy* of child rearing that made their participation at the school feel compromised. Sandra explained, *One family was engaging in risky behavior, and the parents were engaging in that with them, it was drugs specifically, and I have so much sympathy . . . but you have to draw the line somewhere.* Sandra described the behavior as bleeding into the classroom, with outbursts and swearing. I asked them if they felt like the school didn't draw clear boundaries around inappropriate behavior, and Joe declared flatly, *They didn't do anything about it.* Sandra explained that her family tried to talk with the other family and *tell them how they're affecting other people.* But she worried because the mother seemed *so unstable,* the situation *dangerous. And I totally felt that my kids were at risk.* Sandra believed Joe's teacher to be *frustrated.* Sandra was frustrated with the principal's response. *The principal was like, "Well, if it happens at home, we don't need to hear about that and we shouldn't."* In contrast, Joe's Tae Kwon Do instructor aggressively promoted a *healthy lifestyle* among his students that contrasted starkly with the reluctance of public school teachers to step beyond the boundary of the classroom in their exemplary roles.

So, despite its innovative program, Sandra concluded the Family School was caught in the confines of the public school system. *They're exactly what you would imagine someone who was enthusiastic about teaching would be—just incredible. But I think overall the administrative structure is really prohibitive to independent thinkers.* The school staff struggled to hold onto the Garcia family, offering Joe another classroom placement.

Yet, Sandra explained, *I couldn't see any sort of solution. . . . So we made the very difficult decision to leave—um, the biggest part was the relationship with the teacher, because she was fabulous.* Tara felt torn about leaving Family School: *It was hard. It was hard because I had some friends there, but I didn't like being there.* Sandra was impressed when the sixth graders received an exemplary statewide review on their reading skills. The school was *doing really fabulous.*

Sandra concluded, *But we made the decision, and I'm actually happy we made it. . . . So we look back at that experience with a lot of fondness and, I think, a lot of appreciation and just know that we were so fortunate to have a choice. And Family School was right there for us, and now homeschooling is even better.* The family found much more time again for extracurricular activities. Instead of pursuing scholarships to private preparatory schools in Albuquerque, as imagined earlier, Sandra and her husband encouraged Joe to enroll in a flexible computer-intensive charter school, while the younger two were taught at home by Sandra. Other students from Family School, also troubled by the situation in the older classroom, left Family School.

Sandra seemed satisfied with their return to homeschooling. She laughed at the family transformation, *because when I first started, I didn't know anybody. You know, which people homeschool? And now, I'm one of them. I'm one of those weird people, but I get a lot of family support. . . .* More seriously, she reflected that homeschooling had moved from a fringe location to more a mainstream acceptance, *and now I think there are a lot more people who homeschool. For whatever reasons.* With each of their three children's births, Sandra made increasingly alternative attachment parenting-based decisions. With her eldest, Sandra explained, *I just kind of did, what the doctor said.* Then, with the two younger children, Sandra made ad hoc decisions. Joe hardly slept with Sandra and Don when a baby but then *Tara slept with us. And Stéfan, then, he was born in our bed and never left.* One might expect that Sandra would become an unschooler and shun structure and institutionalized schooling. Yet, despite her friendship with Sandra Dodd—an Albuquerque parent and prolific unschooling advocate—Sandra characterized her interest in unschooling as brief. *There was a time when we didn't do a lot of real structured stuff.* When I first talked with her, Sandra characterized their homeschooling days as organized by *a routine more than a schedule.* With the decision to leave Family School, the Garcias returned to such a routine, with more time to *reconnect with all our homeschooling friends who are not in Family School.*

໑໑

The only thing that can help is a conversion which reaches down to our very roots and incorporates into itself the economic foundations of our social life as well. What is also being demanded of us by this revolutionary situation is, therefore, not the bourgeois attitude of unapproachability which has led to the current "liberal" separation of religion and politics, but rather, in opposition to it, a new productive meeting of religion and politics. Only thus will a postbourgeois humanity emerge that involves neither the negation of the individual nor the undialectical rejection of the bourgeois history of freedom.

Johann Baptist Metz, *The Emergent Church: The Future of Christianity in a Postbourgeois World* (1986 [1981])

When I first met Jean Johnston she was bubbling with excitement about all that Family School promised. She invited two other mothers to meet with me in her modest home in Albuquerque and warmly provided us with cookies, tea, and coffee. Her eyes sparkled with delight. She wore jeans and a Christmas sweatshirt. In December, near the close of her daughter's first term at Family School, Jean recounted how she imagined that at Family School *we can do all these other things.* The family—with daughter Kaley and younger brother Adam—could attend Albuquerque's annual fiesta celebration, ballet, and soccer activities and, most important with an afternoon school schedule, could participate in a Wednesday morning fellowship.

Jean's husband Mike, an Anglo from the Midwest like Jean, ran a Christian nonprofit to provide evangelical outreach and social services in an impoverished neighborhood, home to immigrant and Native populations. Before being introduced to Family School, Jean thought she might homeschool to provide her children with a *Christian perspective* and to ensure that her children wouldn't be *sheltered from the world.* Her children's' participation in the family ministry, with its exposure to the poverty and racism in Albuquerque, also guaranteed the children's participation in the world. *We want them to be a part of this world, we see this world and know [else] how can you be Christ in this world to others?* As a former preschool teacher, Jean valued her children's exposure to diverse children and teachers within a school. With its half-time schedule, Family School promised exposure to good teachers and diverse children with time for ministry.

Furthermore, Family School offered Jean development in her vocation as a teacher. Gail Keyes's insistence that parents not only volunteer in the classroom but also attend training workshops to facilitate their role in the children's requisite fifteen hours of outside work appealed greatly to Jean, who self-described as a conventionally trained preschool teacher. In an interesting slip of the tongue, Jean recounted telling her husband, *Now that I've taught Family School, we're not moving until after eighth grade!* In both our conversations Jean asserted a commitment to Family School that was *not for the education* but, rather, *I go there because I want to spend time with my kids and I like to teach, so the two passions just get to go together, you know?* Ironically, thus, her family's participation in Family School became painfully stressful for Jean.

When I next spoke at length with Jean, her family was in the beginning of their third year at Family School. Kaley moved from a kindergarten to second grade classroom to a first through sixth grade class. Adam—a summer birthday child—could have been placed in that class, but Jean chose a classroom geared to younger children. Jean appreciated that Family School allowed choices, since *they give you a lot of freedom.* But this decision was not without its repercussions, despite Jean's initial assertion to me that she was *willing to suffer* the extra meetings. With Adam's attendance in a different class, Jean attended six meetings per month in addition to her hours as a teacher's assistant.

When I asked Jean about her extraordinary commitment to the school, she passionately explained, *Because I love it. I love when I'm there, I love being there. I love being in the classroom, I love learning. I feel like I'm getting my master's degree, basically, you know, because the teachers are so good. And they're all, there's such a community between them, you know, they're a growing organization, they're not stagnant.* Speaking of the Friday curriculum development meetings, Jean enthused about how *it's really quite amazing, for me, as an educator.* Jean dreamed, hopefully, *I do think I might teach at some point.* Yet the difficulty for Jean as a mother and wife lay in upholding her commitment to her family and their ministry outside of Family School. Contrasting the stimulation of being at Family School with the work of fulfilling the home-based education, Jean explained, *there's the chaos, there's the dishes that aren't done, the tears from the child who gets pushed a little bit, and then there's no P.E., so you want to do soccer so they can have some running and playing and being-a-kid time, so your family's not eating together, meals, so there's a lot of issues that revolve, and you really have to be secure in what your family's about in order to make it work, you know?*

The heart of the tension for Jean resided in how to resolve personal development with family needs: *I think that, that's one of the things I've . . . I've struggled with is that I'm an educator and I love being there, but is that what's best for my family? Is it better that I stay home in the mornings and make lunch and make breakfast and get their underwear put in drawers, and . . . or is it better that I go and get challenged and enjoy that? You know, because then I get stressed, and that's not good for them.* Jean confessed that just yesterday she and her husband Mike *had the conversation . . . is this really what's best for our family? Because I was so nervous last week.* Jean granted it was only the beginning of the new school year with new challenges: how to encourage Kaley to complete her work with increasing independence and lend Adam her reassuring presence as he embarked on a new educational endeavor.

But, of even greater challenge, the family's participation in their emergent church ministry led Steve to want to move their family from their lower middle-class neighborhood, with its petty theft and automobile vandalism, to the so-called *war zone* neighborhood of the ministry itself. Jean treasured finding common ground with diverse women in a weekly Bible study. *You know, I grew up in the church, and these people have not, and they view the church very differently, and it's what the world, it's how spreading the Gospel's gonna be like. . . . I'm intrigued with what it means to be in this culture and to share Christ.* Yet Jean did not yet feel herself ready to move their family into the ministry neighborhood. *I shared his vision to be in that neighborhood, he wants us to live in that neighborhood and be a part of that neighborhood, and I went. God hasn't convinced me of that yet! He's still working on me!* Jean steadfastly declared herself and Steve *to be on the same path* as they worked in the ministry neighborhood, despite her reluctance to live *in the neighborhood.*

Jean's commitment to be a more active participant in her husband's ministry led her, however, to assume bookkeeping responsibilities the summer before we last talked. And she proudly underscored how the ministry played *a huge part of our family.* For Jean, work in health clinic, the business enterprise for Native Americans, and the family-centered ministry sparked a political transformation that unsettled her formally comfortable identity as a white middle-class American. *I would desperately love a new couch, but there are people in this world who have no couch. Is that a good use of my money? Or could I help one of those families that can't afford to feed their kids, you know?* Her critique of mainstream consumer consumption rendered Jean the only parent at the Family School she knew to question the school's drive to build permanent buildings.

Jean questioned an upcoming school levy that would garner the Family School a permanent building. *Can't we just be content with what we have? We have luxury. We have an incredibly intelligent administrator who just facilitates beautifully. Our kids are getting the best education—we have the world, you know? Why do we need a building?* Citing the cost of moving even one their portables, Jean wondered why the school couldn't remain in portables as currently located. *I think I'm the only one who's struggling with it. I kind of keep it low-key.* Jean asked a teacher to persuade her, and the teacher responded, *Wouldn't she welcome a library,* but Jean declared herself satisfied with the school's Internet access and the piles of books checked out from the public library in each classroom.

Kaley and Adam experienced a very different childhood than Jean's white middle-class Midwestern upbringing. They participated in a children's club at the ministry and spent hours running around with the other kids while their parents worked. *So they're around the people of that community, and they're around that type of being in work for God, you know?* The desire for the *kids to be exposed to that* has consumed the time available for Girl Scouts and potentially soccer as well. So, while Kaley *desperately wants to go Girl Scouts* with her friends, and Jean would *desperately love her to go to Girl Scouts,* Jean decided that it will not be feasible.

As our conversation wound to a close, Jean asked, rhetorically, *Are my kids missing the joy of childhood?* Jean described a Christian-centered life rich in meaning. *Mike and I have this huge influence over our children because of what we believe and where we're at and what his job is. Our kids very much know what we think is important in life. But . . . sometimes, with Family School, there's no time, and that's killing me. . . . There's not time just to sit and have these devotions together.* The poignancy of Jean's self-directed query near the end of our conversation lingered in my mind: *Do I have to give up Family School in order to get the other things I value? Because I'm not there for the education. I'm there to be with my family and to further nurture my family.*

෴෴

True learning—learning that is permanent and useful, that leads to intelligent action and further learning—can arise only out of the experience, interests, and concerns of the learner.

Every child, without exception, has an innate and unquenchable drive to understand the world in which he lives and to gain freedom and competence in it. Whatever truly adds to his understanding, his capacity for growth and pleasure, his powers, his sense of his own freedom, dignity, and worth may be said to be true education.

Education is something a person gets for himself, not that which someone else gives or does to him.

John Holt, *The Underachieving School* (1969)

I met Clare DeBorst at Jean's home at the end of their first term at the Family School in December of 2003. Clare, an Anglo from the Midwest, struck me as bohemian with her loose brown hair, brightly colored woven hat, and brown cords. She folded her legs under her willowy form and used her hands to outline her philosophical approach to schooling. Clare married a Hispano artist from Northern New Mexico, and they had one child, a son, Clayton. Clare became pregnant with Clay during her first and only year of teaching in a small northern New Mexican town. She acknowledged that, even beginning the education program, *I had concerns* because *of course you always know that there's so much wrong with schools.* But she hoped that she could *be a part of what changes it.*

As Clay approached kindergarten, the family moved from Las Vegas, New Mexico to Española, Juan's hometown. Clay was baptized Catholic, and in Española Clare took him to Catholic mass with Juan's Hispano family. *I never felt entirely comfortable just not being Catholic and not being sure of how am I supposed to follow along and not really knowing what to do.* When Juan *switched*—as Clare humorously put it—from *church to a Sunday bike riding ritual* she no longer felt *compelled to just take him and go, the two of us. We've never gone back to any type of church. It's crossed my mind a couple of times to check out the Quaker Friends House or the Unitarian Church. Actually there's a really great liberal Mennonite group, so I've considered going there.*

Clare imagined homeschooling Clayton but instead sent Clay to the public school in Española. Juan came *an entire family of public school educators*, among which Juan's mother helped found the public school Clay would attend. Clare remembered, *Here I am saying, "I want to homeschool my child!" They were all much to kind to say anything, but I knew that it was very disappointing to them.* Clare's mother told her, however, *"You're going to homeschool?! I don't think that's a good idea!"* Surrounded by Juan's family, Clare yielded and sent Clay to the public school in Española. She explained, *I could not let him miss out on that, you know, it was part of his heritage.*

Clayton resisted getting up for school and complained about kindergarten. Clare was still *sort of veering away from homeschooling*, however, as she felt that she *initiated* many of their conflicts. *So we were back in the mode of looking for schools rather than homeschooling.* The family moved to Albuquerque for Juan's master's degree the next year, and Clare remembered Family School from an *interesting* article in the *Albuquerque Journal*. When we talked after a few months of Family School, Clare explained optimistically, *And here at Family School, they really focus on creative thinking skills and creativity and they give a lot of choices. So I knew that this was a way for him to actually learn to love learning rather than hate school. Although he still spends time hating school, but I can tell he likes it.*

Family School promised a relationship with the teacher and a richer sense of her son's school life. *You get to be a partner with the teacher, you know, another part that really made me happy.* In kindergarten in Española, Clare recounted, *I had no idea what was going on because my son doesn't like to tell me what goes on in his life when I'm not around, so I didn't know what he was exposed to.* Not only did Family School promise a partnership with the teacher, it opened up a community of friends with other children's' parents. *It's really kind of neat to be able to be friends with other children's friends.* In December of Clay's first year only the loss of time for herself seemed a drawback. *The sacrifice is time, a little bit of difficulty for me getting back used to it, after having that year of kindergarten where I did have six hours to call my own. But last year you really don't have anything, time for anything else, so the parents really need to be dedicated.*

As the year progressed, Clare admitted that her approach to the home-based education became increasingly *makeshift*. Rather than require that Clayton read to her, she would sometimes read to him, but logged it as his out-loud reading time. She began to wonder if something was wrong with her son. *The teacher called in a child psychologist or something, and we had a meeting, and [Clay] was becoming a lot more controlling in a lot of areas of life, and I felt as though he was being more and more controlling. And, um, that developed into issues there at school, too. Um, so, you know, I started wondering, well, could this be Asperger's or, or, you know any number of things, OCD, obsessive/compulsive disorder, you know, symptoms of anxiety disorder. He had symptoms of each of those, but never all of them in order to be considered any one of them.*

Before Clay's situation at the school became so fraught, Clare enjoyed her volunteer time in the classroom, *getting to know the kids, getting to help out with their work, and, you know, that all felt kind of fun*, Yet, as the year wore on, her stress about how to do domestic chores infringed on her enjoyment of the classroom. *When you had to rush home and try to squeeze in more work and get dinner ready and, you know, that whole bit, you just felt frantic. . . . If I'm feeling stressed, the whole family is stressed.* She felt like the *emotional barometer* for the entire family. Hence how to manage her stress seemed critical to relieving the family of stress.

Clare took the leap to homeschool inspired by a book she found during her volunteer work in a local art co-op devoted to supporting fair market trade for artists in developing countries. In *Homeschooling and the Voyage of Self-Discovery: A Journey of Original Seeking*, David Albert, a homeschooling Friend (Quaker) and father of two daughters, wrote, *I don't want to overromanticize here, but homeschooling provides us with the opportunity to embrace the world through our children. We are blessed with a second chance. But to do so requires a repertoire that goes beyond what most of us experienced in our own education.* As if writing personally to Clare, he expounded further, *Don't take anything I write for granted. Test it against the light of your own experience, experimentally.*[12] Clare explained to me, *After reading the Albert book, I began to trust it more and I thought, "Well, we can try it, and if it does turn out just miserable, then, you know, yeah, we can go to the public school down the street." No problem. But I felt like I really had to give him the opportunity the book recommended; it felt like somewhere inside me that I was a little scared.*

The first year of homeschooling, Clare recounted, it seemed *as though in a way we had three separate lives. I mean, we interacted, ate together, and had family dinners and things, but really. . . . At first, I think it was a relief, and then I would start worrying a little bit, like it would seem like there would be time when all he would do is lay on the couch and read his Garfield books . . . and it was tough. . . . But, um, it seemed like . . . when I, I'd start worrying about it, he'd pop up and get involved in some big project. I started to see that there was this process of kind of sitting back, and then a bunch of activity when there's a lot of things going on, and then he'd sit back. It's almost like, and now I can see that is how he processes things, it's how he teaches himself and how he learns things.* These first two years of unschooling, Clare *let math go.* She figured *a couple of years with absolutely no math won't do too much harm because . . . either I'll figure out what to do about it, or, if he's interested in it, he'll be able to pick it up.* As Clare reflected on the transition from Family School to unschooling, she explained, *It's been a whole refocus, a shift in everything, you know, just our way of life, and I think we're still going through it.*

Unschooling—as championed by John Holt and, in his footsteps, his early publisher David Albert—critiques schooling as an alienating institutional arrangement that is counterproductive to learning. When children who have been schooled begin homeschooling, they must go through a period of detoxification as part of the process of *unschooling*. Clare, with years of successful schooling—and a former commitment to becoming a schoolteacher—understood not just Clay but herself, and even Juan, to be unlearning schooling. The irony of Juan getting further credentialed to teach in public school as Clay left school did not escape Clare. *Juan hasn't developed a repertoire of doing one thing, and I think that kind of scares him, too, because he also is sort of a schooled kind of person, and I think it's kind of scary to him, being able to let go of a wage and just do what he loves to do. So, yeah, I would really like that for him! Meanwhile . . . right after he graduated from school with a masters, he kind of was shaking his head and saying "What did I do this for? Now I have all the student loans." He could have taught art without an endorsement.*

With the departure from Family School, Clare adopted an approach to mothering more in line with earlier attachment parenting. *In the unschooling lifestyle change, it's all about respecting your children as the human beings that they are and treating them as you would any other adult in your life and any other person that you love. You don't have to be domineering or constantly telling them what to do, you just have to have the trust and faith in them that they know and you don't have to control everything.* Not needing Clayton to wake early for school, Clare realized he could set his own bedtime. Before, she had required that he go to bed when she did, but with unschooling there seemed no reason to enforce this. Clay stayed up until ten o'clock to midnight and then rose between seven-thirty and ten in the morning.

Clare *heartily doubts* that Clay would ever want to return to school. But, after exploring with him *why he wanted to go*, she would help him to find a school. Perhaps more interestingly, Clare held *doubts* that Clay would go to college. She explained, *I do know that, um, homeschoolers and unschoolers are very welcomed at university; they've found that they make excellent college students because they really want to be there. . . . I don't know that he would really do well in college.* Thinking of Clare's commitment to being well schooled, I asked her if this was a change in orientation for her. She responded, hesitantly, *I think I never really thought about it before and I think that now I would approach it differently with him, about it being not a place that you go to get a degree but a place where you can go to learn things you want to learn that, you know, maybe you need guidance for or you know somebody to stimulate your mind in that direction. Um, and not focus on "then you will go there to get a degree."*

Clare's dreams for their family were similarly unconventional. She hoped that when Juan paid off his students loans he could forgo his *wages* from work in the public school system. *He would really love it if he could just earn a living as an artist.* Although they *talked about trying to buy a house this last year* when interest rates were low, they decided to wait. *In a way it's nice to kind of have mobility and the idea that maybe we can go between places. . . . That will give us time to see if he'd really like to stay in this job.* Juan's public school employment seemed less a calling than a means to a distinctly factory-sounding *wage*. Clare wanted Juan to be able to follow his passion and work and live as an *artist*. Meanwhile, the family rented a modest house and lived simply to allow them the lifestyle they desired.

Despite how satisfied Clare seemed with homeschooling, she believed attendance at Family School an important step in the journey to unschooling. *If I had never sent him to school I would have tried schooling at home, and it would have turned into a battlefield. I don't know, I can't say that we never would have never ended up unschooling because maybe I would have found out about the options and/or just naturally fallen into it— I don't know. But I think I would have had a lot more fears around it.* In her accounting of their experience at the Family School, despite the fraught relationship with Clare's teacher and the threatening consultation with the school psychologist, Clare held steady to her positive assessment of Family School as a good school with incredible parent involvement.

When I asked Clare about her short-term goals for the upcoming second year of unschooling, she responded, *Mostly just our relationship. I find that when we reduce stress, in addition to the whole respect issue, we are so much less stressed.* Clare focused on her relationship with Clay *as central to the joy of parenting. Um, it really reminds me more of the times when he was an infant and we were doing the attachment parenting. There's been more of a closeness, and I find myself wanting to focus more on that and on our relationship, and whereas, you know, when he was going to school, it was just a different sort of thing. I found myself not particularly liking being a parent so much.*

THE TIE THAT BINDS

Sociologist Penny Edgell has reported church leaders as identifying time as "the problem" for families in their congregations (Edgell 2000). Joining

Family School seemed to pose as great—or greater—a challenge as con-
gregational participation for families. Enrollment at Family School only
exacerbated the time crunch for mothers already stressed by the rigors
of scheduled time. Sociologist Sharon Hays documented the ascendancy
of what she called the ideology of "intensive mothering in the latter half
of the twentieth century. This ideology which cuts across race and class
has bolstered a psychologically and labor intensive mothering" (Hays
1996). While Family School offers a half-day of structured education and
a guided home-based supplement, school demands consumed the lives of
many families, especially mothers. One mother I interviewed reported
the Family School director as *straightforward* in her message to families: *If
you want this education, you're going to have to work for it.*

In 1989 sociologist Annette Lareau wrote about how some middle-
class children's educational career is compressed into a two-person career
where mothers oversee children's education. This helps us to understand
the intertwining of mothers and children in the educational trajectory at
Family School. Yet, in this more neoliberal era, parents are also striving
to minimize risk, but finding their self-management constrained. Anxiety rebounds at every step.[13] The expectations for the well-educated child
emphasize skills of adaptability and flexibility. In considering how "the
child, family, and community are sacred sites of modern politics and social
welfare systems," educational theorist Thomas S. Popkewitz has described
a typology of cosmopolitism at the turn of the new millennium that ide-
alizes a "lifelong learner who is problem-solving, active, flexible and self-
managed. The parent is pedagogicalized as a surrogate teacher whose
child-rearing practices follow the didactic principles of teaching children."
Schooling prepares the learned to operate within the networks embodied in the "knowledge society" of "globalization" (Popkewitz 2003:35, 37).
Family School not only emerges out of a neoliberal milieu, but, with its
curricular emphasis on self-governance, produces neoliberal subjects of
both parents and children.

Thus, Family School seems the archetypical school at the turn of millennium, with the turn to neoliberal institutions in which consumers act
as managers and advocates for the self. For many parents it is a step-
ping-stone on the risk-assuming path to self-education. In Sandra Garcia's words, *They have a defined curriculum, but they are so flexible I couldn't
imagine any other classroom being that flexible.* Yet families drawn to the
Family School for its apparent flexibility began to chafe at the confines
of not just its curriculum but its time demands too. For the Garcias, the

appeal of Family School faded as Sandra felt their lives constricted by the demands of the institution. After the independence of homeschooling, she begrudged the school's resistance to celebrating religious holidays. All Saint's Day, with its honoring of those who have passed, *is real important to us. But, there's no room in Family School for that. . . . All those celebrations, it's such an important way of keeping peace in the world, understanding other people's religions and their cultures.* Sandra characterized Family School as *still cookie cutter . . . especially about holidays and celebrations in particular.*

Sandra began motherhood as a college student with a hospital birth and an acceptance of vaccinations and most conventional approaches to parenting. When I met her, her youngest had been born at home, and she no longer availed the children of all vaccines. While she acknowledged the relative flexibility of the Family School, she still felt constrained by time regimentation. Her sensibility seemed more aligned with that of La Leche League and its emphasis on following the child's inclination. Although La Leche League refrains from advocating for homeschooling and other social movements or concerns, a review of a recent homeschooling guide posted online by a league leader notes, *Homeschooling is a compelling topic for many LLL members. LLL encourages parents to make their own decisions, following their hearts. While not part of our philosophy, homeschooling can be a natural extension of that self-determination for some families.*[14] Sandra seemed to be guiding her family toward a spiritually reflexive experimentation that moved them out of state schooling, with its institutional compromises into a homeschooling journey that emphasized purity of practice, especially for the last-born child.

Families do opt out of Family School when overwhelmed—or, even more simply, dissatisfied—with its demands. For example, Clare spoke at length of her own *unschooling*. She resisted her own pedagogicalization, first as a teacher, then as a parent. When adaptive measures didn't work, she removed her son from not just school but a track that assumed college and a salaried job as the goal. Serendipity figured centrally in Clare's story as she described last-minute enrollment at the Family School and her many attempts at homeschooling. Seeming rather agentless, she nonetheless steered her family on a path that filled her family life with equanimity, mindfulness, and flow.

Listening to Clare, I was struck by how descriptions of her ideal days resonated with Mihaly Csikszentmihalyi's formulation of "flow experiences" in which one loses one's sense of time while doing an activity perfectly matched to one's skill level. Over a decade ago, sociologists Mary

Jo Neitz and James V. Spickard argued that attention to flow experiences attuned to some otherness move us closer to understanding religious experience (Neitz and Spickard 1990). And, indeed, Clare's homeschooling guru, David Albert, cites Csikszentmihalyi's *Flow* as the single most important book for homeschooling families published in the last decade (Albert 2003:115).

In contrast to Clare, Jean sounded more like the stressed technical contractors described in Stephen Barley and Gideon Kunda's *Gurus, Hired Guns, and Warm Bodies: Itinerant Experts in a Knowledge Economy.* These contractors—often formerly full-time employees of sole companies— sought the rewards of autonomy and self-reliance as they believed themselves to be wresting "control of their time from greedy institutions." Yet Barley and Kunda report that an empirical cross-check and their interviews reveal "an interesting discrepancy between what contractors say and what they do. On one hand, our informants almost universally claimed that they were free to allocate their time as they desired. On the other hand, with few notable exceptions, most contractors minimized downtime, worked long hours, and took little time for themselves" (Barley and Kunda 2004:221, 241). Technical contractors and family schooling mothers share a work practice that necessitates continual adaptation, learning, and flexibility within the neoliberal institution, leaving many stressed and exhausted.

Family School detracted from Jean's involvement in her family's ministry and seemed to disenchant their home. She wondered despairingly, *When we have this crazy schedule, you know, what are we doing? What am I teaching my kids? . . . that I want to be with them but am going to bark at them? And that's not any good.* In contrast to her degrading stress at home, Jean reveled in her role as lifelong learner at the school. Jean's experience—despite her being a committed stay-at-home mother—seemed startlingly similar to those working mothers in Arlie Russell Hochschild's *The Time Bind* who welcomed the relative calm and self-assurance of their workday in contrast to the stress of their home lives managing chores and children in the hours surrounding the workday (Hochschild 1997).

What I came to think of as the *costs of flexibility* were illuminated in these mothers' stories. Jean chose to place her second child in another classroom to maximize his learning experience, but this choice was not without its costs to the family equanimity, as the school-based demands on Jean doubled. Clare entered eagerly into being *a partner* with her son's teacher, but found herself bound by the ties of such partnership. Despite her efforts to treat the home-based work requirements with ingenuity, she felt consumed by the demands of Family School. Those families choosing Family School to obtain an excellent public school education seemed most at ease with the demands of the program. Yet, when time for ministry or a spiritual equanimity guided the decision, the flexibility offered by Family School proved inadequate. The rigors of the home-based education became the tie that binds.

Kim exemplified a parent-teacher well satisfied with the Family School. In an intriguing twist, Kim spoke most often of her experience with Mark as homeschooling. Despite having been a teacher at the Family School, she did not distinguish between family schooling and homeschooling. And in our interview her son, Mark, reflected that he hadn't realized how much homeschooling he had done. Unlike the other mothers portrayed here, Kim was not enthralled by the possibility of a purer homeschooling life. I wondered if she felt more comfortable describing the homework assigned by the Family School as homeschooling, because, unlike the other mothers I described, she wasn't troubled by whether to leave the Family School for homeschooling. Rather, her worries were wrapped up in school choice, where to enroll her son, and when.

Kim words aptly described the potential costs of flexibility: *Everybody comes from a different place into the Family School. Some people come from homeschooling and love it because it's less responsibility for them and because they're starting to have a little trouble with discipline, you know, starting to have their kids not wanting to do the work, and you do have teacher reinforcing "you must do the work," so that's good. Other families come from homeschooling and find that the structure is just way too rigid for them. And one of the things that they learn at that point that they really like about homeschooling is they can do it when they want to. . . . And you just can't do that when you're in a public school classroom. You have to be there on the days that the classroom is there. That's hard for some homeschooling parents.*

Families engaged in school choice often appear at first glance to be self-interestedly "shopping around"—similarly to how women's seeking meaningful birth experiences might appear. Yet, as feminist Barbara Katz Rothman has argued, "In the human struggle to create meaning, to live meaningful lives, we all use the tools we have at hand. The battle is to use those tools and not be used by them." We may be trapped in a consumerist system, but we need not "dismiss the politics, the values, the morality of the issues" engaged as choices are made (Rothman 2004:283, 287). Mothers do much of the work creating and implementing choice programs, and, like social reform movements of earlier years, they often speak the language of "community effort" and "social mission." And, some mothers—like Jean—find meaningful careers in school reform efforts (Stambach and David 2005:1649).

For many mothers, shopping around for an education for their children is anything but spiritually vacuous. Rather than relegate their spiritual ideals to a congregation or ministry, these mothers come to the Family School with the hope that it would offer a flexible arrangement amenable to infusing the entirety of their domestic worlds with meaning. Strikingly absent from their consideration of schooling is criticism of the Family School based on its curriculum. In this milieu of ambivalent attachments, Family School has complicated their lives with its rigorous requirements for homeschooling on top of participation in a demanding organization. For many families the Family School seems a spiritual way station. It opens the door to independent homeschooling but itself becomes the tie that binds. Last I heard, Jean remained there, ambivalent but further committed to her husband's ministry. Clare's domestic questing led her to a dismissal of school and an unschooling identity.

Political scientist Hugh Heclo has written recently on the modern incli-nation to distrust institutions. Academics and the larger public alike are inclined to think critically "about" rather than from "within" institutions. Heclo acknowledges that institutional thinking "resists" utopianism, but argues "it raises[s] us up without flattering us" (Heclo 2008:128). Yet those that leave the Family School take away a different set of lessons, we must assume. Homeschooled children, we can speculate, learn that participa-tion in the dominant society need not be assumed and that one can move in and out of society's large bureaucracies, even refashioning them into new forms. Homeschooling practices articulate easily within a neoliberal society, wherein much of public life is privatized. Consumers of social services—at the nexus of private and public—learn to maintain their own records, be they financial, medical, or educational. Whether they are conservatives dreaming of a revitalized Christian nation or downshifters imagining a community of persuasions untainted by alienating bureau-cracies, for many families homeschooling opens up possibilities for a vaguely imagined but inspired social communion.

And, in homeschooling, as I hope these ethnographic portraits have illustrated, many parents recount what might be described in sociologi-cal terms as a reenchantment of the family. Schooling, with its struc-tured time, disciplining of the child, and bureaucratic organization, is often experienced as stealing away wondrous presence and enchantment from not just the child but the family. Families may be drawn to charter schools such as the Family School for the promise of a professionally validated curriculum and pedagogy and yet still be lured to abandon all formal schooling in favor of homeschooling. The parents encountered here describe Family School as offering *so many resources, just incredible* teachers, *a really specialized curriculum,* but they also disparage *the administrative structure* and its cost to *independent thinkers* and bemoan how *the sacrifice is time,* even in a half-day of schooling. These same parents speak passionately of the turn to homeschooling as *being a gift* that nurtures the *joy of childhood.* Disenchantment with regimentation and structure, even in the most specialized schools, gives way to the enchantment of unfettered time and childish pleasures in learning through homeschooling.

These homeschooling parents are deeply engaged with the intertwined philosophical and pragmatic concerns resulting from the decision to take responsibility for their children's education out of the hands of professionals. Not only does homeschooling—as a lifestyle in Giddens's sense[15]— offer the potential to evade the dangers of schooling, it opens up a more pleasurable way of parenting. While homeschooling may intensify mothering, it offers, rather like participating in new religious movements, the possibility of parenting in an experimental and enchanting way. Similarly to artists struggling to understand and express the spiritual in a context outside of established religions, homeschoolers often seem compelled toward creative spirituality.[16] By not ceding their children's education to public or private schools, parents experience themselves as engaged in meaningful and creative moral decision making.

NOTES

I thank the Spencer Foundation for support of the fieldwork on homeschooling as well as the School for Advanced Research for ongoing support of my scholarly work and the Social Science Research Council for collaborating with SAR in this joint institutional exploration of religion and the secular. Finally, thank you to all the participants in this collaborative endeavor for their feedback, especially to Courtney Bender and Ann Taves for their spirited and sustained commitment to this edited volume.

1. Gary Cross contrasts the "sheltered innocence" of days past to the "wondrous desire" of contemporary childhood. Parents and caregivers delight in giving

gifts and orchestrating experiences to feed the wondrous desire of children in contemporary consumer culture.

2. In writing a history of British occultism, Alex Owen (2004:12) admits he is less interested in religion per se than in what he calls the "broader purchase of enchantment" in the Weberian sense.

3. I use the word *special* in the fashion of Ann Taves (2009:26–29) to designate a "thing set apart" from the ordinary. For many parents, childhood is a time set apart to be attended carefully. Specialness does not insist upon the thing being religious, but marks it with a special status. And, of course, this special status may be disputed by others.

4. Leigh Eric Schmidt (2005) offers a history of the depth and variety of American spirituality.

5. Robert Wuthnow introduces the idea of tinkering in *After the Baby Boomers* (2007).

6. These reports, "Homeschooling in the United States: 1999" (2001) and "1.1 Million Homeschooled Students in the United States in 2003" (2004) may be downloaded at the National Center for Education Statistics Website.

7. Although in the larger project I met homeschooling fathers, often former teachers, at Family School I encountered mothers as the primary homeschooling parent. There was, nonetheless, an interesting way that both descriptions of the Family School and talk among these mothers was often couched in talk about gender-neutral parents. Elsewhere I consider the gendered politics of homeschooling. Let me simply note here that just as women struggle with aligning flexible work with family life, so did the women presented here struggle with making homeschooling fit into the trajectory of their husbands' careers.

8. Gael Keyes thanked me for my interest in Family School, but declined apologetically to talk with me, as she hadn't time for an interview. This information comes from an article on the Family School by Gran 2003.

9. Sociologist of religion Nancy T. Ammerman (2003) writes of the centrality of life stories in contemporary society to religious identities. Such narratives, as she astutely cautions us, rarely address religious concerns alone, but are inflected with multiple expert discourses. Ammerman directs us to listen for the conditions under which these amalgamated narratives touch upon transcendence.

10. Sara Lawrence-Lightfoot writes of her commitment to uncovering evidence of goodness in *The Art and Science of Portraiture* (Lawrence-Lightfoot and Davis 1997:9). Her study of *The Good High School* (1983) exemplifies not only the artistic and empirical nuances of the portraiture method but also how a commitment to evidencing goodness may document the downside of even the best.

11. In *Unequal Childhoods,* Annette Lareau (2003) writes of the labor middle-class parents undergo to cultivate the skills of the child. Yet, as we will see in the case studies that follow, mothers at Family School often felt repelled by the scheduling demands of the school.
12. Albert suggested that a seeking orientation to parenting, suggested by Friends but not exclusive to them, might allow children to flourish in their educational journeys (2003:16–17).
13. Aihwa Ong (2009) shaped my thinking about neoliberalism in a colloquium at the SAR.
14. Melissa Noble (1998), in a review of Mary Griffith's *The Homeschooling Handbook,* points to the "naturalness" of homeschooling for attachment-based parenting as advocated by La Leche League. Other ethnographers have noted La Leche League nudges mothers into homeschooling. For insights into these connections, see, for example, Blum 1999; Stevens 2001; Bobel 2002.
15. I use *lifestyle* with some caution for, while true to Giddens's work (1991) in how it captures the consequentiality of everyday decisions in shaping a life, it is fraught with pejorative meaning when viewed from the perspective of cultural conservatives. And, regardless of political standpoint, taken out of a scholarly context, it often implies an inconsequentiality in relation to weighty ethical concerns. I intend otherwise. As Giddens and many scholars of the family have argued, decisions about how to organize one's family are significant and prescient of political concerns.
16. Characterizing artists as "disciplined seekers," Wuthnow (2001) explores those who are often perceived as being the spiritual vanguard at a time when many in society reject institutional religion as adequate for an understanding of the divine mysteries.

REFERENCES

Albert, David H. 2003. *Homeschooling and the Voyage of Self-Discovery.* Monroe, ME: Common Courage.

Ammerman, Nancy T. 2003. "Religious Identities and Religious Institutions." In Michele Dillon, ed., *Handbook of the Sociology of Religion,* 207–24. Cambridge: Cambridge University Press.

Barley, Stephen R., and Gideon Kunda. 2004. *Gurus, Hired Guns, and Warm Bodies: Itinerant Experts in a Knowledge Economy.* Princeton: Princeton University Press.

Bauman, Kurt J. 2002. "Home Schooling in the United States: Trends and Characteristics." *Education Policy Analysis Archives* 10, no. 26. http://epaa.asu.edu/epaa/v10n26.html (accessed May 16, 2002).

Blum, Linda M. 1999. *At the Breast: Ideologies of Breastfeeding and Motherhood in the Contemporary United States*. Boston: Beacon.

Bobel, Chris. 2002. *The Paradox of Natural Mothering*. Philadelphia: Temple University Press.

Cross, Gary. 2004. *The Cute and the Cool: Wondrous Innocence and Modern American Children's Culture*. New York: Oxford University Press.

Edgell (Becker), Penny. 2000. "It's a Matter of Time: Exploring the Relationship Between Time Spent at Work and at Church." Hartford Institute for Religion Research. http://hirr.hartsem.edu/research/family_Becker-time.html (accessed November 14, 2006).

Family School Reviews. 2009. http://www.greatschools.com (accessed on January 22, 2009).

Fawcett, John. 1740. "Blest Be the Tie That Binds."

Frankenberry, Nancy. 1996. "The American Experience." In Peter H. Van, ed., *Spirituality and the Secular Quest*, 102–26. New York: Crossroad.

Garey, Anita Ilta. 1999. *Weaving Work and Motherhood*. Philadelphia: Temple University Press.

Giddens, Anthony. 1991. *Modernity and Self-Identity: Self and Society in the Late Modern Age*. Stanford: Stanford University Press.

Gran, Susie. 2003. "Uncommon School, Uncommon Success." *Albuquerque Tribune*, May 30.

Hays, Sharon. 1996. *The Cultural Contradictions of Motherhood*. New Haven: Yale University Press.

Heclo, Hugh. 2008. *On Thinking Institutionally*. Boulder: Paradigm.

"Historical Excursus Into the Present." In Marianne N. Bloch, Kerstin Holmlund, Ingeborg Moqvist, and Thomas S. Popkewitz, eds., *Governing the Children, Families, and Education: Restructuring the Welfare State*, 35–61. New York: Palgrave MacMillan.

Hochschild, Arlie Russell. 1997. *The Time Bind: When Work Becomes Home and Home Becomes Work*. New York: Metropolitan.

Holt, John. 1969. *The Underachieving School*. New York: Dell.

La Leche League. 2003. "La Leche League's Purpose." http://www.lalecheleague.org/purpose (accessed on February 3, 2003).

Lareau, Annette. 2000 [1989]. *Home Advantage: Social Class and Parental Intervention in Elementary Education*. Lanham, MD: Rowman and Littlefield Publishers.

—— 2003. *Unequal Childhoods: Class, Race, and Family Life*. Berkeley: University of California Press.

Lawrence-Lightfoot, Sara. 1983. *The Good High School: Portraits of Character and Culture*. New York: Basic Books.

Lawrence-Lightfoot, Sara, and Jessica Hoffman Davis. 1997. *The Art and Science of Portraiture*. San Francisco: Jossey-Bass.

Mason, Charlotte M. 1989 [1925]. *A Philosophy of Education*. Original Homeschooling Series, vol. 6. Wheaton, IL: Tyndale House.

Metz, Johann Baptist. 1986. *The Emergent Church: The Future of Christianity in a Postbourgeois World*. New York: Crossroad.

Mumford, Lewis. 1962 [1922]. *The Story of Utopias*. New York: Viking.

National Center for Education Statistics. 2001. "Homeschooling in the United States: 1999." http://nces.ed.gov/pubs2001/HomeSchool/ (accessed May 13, 2005).

—— 2004. "1.1 Million Homeschooled Students in the United States in 2003." http://nces.ed.gov/homeschool/ (accessed February 16, 2005).

Neitz, Mary Jo, and James V. Spickard. 1990. "Steps Toward a Sociology of Religious Experience: The Theories of Mihaly Csikszentmihalyi and Alfred Schutz." *Sociological Analysis* 51, no 1: 15–33.

Noble, Melissa. 1998. Review of *The Homeschooling Handbook*, by Mary Griffith. http://www.lalecheleague.org/lllleaderweb/LV/LVOctNov98p105.html (accessed February 3, 2003).

Ong, Aihwa. 2009. "The Middle Classes: A Global Perspective." School for Advanced Research Colloquium Series, April 1.

Owen, Alex. 2004. *The Place of Enchantment: British Occultism and the Culture of the Modern*. Chicago: University of Chicago Press.

Partridge, Christopher. 2004. *The Re-enchantment of the West: Alternative Spiritualities, Sacralization, Popular Culture, and Occulture*. London: Continuum International.

Popkewitz, Thomas S. 2003. "Governing the Child and Pedagogicalization of the Parent: A Historical Excursus Into the Present." In Marianne N. Bloch, Kerstin Holmlund, Ingeborg Moqvist, and Thomas S. Popkewitz, eds., *Governing Children, Families, and Education: Restructuring the Welfare State*. New York: Palgrave Macmillan.

Rothman, Barbara Katz. 2004. "Caught in the Current." In Janelle S. Taylor, Linda L. Layne, and Danielle F. Wozniak, eds., *Consuming Motherhood*, 279–88. New Brunswick, NJ: Rutgers University Press.

Schmidt, Leigh Eric. 2005. *Restless Souls: The Making of American Spirituality*. New York: Harper San Francisco.

Shanahan, Suzanne. 2007. "Lost and Found: The Sociological Ambivalence Toward Childhood." *Annual Review of Sociology* 33:407–28.

Stambach, Amy, and Miriam David. 2005. "Feminist Theory and Educational Policy: How Gender Has Been 'Involved' in Family School Choice Debates." *Signs* 30, no. 2 (Winter 2005): 1633–58.

Stevens, Mitchell L. 2001. *Kingdom of Children: Culture and Controversy in the Homeschooling Movement*. Princeton: Princeton University Press.

Taves, Ann. 2009. *Religious Experience Reconsidered: A Building-Block Approach to the Study of Religion and Other Special Things*. Princeton: Princeton University Press.

Wells, Amy Stuart, Alejandra Lopez, Janelle Scott, and Jennifer Jellison Holme. 1999. "Charter Schools as Postmodern Paradox: Rethinking Social Stratification in an Age of Deregulated School Choice." *Harvard Educational Review*. http://www.edreview.org/issues/harvard99/1999/su99/s99wells.htm (accessed September 20, 2001).

Wuthnow, Robert. 2001. *Creative Spirituality: The Way of the Artist*. Berkeley: University of California Press.

—— 2007. *After the Baby Boomers: How Twenty- and Thirty-Somethings Are Shaping the Future of American Religion*. Princeton: Princeton University Press.

MIND MATTERS

Esalen's Sursem Group and the Ethnography of Consciousness

JEFFREY J. KRIPAL

In the last analysis magic, religion and science are nothing but theories of thought; and as science has supplanted its predecessors, so it may hereafter be itself superseded by some more perfect hypothesis by some totally different way of looking at the phenomena—of registering the shadows on the screen—of which we in this generation can form no idea.
—Sir James Frazer, *The Golden Bough*

In the absence of a theory of some kind, it is very difficult to accept the facts.

—Eric Weiss, *The Long Trajectory*

AMBIGUOUS SIGNS: "BENT OUT OF SHAPE"

A flurry of signs.

It is the second week of December of 1998, December 6–11, to be precise. A small collective of about a dozen intellectuals—neuroscientists, psychologists, historians, human potential authors, and philosophers—are meeting at the Esalen Institute in Big Sur, California, in order to discuss "the survival of bodily death." The phrase comes from Michael Murphy, who cofounded Esalen in 1962 with the late Richard Price and called this present group together.

The phrase also functions as a sign, however, since it clearly points to what will become the ultimate inspiration for this group, the two-volume *Human Personality and Its Survival of Bodily Death* by the British classicist Frederic W. H. Myers (1843–1901) (Myers 1903).[1] Always the lover of Greek and Latin, it was Myers who coined the term *telepathy* in 1882 in order to theorize the common "coincidence" of a family member seeing or dreaming of a loved one saying good-bye or otherwise signaling his or her death within a few hours of that death, regardless of the loved one's distance from the visionary or dreamer. It was the emotional bond that counted for Myers, that somehow transcended space and, in some cases, apparently even time. Hence the term: "feeling" (*pathos*) "at a distance" (*tele-*). Myers also wrote poetry, published a significant amount of literary criticism, was a close friend and colleague of William James, and was one of the key founding figures of the London Society for Psychical Research (or S.P.R.). The latter group was founded in 1882 by a group of Cambridge intellectuals in order to study psychic phenomena rigorously and scientifically.[2]

In some ways, one could say that this was an attempted regeneration of the S.P.R. The guest list that fall was impressive enough. It included, among others, Adam Crabtree, a practicing psychotherapist, historian of psychology, and recognized expert on dissociation and multiple personality disorder;[3] Bruce Greyson, the founding editor of the *Journal of Near-Death Studies* and presently the Carlson Professor of Psychiatry in the Division of Perceptional Studies (DOPS) at the University of Virginia; Michael Grosso, a Columbia-trained philosopher and painter who writes bold books about human potential themes and is active in the philosophical counseling movement; Edward Kelly, a Harvard-trained neuroscientist from DOPS; Emily Williams Kelly, a historian of psychology and expert on Frederic Myers, also associated with DOPS; and Charles Tart, a psychologist from the University of California, Davis, who has played central roles in both American parapsychology and the creation and development of transpersonal psychology.

Tart, a scientist with a comedic flare and a most remarkable utility belt that even Batman might envy, is known to be good at naming things. To take the most famous example, he almost inadvertently inserted the phrase "altered states of consciousness" into American English through his edited volume of the same name back in 1969. Hence the movie *Altered States* (1980)—which, in yet another signification, appears to be partly based on Michael Murphy's metaphysical novel *Jacob Atabet* (1977)— begins with a brief homage to Tart and two other psychologists, Arthur Deikman and Robert Ornstein.[4] Tart would also give the classic out-of-body experience an early acronym that would "come back to punish me," as he puts it: people began coming up to Tart after lectures in order to tell him about their OOBE's (pronounced "oobies"). Happily, another form finally stuck—the OBE. Tart tried his hand at naming again when he dubbed this little group "Sursem." His reasoning was innocent enough. He was simply looking for a convenient marker for e-mail and a Web site. Tart assumed the "Sur" stood for (Big) Sur. Others assumed it stood for Sur(vival). An ambiguous sign.

Perhaps the most potent, and certainly the most playful, signs, however, occurred around the dining table in the lodge that week. These began the very first night, on Sunday, but took on their most dramatic shape— literally—when the group gathered for breakfast on the last day of the meeting, Friday. Greyson was eating cereal from a bowl, which he finished and pushed into the center of the table. The conversation wandered on, until Greyson happened to notice his spoon. Oddly, the thing had bent over in the middle, and what was once a concave spoon was now a half-convex one. In Crabtree's description, "it looked like a tongue hanging down." No one saw it happening. No one saw a thing, until, that is, the thing was no longer a thing, but a sign.

But a sign *of what*?

Different witnesses had different readings. According to both Crabtree and Grosso, Greyson was mostly just embarrassed, although it was well known that he had had similar experiences in the past. Indeed, Greyson describes experimenting with spoons with Grosso the night before. He describes the spoons getting warm under his fingers, but he does not think anything necessarily paranormal was involved, and he is sure Grosso was better at it than he was. He does, however, remember telling Michael that night that what would really be impressive is the bowl of the spoon reversing itself, which is of course exactly what happened the next morning.

Crabtree, a trained psychotherapist skilled in the interpretation of dreams and a whole spectrum of unusual states, from hypnagogia and hypnosis to multiple personalities, trance, and possession, saw in these events, and especially in the spoon-become-tongue, a certain playful expression of the group's inner dynamic, a kind of group unconscious at work, as it were.[5]

Ed Kelly's reading is more conservative and skeptical. He doubts that anyone who was there "would be willing to say unequivocally that what seems to have happened actually did happen right there and then at breakfast." For him, this is simply more evidence of "the typical

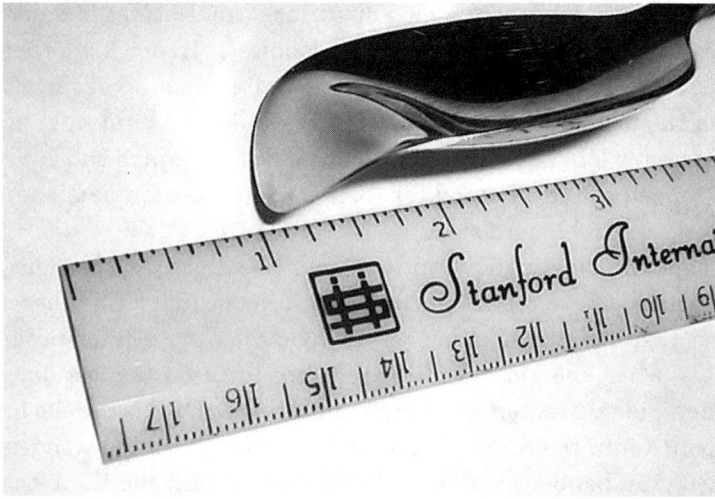

FIGURE 7.1

uncertainties of 'field' observations." Hence his commitment to the controlled laboratory. For all we know, someone could have slipped the spoon in Greyson's bowl while no one was looking.

Tart's reading is different again. He laughs at the latter possibility and sees in the bent spoon "a wonderful mischievous or trickster quality" of the paranormal, as if to say: "Hey, folks, you don't know as much as you think!" Tart's response to being laughed at by a piece of dinnerware? He immediately pocketed "the sacred Sursem spoon," along with three "control spoons," and took them back to his lab for further study (figure 7.1).

Michael Grosso, whose life has been richly punctured by paranormal events, had yet another reading (Grosso 1997). He was sitting at the far end of the table when all of this happened. He prefers to put the scene in a broader context. He confirms that Greyson had softened and twisted some silverware earlier in the week and explains that, in fact, many of the Sursem participants were playing around with the strange art during the week, half in jest, half in earnest.

At one point, probably on Thursday night, Grosso picked up a spoon that Greyson had only slightly bent earlier in the week. As he stroked the handle, the spoon just "melted" under his finger and "became like butter." He easily twisted it into what he calls "a vermicelli" until the thing broke in half. In an attempt to remember this bizarre event and integrate

FIGURE 7.2

its uncertain meanings into his life, Grosso took one of these halves and turned it into art: he used it in one of his metaphysical paintings, which he then named "The Imp of the Perverse" (figure 7.2).[6]

There was certainly nothing either subtle or questionable about the melting, twisting spoon for Grosso. He knew that no one planted the thing, as he was holding it in his hand and personally witnessed it, at point-blank range no less, melt under his own stroking finger. The mind-to-matter effect was patently obvious and essentially unanswerable. Indeed, it was *so* obvious and *so* unanswerable that he experienced it as impish and perverse. Grosso's reading also resonates deeply with Crabtree's. "I definitely associated it with the group." The spoon that he had "reduced to melting butter for a few seconds," after all, "had already been paranormally affected by Bruce." In essence, Grosso is suggesting, like Crabtree, a kind of unconscious group effect—a paranormal power that is neither an alleged fraud nor a special privilege of a few gifted souls, but rather a concrete, *physical* expression of the social body, in this case the Sursem group.

In short, a sociology of the impossible.

☙☙

I do not want to make too much of the melting spoons.[7] And yet I suppose I need those spoons, if only to catch the reader's attention. I suspect that is what the spoons wanted to do too. I wonder about Crabtree's tongue associations, Tart's observations on the well-documented trickster quality of the paranormal, and Grosso's observations on the whole event's impish or perverse nature.[8] Was the spoon trying, like the Sursem group, to speak an impossible truth? Or, better yet, was it sticking its tongue out, as if to mock the very attempt to measure and objectify that which, in the end, is not an object and so cannot be measured? Certainly the bent spoon could be measured, as Tart's photo of it next to a yellow ruler shows. But the mechanism that bent it? Was this a "mechanism" at all?

I invoke the spoon scene, then, not to dwell on the outrageous, much less to suggest that it has constituted some central concern of the Sursem group (it has not), but to treat it as a teasing, intentionally absurd sign of my own thesis, namely, that the present models of the human being dominant in the social sciences and humanities are seriously inadequate to the kinds of weird, uncanny, anomalous experiences that pepper, indeed *define*, the history of religions.

Who, *really*, are we?

I do not want to bend spoons, then. I want to bend minds. I want to bend the academy's present, almost absolute, commitments to materialism (everything is finally reducible to matter, brain, economic production, social class, and so on) and contextualism (there is only local context, identity, or "difference," and any observation of sameness is nothing more than a "grand narrative," a power move, a form of "neocolonialism," and so on). These commitments, I want to suggest, may be perfectly functional, even crucial to what we do as intellectuals, but they also need to be more flexible. They need to bend. I suppose I want my materialism and contextualism even to melt a bit sometimes.

I also want to remind my readers that materialism and contextualism *are* metaphysical commitments, and that neither ontology can be established beyond serious doubt. Scientisms and present enthusiasms aside, the truth is that we simply do not know what consciousness is. I find the current attempts to understand the brain, and with it consciousness, as a kind of biological computer (hence all that language of "processing" and "systems") deeply flawed and, historically speaking, incredibly naive: has not every other technological advance produced a similar flurry of models, none of which have ever proved adequate?

Then there are the humanities and the social sciences. Although they too are hardly ready for a discussion of consciousness as consciousness (instead of as culture, politics, economics, or some very particular political identity), these fields of inquiry understand the hermeneutical or mirrorlike nature of consciousness quite well. Hence all that "mirror-talk" of reflexivity, reflection, speculation (the mirror or *speculum*), and the fundamental paradoxes of what has come to be called the hermeneutical circle—essentially, a looking into the mirror.

Such real humanist and social scientific insights, however, generally restrict themselves to a purely rational or discursive level. What we really need to do is stop looking in the mirror and figure out how to get *behind* the mirror in order to see the seer and observe the observer. I recognize, of course, that this is pure heresy in our present intellectual context, where any such direct knowledge of consciousness, much less the true nature of reality itself, is completely denied as completely impossible.

But this is hardly a new or strange idea, much less an impossible one, in the broader historical context of my own field, comparative mystical literature, where phrases like "the eye with which I see God is the same eye with which God sees me" and remarkable phenomenological descriptions of pure consciousness beyond the usual limitations of culture and context are utterly commonplace. Do we really think that the Buddha intended his teaching about the impermanence of the social self, the universal nature of suffering, and the blissful dissolution of both in a timeless, spaceless *nirvana* only for north Indians of his own generation? The truth is that all forms of Buddhism, like so many other religious traditions, assume a shared psychic unity. Indeed, most religions make little or no sense without just such a conviction.

Now we can certainly deny such a psychic unity for our own political or intellectual commitments. But what, it seems to me, we cannot logically do is a. deny in principle that such a psychic unity exists, and then b. claim that we are deeply engaging religion. We may be engaging a whole lot of very important things, but religion is not one of them. To even begin to engage the truth claims of the religious traditions at their best (as opposed to their worst), we must engage the principle that the human species shares common forms of consciousness, agency, and moral integrity, and that these are transmissible and replicable and not simply epiphenomena of local political, economic, and social practices.

Many intellectuals, of course, working from their own metaphysical commitments to contextualism and materialism, want to deny all this, since, obviously, there can be no such thing as consciousness as consciousness. There are only the infinitely recursive reflections in the mirror of language, history, culture, and identity. There is only the mirror. There is no behind the mirror.

Or is there?

What follows is a brief ethnography of the Sursem group toward this question. I will proceed in three parts: 1. a brief history of the group and its intellectual lineages; 2. a synopsis of the group's most significant publication to date, the aptly titled *Irreducible Mind*; and 3. a personal reflection on what the Sursem group might offer our present discussion of secularism and religion and "what really matters."

History and Lineages

Put in its immediate historical context, the Sursem group is the latest expression of the Esalen Institute's half-century search for an ontological foundation adequate to the modern world and its remarkable scientific advances. Hence the very first brochure, sent out in the fall of 1962, featured on its cover a calculus equation from Bertrand Russell and an Indian lotus, the classic Hindu and Buddhist symbol of pure consciousness. The message could not have been clearer: the institute was about the "integral" synthesis of East and West, of reason and mysticism, of science and spirit. Although the cover of that first brochure was silent on the matter, another dualism would also come to focus the institute's energies and seminars, that of soul and body or, framed in more contemporary terms, mind and matter. I have written about this elaborate history elsewhere (Kripal 2007a).[9] Here it is perhaps enough to point out that the Sursem group sits in this half-century lineage of intellectuals trying to forge a new, more integral worldview.

As a social institution, the primary format of the Sursem group is the five-day invitational seminar organized and hosted by Esalen's Center for Theory and Research (or CTR), the formal name for the institute's research and development arm. As an official branch of the institute, the CTR goes back to 1998 (the same year Sursem began), when it was organized as such, but the invitational symposium has in fact functioned as one of the centerpieces of Esalen from the very beginning. Indeed, the first seminars of the earliest brochures were symposia of sorts in that they routinely featured two or three speakers on a particular topic. But they were hardly invitational conferences. They were entirely open to any interested person willing to pay a small attendance fee and they generally lasted only one, two, or three days. The more extended invitational, private, five-day model took time to develop.

Murphy considers the first real invitational conference to have taken place on January 29–31, 1965, when Esalen sponsored a discussion of one of the hottest political issues of the day, Sino-American relations. Entitled simply "America and China," the event was open to the public and advertised as "[a] critique of American policy toward Red China." It featured not one or two or three speakers, but six, including such names and institutions as the double Nobel-prize winner Linus Pauling from the Center for the Study of Democratic Institutions in Santa Barbara and Dennis Doolin of the Hoover Institute at Stanford.

Things developed gradually from these beginnings. A standard five-day format evolved over the next decade and was solidly in place by the mid-1970s, when the practice hit something of a peak with almost twenty invitational seminars taking place each year. Although expenses have pushed down this number to around five or six per year, the format has remained more or less the same. Twenty or so individuals are invited to discuss a specific topic. Participants show up on Sunday afternoon and are welcomed to the Big House, where most of them will also be staying. This stately structure sits at the edge of a cliff on the north end of the property. It was originally built by Murphy's grandfather as the family vacation home, but it has since been refashioned, with a grant from Laurence Rockefeller, into what might be described as an intimate convention center.

Sunday night is dedicated to social icebreaking. Morning, afternoon, and evening sessions then follow Monday through Thursday. The meals are taken in the lodge, and participants are given free time to enjoy the baths, arrange for a massage, or enjoy the grounds and local Big Sur community. Traditionally, Thursday dinner functions as a kind of capping event and is served more formally in the Big House's main meeting room by Esalen's own chefs.

Four- to five-year commitments to a particular topic are not unusual, although most will only see one or two meetings. In other words, a typical conference series at Esalen might extend over a number of years and involve the participation of between twenty and seventy-five individuals (depending how much overlap there is from year to year). By far, the majority of these participants come from academic institutions or have advanced graduate training in some field of study. The PhD is as common in the Big House as the water running through the pipes. In essence, the CTR is a think tank.

The topics of the invitational conference events range widely, but they usually revolve around a particular set of ideas or a broad comparative theme whose integral nature (at once rational and mystical) has rendered the idea too anomalous and too technical for either the traditional halls of the academy or the popularizing bookstores. The first five series of the CTR, for example, were: 1. subtle energies (that is, the widely reported nonordinary energies of *chi, prana, psi*, and so on); 2. the ethical urgency of ecological and sustainability issues; 3. the philosophical implications of evolutionary theory, led by the philosopher Jay Ogilvy and molecular biologist David Deamer; 4. transformative practice (an Esalen code term for psychophysical practices that help actualize the human potentials that are said to lay dormant in each of us); and 5. postmortem survival research (the Sursem group).

As the years ticked by, the survival series was the only one of these first five to survive. Two other topics were eventually added: 1. the history of Western esotericism, an explicitly joint American-European venture that I codirected with Wouter Hanegraaff of the University of Amsterdam; and 2. contemporary fundamentalist challenges to scholarship on religion, which quickly morphed into the psychodynamics of global fundamentalism under the direction of the career diplomat and political psychology theorist Joseph Montville and the rubric of "the Abrahamic Family Reunion." At present the CTR is also heavily involved in major outreaches to China on the subject of economics and Russia on the subject of transpersonal psychology and human potential. As such examples make clear, the invitational conferences tend strongly to go after "the big picture," and they often constitute themselves as forms of social and intellectual activism.

The Sursem group, which has been meeting now for thirteen years (1998–2011), is a perfect example of this kind of big thinking.[10] As already explained, the series was initially dedicated to the question of postmortem survival. The series participants, however, quickly chose not to attack this question quite so directly. Instead, they chose to address an even more basic issue: What is the relationship between mind and matter? Their reasoning to focus on the mind-body problem was simple. If mind is *produced* by matter, as in most present neurological models, then mind necessarily ends when the brain stops functioning, and none of us will survive bodily death in any form. If, however, mind is *transmitted* or *filtered* or *permitted* by the brain, as a kind of biological TV or radio (or, as in Kant's categories of understanding and his famous distinction between the noumenon and the phenomenon), then it is quite possible that mind does not end when the brain-receiver stops working and, in Myers terms now, human personality, or at least some aspects of it, may actually survive bodily death.

And so they began to arrive. At the top of Murphy's list was Ian Stevenson, who then held the Carlson Chair of Psychiatry at the University of Virginia (funded by Chester Carlson, the inventor of the xerox process). Stevenson, now deceased, was probably the most impressive researcher in the survival studies field at that time. His work is very much worth dwelling on for a moment, as his University of Virginia colleagues have played major roles in the history of the Sursem group, and the group cannot really be understood without first understanding something about Stevenson and his successors.

For over forty years, Stevenson studied what he came to call CORT or Cases Of the Reincarnation Type. His methods were primarily ethnographic, that is, he traveled around the world and worked with local translators in order to interview families whose children claimed to remember previous lives. He also worked closely with autopsy reports and criminal records, since, as we will see, many of these cases involved violent deaths with significant and very helpful paper trails.[11] In book after book, Stevenson documented and analyzed these impossible narratives from his collection of hundreds, then thousands of case studies of past-life memories, particularly in Hindu and Buddhist South and East Asia (India, Sri Lanka, Thailand, and Burma), Shiite Lebanon, Turkey, West Africa, and Northwest

America.[12] As of 1997, he had collected 2,600 reported cases of past-life memories and had published 65 detailed reports on individual cases, including the phenomenon of unlearned languages and a massive and eerily suggestive study of 225 cases detailing what he calls "the biology of reincarnation," that is, the phenomenon of birthmarks or birth defects as physical "marks" from a previous life's violent ending by knife, rope, or bullet wound (Stevenson 1997a).[13] This last study extends to almost 2,300 pages of text.

I strongly recommend reading this volume (or, to be more reasonable, some large chunk of it), as these two thousand pages plus will quickly dispel much of the nonsense written about parapyschological literature, namely, that it is somehow always fraudulent, sloppily collected, imprecise, unreliable, or—perhaps the ultimate dodge now—"anecdotal." There are certainly major interpretive, philosophical, and cross-cultural issues that could be discussed here, but these false stereotypes are not among them. Indeed, even arch-skeptics like Carl Sagan and Sam Harris have recognized that Stevenson's material cannot be easily dismissed. Sagan, who also thought that telepathy and mind-to-matter interactions deserved more scientific attention, was persuaded that Stevenson's material is worth examining further (Sagan 1996:302). Similarly, Harris's otherwise famous ideological reductionism generously leaves open the possibility that psychic phenomena may have something to teach contemporary neuroscience. He even writes of "some credible evidence for reincarnation" in his rationalist manifesto, The End of Faith (Harris 2005:232n18). He means Ian Stevenson's work.

Anthropologist and cultural psychologist Richard Shweder has also made a special point to flag Stevenson's work as unusually suggestive. "What are we to make," he asks with reference to this corpus, "of those cases in which a child claims to have memory of a former life in another family at another time and many of the details in the child's account of that family turn out to be accurate?" The facts, as he rightly notes, seem "resistant to either genetic or environmental explanations" (Shweder 1991:61). That is putting it mildly. But it is also putting it correctly. Again and again (and again), Stevenson minutely documents "cases of the reincarnation type" in which people, generally young children, appear to remember extremely accurate, detailed, and otherwise unavailable information about a former life that is then confirmed empirically and objectively.

Through his entire database (still being coded, organized, and analyzed by his colleagues), Stevenson isolated what he calls "four universal features" found in every cultural complex that he studied, including, inter-estingly enough, Europe (where the cases were much more rare but still present). These four universal features are: "an early age (usually between 2 and 4 years) of a subject's first speaking about a previous life; a slightly older age (usually between 5 and 7 years) when the subject stopped speaking spontaneously about a previous life; a high incidence of violent death in the previous life; and frequent mention of the mode of death in the child's statements" (Stevenson 2003:250).

The pattern of a violent death is particularly interesting, as it correlates strongly with two other features of the database: the violent birthmarks and the high number of male memories. The data, in other words, is gendered. The Virginia group, particularly in the voice of Jim Tucker, another Sursem participant associated with DOPS whom I witnessed give a presentation on the CORT data at the 2007 Sursem meeting, offers this gendering a most provocative and eerily plausible interpretation. In almost any culture, Tucker pointed out, males are much more likely to die violent deaths than females. He further speculated that a life suddenly or violently ended is much more likely to be remembered (much like a dream, I would add, out of which one is suddenly awakened) than a life that ends naturally and is sufficiently processed (like a gradual awakening from a long night's sleep). Which raises, for me anyway, another paradoxical or mirror question with respect to the afterlife well known in comparative mystical literature: Which is the sleep? And which the awakening?

Ian Stevenson, however, could not come to that original Sursem conference, so he sent his colleague, Emily Williams Kelly, in his place. Kelly was a natural pick for the series, since she had written her dissertation at the University of Edinburgh on the psychology of Frederic Myers (Cook 1992). She chose that university because no one in the States was willing to work with her on this subject, and because Edinburgh was emerging as a kind of global center for parapsychology since the writer Arthur Koestler had endowed the university toward this same end.

Kelly's husband, Ed, tagged along to the first conference in 1998, "to carry the bags," as he puts it. Actually, however, he too had considerable experience in the field. After completing his PhD at Harvard in psycholinguistics, Ed had done a stint at J. B. Rhine's parapsychology lab in Durham, North Carolina, before getting involved in EEG research in the electrical engineering department at Duke University and moving into neurophysiological studies at the University of North Carolina, Chapel Hill. By carrying his wife's bags into the Big House, Ed was effectively reentering the field of his first intellectual love: psychic research, as broadly conceived by Myers, James, and contemporary figures such as Ian Stevenson and Michael Murphy.

The Transmission Thesis and the Meaning of Meaning

Within a few years, the man carrying the bags was appointed series leader and eventually led the effort in editing Sursem's most lasting testament to date, the eight-hundred-page edited volume entitled *Irreducible Mind* (parapsychologically oriented scientists and intellectuals often write immense tomes, perhaps because they know what they are up against). Everyone with whom I spoke about this volume confirmed that it is very much "Ed's baby," that Ed Kelly was the main intellectual force behind the book, that the spirit and core arguments of the book were Ed's.

Here is how the book came to be.

Crabtree had brought Frederic Myers's *Human Personality* with him to the first meeting. He began each morning session by reading a passage from Myers to the group. Everyone there admired Myers, even though they had not come to Esalen to talk about him or his work. Ed Kelly, having read both Myers's *Human Personality* and Murphy's *The Future of the Body*, playfully asked Murphy if he might be Myers reincarnated. It was a joke, but also a quite accurate observation about intellectual resonances and spiritual lineages.

At end of the second year's meeting, in the spring of 2000, Ed made a proposal to the group to engage in a book project that would appear in 2003, on the hundredth anniversary of Myers's *Human Personality*. More specifically, he proposed they write a book together that would take Myers as its starting point in order to address what the fields of psychology have done with these issues over the last century. Such a project might also function to signal a clear intellectual link between the S.P.R. and their own Esalen group. Despite their best intentions, they overshot that centenary by four years.

Close enough.

Intellectually speaking, it would be difficult to overestimate the importance of Frederic Myers for the Sursem group. There are other major intellectual lineages at work here, of course. James, Bergson, Whitehead, Aurobindo (a twentieth-century Indian freedom fighter become metaphysical writer and guru), and Murphy himself are probably the most cited. One key expression of some of these multiple influences is the metaphysical writing of Eric Weiss, whose Sursem-sponsored book manuscript, *The Long Trajectory*, synthesizes Whitehead and Aurobindo to offer a new model of transphysical worlds and their importance for thinking about postmortem survival and reincarnation.

The much-discussed participatory effect of human observation in quantum physics (a hermeneutical insight if ever there was one), particularly through the work of the quantum theorist Henry Stapp, also plays a major role in the Sursem group. Stapp has now written two major books and multiple technical essays on the philosophical implications of quantum mechanics and QM models of what he calls the mind-brain interface, particularly via the interpretation of quantum mechanics advanced by mathematician John von Neumann. Von Neumann's interpretation puts conscious will at the very center of quantum mechanics via the initial probing question and the manner in which the experiment is intentionally set up, what he calls "Phase 1" (Stapp 2007, 2009).

More stunning still, Stapp argues that consciousness has a physical effect on matter itself through the ability of mental concentration to focus the Zeno effect of quantum "smearing" within the brain and so collapse the quantum wave functions occurring between the synapses into discrete and desired ends. For Stapp, all this leads to the inescapable conclusion that physicalism can no longer be sustained as an adequate ontology—some dualist or interactional dualist model of mind/brain must be entertained as the most likely candidate. In short, materialism has effectively imploded within the most fundamental and privileged form of modern science—theoretical physics. Although I am certain not everyone in the Sursem group understands all of technical details here (I don't), the philosophical implications are certainly clear enough, and Stapp's presence in the group an absolutely central one.

But Myers is clearly the *origo et fons* of the group. The group especially admires what they call his *synoptic empiricism*, a particularly broad approach to the study of consciousness incorporating both first-person and third-person data that was all but lost in the narrower behaviorist and neurological approaches of the twentieth century. By synoptic they also mean an approach that is at once empirically grounded and theoretically bold. They intend something along the lines of what James called a *radical empiricism*. This was James's notion that, if we are going to be truly empirical in our thought, we must examine *all* forms of human experience, even and especially those that offend our present categories.

Nothing can be dismissed as unimportant or too strange. If we are going to be empirical, well, then let's be empirical. Here an *experience* is as important as an *experiment*.

The group often cites J. B. Rhine's parapsychology at Duke University as a historically important methodology that was not sufficiently synoptic and radical in its empiricism. In the hands of Rhine, Ed Kelly observes, the field suffered a kind of "identification with the aggressor," that is, with the reductive models of academic psychology (Kelly et al. 2007:584). The results were predictable enough. Rhine's methods, with their restrictive reliance on artificial laboratory settings and statistical methods (Zener cards, random number generators, bored or tired undergraduate volunteers), did produce some statistically significant data, which has never really been answered, but it also ended up missing almost entirely the strongest empirical evidence, the dramatic real-world appearances of psychic phenomena that seem to be usually (not always) invoked as responses to traumatic contexts. Staring at abstract shapes on playing cards and suffering the physical terrors of a car accident are simply two different things, and it is the latter, not the former, that most effectively calls forth psychic events.

Charley Tart captures the same insight in the form of a joke, with his definition of academic psychology as "the study of college sophomores by former college sophomores for the benefit of future college sophomores" (Tart 2009:133n1). And, indeed, I have also heard Tart joke that what Rhine really figured out how to do in his parapsychological lab, with all those bored sophomores, is how to *extinguish* psi. Study it enough with these methods, and you can be sure it will disappear. It's as if all one had to understand a mirror were a hammer.

Irreducible Mind is dedicated to two figures: Ian Stevenson and Michael Murphy. The Kellys understand Stevenson and Murphy to be among the few true descendants of Myers, James, and other nineteenth-century founders of psychic research who took a similarly broad-based empirical and theoretical approach to important human questions. They also point out that, again like Myers, Murphy has lived his entire professional life outside academia, even as he has embodied what they call the best of that world, a combination of an intellectual openness and a critical rigor that will not allow him to accept any cheap solutions. Ed in particular points to some of the "new age bullshit" he sees represented at Esalen and notes that he believes Murphy has grown impatient with much of this and is now looking for a more solid and lasting accomplishment. "The CTR is his vehicle for this," Ed observes, "and *Irreducible Mind* is meant to be a part of this legacy."

It is certainly true that Murphy has grown impatient, although *impatient* is probably not the best word after fifty years of almost preternatural tolerance and literally millions of spent Esalen dollars. With the survival question in particular, Murphy has grown increasingly frustrated with what we might call faith and belief, neither of which the Sursem group are particularly interested in affirming. As Murphy once put it to me: "The older I get, the more impatient I get with religion." Certainly the survival group certainly does not want yet another religious model of the afterlife. Like Myers, they operate with the conviction that the question of the afterlife is not simply a conceptual or metaphysical question; it is also an *empirical* one. The group thus believes that the survival of the human personality after death is simply the most extreme case of the question of mind and matter and that this question can and should be explored empirically as well as philosophically and speculatively.

In terms of its actual content, *Irreducible Mind* argues that the best model available to us at this moment to explain *all* the empirical evidence is not the standard, indeed orthodox epiphenomenon thesis (mind is a surface product of the brain and its neural net), but the transmission thesis developed by Myers and James and subsequently reimagined by authors like Henri Bergson and Aldous Huxley (mind as transmitted through the brain, which acts as a kind of filter or suppressor). The authors also insist on looking at the full data of human functioning, even and especially in its most extreme or "rogue" forms, which they argue—very much with Myers and James—constitutes our best evidence of what consciousness really is behind and beyond its surface functions as social ego, cognitive function, culture, and, yes, religion.

With this "transmission" or "filter thesis" in place, consciousness now appears as a fundamentally irreducible mind or trans-subject that is not produced by the brain but filtered or transmitted through it in massively complex ways, involving everything from neurobiology and psychology to culture and language. Just as it is both foolish and futile to go looking for "little people in the TV set" by taking apart the transmission tube and electronics, so too it is both foolish and futile to go looking for human consciousness in the organic technology of the brain. It is not there, although it does exist, again much like the TV signal that surrounds us at all times but needs a very special receptor to be picked up and broadcast as a meaningful experience. In essence, then, the brain is a super-sophisticated biological organ that has evolved precisely to pick up and socialize these transcultural transmissions.

The group is perfectly aware that the metaphors of the "filter" and "transmitter" are crude ones that will no doubt be replaced by more adequate analogies in the future. Crabtree is especially unhappy with the implied dualism, and both Ed Kelly and Eric Weiss, partly inspired by Henry Stapp, are moving toward a Whiteheadian world of "occasions" or "experiences" as the base building blocks of reality. The reader should not imagine a traditional spirit-body dualism at work here, then. The group is much more drawn to ontological theories that might be described as panpsychism, neutral or dual aspect monism, or nondual interactionism, that is, models that understand mind and matter as *always* joined, as two sides of some deeper cosmic coin, if you will.

Taken as a whole, *Irreducible Mind* advances a sustained, empirically based critique of contemporary cognitive psychology and mainstream neuroscience as it moves toward a more adequate philosophy of consciousness. By "more adequate," they mean more capable of embracing the full range of empirical data, including and especially the phenomenology of anomalous psychic, paranormal, and mystical experiences. Put much too simply, what this project involves is a firm rejection of psychology's monistic materialist assumptions, its historically naive commitment to computational models of the mind, and its consistent conflation of correlation and causation, whereby a specific neurological location of brain activity is taken to be definitive evidence for a local materialist cause of that mental event.

Obviously, if these authors are even approximately correct about the nature of human consciousness and the brain, the implications for the study of mind, consciousness, and religion border on the unimaginable.

෴

The Sursem group is now moving into a second stage of questioning, one that involves more the speculative construction of actual psychophysical causal mechanisms and possible postmortem scenarios. The question is this: given the empirical evidence we now have, what would a reasonable model of mind-matter interactions look like? And, more to the point, what sorts of possible afterlives do these models suggest? Most basically, are we talking about something that resembles the single-life model of the Western religions (single birth, single life, single death, judgment, followed by some sort of eternal state), or perhaps something more along the lines of what the Asian religions have imagined (multiple births, lives and deaths toward some sort of liberation or enlightenment)? Or something entirely different?

It should be pointed out here that, from Myers to Murphy, it is the transmigration models that carry the most weight, but not because of their traditional foundations or any appeal to religious authority. Rather, it is because of their resonance with evolutionary theory. Essentially, for thinkers like Frederic Myers, Michael Murphy, Eric Weiss, and Michael Grosso, reincarnation becomes the most likely ontological mechanism through which the human spirit evolves into higher and higher forms. Theirs, in other words, is fundamentally an evolutionary spirituality. Murphy is an interesting and key example here. Long agnostic on the question of reincarnation, he has recently relinquished this public position as "cowardly" and "dishonest." Basically, he came to the conclusion that the evidence as a whole simply could no longer support an agnostic position. Something somehow reincarnates. Of this he is convinced.

This has long been implicit in his thought, however. For example, when I pressed him four or five years ago on the differences between the one-life models of the Western near-death experience and the multiple life models of the Asian religions, he already had a clear answer for me then. He pointed out that the modal Western near-death experience does not seem to be a true death experience. It is rather a *near*-death experience. The researchers consistently stand in a consensus that the person does not actually die in these events. The past-life memories, on the other hand, clearly represent, or at least claim to represent, a death that was carried through. In other words, the easiest way to synthesize both the Western and the Asian models for Murphy was to adopt a model of reincarnation and assume that the Western near-death experiences are just that—*near*-death experiences, which, if carried through, would have led to a next-life scenario. This, of course, is very much what we find in Stevenson's literature, where such Cases Of the Reincarnation Type have been freed from local culture by a comparative method, discovered in all parts of the world, and recentered in a single species within a scientific methodology.

Obviously, such a conclusion does not constitute a ringing endorsement of religions, Asian or otherwise. Quite the contrary, Murphy's fiction and analytical works are filled with serious criticisms of these traditions' common antiworld and antibody attitudes, all of which flow into their postmortem models as well. Moreover, he is intriguingly insistent that the soul is never without a body of some sort, that is, that mind and matter are *always* united. For Murphy, in other words, the possibility that the always embodied human personality lives on again and evolves into another form of life, here in another birth or on some other plane or dimension, is a possibility that finally escapes all previous religious models and explanations.

That is Murphy's position. The Sursem group has yet to arrive at a consensus on this. Indeed, at one point, the group separated into two different working groups, "the empiricals" and "the theoreticals." The two groups met both separately in the fall and winter and together in the spring in the original "synoptic" spirit of the Sursem group. Now back together again, theirs is an attempted synthesis of third-person laboratory science committed to objectivity, falsifiability, and replicability and first-person, humanistic modeling dedicated to theory building and a rich phenomenology of the rogue. One can easily observe at least three major mediating methodologies between the empiricals and the theoreticals— 1. comparison, 2. classification or natural history, and 3. ethnography. One can also observe one central and still unresolved issue—the question of semiotics or the science of meaning.

COMPARISON AND CLASSIFICATION

The disciplines and cultures of science now evoke in the imagination elaborate technologies, multimillion dollar labs, and mathematical equations that no lay reader can hope to understand. In such a highly specialized, hypertechnical climate, it is often forgotten that Darwin's theory of descent by modification, or natural selection, required no such equations, no such labs, and was the direct result of comparative and classification methods. Comparing this beak to that beak, this wing to that limb, Darwin classified his field data toward a grand theory of the natural world that turned out to be, well, true. He knew nothing of DNA or genetics for that matter. He was a comparativist through and through, and his primary intellectual method was classification.

ETHNOGRAPHY

This simple truth bears directly on the Sursem group and its central ideal of synoptic empiricism. Frederic Myers, after all, was a trained classicist, accomplished poet, and literary critic who, with his Cambridge colleagues, anthropologized their own British society in order to collect thousands of deeply personal narratives of crisis and apparition toward a classificatory system that produced categories like the subliminal and the telepathic. For William James, at least, Myers was a kind of "taxonomic genius" whom he compared to Darwin (Kelly et al. 2007:584). Similarly, the methods of Ian Stevenson were primarily ethnographic, comparative, and narrative. He traveled all around the world for four decades collecting and classifying stories of unusual human experiences until they fell into patterns from which he could draw tentative, but plausible conclusions. Similarly, again, Michael Murphy takes up Darwin's comparative methods in his *The Future of the Body* in order to look at different types or "species" of extraordinary human experience and arrive at his own classification schema and theory about metanormal functioning. Clearly, this is where the empiricals and the theoreticals of the Sursem group meet—in the practices of comparison, classification, ethnography, and narrative collection and analysis.[14]

SEMIOTICS

Where the empiricals and theoreticals have not yet come to any clear resolution is on the meta-issue of meaning. Henry Stapp, for example, often explains that in quantum physics the deepest nature of reality is understood to be organized around bits of information, that is, around meaning. Adam Crabtree, a deep reader of Charles Sanders Peirce (often considered to be the founder of modern semiotics), also speaks eloquently of meaning as the fundamental structure of anomalous experiences like precognition and synchronicity, including his own. It is not at all clear, however, whether these two men are referring to the same processes, that is, whether they agree on the meaning of meaning.

In terms of the history of the philosophy of language, it is easy to identify at least two major understandings of representation: one premodern model that we might call a performative, occult, or magical theory and one modern model that we might call a purely referential or semantic theory. In medieval philosophy these two theories of language went under the general names of realism and nominalism and aligned themselves with the more general worldviews of Platonism and Aristotelianism.

In different versions of the former—as we find, for example, in Plato's philosophy of Ideal Forms, in many forms of religious ritual, in occult and mystical traditions like ancient Hermetism and medieval Jewish Kabbalah, and in certain radical theories of poetry—reality itself is understood to be linguistically structured by words and letters. Accordingly, language becomes a privileged means to pass back and forth between the visible and invisible levels of reality. Correspondences, moreover, are intuited between signs and the realities that they signify, and so language—more precisely, the correct, highly specialized ritual, revealed, or inspired use of language— is understood to literally effect, *to be*, that which it signifies. Here representation is quite literally re-presentation, a "making present again" of the signified. Such a world of correspondences was famously captured in the Hermetic sound bite "as above, so below," which we might translate for our own purposes here this way: since the human being is a microform of the macroform of the universe, the human body and human mind—of which language is one of the most intimate expressions—can, in very special cases, reflect and refract the most fundamental structures of the cosmos.

In the latter, modern model, language is understood to have no direct connection to reality; its letters and words are considered to be purely arbitrary cultural constructions. Accordingly, it is used in simply semantic ways, as culturally agreed on signs that point to but do not participate in that which they signify. The Hermetic dictum of "as above, so below" is reread here as nothing more than a naive projection of human nature and human consciousness into the natural world, where neither in fact exists in any form. Religious referents are "reduced" to purely human referents—brain processes, social processes, political processes, wish fulfillments, false forms of consciousness, and so on. Certainly there is nothing human, nothing essentially meaningful "out there."

So which is the meaning of meaning in quantum physics and, more to my present point, paranormal experience? Should we be realists or nominalists? Platonists or Aristotelians? Should we be Hermetic mystics or secular reductionists? Or, perhaps most interesting of all, some artful integration of both?

Very roughly speaking, modern mainline science has aligned itself with a purely semantic or nominalist philosophy of language. Much as they did with respect to subjectivity and mind, the sciences have denied language any real place or role in the nature of things. What sets apart the sciences is the fundamental conviction that *the world is made of numbers*, not words or letters, that mathematical, not linguistic, structures are constitutive of the deepest dimensions of the universe, and, perhaps most radically of all, that these numbers can be used to predict and manipulate the workings of nature and matter itself.

Interestingly, the only academic disciplines that still preserve any echo of the older magical view of language are the humanities. Indeed, what sets apart the practices of the humanities is the fundamental conviction that *the world is also made of words*: language and culture precede and are constitutive of the most intimate dimensions of human experience and meaning and these worlds of meaning are everywhere and always human creations that can be deconstructed and created anew. A few humanists take such a line of thought further still and suggest that reality may in fact behave differently in different cultural zones, that different languages produce different reality posits, as it were.[15] Regardless, the reality of the humanist is seldom, if ever, mathematically certain or predictable in a laboratory fashion. Reality for the humanist is not an objective reality to reflect and describe fully. It is a participatory reality to engage and realize through social, ritual, and linguistic practices.

There are two deep complications here, however. The first is the phenomenological fact that the very structure of many paranormal experiences replicate, perfectly, the old Hermetic dictum "as above, so below," which now becomes, in Eric Weiss's insightful transform, "as without, so within" (Weiss 2009:10). That is to say, in a paranormal experience the external world "without" behaves as if it were in intimate dialogue, as if it "corresponds," to use the old occult language, with a subjective state of mind "within." The paranormal, in other words, appears to operate more or less exactly like a real-world magical event or Hermetic transform.

The second complication boils down to the truly embarrassing fact that there is another modern correspondence theory, a magical or Hermetic language that exists only inside the human mind but turns out to conform, precisely, to the deepest structure and most distant behavior of the cosmos. We call that Hermetic language mathematics. As already noted, for the modern sciences, reality *really is* structured according to this universal language, and this language, moreover, can be used to manipulate the behavior of the real anywhere at anytime. No one has really explained this utterly bizarre fact. For God's sake, what *is* a number? And how can these purely abstract signs, these Ideal Forms that exist only in our heads, turn out to explain and map out the entire history of the universe?

Sociologist of religion Peter Berger beautifully summed up these semiotic conundrums in an appendix to his classic analysis of religion, *The Sacred Canopy* and, in the process, offered us the possibility of a both/and approach to the meaning of meaning:

The sociological theory must, by its own logic, view religion as a human projection, and by the same logic can have nothing to say about the possibility that this projection may refer to something other than the being of its projector. In other words, to say that religion is a human projection does not logically preclude the possibility that the projected meanings may have an ultimate status independent of man. Indeed, if a religious view of the world is posited, the anthropological ground of these projections may itself be the reflection of a reality that includes both world and man, so that man's ejaculations of meaning into the universe ultimately point to an all-embracing meaning in which he himself is grounded. . . . Put simply, this would imply that man projects ultimate meanings into reality because that reality, is, indeed, ultimately meaningful, and because his own being (the empirical ground of these projections) contains and intends these same ultimate meanings.[16]

In other words, "as above, so below." And then a most provocative act of comparison:

The case of mathematics is rather instructive in this connection. Without any doubt mathematics is a projection onto reality of certain structures of human consciousness. Yet the most amazing fact about modern science is that these structures have turned out to correspond to something "out there." . . . So far nobody has suggested that *therefore* modern science is to be regarded as a great illusion. The parallel with the case of religion, of course, is not perfect, but it is worth reflecting on.

(Berger 1969:180–81)

It is very difficult not to be a Platonist, even when one is trying to be a good Aristotelian.

The Tertium Quid: On Consciousness and Culture

As the above (so below) discussion makes clear, I am by no means an objective reporter on the Sursem group and its proceedings. Nor am I a participant-observer, as we say in anthropology to hedge our subjectivist-objectivist bets. I am a participant, pure and simple. Moreover, I am not sure what it means, but my introduction to the Esalen Institute coincides exactly with the birth of Sursem. The first symposium I attended was on transformative practice, and it took place the week before the first Sursem meeting. Indeed, I remember riding back to the airport in a car with Ed Kelly, who had just arrived for his first Sursem meeting, "carrying the bags," as he says. Actually, he *was* carrying bags. He was coming along to pick up some Sursem participants at the same airport, luggage and all. Somewhere between Big Sur and San Jose, I told him that his voice, which is quite distinctive, reminded me of Gomez Addams of *The Addams Family*.

I still think it does.

I am not a participant, though, because of such historical accidents. I am a Sursem member for very specific philosophical and epistemological reason, namely, because I see reflected in the Sursem's synoptic methodology and radical empiricism my own previous writings on theory and method in the study of religion. I also happen to think these attempted fusions of neuroscience and the history of religions might be very fruitful ones. Indeed, with a wink at Charles Tart, I would go so far as to suggest that it would be useful as an experiment to refigure the history of religions as a disciplined study of the "altered states of history," that is, of the ways paranormal events have guided, shaped, and even inspired the most basic religious ideas, practices, and texts of human history.

Tart has written famously of what he calls "state-specific" truth claims, by which he means that particular states of consciousness produce different sorts of truth claims (Tart 1972:1203–10). He was writing about the sciences, but the same insight can easily be extended into the social sciences and the humanities. Both fields of inquiry are often, if not almost always, "state specific" to the ego and social-political processes. They thus ignore, almost completely, those altered states of consciousness that are the specific concern of someone, like myself, who studies comparative mystical literature. Once such altered states and their state-specific truths are taken seriously, however, just about everything, including and especially historiography, begins to look very different indeed.

This is more or less what I proposed in my history of Esalen, where the phrase "altered states of history" functions as one of four terms of my hermeneutical art. Not that anyone was listening. Heard or not heard, I remain convinced that 1. paranormal events are real historical events that are often experienced as overwhelmingly meaningful, if also in profoundly ambiguous ways; 2. as such, these events or "ambiguous signs" play a major role in the history of religions, where they are subsequently encoded in revelation, scripture, mythology, folklore, doctrine, institution, magical practice, and ritual; 3. these indirect socialized forms or crystallizations of the anomalous event or ambiguous sign powerfully inform and shape subsequent human experience and hence the neural patterning of human brain aggregates (read: cultures); 4. these brain patternings then continue to experience anomalous events and ambiguous signs, which . . . well, you get the picture.

This mirroring feedback loop between consciousness and culture, between anomalous event and public mythology, between ambiguous sign and religious doctrine, between brain and ritual loops and loops until, I gather, it produces different neural networks and different sorts of brains and thus different experiences of reality or what Richard Shweder has so eloquently called "reality-posits." In other words, anomalous events have real effects on public culture, which in turn has real effects on human brains, which in turn have real effects on public culture, and so on in a never-ending process.

I would stress the word *process* and propose that we set it in deep dialogue with emergence theory. Again, it is not a matter of imagining some simple essence, tiny *homunculus*, traditional "soul," or immortal ego hovering about somewhere. Nor, however, is it a matter of denying the universalism of something called consciousness or mind in the human species. We need not choose between the false absolutes of complete difference, as if a fifteenth-century Parisian were a Martian to us, or complete sameness, as if a fifteenth-century Parisian pondered the challenges of two mysterious things called secularism and religion. It is a matter of choosing *both* sameness (consciousness) *and* difference (culture) within a mind-bogglingly complex dialectic or feedback loop, all expressed through a shared, universal neurobiology that is itself being rewired and refigured as this historical process continues. This, anyway, is how I would imagine, or begin to imagine, a neurohistory of religions.[17]

All of this, it seems to me, bears directly on the subject of the present volume, that is, the issue of secularism and religion in our present intellectual climates. After all, if difference/sameness, local/universal, brain/mind, and consciousness/culture are ultimately false dichotomies, it seems extremely unlikely that secularism/religion or, for that matter, science/religion will withstand the same sorts of analysis. Such a both/and move should not be construed as a simple compromise, as an act of practical diplomacy, or as an easy abstract solution without real costs. My thinking is much closer to Roland Barthes's thoughts on interdisciplinarity: "Interdisciplinary work," he wrote, "is not about confronting already constituted disciplines (none of which, in fact, is willing to let itself go). To do something interdisciplinary it's not enough to choose a 'subject' (a theme) and gather around it two or three sciences. Interdisciplinarity consists in creating a new object that belongs to no one" (Gordon 1997:7). I am thinking of Frazer's stunning sentences, with which I began.

The truth is that such a both/and reading comes with a heavy cost for both the traditionally religious and the traditionally scientific readings. Specifically, the epistemology of faith would have to surrender its common literalisms and the epistemology of reason would have to surrender its absolute commitment to materialism and recognize, fully, that rationalism and materialism are not the same thing at all.

In essence, I am suggesting a kind of double move that can take the most fantastic expressions of religious experience as reflective of real-world paranormal events, but as inherently ambiguous signs now, hence my own semiotics is neither purely magical nor semantic but a bit of both. This is hardly a new idea. Consider what Ed Kelly has to say about the Myers-James lineage and its attempt to chart a *tertium quid* or "third thing" through and beyond the materialist and literalist epistemologies of reason and faith. The same lines could easily function as a kind of mission statement for the Sursem group: "Myers's central impulse and long-term goal is to overcome the historical opposition between science and religion by means of an expanded and enlightened science capable of penetrating into the psychological territory previously occupied by the historical religions alone, with their mutually inconsistent teachings and decidedly mixed impacts on human welfare. He aspires ultimately to re-ground this entire domain of vital human experience in real scientific knowledge rather than faith and dogma" (Kelly et al. 2007:582).

I would reframe the statement in humanist and hermeneutical terms, but the spirit would be much the same. It is also this third space that I would propose here as one possible direction for our intellectual interventions around secularism and religion. It is, after all, quite possible to treat religious experience seriously and critically at the same time. We've been doing it for two centuries now. Serious questions remain, though, like: Is anyone listening? Can we muster consensus on the issues so as to speak to the public with any authority? Do we *really* want to speak to a public that will almost certainly reject—probably hysterically reject—what we have to say?

PERSONAL POSTSCRIPT

I have spent the last two decades studying what I like to call the erotics of comparative mystical literature, by which I mean the elaborate

patterns through which gender, sexual orientation, and religious experience are intertwined in texts expressing the intimate communion, union,
even identity, of the human and the divine. In my earlier writings I cat-
egorized the common polarities of spirit/sex, soul/body, consciousness/
energy, and mind/matter within the history of religions as surface expressions of a much deeper and fundamental unity that expresses itself
through countless cultural shapes. From Plato's *Symposium* and early
Christian gnosticism, through medieval Christian bridal mysticism,
Islamic Sufism, and Jewish Kabbalah, to Indian Tantra in colonial Cal-
cutta and the American human potential movement in countercultural
California, I argued, the history of comparative mystical literature cannot
be separated from the history of human sexuality. They are joined at the
hip, sometimes even literally.

I occasionally took a great deal of flak for such a conclusion, mostly
from conservative religious voices, and came to be known as the scholar
who thinks religious experience is really about sexual experience. In other
words, my radically dialectical writings about the mystical as the erotic
and the erotic as the mystical were read—or, more often, not read—in
grossly dualistic ways, as if I were simply writing about "sex" (as if it is
apparent what that *is*).

I fear the same gross and silly misreadings here, only in reverse. I have
no doubt that what I have written in this chapter about the dialectics of
mind and matter and consciousness and culture will be read by some as
denying the material, historical, social, local, and neurological dimensions
of religious experience, as if I were now simply writing about "spirit" (as
opposed to "sex" now). I also have no doubt that what I have recently
written in *Authors of the Impossible* about the sacred as a radically dialectical and hermeneutical process between consciousness and culture,
as the act of "reading the paranormal writing us," will be read by some
as somehow advancing a simple substance or now defunct universalism
or perennialism.

I am doing no such thing. What I am doing is offering a model of mind-
matter and consciousness-culture interactions at once more paradoxical
and more humble, one that can recognize, with Emily Williams Kelly, that
precisely because our present pictures of both mind (through abnormal
psychology, the study of dissociation, and psychic research) and matter
(through quantum physics) are so thoroughly surprising and frankly puzzling we should also expect that the real relationship of mind and matter
radically overflows our present philosophical options and psychological

models. "It is no longer safe to assume any sharply-defined distinction of mind and matter," Kelly writes. "Our notions of mind and matter must pass through many a phase as yet unimagined" (Kelly et al. 2007:610).

I am also trying to advance an argument—which may be more of a provocation—that historical and cultural contexts, as crucial as they are, remain contexts or correlations, not adequate explanations, and they do not and *cannot* exhaust the meanings of some particularly excessive religious experiences we have come to call, for our own theoretical and historical reasons, mystical, psychic, and paranormal.

Present academic correctness aside, such anomalous experiences, marvels, wondrous events, or what Ann Taves calls "special things" are universal, even as their specific meanings, nuances, conscious attributions, and unconscious ascriptions are also profoundly constructed, shaped, disciplined, and even determined by local culture, ritual, doctrinal system, and religious institution.[18] As universal human experiences that violate—really mock—our present Cartesian epistemologies that have divided the world up neatly into mental and material realities (the former of which are then subsequently denied as lacking any truly independent existence), robust paranormal events should lie at the core of any adequate philosophy of mind or history of religions methodology. They, of course, do not lie at the core of any present philosophy or methodology, or of any academic project for that matter. On the contrary, they are completely and totally ignored.

And for a very good reason. Given our present assumptions about subjectivity and objectivity, about mind and matter, about consciousness and culture, about religion and secularism, they are in fact impossible and *must* be ignored.

And so our silverware melts.

NOTES

My thanks to the following individuals for helping me with this essay: Adam Crabtree, Bruce Greyson, Michael Grosso, Edward Kelly, Emily Williams Kelly, Michael Murphy, Charles Tart, and Eric Weiss.

1. The Society for Psychical Research (or S.P.R.) was founded in the winter of 1882.
2. For a much fuller discussion of Myers from a key Sursem member, see Kelly et al. 2007. For my own readings of Myers, see Kripal 2010: chapter 1.

3. Crabtree's work on dissociation and multiple personality disorders is well represented in the recent state-of-the-art statement on the subject by John A. O'Neil and Paul F. Dell (2009). As is that of another Sursem participant, analytic philosopher Stephen E. Braude, whose essay on "The Conceptual Unity of Dissociation: A Philosophical Argument" helps introduce the volume. Braude has written extensively on mind-matter issues, especially psychokinesis, a phenomenon that he personally and dramatically experienced as a graduate student. See Braude 1979, 2008.

4. The character of Dr. Edward Jessup, a Harvard professor of abnormal psychology, seems to be a kind of "condensation" of numerous countercultural and human potential figures, including Charles Tart, John Lilly, who became well known for his research into sensory deprivation, and Timothy Leary, the Harvard psychologist who became the psychedelic guru of the 1960s. But the climactic scene in which Jessup regresses or "devolves" back to the Big Bang looks most like what happens to the character of Jacob Atabet toward the end of Murphy's novel.

5. In later conversation with me, Crabtree also suggested a common parapsychological hypothesis, namely, that paranormal events often happen in groups or in the dark so as to mask who is responsible for the bizarre happenings. In a group, after all, no one has to take responsibility for the event. This phenomenon is called "ownership resistance" in the parapsychological literature.

6. Grosso was thinking of two works here: the short story of Edgar Allen Poe with the same title and "the perversity of physics" as discussed in Arthur Koestler's *The Roots of Coincidence*.

7. Historians sometimes speak and write of a *petite histoire,* a "little history," performed through a focus on ordinary objects, like clothing fasteners, hats, or beds. Someone needs to write just such a *petite histoire* of the bent spoon: When did this begin? What has it signified? And, most of all, why, of all things, *spoons*? For a beginning, consider the bent spoon in the history of the U.S. Army and its secret paranormal training program (Smith 2005:20–22). For a scientific study by an experimental physicist, see Halsted 1981.

8. For a sophisticated and provocative study of the paranormal-as-trickster, see Hansen 2001.

9. The present section on the history of Sursem is in part a revised version of a subsection of chapter 19, used here with the permission of the University of Chicago Press.

10. Summaries of the first ten meetings, including lists of the participants, can be accessed at http://www.esalenctr.org/display/survival.cfm.

11. For a sympathetic treatment of Stevenson's life and work, see Shroder 1999. For a recent special issue dedicated exclusively to Stevenson's life and work, see *Journal of Scientific Exploration* 22, no. 1.

12. Stevenson's corpus is immense. For an accessible and excellent introduction to his lifework, see Tucker 2005.
13. An abridged version of this work has also been published (see Stevenson 1997b).
14. As a kind of disciplinary footnote, it seems worth pointing out that one of the premiere theorists of comparison in the study of religion, J. Z. Smith, was a plant botanist before he turned to the comparative study of religion. This, no doubt, is why so much of his work is about the intricacies, possibilities, and problems of classification. The assumed divisions between the sciences, the social sciences, and the humanities are not so stable, after all.
15. The most provocative case for this position of which I am aware is Richard Shweder's "ontological polytheism," a radical philosophical stance in which "realism and rationality are compatible with the idea of multiple worlds" (Shweder 1991:69). Such an anthropology, which he calls a cultural psychology, displays a real resonance with the human potential movement and its commitment to cultural pluralism and the dual language of potentiality and actualization. Here, after all, the vocation of the anthropologist is to "honor and 'take literally' (as a matter of belief) those alien reality-posits in order to discover other realities hidden within the self, waiting to be drawn out into consciousness" (Shweder 1991:68–69).
16. I performed this very "reversal" of projection theory in Kripal 2007, chapter 2, "Restoring the Adam of Light."
17. I have developed this consciousness and culture dialectic in much more detail in *Authors of the Impossible: The Paranormal and the Sacred* (Kripal 2010).
18. See Taves 2009. Taves advances attribution theory, which incorporates both conscious "attributions" and unconscious "ascriptions" of meaning, as a strong contender for bringing the study of religion into serious collaboration with the cognitive sciences. My thought resonates deeply with many aspects of Taves's project, including her insistence on unconscious processing, her refusal to enter the dichotomous simplicities of the essentialist/constructivist debate, and her related insistence that attribution theory does not equal complete constructivism (Taves 2009:92). Leaving open the possibility of shared structures of mind across temporal and cultural boundaries, her methodology is, finally, a robust comparative one that, in my own terms now, balances difference and sameness. Where, I take it, we differ is in our final metaphysical commitments. I lean strongly to a dual aspect monism (the position that mental and material phenomena are complementary domains "split off" from a deeper shared reality) and the subsequent paradoxical position that mind, although never entirely separated from matter, cannot be reduced or explained by the material brain (as represented in the text by "the More" of William James [4–5], the luminous and universal Mind of Tibetan Buddhism

[37], the filter-thesis of *Irreducible Mind* [88], and the mystical experience and scholarship of William G. Barnard [chapter 3]), whereas I read Taves as leaning in the opposite direction, toward a materialist or emergentist position. Regardless, there is a great deal to agree on "in the middle," and attribution theory could clearly be used from within either commitment, neither of which can be established with any certainty at this time.

REFERENCES

Berger, Peter. 1969. *The Sacred Canopy: Elements of a Sociological Theory of Religion.* New York: Doubleday.

Braude, Stephen E. 1979. *ESP and Psychokinesis: A Philosophical Examination.* Philadelphia: Temple University Press.

—— 2007. *The Gold Leaf Lady and Other Parapsychological Investigations.* Chicago: University of Chicago Press.

Cook, Emily Frazer Williams. 1992. "Frederic W. H. Myers: Parapsychology and Its Potential Contribution to Psychology." PhD diss., University of Edinburgh.

Gordon, Avery. 1997. *Haunting and the Sociological Imagination.* Minneapolis: University of Minnesota Press.

Grosso, Michael. 1997. *Soulmaking: Uncommon Paths to Self-Understanding.* Charlottesville: Hampton Roads.

Halsted, John. 1981. *The Metal-Benders.* London: Routledge and Kegan Paul.

Hansen, George P. 2001. *The Trickster and the Paranormal.* XLibris.

Harris, Sam. 2005. *The End of Faith: Religion, Terror, and the Future of Reason.* New York: Norton.

Kelly, Edward F., Emily Williams Kelly, Adam Crabtree, Alan Gauld, Michael Grosso, and Bruce Greyson. 2007. *Irreducible Mind: Toward a Psychology for the Twenty-first Century.* Lanham: Rowman and Littlefield.

Kelly, Emily Williams. 2001. "The Contributions of F. W. H. Myers to Psychology." *Journal of the Society of Psychical Research* 65.2, no. 863 (April): 78–79.

Kripal, Jeffrey J. 2007a. *Esalen: America and the Religion of No Religion.* Chicago: University of Chicago Press.

—— 2007b. *The Serpent's Gift: Gnostic Reflections on the Study of Religion.* Chicago: University of Chicago Press.

—— 2010. *Authors of the Impossible: The Paranormal and the Sacred.* Chicago: University of Chicago Press.

Myers, F. W. H. 1903. *Human Personality and Its Survival of Bodily Death.* London: Longmans, Green.

O'Neil, John A., and Paul F. Dell. 2009. *Dissociation and the Dissociative Disorders: DSM-V and Beyond.* New York: Routledge.

Sagan, Carl. 1996. *A Demon-Haunted World: Science as a Candle in the Dark.* New York: Ballantine.

Shroder, Tom. 1999. *Old Souls: Scientific Evidence for Past Lives.* New York: Simon and Schuster.

Shweder, Richard. 1991. *Thinking Through Cultures: Expeditions in Cultural Psychology.* Cambridge: Harvard University Press.

Smith, Paul H. 2005. *Reading the Enemy's Mind: Inside Star Gate, America's Psychic Espionage Program.* New York: Forge.

Stapp, Henry P. 2007. *Mindful Universe: Quantum Mechanics and the Participating Observer.* Berlin: Springer.

—— 2009. *Mind, Matter, and Quantum Mechanics.* Berlin: Springer.

Stevenson, Ian. 1997a. *Reincarnation and Biology: A Contribution to the Etiology of Birthmarks and Birth Defects.* Westport, CT: Praeger.

—— 1997b. *Where Reincarnation and Biology Intersect.* Westport, CT: Praeger.

—— 2003. *European Cases of the Reincarnation Type.* Jefferson, NC: McFarland.

Tart, Charles. 1972. "States of Consciousness and State-Specific Sciences." *Science* 176:1203–10.

—— 2009. *The End of Materialism: How Evidence of the Paranormal Is Bringing Science and Spirit Together.* Oakland: New Harbinger.

Taves, Ann. 2009. *Religious Experience Re-Considered: A Building-Block Approach to the Study of Religion and Special Things.* Princeton: Princeton University Press.

Tucker, Jim B. 2005. *Life Before Life: A Scientific Investigation of Children's Memories of Previous Lives.* New York: St. Martin's.

Weiss, Eric. 2009. *The Long Trajectory: The Metaphysics of Reincarnation and Life After Death* (iUniverse, 2011).

TRIBALISM, EXPERIENCE, AND REMIXOLOGY IN GLOBAL PSYTRANCE CULTURE

GRAHAM ST JOHN

It's dusk, and I'm caught in a blizzard of sensory impressions. Psycho-tropic projections, morphing geometric laser patterns, hanging three-dimensional string-art structures, "galactic shields," and other mysteri-ous glyphs, flash across my visual field. A DJ occupies center stage mixing from CDs that orchestrate a sonic broadside incorporating hypnotic mel-ody lines around persistent and seductive bass lines. Possibly the largest dance floor on the planet, it features a high-performance audio system and is encompassed by towering ultraviolet reactive art installations, with an overhead water misting system now switched off as the sunlight fades and the moon rises full in the midsummer night. Transiting from the withering daytime weather conditions, emerging from their tents and campsites, thousands of festival inhabitants appear in outfits with vivid fractal designs, alien insignia, om symbols, and a host of personal emblems. Dreadlocks of varying styles are prominent, sometimes braided with beads, and facial piercings and elaborate tattoos are common, as are ground-scruffing phat pants with personal patches and badges, leather skirts, fleece boot covers, and pixie sleeves. Many have chic multipocket utility belts slinked about their waists, while others are smoking *charas* shared from thick wood chillums. Around the edge of the floor, dancers are engrossed in acrobatic displays, skillfully manipulating fire staffs and twirling illuminated poi with light-trail effects. It's mid-August 2008,

central eastern Portugal, near the protected area Parque do Tejo Interna-
cional and the village of Idanha-a-Nova. Over the next seven days, this
dance floor will attract twenty-five thousand people holding passports
from approximately eighty-five countries.[1]

From clubs to raves, from small outdoor parties to weeklong international psytrance festivals, like Portugal's Boom Festival described here,
electronic dance music culture (EDMC) flourishes in the global present.
The religious and/or spiritual characteristics of EDMC are a growing field
of study for anthropologists, sociologists, and other scholars of religion,
music, and culture employing a diverse range of theoretical and methodological approaches.[2] Through attention to the aesthetics and techniques
of *transition* axiomatic to psytrance (or psychedelic trance)—an international EDM genre rooted in both the psychedelic counterculture of the
1960s and 1970s and developments in EDM over the 1980s and 1990s—
this chapter addresses those themes of greatest weight among participants: 1. the self-identified *tribal* characteristics of psytrance and its festivals; 2. the *experiential aesthetic* integral to this technocounterculture,
and; 3. the technique and sensibility of the "sampledelic" *remix*. These
themes will be explored with attention to the premier event in the global
psytrance calendar, Portugal's Boom Festival, and through more general
observations of psytrance culture.[3] From states of self-transcendence to
commitments to cultural transformation, the transitional character of
psytrance most pronounced in the context of its festivals warrants the
attention of contemporary approaches to religion and spirituality. Yet,
recognizing that this phenomenon cannot be rendered sensible according
to the religious/secular binary conventional to social scientific studies of
religion, the chapter uses emic data to fashion appropriate heuristics.

TRANCE, TRIBALISM, AND THE BOOM FESTIVAL

The growing interest in the religiospiritual dimensions of EDMC is characterized by a diversity of analysis and debate. That EDMCs contextualize collective alterations of consciousness, especially among youth, has
triggered a range of passions: from moral panics and hysteria like that
expressed by Christian fundamentalists,[4] the zealous architects of the
RAVE Act (2003) in the United States,[5] or the Zionist reaction to trans-
nationalizing youth culture in Israel (see Meadan 2001), to statements of
self-awakening,[6] and other material produced by raving evangelists (see

Fritz 1999). While some studies seem loath to recognize the religiosity of their research subject—sometimes in reaction to Christianity where religious experience appears conflated with institutionalized religion (see Jackson 2004:22)—in diverse scholarly approaches research consistently identifies scenes as contexts enabling an immediate and extraordinary sociality approximating a religious or spiritual experience for its participants. Insights have been forged, for example, about ritual, transgression, and the sacred (Gerard 2004; Gauthier 2004), new age and alternative spirituality (St John 2004b, D'Andrea 2006; Partridge 2005, 2006a,), and millenarianism and revitalization (Olaveson 2004; St John 2004c). The study of clubbing (Lynch and Badger 2006) exemplifies the turn to secular spirituality, or "spiritualities of life," which Paul Heelas observes downstream from the "revolutionary" turn to subjective or "expressive life" and the self-spirituality of the 1960s (Heelas 1996, 2008; Heelas and Woodhead 2005). Often interpreted via Victor Turner's concept of "communitas" in which participants, typically strangers to one another, may experience a spontaneous "flash of mutual understanding on the existential level, and a 'gut' understanding of synchronicity" (Turner 1982:48), the EDMC party *vibe* is addressed by numerous commentators (e.g., Fikentscher 2000:80; Taylor 2001; Takahashi and Olaveson 2003:81; Gerard 2004:178–79; Olaveson 2004:90; Rill 2006; St John 2008 and 2009a). The empathetic sociality of the vibe reveals a compulsion consistent with the "neotribes" identified by sociologist Michel Maffesoli (1996 [1988]): the motivation for *being together*. The "orgiasm" of the EDMC *vibe* offers an interstitial context for vitality, belonging, and identification (Malbon 1999) outside the "dictated life" of primary institutions and in ways reminiscent of the sociality connected with what Thomas Luckmann (1967) identified as "secondary institutions." This is a spirituality in which the self has assumed divine authority, yet in a "deindividualized" context outside traditional sources of belonging (family, church, state).

Research on psytrance provides especially significant insights for studies of social aesthetics, transnational religiosity, and the anthropology of contemporary religion (Tramacchi 2000; see D'Andrea 2007; St John 2010a, 2012a). Psytrance is a cultural movement amplifying the liminal and transcendent qualities thought and felt to be inherent to music, especially psychedelic music, such as psychedelic rock, but also ambient, cosmic jazz, dub reggae, and techno. In this sense its cultural timbre is rather different from most other EDM movements. Indeed transcendence is a critical motivation for enthusiasts as well as label managers, party collectives, and event organizers and is given expression across personal, social, and cultural vectors. That is, while participants may be committed to states of self-transcendence, by virtue of the intensely social nature of the experience, they become involved in states of radical immanence that have long been associated with ecstatic dance cults, subcultures, and scenes. Furthermore, the entire assemblage resounds with an expectancy of the kind animated by the recognition of crisis (or crises), which inspires the engineering of projects, organizations, and initiatives motivated to make transit into an alternative future, a transition in which the festival performs a critical role.

The typical identification with "tribalism" signals the role of the festal. As I discuss elsewhere (St John 2009b, 2010a, 2012b), trance danc-escapes possess a "tribal" dynamic whereby the term *tribe* is adopted by participants to connote a particular aesthetic, practice, technique, or language by which an individual or group is distinguished from an other *and/or* designates the dissolution of such differences. This elective festal dynamic lies at the heart of psychedelic trance, which calls for interpretation deviating from conventional theories of *trance* (and possession)— from traditional (e.g., Winkleman 1986) to Western manifestations (e.g., Taves 1999). This *neotrance* also diverges from Maffesolian sociality in *The Time of the Tribes*, which offers a conservative heuristics in which social aesthetics are divorced from proactive or movement pretensions. Trance formations are movement oriented, and this also finds expression in the typical self-identification as "tribal" (e.g., Moontribe, Tribedelic, Tribal Records and Blood Tribe Records). As evidenced in participant discourse, the tribal designation signifies a romantic desire for a sociality, howsoever temporary, perceived to have been lost or forgotten in the separation, privatization, and isolation of the present. This is clearly a response to social conditions in the present from which producers and participants seek alternatives. There is thus a *responsibility* in this form of tribalism (a self-identified tribalism) unrecognizable to Maffesolian heuristics that nevertheless makes claims to uncovering evidence of "reenchantment" in the present. This responsibility may be expressed in primitivist signifiers and essentialist fantasies of the "tribal" other (see Luckman 2003), yet the term *tribe* is more than often adopted as a nonspecific signifier for community (or, more accurately, *alternative community*). This *tribalism* may manifest in reaction to those elements threatening to undermine the source of identification and vitality (e.g., competing aesthetics, commercialism, environmental pollution, state repression), with participants defending their sites of significance. Yet the trance festival is also a proactive staging ground for the pursuit of manifold causes, accommodating a variety of performance frames through which diverse alternative agendas within a movement consciousness are expressed (see St John 2010b, 2012a).

From overnight parties to all-week campouts, psytrance events are favorably held in open-air locations with dance floors positioned in bushland, forests, beaches, and deserts where participants will hold events to mark seasonal transitions or celebrate celestial events. As an exotic location for full moon beach parties held since the early 1970s near the villages of Anjuna and Vagator, the former Portuguese colony of Goa, India, was formative to this development. Populated by self-exiled Westerners seeking spiritual liberation and enlightenment in the East, projects popularized by Timothy Leary and the Beatles, these parties were spearheaded by Goa Gil, an expatriate from Marin County who arrived in Goa in 1970, later becoming a *sadhu* and advocating "re-creating ancient tribal ritual for the twenty-first century."[7] Through the 1970s and 1980s, Goa would evolve into a highly eclectic and experimental dance and music scene. During the 1980s, as this traveler enclave was infused with rapid developments in electronic music production and performance, a distinct "Goa trance" sound and sensibility emerged and would be transported around the world. Following the success of Goa trance in the mid-1990s, with no small assistance from the Internet, the genre exploded into various subgenres, scenes, and aesthetics. By the late 1990s, the psytrance underground was apparent in Western Europe, Israel, North America, Australia, Japan, South Africa, and elsewhere, gaining popularity more recently in Russia, Brazil, and Mexico. Public events range from small-scale parties to large international festivals, like the events held on the line of totality during a solar eclipse.

Of the regular calendar festivals, Boom would become a popular site for trance enthusiasts. Initiated in 1997, and held on a lake in the mountainous Beira Baixa region of Portugal, the Boom Festival has become a pilgrimage center for the global electronic trance dance community. The festival features a range of trance genres, but it is not strictly a music or dance festival—it is what organizers regard as a "visionary arts and lifestyle festival" or an innovation in "sustainable entertainment." Promoted as a "harmonic convergence of people, energy, information and philosophies from around the planet earth and beyond," and "reflecting a balance of the organic and the cyber-technologic,"[8] Boom accommodates diverse countercultural strands drawn toward ecstatic trance and proactivity. That is, it is a context for both the self-transcendent/transgressive (*ecstatic*) and conscious alternative (*reflexive*) trajectories persistent within a countercultural trajectory that achieved a critical threshold in the post-WWII period. The event features four sound stages that host a diversity of psychedelic music, from progressive psychedelic to dark trance (or darkpsy), from ambient to electro, and from dub styles to global music trance fusion ensembles. Operating for twenty-two hours a day for six days and catering comfortably to approximately five to six thousand people in 2006, the Dance Temple (Main Stage) featured a tall bamboo pagoda design with a sophisticated audiovisual assemblage designed for enhancing expressive/transcendent states. In this arena, over one hundred DJs and fusion bands from many different countries performed a range of electronic trance genres. While the Dance Temple constitutes something of a hallowed ground, there are three other sound areas: the Ambient Forest (for the performance of ambient music); the Groovy Beach stage (where a profusion of broken-beat, electro, and dub styles are performed), and the Sacred Fire "world music" stage (which is the responsibility of many living in self-sustainable communities and featured a fire pit constructed according to principles derived from Rainbow Family Gatherings).[9] Other significant areas of Boom include a Flea Market (with a variety of handicraft, clothing, and jewelry stalls); Eco-Centro (with displays and workshops on the ecological sustainability projects undertaken by Boom);[10] the Liminal Village (an area for contemporary "visionary" pursuits including workshops, presentations, panels, and films—e.g., yoga, capoeira, belly dancing, entheogens, biodynamics, and shamanism);[11] the Theatroom (an interactive multimedia arts space including circus, fire arts, cabaret, puppet shows, Butoh dance); the Divine Flower Healing Area (with various alternative healing modalities including homeopathic consultation, yoga, Tantra, Thai massage, Shiatsu, Reiki); a Restaurant area (with bakeries, vegan, vegetarian options, chai tents, macrobiotics, etc); and Baby Boom (a children's entertainment and babysitting zone). This complexity reveals that Boom, through its managing body Good Mood Productions, has evolved into a sophisticated and highly organized event whose reliance on advanced multimedia technologies, whose connections with the trance and world music industry, whose growing technical bureaucracy, and whose compliance with state regulatory requirements are all modulated to effect transformation according to the specifications of ecstatic and reflexive countercultural modalities.

THE QUEST FOR EXPERIENTIAL AUTHENTICITY

Psytrance offers evidence that, as reported by Jeffrey Kripal in this volume, Timothy Leary did not go about his business *quietly* as Aldous Huxley advised. To recognize that psytrance evolved from the 1960s counterculture is to acknowledge its legacy in the search for experiential authenticity, a seekership integral to the psychedelia emerging in that period.[12] The quest for experience is redolent in psytrance's most renowned act, Shpongle (the collaboration of Ron Rothfield and Simon Posford), whose 1998 debut album *Are You Shpongled?* (Twisted Records) evoked the inquiry of the title track on the monumental 1967 LP *Are You Experienced* (Track Records), by the Jimi Hendrix Experience. From the original to the new "summer of love," we recognize the common desire for *real experience*. Such would be sought through altered states of being, typically characterized, across three decades, by Dionysian pleasure and visionary states. In his astute observations of Goa trance, what Erik Davis (2004) identified as "spiritual hedonism"—the dynamic of erotic/immanent and cognitive/transcendent experience—is a persistent quest for immediacy linking the present with earlier countercultures. From Hendrix to Shpongle, acid rock to psytrance, the authenticity desired is a raw and untrammeled life, not dictated by the conniptions of the advertising industry nor performed for "the Man." Not ruled by religious dogma nor mediated by Fox News. It was the radical immanence championed by the Beats and their predecessors. It was the freedom from the sexual inhibitions of the parent culture characterizing the "hippy" trajectory. It was the exploration of new and subversive forms of art, leisure, and sociality. It was experimentation with psychotropic mind alterants—LSD and psychotropic mushrooms in particular—affording visionary insights, often reinforcing suspicions concerning the corruption, greed, and "soullessness" of official culture. With its pastoral sensibility (see Reynolds 1997), in the proto acid, or cosmic, rock of the 1960s and 1970s, adherents to alternative lifestyles were laying claim to the possibility of the Self's direct encounter with the Other, a mystical experience we might identify as the epiphanic field of the sacred variously encountered in this period as "the One," "godhead," "Great Spirit," "life-force," the "source," "cosmic consciousness," or "Nature." In the U.S., radical immanence would be found in alternative cultural lifestyle trends exemplified by the followers of the Grateful Dead (the "Deadheads," see Sardiello 1994; Adams and

Sardiello 2000) and members of the "Rainbow Family" (Niman 1997). In the UK, these tendencies were embodied by the alternative Travellers of Albion (McKay 1996; Hetherington 2000; Partridge 2006), and in Australia, those who inhabited the New South Wales town of Nimbin (born from the 1973 Aquarius Festival) and/or participated in the alternative lifestyle event ConFest (Newton 1988; St John 2001). More recently, we could filter "Burners" into the list, those inhabitants of the annual Burning Man Festival in Nevada's Black Rock Desert, who Lee Gilmore, in her ethnography *Theater in a Crowded Fire* (2009:96), indicates are performing a "spirituality" that is fundamentally "experiential" (see also Gilmore and Van Proyen 2005). As research on Burning Man illustrates, that event has attracted a significant neopagan population (see Kozinets and Sherry 2004), an alternative spiritual commitment dedicated to radical immanence in festal contexts (Pike 2001).

The encounter with the Other (and the concomitant process of self-othering) within Western countercultural contexts presupposes the highly personal *journey of transformation* integral to what Linda Woodhead (2001) referred to as the "New Spirituality." The spiritual *transit* typically implies movement *from* a condition of separation and alienation (from inner God, Nature, the cosmos, humanity) implicit to monotheism, possessive materialism, patriarchy, and patriotism and, in sympathy with a Western Romantic idealism which has "for over two centuries, expounded an optimistic, evolutionary, de-traditionalizing, mystical immanentism" (Woodhead 2001:96), a corresponding movement *toward* a resolution: realization, utopia, an age of awareness, peace, unity, an ideal state where notably "all" is reputedly "one." Importantly, in this trajectory, self possesses a mind not disconnected from body and spirit, the holistic departure from which was embodied in the teachings of the human potential movement (Kripal 2007) and the integral movement.[13] Nor is this self isolated from other selves, but a person whose identity is formed in the intimate presence of others, and, notably, strangers (e.g., not only beyond family, but outside the church, ethnicity, or one's nationality). For practitioners of this progressive and holistic movement, everyday reality can elicit a profound unifying spirit, "life-force," or vitality that can be accessed and reaffirmed through activities in the phenomenal world like meditation, yoga, dance, and travel to places of spiritual significance.

The journey of transformation is integral to psytrance, and dance—the context in which bodies respond to music in the presence of others—is the corporeal context for transition. From its inception on the beaches

of Goa—those exotic locales to which well-resourced (and resourceful)
young Westerners journeyed a great distance from their homes and routines—trance has provided the context for Oriental/Dionysian abandonment. There, in a relatively licentious realm, free from responsibilities and
roles at home, an exotic "temporary autonomous zone" (Bey 1991) located
beyond and between "Apollonian" rules of moral propriety, repressive
criminal laws, and disciplinary codes of conduct,[14] travelers were free to
interact with fellow seekers in the context of ecstatic pleasure and self-
liberation. Disembarking from their routines and smoking *charas* within
a legal context, their experience was flavored by well-circulated images of
timelessness, innocence, and mystique imagined to encapsulate the Orient, a "timelessness" often interrupted by the realities of life—e.g., poverty, crime, begging—in a "contact zone" like India. If this liminal *contact
experience* constitutes an embracing of inviolability, an opening outward
to others, for "freaks" undertaking the simultaneous "horizontal" (geo-
spatial) and "vertical" (spiritual-psychedelic) journey from home states to
and in Goa (D'Andrea 2007), the concord would be experienced primarily
with those sharing in the journey (i.e., their fellow travelers). As such, it
generally constitutes a circumstance offering a rather different quality of
"realism," and a radically different "trip," than the typically liminal philanthropic practice of volunteering engaged in by Westerners in poverty-
ravaged rural India observed by Erica Bornstein in this volume.

Furnished with the essence of the Orient, travel to the East was imagined to enable an escape from the cage of Occidental rationality and
facilitate insight or gnosis, philosophies, and practices pursued long
after the scene left Goa.[15] To implement this *Orientation*, Goa trance
labels, albums, and events emerging in the mid-1990s would promote
and package the trance experience as a transcendent journey adopting
Oriental imagery and iconography to assist the telos. For instance, in
efforts to reproduce the Goa party vibe outside Goa, early label Javelin
Records released material like their 1995 album *Techno Spiritual Trance
from Goa*, compiled by Goa Gil. An effort to reproduce the Goa trance
experience, the album began with his trademark offering to Shiva, "Om,"
followed by Astral Projection's "Let There Be Light," with their mystical
remix "Mahadeva" positioned near the conclusion. Replete with Hindu
and Buddhist imagery, the first Return to the Source compilation, *Deep
Trance And Ritual Beats* (1995), consisted of a double CD and featured
a booklet with stylized images of the elephant-headed Ganesh, son of
Shiva, the Goddess Parvati, and the sitar-playing Hindu muse Sarasvati.

With the Goa aesthetic so transportable, enthusiasts on the dance floor could consume the Goa experience, be exposed to the mystique, and access the metaphysical lore without ever having set foot in India. In efforts to induce Visions of Shiva, the name Paul van Dyke chose for his outfit formed in 1992 with Harald Blüchel (aka Cosmic Baby), or to reduce the *Distance to Goa*, the successful compilation series released by French label Distance (founded in 1995), promoters, producers, and designers were concocting label aesthetics, album cover art, track titles, music structures, and festival concepts saturated with Orientalism. Getting Oriented could never have been easier. At the time the renowned Italian outfit Etnica released their *Kumba Mela* EP (Matsuri, 1995), TIP Records was releasing its Colour of Shiva compilations, and tabla, conch horns, and chanting Tibetan Buddhist monks were becoming ubiquitous samples. The Shiva Moon festival had begun in postunification Germany; the name of that event later used by one of several party organizations on Thailand's Koh Pangan, a popular destination for trance travelers and rave tourists through the 1990s and into the present. All through this period, trance was saturated with om symbols and mandalas, an iconic pandemic reminiscent of the essentializing motifs of the earlier counterculture.[16] But the "Easternisation of the West," to use the phrase Colin Campbell chose for the title of his book (2008), is not one-dimensional, and it never was. While evidence of superficiality and contradiction is readily apparent, analyses cannot ignore the actual life practices of those for whom, for instance, the worldview of an interior God holds greater salience than an external creator. Whether studies attend to the gifting of Oriental pathways to Westerners, as is exemplified by the Krishna movement founded by Bhaktivedanta Swami Prabhupada, offered to the West as a form of "consciousness expansion" (Ziguras 1996:74), a recognition of the life experience of "expressive expatriates" (D'Andrea 2006, 2007) who may have "gone native" like Goa Gil or Erik Cohen's (1979) "existential tourist," or contexts in which the inhabitants of contact zones draw livelihoods from cultural and spiritual tourism, requisite comparative, cultural, and phenomenological methodologies are required. In any case, these days, most psytrance participants find Oriental motifs passé, and the party scene has been seriously impacted by police corruption, organized crime, and a succession of laws aimed at curtailment. While enthusiasts still travel to Goa, by the current decade, the scene had by and large migrated from the East to various, mostly domestic, settings.

While from the 1960s the East had become a popular destination for Westerners in search of spiritual maturity, others sought alternative experimental frontiers, including the Americas. On an expedition to the Amazon in 1971, in one formative instance, philosopher and entheogenesist Terence McKenna, with his ethnobotanist brother Dennis McKenna, sought a rendezvous with *ayahuasca*-using shamans, stumbling across *psilocybe cubensis* ("magic mushrooms") instead. The lore, practice, artifacts, psychotropes of Native American cultures have long exerted influence on those desiring departure from core Western values and practice. The desirable practices, the appropriations, and the outcomes are uneven. From the U.S., to Germany and Australia,[17] and indeed among Brazilians, Mexicans, Chileans of Portuguese and Spanish descent, countercultural participants have long found Native Americans to embody an originary power, a spiritual purity, a remedy for their alienated selves. The trend has ordinarily received reactionary criticism within academia, where contemporary symbolic appropriations are held as neocolonial in practice.[18] Psytrance is not above reproach. Native American cultures have been romanticized by artists and enthusiasts who sculpt fantasies using sound and images sampled from popular cultural sources in music and at festivals. Generic American Indians have been the source to which initiates journey to obtain wisdom to remedy their modern afflictions. Primitivist signs are replete in the promotions, the decor, and even the name of one German psytrance festival, Indian Spirit. Here, indigenes are consigned to the status of essential difference, cultures with great variation homogenized in sonic fictions and consumer fantasies standardizing peoples according to primitivist specifications and potentially disadvantaging those who deviate from those icons.

The practices by which "Others" are pirated and distorted as profitably "pure products" (Clifford 1988) and marketed to those seeking spiritual growth, restoration, and status enhancement deserves attention as an appendage to more conspicuous histories of dispossession. But how should we approach cultural borrowing and exchange within the world's most culturally diverse dance music scene? To begin with, we need to avoid conflating appropriation with expropriation, as unfortunately appears typical to critics far removed, and scholarship comfortably detached, from the objects (or subjects) of their scorn (e.g., Marcus 1988; Cuthbert and Grossman 1996; Thomas 2005; Cooke 2006). Furthermore, critics show a tendency to advocate for and defend an authentic Other who may be as idealized as that pursued by those routinely dismissed as one-dimensional cannibals of the Other. The situation can foreseeably result in a kind of "cultural apartheid" managed and policed by secular humanist social scientists and culture experts.[19]

As McKenna's adventures illustrate, the practices of native inhabitants of the Central and South Americas have generated appeal among dissidents of the West, many of whom, especially following the popularity of the dubious works of Carlos Castenada, but likely also as much Lewis Carol, went in search of what is now dubbed entheogenesis (literally the awakening of the divine within) with the assistance of plants, fungi, and herbs such as *psilocybin, Salvia divinorum, ayahuasca,* and DMT (dimethyltryptamine), all used by various indigenous inhabitants of Mexico and the Amazon.[20] In another, not unrelated, development, in the 1980s and 1990s, as a sophisticated adaptation of the Mayan calendar, José Argüelles initiated the "movement for a New Time" and its Dreamspell calendar, which has been adopted by groups in over ninety countries (Argüelles 1987, 2002; Sitlar 2006; Gelpher 2010). The use of entheogens and the adoption of elements of the Mayan calendar are clear examples of "appropriation," which, as John Morton reminds us, means to take something "unto oneself and devote it to a special purpose" (1996:134), a definition that indeed hails our very human capacity to learn, create, innovate, interact, and grow. A key question then becomes, repurposing to what ends? The practices I have introduced are not equivalent to the cannibalizing of the authentic other, nor do they simply represent the pursuits of self-seeking aesthetes or illustrate the theft of cultural property. These are projects, both personal and social, through which activists of the mind, and indeed of "time" itself, have sought radical transformations of the social and cultural worlds into which they were born. After all, as McKenna held, "our world is endangered by the absence of good ideas," by the "absence of consciousness," and the objective of the entheogenic experience was "to participate in the redemption of the human spirit," charging neoshamanic experimentalists in one mid-1990s presentation to "bring back a small piece of the picture and contribute it to the building of the new paradigm."[21] As an "entheonaught" himself, McKenna's journey to the Amazon, recounted in *The Invisible Landscape* (McKenna and McKenna 1994 [1975]), enabled an experience that would catalyze his speculative contribution to the entheogenic theory of religion (McKenna 1993), grist for an ecospiritual revitalization movement (see St John 2004c). Boom's Liminal Village offers something of a dedication to McKenna and the self-shamanizing theme. A "global hub of visionary

arts and culture," the space represents a conscious effort to adopt a language, architecture, and vision of transformation using anthropological
discourse forged in the study of traditional ritual, and specifically ritual,
thresholds. Consciously emulating the demarcated and sacred zones of
passage rites, the "village" facilitates the transmission of alternative cultural *sacra* (including ecological consciousness, cognitive freedom, personal well-being, diversity, and peace), becoming an environment enabling
the distillation of novelty ("seeding" the future). As for Argüelles and his
followers in the international Planet Ark Network (PAN), the Dreamspell
calendar is a technology, partly based on an interpretation of the Mayan
calendar, for redressing global ecological and humanitarian crises.

Both examples, and both figures, are central to the study of psytrance
and its association with indigeneity. McKenna's ideas have been hugely
influential (he is himself likely the most sampled individual in the whole
of the genre), and an entheogenic consciousness, in which the real and
imagined shamanic practices of indigenous peoples are valorized, is rife.
For instance, the psychedelic ambient outfit Entheogenic Sound Explorers, whose first release, *The Shroom Experience* (Practising Nature Records,
2008), offers little doubt as to where their affinity lies. Indeed, on album
covers, event fliers, banners, in decor, "magic mushrooms" form ubiquitous iconography, often depicted in proximity to images of natives.
And besides *psilocybin*, a palette of substances used in world shamanic
practices would become popular: "the ritual use of tobaccos; the Carib-
bean *Cohoba* snuff; morning glories; *Datura* . . . entheogenic cacti; and the
vast pharmacopeia of South American psychointegrator plants" would
form the "constellation of New World entheogen use" identified by Des
Tramacchi (2006:32). In psytrance, shamanic and entheogenic practices
hold widespread appeal among a curious population of DIY investigators, exploring, reenvisioning, and mulling source practices. Herb shops
are common at festivals, where a range of products can be purchased,
from Indian style chillums to packets of *Salvia divinorum*.[22] Festival zones
have appeared, facilitating discussion of the role of "teacher plants" in the
evolution of consciousness, as at Boom's Liminal Village, which, in 2006,
hosted presentations from, among others, Daniel Pinchbeck, author of
the popular *Breaking Open the Head: A Psychedelic Journey Into the Heart of
Contemporary Shamanism* (2002).

And the quest for visions is redolent in the music, as apparent in the
debut self-titled album of the group 1200 Mics. Featuring the tracks listed
as "Ayahuasca," "Hashish," "Mescaline," "LSD," "Marijuana," "Ecstasy,"

"Magic Mushrooms," "Salvia Divinorum," and "DMT" (1200 *Micrograms*, TIP World, 2002), the outfit stridently served up an entheogenic fusillade. The opening offering, "Ayahuasca," begins with exotic birdlife in the canopy, and then a voice: "A thousand years ago deep in the darkest jungles of the Amazon, the ancient Incas discovered the mystical vine to brew up the sacred psychoactive hallucinogenic drink, the holy Ayahuasca. . . . You enter a special magical dimension, the dimension of the spirit world." A polyphonic percussion builds with the faint suggestion of a wet burp repeated behind the pace, a not especially pleasant realization for anyone who has drunk the "vine of the souls," a translation of the Quechua term *ayahuasca* (also *yajé, caapi*). In western Amazon healing traditions, *ayahuasca* is a brew typically mixing the roots of the *B.caapi* vine with leaves of DMT (Reichel-Dolmatoff 1975), which, when drunk, induces vomiting, diarrhea, and probably the most powerful entheogenic experience available. With the vomiting having begun, the session is in full swing and 1200 Mics guide their listeners (dancers) through a substance-induced odyssey, distributing their product to DJs who will cut, mix, and deal the sonic stash to packed dance floors across the planet.

Furthermore, psytrance festivals are common ground for the pedagogical transmission of the Dreamspell calendar, as the broader culture remixes Mayan, Aztec, and other symbolism (see St John 2011b). In 2006 Boom featured PAN's "13 Moon Temple," which offered daily workshops on the "13 Moon Calendar." While an entheogenic sensibility and the 13 Moon Calendar are pursued more broadly, psytrance is a critical clearinghouse for these ideas, a medium for indigeneity beyond their sources. But these aren't simply arenas remote from traditional cultures, for we find collaborations between peoples holding multiple ethnic backgrounds, including those from indigenous groups. Some of the better examples of sound alliances are evident in Australia where the Rainbow Serpent Festival, Exodus Festival, and Earthdream (see St John 2005) exemplify the independent quest for intercultural reconciliation among citizens seeking alternative routes toward coexistence and legitimacy. The former events have featured opening ceremonies involving local Aboriginal performers and artists functioning as "permission ceremonies" reminiscent of those transpiring at Queensland's Woodford Festival (Lewis and Dowsey-Magog 1993). As Morton suggests, "reconciliation necessarily entails a logic of redemption . . . [which is] at the same time, personal and political, not simply subject to 'discourse'" (1996:134). Further, a "mutually satisfying future" for Australians, he argues, depends upon appropriative

exchanges. In a further example of intercultural exchange and performance, Boom's Sacred Fire stage has accommodated artists from diverse
trance dance traditions, with performance including African djembe, Jap-
anese talko, Balinese gamelan, Australian Aboriginal didjeridu, Moroccan
gnawa, and Turkish sufi. The presence of performers from a multitude of
cultural and ethnic traditions reveals the complex landscape of appropriation. In the last decade, scholars have felt the need to carefully traverse
this landscape, holding that cultural borrowing cannot be dismissed out
of hand as pernicious. Observing new agers' "genuine attempts to honour indigenous people," Jane Mulcock (1997:15n8) pressed for recognizing
the lived experience of those participating in alternative discourses. Bron
Taylor (1997) argued that, in some circumstances, cultural borrowing promotes *respect*, furthers the establishment of concrete political alliances,
even enhancing the survival prospects of indigenous cultures. Researchers have also recognized how agents have been strategically involved in
manufacturing, selling, spending, and buying their own authenticity (see
Conklin 1997; Welch 2007).

REMIXOLOGY: NATIVES OF THE DIGITAL AGE

In the quest for the experience of the other, and of the self—indeed one's
other-self—from its inception in the Goa period, psytrance has been reliant on the development and repurposing of new technologies, from LSD
to computers. New chemical, audio, digital, and cyber innovations are
adopted and reprogrammed in order to upgrade or enhance the means
for ecstatic dance, the perennial desire for which is said to be facilitated
through modern means. In the early to mid-1990s, from to London to
Berlin to San Francisco, and from samplers to brain machines, a host of
"cyberdelic" mind-body technologies was being harnessed to the project
of self-realization, enabling what was being touted in the magazine *Mondo
2000* as the "new edge." Virtualizing travels to outer- and cyberspace, progressive "new edge" technologies were facilitating the modes of gnostic
awakening that such travel tropes potentiate. As a technologically mediated spirituality, psytrance possesses something of the "techgnostic"
adventure identified by Erik Davis (1998) in his *Techgnosis: Myth, Magic,
and Mysticism in the Age of Information,* which documents how the tech-
noliberationist flame, reignited throughout Western history and promising the millenarian dispensation, has conflagrated with the advent of the

digital age. Like their forebears, the experimental habitués of psytrance can be considered, in Davis's terms, "children of technique," heirs to a heterogeny of pathways toward the truth, oneness, eternity, belonging. As Davis (1998:146) observes, "for meditators, mystics and Caucasian shamans, the only legitimate course into the blazing dawn of enlightenment was to cobble together experimental protocols from a wide range of traditions."

Exemplary producers of what has been dubbed "ethnodelia," and exemplars of the "sampledelic" practice common to EDM, Shpongle are known for sampling a wide range of sounds from different world regions, exotic instruments, tribal chants, nature sounds. The audio feast, such as that served up on their *Nothing Lasts* (Twisted Records, 2005), caters to the appetites of enthusiasts desiring new and strange sounds. These and other producers use exotic soundscapes to structure and arrange the transformative context demanded. Whether sampling bass lines, melodies, or vocals lifted from cinema, TV, documentaries, radio, or live recordings, the rearrangement of found sound is endemic to EDM, where samples are selected, repurposed in production (e.g., using synthesisers or MIDI sequencers), and/or treated in performance (e.g., using mixing desks, turntables, CD decks, or software like Ableton Live) to fashion new works. Psytrance producers and/or DJs, thus, take possession of existing artifacts, remastering them in the process. The artifice has its roots in Jamaican dub-platting and in the studio techniques subsequently known as "dubbing" (see Partridge 2007), the art of the remix seeding the emergence of EDM (disco, hip-hop, techno, trance, etc.), the practitioners of which were manipulating a suite of tools to perform the practice native to the electronicage: copying. Yet, this is not direct imitation, just as appropriation is never absolute simulation, for it involves improvisation and extemporization, which means manipulating existing repertoires and idioms, and implies varying degrees of competence, respect, technical skills, and risk taking. At a further level, dancers, who interpret the music through physical expression, effectively embody the sonic fiction, an aesthetic that is interiorized and enables individuals to fictionalize and remaster themselves in the dance. And, further yet, enthusiasts participate in a re-creational sensibility that extends beyond music and sound to an assemblage of dress options, body modifications, hairstyles, and selected symbols from diverse and often unknown origins. "Freaking" their selves, participants are performing mimesis, where mimicry, the copying of otherness, is central to play, creativity, and the production and reproduction of the self.

The lifestyle practice of participants is then contiguous with the "sampledelic" sensibility of EDM culture, as practiced in the techniques of the DJ and producer, in which novel works are perpetually remastered from found sounds. At Boom and other psytrance festivals, with the imitation of the authentic via corporeal inscriptions and elaborate performances, enthusiasts enter, through the laws of sympathetic magic, into physical contact with that authentic Other whose raiment, whose very image, enhances condition and status. Such othering demonstrates the possibilities arising out of what Michael Taussig (1993) calls the "mimetic faculty"—the very human capacity and desire to *other*. In the "mimetic faculty" lies the potential for "copying or imitation and a palpable, sensuous, connection between the very body of the perceiver and the perceived" (1993:21). Yet, since the festival encourages the "freaking" of the self using a multitude of sources, mimesis is glaringly complex. Using an assemblage of dress options, body modifications, hairstyles, adornments, and inscriptions, participants cobble together their identity from a multitude of religious and esoteric sources (e.g., Oriental, Amer-Indian, African, Aboriginal, Rastafarian, Celtic, but also aliens, zombies, and other figures from cinema and popular cultural sources). Indeed, with influences from psychedelic rock and Afropsychedelia the figure of the alien is almost axiomatic: psytrance productions are heavy populated with UFO sighting and alien abduction narratives sampled from feature and documentary films, and festivals are decorated with an off-planetary sensibility, reinforcing belief in one's "galactic citizenship." Thus while some tend to display atavistic tropes, deploying symbols to display a rustic appearance, others convey sophisticated futurist and cyborg repertoires, while others tactically combine reenchantment and ascensionist aesthetics.

As participant identities are a tangled web of signifiers/inscriptions, they are bricoleurs whose practices embody a kind of syncretic cut-and-paste spirituality resonant with that identified in the occult. Indeed, the connection has already been made by Christopher Partridge discussing the role of psychedelic trance in the history of the popular occult or "occulture" and, more broadly, the "re-enchantment of the West" (2004:166–75, 2005). The immediate occultural character of psytrance is illustrated by its proponents' pursuit of a checklist offered by Partridge (2004:69): "direct experience of the divine, in secret gnosis, in alchemy, in theurgy, in a *philosophia perennis*, and in ancient religion and mythical figures, texts and civilizations," along with UFOs and alien abduction narratives. Pruning from Western esoteric and mystery traditions, Oriental and indigenous sources, along with Afrofuturist "sonic fictions" (Eshun 1998) and science fiction narratives, these eclectic worldviews return us to the advocates of the "New Spirituality," who, according to Linda Woodhead (2001), in their pursuit of experience, gave expression to a spiritual relativism in which a profusion of religious and symbol systems are adopted in the belief that they offer access to similar divine truths—truths housed, for instance, in "Nature," "God," the "alien," etc.

Expatriate German artist Jörg Kessler (aka Shiva Space Technology) would form an exemplary product of the marriage of new age and techno cultures. In 1997 Kessler's label released the self-titled compilation, which featured Shiva Shidapu's (Kessler and Infected Mushroom's Erez Alzen) track "India Spirit." But while the album was dedicated to Shiva, it also featured the same artist's "Power Of Celtic," indicating that the album drew from multiple traditions. Indeed, the liner notes of the CD prominently feature an iconoclastic profusion of symbols, including the crescent, the Star of David, the Cross, the ying/yang symbol, and a prominent om along with Shiva's trident. Goa Gil is also exemplary here, his compilation *World Bridger* (Avatar, 2007) evincing his mobilization across multiple religions, sampling those icons and sounds felt to express eternal truths, the sampling techniques adopted by electronic artists amplifying the integralist sensibility of the times.

In the psytrance carnival of symbols, where the remix spins continuously in the decks, habitués are bricoleurs synthesizing signification. Here the origin of sounds, signifiers, and artifacts adopted becomes unclear, since meaning has been repurposed and recreated in diffuse iterations, even as individuals remaster themselves in the syncretism. Thus the culture of the spiritual remix throws up unique products and people from its wash cycle, challenging simplified assessments of cultural appropriation. People like Chris Deckker, founder of the band Medicine Drum and London label/club Return to the Source. Deckker's early objective was to produce an "electro-organic" soundscape that expressed "a connection between the modern, futuristic dance music sounds and the primal, ancient trance-inducing rhythms of tribal drummers." His formative Return to the Source compilations, such as *Sacred Sites* (1997), offered a journey across global sacred centers, a fusional impulse later manifesting in the his global Earthdance project, which, among other charitable work, raises funds for various threatened indigenous populations.[23] Or Olli Wisdom (aka Space Tribe), who has regularly sampled the voice of Timothy Leary and pursues an off-planetary lifestyle as a "galactic citizen."

Or Kwali, who is a Red Magnetic Skywalker, according to her Dreamspell Galactic Signature, and who works for the Planetary Art Network and identifies as a fairy. Or Delvin Solkinson, cocreator of the Liminal Village, permaculturalist, "unified systems" enabler, and member of "an elvish tribe of galactivators and technomystics" based in Mount Elpinstone in British Columbia.[24] Such spectacular and shifting self-assemblages transpire within a (counter) culture of the sample and remix. To negotiate this complex terrain of symbolic transactions and intercultural collaboration is a challenging task for researchers. In the remixological world of psytrance, as interethnic, cultural, and national diversity multiplies— remember that Boom, for instance, has reported the attendance of participants from eighty-five countries—the prospect of locating an authentic original or a true fake becomes increasingly difficult, if not impossible.

ᘐᘐ

Where Jeffrey Kripal, in his philosophy of consciousness conveyed in this volume, offers evidence of what he calls the "mind filter," in this chapter I have explored the socioexperiential aesthetics, the techniques through which such aesthetics are realized and performed, and the *cultural island* (apropos Aldous Huxley) upon which psytrance flourishes. Downstream from ecstatic and reflexive countercultural trajectories, it seems possible to argue that these aesthetics offer a cultural expression of the "filter" with which Kripal is concerned. With the Boom Festival, though, we have transited from the island to the festival, from utopia to heterotopia, or, more to the point, an alternative cultural heterotopia, a sociocultural expression of the multiplicity of that which "matters" among its transnational participants. Whereas a utopian space is a place that is not a real place, psytrance festivals like Boom are actual social contexts, empirical sites where participants are encouraged to experiment with otherness, re/discovering their selves in an experiential authenticity at the root of the countercultural quest. The chapter has shown that various experimental practices, including travel, psychoactive drug use, dance, and music, have been integral to this quest. And recognition that identities are shaped and reshaped in accordance with the logic of the perpetual remix endogenous to EDM, and in accordance with digitized lifestyles, contributes to our understanding of the role of mimesis and recombinant techniques in projects of the self and culture. Such experimental techniques reveal a quest for transcendence not exhausted by an expenditure of energy on the dance floor, one that expresses a desire for (personal and cultural) transition. A "tribal" social aesthetic rooted in an ecstatic romanticism (the Dance Temple), and a pedagogical hub for the transmission of alternative cultural *sacra* (the Liminal Village), powered by an assemblage of chemical, sound, and cybertechnologies, Boom is an optimized mechanism for the transitional experience. As the most important pilgrimage center in the psytrance movement, the event hosts this diverse religiospiritual legacy, illustrating an interfacing of the "religious" and the "spiritual" facilitated by a sophisticated, technologically advanced ("secular") institution.

NOTES

1. This was the official figure.
2. See especially St John 2004a and 2006 and the other contributions to that special edition of *Culture and Religion*. For accounts specifically addressing the religiospirituality of EDMC, see D'Andrea 2007; Gauthier 2005; Hutson 2000; Sylvan 2005; Takahashi 2005; Takahashi and Olaveson 2003; and Tramacchi 2000.
3. I conducted field research at the Boom Festival in August 2006 and August 2008.
4. For example, the now removed fundamentalist Christian Web site "truthaboutrave.com," which had revealed the "awful truth" that raves are "a means of the devil to solicit worship."
5. RAVE is an acronym for Reducing America's Vulnerability to Ecstasy, the apparent vocation of Democrat Senator Joe Biden and Republican Senator Chuck Grassley. Constituting an update on the repressive "crack house" laws extended to temporary, one-off, and open-air events, the Rave Act legislation was embedded in the Child Abduction Protect Act of 2003.
6. See Richard Spurgeon's "Rave—The Awakening": http://www.rave-theawakening.com (accessed June 15, 2007).
7. http://www.goagil.com/ (accessed June 15, 2008). Also see McAteer (2002:29) and St John (2011a).
8. http://www.boomfestival.org (accessed August 21, 2008).
9. http://www.welcomehome.org/rainbow/index.html (accessed June 6, 2008).
10. Boom promotes and practices permacultural principles, builds community gardens, uses recycled material for major installations, features composting toilets, biological treatment of waste waters, and recycles vegetable oil to fuel power generators (as "biofuel").

11. The Liminal Village features a Visions Gallery presenting works from the global visionary art movement, and the Temple Gardens designed according to permaculture principles. The dramatizing of participant causes within the framework of Boom's "visionary" trajectory is discussed in St John (2009b, 2010b).

12. But which has deeper historical roots (i.e., Transcendentalist and romantic traditions).

13. Among whom figure Sri Aurobindo (whose work provided the inspiration for the founding of the California Institute of Integral Studies); George Burr Leonard, who coined the term "human potential movement"; Michael Murphy, cofounder of the Esalen Institute in Big Sur and "Integral Transformative Practice" (with Burr Leonard); and Ken Wilber, who articulated "integral theory" and founded the Integral Institute.

14. Though not without their own elitist codes and norms, as configured by Arun Saldanha 2007.

15. The Hindu idea of moksha, which in Sanskrit refers to liberation from suffering, has been frequently adopted as a motivating theme.

16. As illustrated by Space Tribe's (Olli Wisdom) debut album *Sonic Mandala* (Spirit Zone, 1996) and the collaborative project, Mandala. Whether in the form of a Tibetan sand mandala or a crop circle, mandalas are often regarded as spiritual teaching tools, and as an aid to meditation and trance induction.

17. Of course, in Australia, settler inhabitants have more commonly turned to Aboriginal peoples, often held to embody timeless archetypal symbols, the proximity to which promise spiritual sustenance and "redemption" for alienated setters (Marcus 1988; Hamilton 1990; Lattas 1990, 1992).

18. We thus encounter challenges to dubious claims to indigeneity (Kehoe 1990; Rose 1992), "fakelore" (Niman 1997:131–48), "imperialist nostalgia" (Rosaldo 1989), a "salvage paradigm" (Root 1996:100), and entrepreneurial expropriation and commodification (Aldred 2000; Jenkins 2004). Within cautionary tales the common conviction is that an "equivalence of agency" is impossible (Johnson 1995:164) and that "appropriation goes hand in hand with colonialism" (Root 1996:102).

19. The phrase is used by David Tacey (2000:151) in his response to critics.

20. Indeed, these days, illustrating the growth of a therapeutic ethnotourism industry, growing numbers are undertaking journeys to religious specialists such as Amazonian *ayahuasceros* ("ayahuasca shamans") and Hispanic *curanderos* (healer/shaman) who offer entheogenic retreats.

21. These lines form vocal samples in Burn in Noise's "Transparent" (*Passing Clouds*, Alchemy, 2008).

22. Also known as diviner's sage, *Salvia divinorum* has a long and continuing

tradition of use by indigenous Mazatec in Oaxaca, Mexico, where shamans employ it to facilitate visionary states of consciousness during curing or divination sessions as well as to treat remedial ailments.

23. http://www.earthdance.org/ (accessed September 14, 2008).

24. Delvin is also a member of the Crystal and Spore collective and is creator of the Galactic Trading Card Oracle Complex. Variously used as altar icons, for random gifting, or for divination, these cards feature designs/numerology drawn from the Tarot and Argüelles's Dreamspell, and involve I Ching trigrams, chakras, Platonic solids, and Mayan numbers. http://www.elvism.net/ (accessed September 29, 2008).

REFERENCES

Adams, Rebecca, and Robert Sardiello, eds. 2000. *Deadhead Social Science: You Ain't Gonna Learn What You Don't Want to Know*. Walnut Creek, CA: AltaMira.

Aldred, Lisa. 2000. "Plastic Shamans and Astroturf Sun Dances: New Age Commercialization of Native American Spirituality." *American Indian Quarterly* 24, no. 3 (Summer): 329–52.

Argüelles, José. 1987. *The Mayan Factor: Path Beyond Technology*. Santa Fe: Bear.

—— 2002. *Time and the Technosphere: The Law of Time in Human Affairs*. Rochester, VT: Inner Traditions.

Bey, Hakim. 1991. *TAZ: The Temporary Autonomous Zone—Ontological Anarchy and Poetic Terrorism*. New York: Autonomedia.

Campbell, Colin. 2008. *The Easternization of the West: A Thematic Account of Cultural Change in the Modern Era*. Boulder: Paradigm.

Clifford, James. 1988. *The Predicament of Culture: Twentieth Century Ethnography, Literature and Art*. Cambridge: Harvard University Press.

Cohen, Erik. 1979. "A Phenomenology of Tourist Experiences." *Sociology* 13:179–201.

Conklin, B. 1997. "Body Paint, Feathers, and VCRs: Aesthetics and Authenticity in Amazonian Activism." *American Ethnologist* 24, no. 4 (November): 711–37.

Cooke, Del. 2006. "Delirious Expenditure: Post-Modern Ghost Dances and the Carnivalesque." *eSharp* no 7 (Spring). http://www.gla.ac.uk/departments/esharp/issues/7/ (accessed July 12, 2011).

Cuthbert, Denise, and Michelle Grossman. 1996. "Trading Places: Locating the Indigenous in the New Age." *Thamyris* 3, no. 1: 18–36.

D'Andrea, Anthony. 2006. "The Spiritual Economy of Nightclubs and Raves: Osho Sannyasins as Party Promoters in Ibiza and Pune/Goa." *Culture and Religion* 7, no. 1(March): 61–75.

—— 2007. *Global Nomads: Techno and New Age as Transnational Countercultures.* New York: Routledge.

Davis, Erik. 1998. *Techgnosis: Myth, Magic, and Mysticism in the Age of Information.* New York: Harmony.

—— 2004. "Hedonic Tantra: Golden Goa's Trance Transmission." In Graham St John, ed., *Rave Culture and Religion,* 256–72. London: Routledge.

Eshun, Kodwo. 1998. *More Brilliant Than the Sun: Adventures in Sonic Fiction.* London: Quartet.

Fikentscher, Kai. 2000. *"'You Better Work!': Underground Dance Music in New York City.* Middletown: Wesleyan University Press.

Fritz, Jimi. 1999. *Rave Culture: An Insider's Overview.* Canada: Smallfry.

Gauthier, François. 2004. "Rapturous Ruptures: The 'Instituant' Religious Experience of Rave." In Graham St John, ed., *Rave Culture and Religion,* 65–84. London: Routledge.

—— 2005. "Orpheus and the Underground: Raves and Implicit Religion—From Interpretation to Critique." *Implicit Religion* 8, no. 3: 217–65.

Gelfer, Joseph, ed. 2011. *2012: Decoding the Countercultural Apocalypse.* Sheffield: Equinox.

Gerard, Morgan. 2004. "Selecting Ritual: DJs, Dancers, and Liminality in Underground Dance Music." In Graham St John, ed., *Rave Culture and Religion,* 167–84. London: Routledge.

Gilmore, Lee. 2009. *Theater in a Crowded Fire: Ritual and Spirituality at the Burning Man Festival.* Berkeley: University of California Press.

Gilmore, Lee, and Mark Van Proyen, eds. 2005. *Afterburn: Reflections on Burning Man.* Albuquerque: University of New Mexico Press.

Hamilton, Annette. 1990. "Fear and Desire: Asians, Aborigines and the National Imaginary." *Australian Cultural History* 9:14–35.

Heelas, Paul. 1996. *The New Age Movement. The Celebration of the Self and the Sacralization of Modernity.* Cambridge: Blackwell.

—— 2008. *Spiritualities of Life: From the Romantics to Well-being Culture.* Oxford: Blackwell.

Heelas, Paul, and Linda Woodhead, with Benjamin Seel, Bronislaw Szerszynski, and Karin Tusting. 2005. *The Spiritual Revolution: Why Religion is Giving Way to Spirituality.* Malden, MA: Blackwell.

Hetherington, Kevin. 2000. *New Age Travellers: Vanloads of Uproarious Humanity.* London: Cassell.

Hutson, Scott. 2000. "The Rave: Spiritual Healing in Modern Western Subcultures." *Anthropological Quarterly* 73, no. 1(January): 35–49.

Jackson, Phil. 2004. *Inside Clubbing: Sensual Experiments in the Art of Being Human.* Oxford: Berg.

Jenkins, Philip. 2004. *Dream Catchers: How Mainstream America Discovered Native Spirituality*. New York: Oxford University Press.

Johnson, Paul, C. 1995. "Shamanism from Ecuador to Chicago: A Case Study in New Age Ritual Appropriation." *Religion* 25:163–78.

Kehoe, Alice, B. 1990. "Primal Gaia: Primitivists and Plastic Medicine Men." In J. Clifton, ed., *The Invented Indian: Cultural Fictions and Government Policies*, 193–209. New Brunswick, NJ: Transaction.

Kozinets, Robert V., and John F. Sherry Jr. 2004. "Dancing on Common Ground: Exploring the Sacred at Burning Man." In Graham St John, ed., *Rave Culture and Religion*, 287–303. New York: Routledge.

Kripal, Jeffrey. 2007. *Esalen: America and the Religion of No Religion*. Chicago: University of Chicago Press.

Lattas, Andrew. 1990. "Aborigines and Contemporary Australian Nationalism: Primordiality and the Cultural Politics of Otherness." *Social Analysis* 27:50–69.

—— 1992. "Primitivism, Nationalism, and Individualism in Australian Popular Culture." In *Power, Knowledge, and Aborigines: Journal of Australian Studies* 35 (December): 45–58.

Lewis, J. Lowell, and Paul Dowsey-Magog. 1993. "The Maleny Fire Event: Rehearsals Toward Neo-Liminality." *Australian Journal of Anthropology* 4, no. 3 (December): 198–219.

Luckman, Susan. 2003. "Going Bush and Finding One's 'Tribe': Raving, Escape, and the Bush Doof." *Continuum: Journal of Media and Cultural Studies* 17, no. 3: 315–30.

Luckmann, Thomas. 1967. *The Invisible Religion: The Problem of Religion in Modern Society*. New York: MacMillan.

Lynch, Gordon, and Emily Badger. 2006. "The Mainstream Post-Rave Club Scene as a Secondary Institution: A British Perspective." *Culture and Religion* 7, no. 1 (March): 27–40.

McAteer, Michael. 2002. "'Redefining the Ancient Tribal Ritual for the Twenty-first Century': Goa Gil and the Trance Dance Experience." Paper for Division of Philosophy, Religion, and Psychology, Reed College. http://www.goagil.com/thesis.html (accessed August 29, 2008).

McKay, George. 1996. *Senseless Acts of Beauty: Cultures of Resistance Since the Sixties*. London: Verso.

McKenna, Terence. 1993. *Food of the Gods: The Search for the Original Tree of Knowledge*. New York: Bantam.

McKenna, Terence, and Dennis McKenna. 1994 [1975]. *The Invisible Landscape: Mind, Hallucinogens and the I Ching*. San Francisco: Harper.

Maffesoli, Michel. 1996 [1988]. *The Time of the Tribes: The Decline of Individualism in Mass Society*. London: Sage.

Malbon, Ben. 1999. *Clubbing: Dancing, Ecstasy, and Vitality*. London: Routledge.

Marcus, Julie. 1988. "The Journey Out to the Centre: The Cultural Appropriation of Ayers Rock." *Kunapipi* 10, nos. 1 and 2: 254–75.

Meadan, Bryan. 2001. *TRANCENational ALIENation: Trance Music Culture, Moral Panics, and Transnational Identity in Israel*. Lulu.

Morton, John. 1996. "Aboriginality, Mabo, and the Republic: Indigenising Australia." In Bain Attwood, ed., *In the Age of Mabo: History, Aborigines, and Australia*, 117–35. Sydney: Allen and Unwin.

Mulcock, Jane. 1997. "Cultural Consumerism and the Quest for Indigenous Identities: Differing Perspectives on Cultural Appropriation." Paper presented at Objects of Belonging: Consumption, Culture, and Identity, RCIS, University of Western Sydney, October 11.

Newton, Janice. 1988. "Aborigines, Tribes, and the Counterculture." *Social Analysis* 23:53–71.

Niman, Michael. 1997. *People of the Rainbow: A Nomadic Utopia*. Knoxville: University of Tennessee Press.

Olaveson, Tim. 2004. "'Connectedness' and the Rave Experience: Rave as New Religious Movement?" In Graham St John, ed., *Rave Culture and Religion*, 85–106. London: Routledge.

Partridge, Christopher. 2004. *The Re-Enchantment of the West: Alternative Spiritualities, Sacralization, and Popular Culture and Occulture*. Vol. 1. London: Clark International.

—— 2005. *The Re-Enchantment of the West: Alternative Spiritualities, Sacralization, and Popular Culture and Occulture*. Vol. 2. London: Clark International.

—— 2006. "The Spiritual and the Revolutionary: Alternative Spirituality, British Free Festivals, and the Emergence of Rave Culture." *Culture and Religion* 7, no. 1 (March): 41–60.

—— 2007. "King Tubby Meets the Upsetter at the Grass Roots of Dub: Some Thoughts on the Early History and Influence of Dub Reggae." *Popular Music History*, 2, no. 3: 309–31.

Pike, Sarah. 2001. *Earthly Bodies: Magic Selves: Contemporary Pagans, and the Search for Community*. Berkeley: University of California Press.

Pinchbeck, Daniel. 2002. *Breaking Open the Head: A Psychedelic Journey into the Heart of Contemporary Shamanism*. New York: Broadway.

Reichel-Dolmatoff, Gerardo. 1975. *The Shaman and the Jaguar: A Study of Narcotic Drugs Among the Indians of Colombia*. Philadelphia: Temple University Press.

Reynolds, Simon. 1997. "Back to Eden: Innocence, Indolence, and Pastoralism in Psychedelic Music, 1966–1996." In Antonio Melechi, ed., *Psychedelia Britannica: Hallucinogenic Drugs in Britain*, 143–65. London: Turnaround.

Rill, Bryan. 2006. "Rave, Communitas, and Embodied Idealism." *Music Therapy Today* 7, no. 3 (October): 648–61.

Root, Deborah. 1996. *Cannibal Culture: Art, Appropriation, and the Commodification of Difference.* Boulder: Westview.

Rosaldo, Renado. 1989. "Imperialist Nostalgia." *Representations* 26:107–22.

Rose, Wendy. 1992. "The Great Pretenders: Further Reflections on Whiteshamanism." In M. Jaimes, ed., *The State of Native America: Genocide, Colonization, and Resistance*, 403–21. Boston: South End.

St John, Graham. 2001. "Alternative Cultural Heterotopia and the Liminoid Body: Beyond Turner at ConFest." *Australian Journal of Anthropology* 12, no. 1 (April): 47–66.

—— ed. 2004a. *Rave Culture and Religion.* London: Routledge.

—— 2004b. "The Difference Engine: Liberation and the Rave Imaginary." In Graham St John, ed., *Rave Culture and Religion*, 19–45. London: Routledge.

—— 2004c. "Techno Millennium: Dance, Ecology, and Future Primitives." In Graham St John, ed., *Rave Culture and Religion*, 213–35. London: Routledge.

—— 2005. "Outback Vibes: Sound Systems on the Road to Legitimacy." *Postcolonial Studies: Culture, Politics, Economy* 8, no. 3: 321–36.

—— 2006. "Electronic Dance Music Culture and Religion: An Overview." *Culture and Religion* 7, no. 1 (March): 1–26.

—— 2008. "Trance Tribes and Dance Vibes: Victor Turner and Electronic Dance Music Culture." In Graham St John, ed., *Victor Turner and Contemporary Cultural Performance*, 149–73. New York: Berghahn.

—— 2009a. *Technomad: Global Raving Countercultures.* Sheffield: Equinox.

—— 2009b. "Neotrance and the Psychedelic Festival." *Dancecult: Journal of Electronic Dance Music Culture* 1, no. 1 (Fall): 35–64.

—— ed. 2010a. *The Local Scenes and Global Culture of Psytrance.* London: Routledge.

—— 2010b. "Liminal Culture and Global Movement: The Transitional World of Psytrance." In Graham St John, ed., *The Local Scenes and Global Culture of Psytrance*, 220–46. London: Routledge.

——2011a. "DJ Goa Gil: Kalifornian Exile, Dark Yogi, and Dreaded Anomaly. *Dancecult: Journal of Electronic Dance Music Culture* 3, no. 1: 97–128.

—— 2011b. "The 2012 Movement, Visionary Arts and Psytrance Culture." In Joseph Gelfer, ed., *2012: Decoding the Countercultural Apocalypse*, 123–43. London: Equinox.

—— 2012a. *Global Tribe : Technology, Spirituality and Psytrance.* London: Equinox.

—— 2012b. "Freak Media: Vibe Tribes, Sampledelic Outlaws and Israeli Psytrance." *Continuum: Journal of Media and Cultural Studies* 26, no. 2 forthcoming.

Saldanha, Arun. 2007. *Psychedelic White: Goa Trance and the Viscosity of Race.* Minneapolis: University of Minnesota Press.

Sardiello, Robert. 1994. "Secular Rituals in Popular Culture: A Case for Grateful Dead Concerts and Dead Head Identity." In John. S. Epstein, ed., *Adolescents and Their Music: If It's Too Loud, You're Too Old*, 115–38. New York: Garland.

Sitler, Robert. K. 2006. "The 2012 Phenomenon: New Age Appropriation of an Ancient Mayan Calendar." *Nova Religio* 9, no. 3 (February): 24–38.

Sylvan, Robin. 2005. *Trance Formation: The Spiritual and Religious Dimensions of Global Rave Culture*. New York: Routledge.

Tacey, David. 2000. *Re-Enchantment: The New Australian Spirituality*. New York: Harper Collins.

Takahashi, Melanie. 2005. "Spirituality Through the Science of Sound: The DJ as Technoshaman in Rave Culture". In Michael J. Gilmour, ed., *Call Me the Seeker: Listening to Religion in Popular Music*, 239–66. New York: Continuum.

Takahashi, Melanie, and Tim Olaveson. 2003. "Music, Dance, and Raving Bodies: Raving as Spirituality in the Central Canadian Rave Scene." *Journal of Ritual Studies* 17, no. 2: 72–96.

Taussig, Michael. 1993. *Mimesis and Alterity: A Particular History of the Senses*. New York: Routledge.

Taves. Ann. 1999. *Fits, Trances, and Visions: Experiencing Religion and Explaining Experience from Wesley to James*. Princeton: Princeton University Press.

Taylor, Bron. 1997. "Earthen Spirituality or Cultural Genocide? Radical Environmentalism's Appropriation of Native American Spirituality. *Religion* 27:185–215.

Taylor, Timothy. 2001. *Strange Sounds: Music, Technology, and Culture*. New York: Routledge.

Thomas. Nicholas. 2005. "Introduction." In Nicholas Thomas, Anna Cole, Bronwen Douglas, eds., *Tattoo: Bodies, Art, and Exchange in the Pacific and the West*, 7–30. Durham: Duke University Press.

Tramacchi, Des. 2000. "Field Tripping: Psychedelic Communitas and Ritual in the Australian Bush." *Journal of Contemporary Religion* 15, no. 2: 201–13.

—— 2006. "Vapours and Visions: Religious Dimensions of DMT Use." PhD diss., School of History, Philosophy, Religion, and Classics, University of Queensland.

Turner, Victor. 1982. *From Ritual to Theatre: The Human Seriousness of Play*. New York: PAJP.

Welch, Christina. 2007. "Complicating Spiritual Appropriation: North American Indian Agency in Western Alternative Spiritual Practice." *Journal of Alternative Spiritualities and New Age Studies* 3: 97–117.

Winkleman, Michael. 1986. "Trance States: A Theoretical Model and Cross-Cultural Analysis." *Ethos* 14:174–203.

Woodhead, Linda. 2001. "The World's Parliament of Religions and the Rise of Alternative Spirituality." In Linda Woodhead, ed., *Reinventing Christianity: Nineteenth-Century Contexts*, 81–96. Aldershot: Ashgate.

Ziguras, Christopher. 1996. "Paying Your Respects to Someone Else's Elders: The Western Appropriation of Asian and Indigenous Religious Discourses." *Aedon* 4, no. 1: 67–76.

ACKNOWLEDGMENTS

The initial questions that provided the impetus for this volume were voiced during vigorous and stimulating conversations at the School for Advanced Research in Santa Fe, New Mexico, at a meeting titled "Can there be a social science of spirituality?" The meeting, sponsored by the Social Science Research Council and the School for Advanced Research, proved most conducive to reflection and discussion. The majority of the contributors to this volume met for the first time at the SAR; we were joined at that stimulating meeting by SSRC president Craig Calhoun, SAR president James F. Brooks, Omri Elisha, and Julie Velasquez Runk, each of whom made important contributions to our discussions.

A subsequent meeting in New York extended the conversation and questions in different ways, thanks in part to the active participation of our growing list of contributors and other invitees to the meeting: Jeremy Stolow, Webb Keane, Tanya Luhrmann, Charles Hirschkind, and Gauri Viswanathan. Their insights, challenges, and thoughtful engagement helped to shape the next stage of the process, where we began to see this project take shape as a book.

As the project moved from conference to book, we received support and assistance from the Social Science Research Council and the SSRC's expert staff, particularly Jessica Polebaum, as well as from Columbia

University's Institute for Religion, Culture, and Public Life. We are fortunate to have had their institutional support.

As editors, we are nonetheless most grateful to the authors of the individual chapters in this volume. Our colleagues are without exception conscientious contributors and discussion partners. We have enjoyed and appreciated the gifts of time, thought, and argument they each offered to us and to the larger whole.

CONTRIBUTORS

REBECCA ALLAHYARI is research associate at the School for Advanced Study in Santa Fe, New Mexico. Her ethnographic work centers on moral self-betterment in everyday practice and politics. She is completing a project, "Utopian Devotions: Enchantment and Anxiety in Homeschooling," which explores homeschooling as an everyday experimental practice interwoven with urgent visions of sacred childhoods and the constraints of mundane life. A new fieldwork project, "Witnessing Dementia: Generosity, Surrogacy, and Conflict in the Guardianship of the Elderly," will compare the experience of guardianship and elder care between professional guardians and family guardians. She is the author also of *Visions of Charity: Volunteer Workers and Moral Community* (University of California Press, 2000).

COURTNEY BENDER is associate professor of religion and sociology at Columbia University. Her work centers broadly on lived religious practice and public religious interactions in American life. She is the author of *Heaven's Kitchen: Living Religion at God's Love We Deliver* (University of Chicago Press, 2003) and *The New Metaphysicals: Spirituality and the American Religious Imagination* (University of Chicago Press, 2010) and the coeditor, with Pamela Klassen, of *After Pluralism: Reimagining Models of Interreligious Engagement* (Columbia University Press, 2010).

ERICA BORNSTEIN is associate professor of anthropology at the University of Wisconsin-Milwaukee. Her research interests include philanthropy, religious charity, humanitarianism, nongovernmental organizations, political anthropology, and the anthropology of religion. She is the author of *The Spirit of Development: Protestant NGOs, Morality, and Economics in Zimbabwe* (Stanford University Press, 2005), and her current research project, *Disquieting Gifts: An Ethnography of Humanitarianism in New Delhi* (Stanford University Press, 2012), and coeditor, with Peter Redfield, of *Forces of Compassion: Humanitarianism Between Ethics and Politics* (SAR, 2011).

JEFFREY J. KRIPAL holds the J. Newton Rayzor Chair in Philosophy and Religious Thought at Rice University. His current areas of interest include the comparative erotics of mystical literature, American countercultural translations of Asian religious traditions, and the history of Western esotericism from ancient gnosticism to the new age. He is the author, most recently, of *Mutants and Mystics: Science Fiction, Superhero Comics, and the Paranormal* (University of Chicago Press, 2011), *Authors of the Impossible: The Paranormal and the Sacred* (University of Chicago Press, 2010), and *Esalen: America and the Religion of No Religion* (University of Chicago Press, 2007).

BIRGIT MEYER is a professor in the Department of Religious Studies and Theology at the University of Utrecht. Her research explores the anthropology of religion and modernity in the context of West Africa. She is the author of *Translating the Devil: Religion and Modernity Among the Ewe in Ghana* (Africa World Press, 2000) and the editor of *Aesthetic Formations: Media, Religion, and the Senses in the Making of Communities* (Palgrave, 2009) as well as coeditor of *Readings in Modernity in Africa* (Indiana University Press, 2008) and *Religion, Media and the Public Sphere* (University of Indiana Press, 2006).

PETER REDFIELD is associate professor of anthropology at the University of North Carolina at Chapel Hill. Trained as a cultural anthropologist sympathetic to history, he concentrates on circulations of science and technology in colonial and postcolonial contexts. He is the author of *Space in the Tropics: From Convicts to Rockets in French Guiana* (University of California Press, 2000) and *Life in Crisis: The Ethical Journey of Doctors Without Borders* (University of California Press, forthcoming), as well as coeditor, with Erica Bornstein, of *Forces of Compassion: Humanitarianism Between Ethics and Politics* (SAR, 2011).

GRAHAM ST JOHN is a research associate at the University of Queensland's Centre for Critical and Cultural Studies. A cultural anthropologist with an interdisciplinary research interest in electronic dance, dance cultures, ritual, and performance, he is the author of *Global Tribe: Technology, Spirituality, and Psytrance* (Equinox, 2012) and *Technomad: Global Raving Countercultures* (Equinox, 2009) and the editor of *The Local Scenes and Global Culture of Psytrance* (Routledge, 2010). He is executive editor of *Dancecult: Journal of Electronic Dance Music Culture*.

ANN TAVES holds the Virgil Cordano OFM Endowed Chair in Catholic Studies and is professor of religious studies at the University of California, Santa Barbara. She is a historian of Christianity specializing in the modern period in the United States, England, and France with a focus on the historical and contemporary interplay of psychology and religious experience. She is the author of *Religious Experience Reconsidered: A Building Block Approach to the Study of Religion and Other Special Things* (Princeton University Press, 2009) and *Fits, Trances, and Visions: Experiencing Religion and Explaining Experience from Wesley to James* (Princeton University Press, 1999).

SILVIA TOMÁŠKOVÁ is associate professor of women's studies and anthropology at the University of North Carolina at Chapel Hill. Trained as an anthropological archaeologist, her professional interests combine an inquiry into the prehistoric past with a concern for present social and political contexts in which the science of archaeology operates. She is the author of *The Nature of Difference: History and Lithic Use-Wear at Two Upper Paleolithic Sites in Central Europe* (Archaeopress, 2000) and *Traveling Spirits: The History of Shamans and the Prehistory of Gender* (University of California Press, forthcoming).

CHRISTOPHER WHITE is associate professor of religion in America at Vassar College. His research is particularly focused on religion and science, the history of Christianity, spirituality and "unchurched" religion, religion and popular culture, and new religious movements. He has published articles on these and other subjects in scholarly journals and edited books and is the author of *Unsettled Minds: Psychology and the American Search for Spiritual Assurance* (University of California Press, 2009).

INDEX

Adusei, Kwadwo, 113n20
Akosah-Sarpong, Kofi, 103–5, 107
Albert, David, 201, 202, 206
Albert I of Monaco, Prince, 48, 54, 56
Allahyari, Rebecca, 23, 26
Ammerman, Nancy, 210n9
Angell, James, 68
anthropology, *see* France; prehistory; science
archaeology, *see* France; prehistory
Arendt, Hannah, 25, 144, 168–69
Argüelles, José, 259, 260
Aron, Raymond, 163
Asad, Talal, 4, 87
atheism, 6
Atta Mills, John Evans, 106, 113n20
authenticity, 2, 3, 19; and childhood, 2, 23,
    179–82, 184, 209; contexts of, 22–24; and
    prehistory, 24; and psytrance culture,
    249–51, 254–55, 262, 264, 266–67; and
    spirituality, 24, 96–97; and suggestibility,
    71, 77–81; and voluntarism, 124, 126, 128
authority, 3, 19; and American context, 26, 64,
    108–9, 180; and colonialism, 156; contexts
    of, 24–28; and crowd behavior, 64–65; and
    education, 180–182, 192, 202, 208; and
    science, 26–27, 146; and secular-religious
    binary, 25–26; and spirituality in Ghana,

96–97, 103–6; and suggestibility, 70–77;
    and valuation, 27, 146

Barley, Stephen, 206
Barthes, Roland, 163, 240–41
Bauman, Kurt, 182
Bayart, Jean-François, 104
Beauvoir, Simone de, 163
belief: and practices, 14–15, 148; and social
    constructivism, 16, 236–38; and suggest-
    ibility, 77–82; *see also* religion; spirituality
Berger, Peter, 237–38
Besant, Annie, 8
Blumenberg, Hans, 146
Bonsam, Kwaku, 92, 102–3, 113n20
Boom Festival (Portugal), 21–22, 25, 266–67;
    and counterculture, 253, 264, 266; descrip-
    tions of, 248–49, 252–53, 259–62; *see also*
    psytrance culture
Borel, Raymond, 160
Bornstein, Erica, 21, 256
Boule, Marcellin, 48–51
Bouyssonie, abbé brothers Amédée and Jean,
    38, 52
Braude, Stephen, 244n3
Brauman, Rony, 148, 162–64, 165
Bremond, Abbé Henri, 52

Price, Richard, 215
primitivism, 1, 64, 258
Protestantism, 20–21, 28, 82n2, 108, 151; and
    colonial Africa, 89, 154, 156; and Ghana,
    95; and suggestibility, 69
psychology: and American evangelicalism,
    63, 69, 74–75, 80; and controlling religious
    credulity, 61–62, 67–77; and crowd
    behavior, 63–65; and hypnotism, 64; and
    suggestibility experimentation, 72–75; and
    the unconscious, 62–65, 67, 78; see also
    suggestibility
psytrance culture, 2, 21–22, 255, 257;
    development of, 254–55; and drug use,
    258–61; and electronic dance music culture
    (EDMC), 249–50, 262–64, 266; and Mayan
    calendar, 259, 261; and music, 254–57,
    262–63, 265; and Native American culture,
    258–59; and occultism, 264–65; and Ori-
    entalism, 256–57; religious and spiritual
    characteristics of, 249–50, 254–55, 259,
    262, 264–67; and transcendence, 249–51,
    267; and tribalism, 251–52

RAVE Act (United States), 249, 267n5
Rawlings, J. J., 90, 91, 98, 105
Red Cross, 23, 145, 149–53, 156, 157, 158, 159,
    160, 161, 162, 166, 169, 171n6; see also
    Durant, Henry
Redfield, Peter, 23, 27
reincarnation, 20–21, 225–27, 233–34
religion: and authority, 25–26, 98, 108–9; and
    belief 14–15, 19; and biblical reference,
    66–67, 78; and humanitarianism, 144, 148,
    154–57; and intersections with spiritual-
    ity and secularism, 86–92, 93, 106–7,
    119–20, 139, 144–46, 151–53, 154–57, 161,
    168–70, 179–81, 209, 222, 238–41, 243,
    249–50, 267; lived religion, 12–13, 29n5;
    and politics, 103–6, 108–9, 195; religious
    choice, 8–9; religious scientists, 37–39,
    51–57; and science dualism, 35–36, 38–39,
    54–57, 69, 81–82, 215, 220, 222, 238–41,
    243; and scientific refutation, 61, 67–68;
    and suggestibility, 62–63, 66, 70–71; and
    technology, 99–101
Rhine, J. B., 230
Richards, Graham, 64
Rothman, Barbara Katz, 207
Royer, Clémence, 40, 46–47

Russell, Bertrand, 222
Sadler, William, 81
Sagan, Carl, 226
Saint-Hilaire, Geoffrey, 36, 41
Sartre, Jean-Paul, 163
Sautuola, Marcelino Sanz de, 50
Schmidt, Leigh Eric, 210n4
Schweitzer, Albert, 23, 145, 154–57, 158, 162,
    163, 165, 169; early life, 154–55; and mis-
    sionary context, 154–56, 172n13
science: and authority, 26–27; and French
    Catholicism, 34–35, 41; and material-
    ism, 229, 238, 241–43; and mind-matter
    relation, 225, 229, 231–32, 238–40, 242–43;
    and neurohistory of religions, 239–41; and
    paranormal experience, 216, 220, 239–40;
    and prehistory, 50–51; religious scientists,
    37–39, 51–57; scientific method, 3, 4, 230,
    234–35; and suggestibility, 78–79; see also
    psychology; religion
Scott, Joan, 140n3
Scott, Walter Dill, 63
secularity: and authority, 25–26, 161;
    and homeschooling, 183, 192–93; and
    humanitarian morality, 144–46, 147–49,
    152, 154–57, 161, 165–70; and intersec-
    tions with religion and spirituality, 87–92,
    93, 103–9, 119–20, 139, 144–46, 151–53,
    154–57, 161, 168–70, 222, 238–41, 243, 267;
    meaning and context of, 1, 2, 4, 28–29,
    29n2; and practice, 13–15, 92; secularism,
    4, 5, 8, 9; secularization, 3, 4, 15, 62, 86–87,
    106–7, 108; secular-religious binary, 3–12,
    17–19, 24, 86, 154, 240–41, 243, 249; and
    suggestibility, 82
Shanahan, Suzanne, 181
Shpongle, 254, 263
Shweder, Richard, 226, 240, 245n15
Sidis, Boris, 64–65, 66
Sinclair, R. D., 72, 74
Singh, Manmohan, 122
Smith, Adam, 147, 148, 149
Smith, J. Z., 245n14
Snow, A. J., 82n1
Solkinson, Delvin, 266
Spickard, James, 206
spirits, 3, 6, 28, 56, 66, 81–82, 89–91; and
    Ghanaian context, 86–97, 98, 102–9,
    111n9; and materialism, 48, 93–97,
    231–32; and politics, 103–6, 108; and

CW01455185

The Essential Good Hotel Guide UK 2025–2026

Trusted Picks for Comfort, Quality, and Memorable Stays Across Britain

Tavian Q. Marlowe

DISCLAIMER

While every precaution has been taken in the preparation of this book, the publisher assumes no responsibility for errors or omissions, or for damages resulting from the use of the information contained herein.

The Essential Good Hotel Guide UK 2025–2026 : Trusted Picks for Comfort, Quality, and Memorable Stays Across Britain

First edition.

COPYRIGHT © TAVIAN Q. MARLOWE 2025.
ALL RIGHTS RESERVED

Before this document can be legally duplicated or reproduced in any manner, the publisher's consent must be gained. Therefore, the contents within this document can neither be stored electronically, transferred, nor kept in a database. Neither in part, nor in full can this document be copied, scanned, faxed, or retained without approval from the publisher or creator.

TABLE OF CONTENTS

INTRODUCTION

HOW TO USE THIS GUIDE EFFECTIVELY

Every traveller seeks that elusive balance between comfort, authenticity, and value — the feeling of stepping into a place that welcomes you as though you belong there. Yet, in a world overflowing with polished marketing, digital advertising, and star ratings that often tell only half the story, finding such a place requires more than a quick search or glowing online review. The process calls for discernment — a way of reading between the lines, understanding what makes a stay truly memorable, and learning to see past the surface of glossy hotel descriptions.

This guide is designed to help you do just that. It invites you to read with curiosity, cross-reference what you see, and use your own instincts as much as the information presented. Each section is built to give you a deeper understanding of what distinguishes a genuinely good hotel from one that merely looks good on paper. Rather than relying on promotional descriptions or overused buzzwords, it focuses on experience, atmosphere, and the subtleties that turn a night's stay into something worth remembering.

The most effective way to approach this material is with an open but attentive mindset. Every chapter serves a particular purpose — from helping you interpret hospitality standards and guest reviews, to guiding you through Britain's regional differences and cultural nuances. Instead of skimming through the pages in search of the highest-rated hotels, take the time to absorb the reasoning behind each recommendation. When you understand *why* a hotel is exceptional, you gain the tools to identify excellence anywhere, even beyond the properties listed here.

At its heart, this journey is about connecting with places that express genuine care for their guests. When you read about a hotel, notice the descriptions of service, setting, and design. A great stay is rarely just about luxury; it's about the details that reveal the soul of the establishment — how the staff interact, the thoughtfulness of the design, the warmth of the welcome, and even the sincerity of a handwritten note left by a housekeeper. These are the signs of hospitality that no marketing campaign can fabricate.

To use this resource effectively, think of it as a conversation between travellers rather than a static reference. The language and tone reflect honest impressions drawn from direct experience, not advertisements. When something stands out, pause and reflect on how it resonates with your own expectations. Does it evoke curiosity? Comfort? A sense of adventure? The more personally you connect with the descriptions, the easier it becomes to identify what kind of stay suits your personality and travel goals.

It is also helpful to read regionally, not randomly. Britain's hospitality landscape is a rich tapestry of contrasts — a boutique hotel in Edinburgh offers a very different experience from a coastal retreat in Cornwall or a countryside inn in the Cotswolds.

Each region carries its own rhythm, influenced by history, landscape, and local culture. By approaching the guide geographically, you begin to see patterns: the craftsmanship of Scottish design, the culinary pride of Welsh inns, or the warmth and intimacy of English bed-and-breakfasts. This way of reading allows you to understand not only the hotels themselves but the character of the regions they inhabit.

Another key to using this material well is to read comparatively. When you examine two or three recommended stays within the same area, you start to perceive the nuances of what makes each one special. Some may excel in culinary excellence, while others shine through their tranquil gardens, design philosophy, or sustainability practices. By comparing, you sharpen your ability to distinguish what type of comfort matters most to you.

As you move through the listings and regional gazettes, consider what kind of traveller you are. Do you value discretion and peace above all else? Are you drawn to places that tell a story through their architecture or heritage? Or are you seeking the balance of affordability and authenticity that defines the modern independent stay? Your personal priorities will act as a filter, allowing you to make the most of the information provided without being swayed by star ratings or marketing phrases.

Remember that true quality in hospitality often lies in the intangible. It's in the graciousness of a host who anticipates your needs before you speak, in the soundproofing that ensures a silent night, or the sense of belonging that lingers long after you check out. When reading about each property, try to sense these invisible threads — the aspects that cannot be measured by numbers or awards. They are often what separate a stay that satisfies from one that transforms.

The accompanying checklists and thematic sections are not meant to be followed mechanically but rather to sharpen your awareness. As you explore them, reflect on how each point aligns with your experiences as a traveller. You may notice that what once seemed secondary — such as the character of a dining room or the friendliness of staff — becomes a primary consideration once you understand its impact on your overall comfort. The value of the information here lies in how it trains your perception, helping you to recognize excellence instinctively.

When you come across the Recommended Hotels Gazette, read beyond the ratings and brief descriptions. Each entry represents more than just a place to sleep; it reflects a standard of integrity and personality. Take note of how the descriptions mention atmosphere, service quality, and guest satisfaction rather than price alone. If you keep a travel journal, it can be rewarding to note which properties appeal to you most and why. Over time, this becomes a personal record of your own hospitality preferences — a kind of compass for future travel.

Equally important is to approach every recommendation with flexibility. Hotels evolve; management changes, renovations occur, and seasons influence atmosphere. A stay that feels serene in spring may feel lively in summer or introspective in autumn. The key is to treat these descriptions as a snapshot of excellence at a

moment in time — an invitation to discover, not a rigid instruction. By remaining adaptable, you preserve the sense of exploration that makes travel meaningful.

As you move through the later chapters, you'll encounter discussions of themed stays — romantic, sustainable, or food-focused — and insights into the future of hospitality. These are meant to expand your understanding of what makes a stay "good" in the modern era. Reading them in sequence enriches your awareness, revealing how contemporary hotels balance tradition with technology, comfort with conscience. Understanding these shifts allows you to make decisions not just for today's trip but with a sense of where the industry is heading.

Ultimately, the best way to benefit from this collection is to engage actively with it. Treat it as a companion before, during, and after your travels. Before your trip, read the regional sections to narrow your choices; during your stay, notice how the details align with what you've learned; and afterwards, reflect on your experience through the lens of what defines good hospitality. In doing so, you participate in a broader culture of travel appreciation — one that values sincerity, attention to detail, and respect for both guest and host.

Good hotels, in the truest sense, are about connection: between people, between past and present, and between place and memory. When you learn to read about them thoughtfully, you begin to see travel not just as movement but as enrichment. Every paragraph here offers a key to understanding that connection — a reminder that the most memorable stays are never accidents. They are the result of craftsmanship, empathy, and the quiet art of making strangers feel at home.

And when you finish reading, carry that awareness with you. Let it guide how you plan, how you choose, and even how you respond as a guest. Because the true value of understanding what makes a hotel "good" lies not only in finding exceptional places but also in becoming a more mindful, appreciative traveller — one who recognizes that every stay, great or small, holds the potential to become part of your life's unfolding journey.

WHAT "GOOD" REALLY MEANS IN MODERN HOSPITALITY

The idea of what makes a hotel "good" has changed profoundly in recent years. Once, the measure of quality in hospitality was largely confined to grandness — plush interiors, uniformed staff, and perhaps the glint of polished silverware. Comfort was defined by visible luxury and standardized service. Yet, the world has shifted. Travellers today are more discerning, more experienced, and far less impressed by showmanship. The meaning of "good" has evolved from appearances to authenticity, from opulence to experience, from mere service to genuine care. Modern hospitality is not about perfection in presentation; it is about connection, intention, and the quiet art of making guests feel they truly belong.

At its heart, a good hotel is one that understands people. It recognises that every guest arrives with expectations, emotions, and needs that extend beyond a place to sleep. Whether someone is travelling for business, leisure, or recovery, what they seek

is not simply accommodation but reassurance — the feeling that they are seen, valued, and respected. The finest hotels achieve this without extravagance. They anticipate comfort rather than advertise it, offering a kind of effortless grace where everything seems to work just as it should. From the temperature of the room to the tone of a welcome, each detail contributes to a seamless sense of care.

In the modern sense, "good" is not synonymous with luxury, although the two may coexist. A boutique guesthouse overlooking the Cornish coast can be just as "good" as a five-star London landmark if it captures the essence of genuine hospitality. What matters is how well a place reflects thoughtfulness — the difference between being served and being cared for. Luxury can be bought, but sincerity cannot. Guests today crave warmth over extravagance, quiet over spectacle, and meaningful experiences over mechanical efficiency. The best establishments understand that comfort begins with empathy.

Good hospitality also thrives on consistency. In an age when travellers can instantly share their opinions online, reputation depends on delivering reliability without losing character. The good hotel manages to offer predictability in standards while maintaining individuality in spirit. Guests should never wonder whether the shower will work or if breakfast will disappoint; these basic assurances form the bedrock upon which charm and distinctiveness can flourish. Yet consistency does not mean sameness. Each good hotel has a personality — sometimes discreet, sometimes bold — that arises from its people, its design, and its setting.

The human element remains the soul of good hospitality. Technology has introduced convenience, but it has not replaced the irreplaceable warmth of human interaction. A gracious greeting, a thoughtful recommendation, or the simple courtesy of remembering a guest's preference carries more weight than any digital innovation. When staff serve with authenticity rather than routine politeness, they transform transactions into relationships. Guests can sense the difference between obligation and genuine care, and it is this sincerity that lingers long after departure. The finest hotels cultivate teams who see hospitality not as a job but as a craft — people who take pride in the atmosphere they help create.

Modern travellers also associate "good" with awareness — awareness of the environment, the community, and the changing expectations of the world. Sustainability has become more than a marketing slogan; it is now an ethical cornerstone of responsible hospitality. A hotel that values its surroundings by sourcing locally, reducing waste, and supporting nearby artisans reflects a deeper understanding of what it means to offer a meaningful stay. Guests notice when a property's values align with their own, and that recognition builds trust. The good hotel does not merely occupy a location; it belongs to it, participating in the life of its region rather than standing apart from it.

Equally important is the sense of place. A truly good hotel tells a story through its setting, architecture, and design. It feels rooted rather than generic. A thatched inn in Devon should not resemble a townhouse in Bath, and a lakeside retreat in the Scottish Highlands should express its landscape in both tone and texture. Travellers

today appreciate individuality — the sense that their stay could not have happened anywhere else. This connection between place and experience transforms accommodation into memory. When the scent of a wood fire or the view from a breakfast table lingers in the mind, the hotel has achieved something beyond service: it has created belonging.

The notion of value also shapes modern definitions of "good." Price alone no longer determines quality; satisfaction does. A modestly priced country inn that offers heartfelt service and simple, well-prepared food can deliver far greater worth than an expensive establishment that feels impersonal. The essence of value lies in proportion — the harmony between what a guest pays and what they receive in comfort, atmosphere, and attention. Good hotels understand that generosity need not be lavish; it can be as simple as flexibility with check-in times, a complimentary upgrade, or an unasked-for kindness that demonstrates thoughtfulness.

Food, too, plays a vital role in defining hospitality. The modern guest expects meals that express both place and quality — dishes prepared with care, ingredients sourced responsibly, and menus that balance creativity with familiarity. A good hotel understands that dining is not merely sustenance but storytelling. Whether it's breakfast served with local preserves or a dinner that highlights seasonal produce, cuisine is an opportunity to deepen a guest's connection to the area. Even modest establishments can excel when they treat food as part of the experience rather than an afterthought.

The design of a good hotel is another subtle but essential element. Beauty, in this context, does not depend on extravagance but on coherence and intention. Everything from the furniture to the lighting should serve a purpose: to soothe, to inspire, or to welcome. Good design feels effortless because it functions intuitively — rooms that breathe, spaces that invite, and materials that feel honest to their purpose. Guests may not consciously analyse these details, but they feel them. A well-designed space restores calm and encourages presence, turning a stay into a restorative experience rather than a temporary stop.

Modern hospitality also recognizes that "good" must mean inclusive. A truly good hotel makes all guests feel equally valued, regardless of background, ability, or circumstance. Accessibility is no longer an optional feature; it is an expression of respect. The same applies to diversity in staffing and representation, which broadens the cultural intelligence of an establishment and enriches the guest experience. The essence of hospitality is to welcome the stranger — and in today's world, that principle must extend to everyone.

Another defining quality of the good hotel in this era is emotional intelligence. Beyond efficiency and professionalism, the finest establishments cultivate an ability to read moods, sense unspoken needs, and adapt seamlessly. When a guest arrives tired from travel, the best hosts know instinctively when to offer conversation and when to offer silence. This subtlety — the art of noticing — is what sets truly exceptional hospitality apart. It transforms the experience from procedural to personal, from expected to memorable.

Good hotels are also those that evolve gracefully with time. They honour their traditions while embracing progress. A centuries-old manor that incorporates modern comforts without sacrificing its historical charm shows that respect for heritage can coexist with innovation. Similarly, a new urban retreat that combines smart technology with handcrafted detail demonstrates that modernity need not mean sterility. The finest establishments understand that continuity and change are not opposites but partners in refinement.

Ultimately, "good" in hospitality cannot be reduced to ratings or amenities. It is a feeling — an atmosphere that cannot be manufactured. It exists in the quiet confidence of a place that knows who it is and what it stands for. Guests recognise it instinctively, even if they cannot articulate it. It is the difference between checking out satisfied and checking out grateful.

To experience a genuinely good stay is to encounter the best of human intention: care without pretence, service without servility, and comfort without excess. The modern definition of "good" is, therefore, both timeless and progressive — rooted in kindness, shaped by awareness, and elevated by craftsmanship. As travellers continue to seek meaning as well as rest, the hotels that thrive will be those that understand this truth: hospitality, at its finest, is not about impressing guests but about honouring them. And in that understanding lies the quiet, enduring art of what it truly means to be good.

HOW WE SELECTED OUR RECOMMENDED HOTELS

Selecting hotels worthy of genuine recommendation is not a matter of glamour, reputation, or advertising; it is an act of careful discernment that balances the tangible and the intangible. A truly outstanding place to stay is not defined solely by luxury, nor by price, nor even by location. It is distinguished by an alignment of quality, authenticity, and care that reveals itself in every aspect of a guest's experience. The process of identifying such establishments requires patience, experience, and above all, integrity — the commitment to look beyond marketing gloss and uncover what truly makes a hotel exceptional in the eyes of the traveller.

The first principle of sound selection lies in independence. No recommendation can hold value if it has been influenced by payment or persuasion. Every property chosen must earn its place on merit alone. That means no advertisements, no hidden arrangements, and no preferential treatment. The most reliable way to understand whether a hotel deserves to be recognised is to experience it as a guest would — to see it not through the lens of publicity, but through the small, revealing moments that shape a stay. The way a reservation is handled, the warmth of a welcome, the attention given to comfort, and the consistency of service all speak volumes about the ethos of a hotel.

Understanding the true quality of a property begins long before one steps through its doors. Research plays a vital role in determining which hotels even merit consideration. Independent guest feedback, historical reputation, and regional

distinction help to identify places with enduring character and excellence. However, these signals alone are not enough. The modern traveller's expectations have evolved, and so must the criteria by which hotels are judged. Comfort and cleanliness remain fundamental, but now the evaluation extends to atmosphere, sustainability, cultural connection, and the emotional intelligence of service.

When visiting a hotel, the first impression often reveals more than any formal review could capture. A sincere welcome, offered naturally rather than rehearsed, immediately sets a tone of genuine hospitality. Attention to detail — such as the ease of check-in, the readiness of the room, and the quiet efficiency with which requests are handled — reveals the depth of a team's training and commitment. Staff who act with quiet confidence rather than formality suggest a workplace where respect, not hierarchy, defines professionalism. In contrast, a hotel where charm feels forced or where systems seem strained often betrays a gap between image and reality.

The quality of accommodation itself forms another crucial measure. A room need not be grand to be good; it must simply be designed with care and maintained with pride. The comfort of the bed, the cleanliness of the space, the functionality of lighting and temperature control, and the thoughtful arrangement of furnishings all contribute to how a guest feels. What matters is the sense of calm, privacy, and balance — that subtle harmony between beauty and practicality. Great hospitality lies in anticipating needs before they are expressed: a bedside socket where one expects it, a reading light that works, curtains that truly block morning light, and water that runs both hot and reliably. These are not luxuries but essentials, and they speak to the professionalism of an establishment.

Beyond the room, the atmosphere of the entire property must tell a consistent story. Each hotel has its own identity — sometimes rooted in history, sometimes in innovation — and that character should be both authentic and intentional. A family-run inn in the Cotswolds should feel intimate and personal, while a contemporary city retreat in Manchester might express sophistication and energy. The setting should feel true to its environment rather than copied from a global template. Originality is a sign of care, and care is the surest indicator of quality.

Food and drink, too, are a window into a hotel's standards. Even a simple breakfast, when prepared with fresh, local ingredients and served with warmth, can define a guest's impression of value and thoughtfulness. In contrast, uninspired menus and mechanical service quickly erode trust. For establishments with restaurants, the link between cuisine and place becomes even more important. A good hotel supports its community by sourcing from nearby producers, adapting to seasons, and reflecting regional flavours. Dining in such an environment is not just about nourishment; it becomes a continuation of the destination itself.

Equally central to selection is the behaviour of staff. True hospitality is emotional as much as operational. A guest's experience depends as much on human connection as it does on comfort. Hotels that encourage staff to act naturally and empathetically create an atmosphere of ease. When service feels personal — when one is greeted by name, when assistance is offered before it is asked for, when a member of staff shows

quiet pride in their role — that signals an establishment led by principle rather than policy. Good management cultivates kindness as much as efficiency, understanding that warmth cannot be faked or forced.

The best hotels also respect their surroundings. Sustainability has become not merely desirable but essential. Establishments that use renewable energy, minimise waste, and engage with local communities demonstrate an awareness of their place in the broader world. The modern traveller increasingly seeks meaning alongside comfort; they wish to stay somewhere that contributes positively to its environment rather than detracts from it. Such properties reflect a quiet form of integrity — one that prioritises responsibility over excess.

Cleanliness remains one of the most telling measures of all. It speaks directly to standards, organisation, and care. In a truly good hotel, cleanliness extends beyond visible surfaces; it exists in the air, in the freshness of linens, in the scent of the corridors. It conveys discipline without sterility. The same can be said of maintenance — an often overlooked but critical marker of excellence. Flickering bulbs, scuffed furniture, or malfunctioning fixtures reveal a neglect of detail that undermines confidence. In contrast, a well-maintained property signals pride and attentiveness, qualities that often mirror the calibre of its service.

The process of selection also values consistency over time. A single glowing stay does not guarantee enduring quality. The most trustworthy hotels are those that maintain high standards season after season, regardless of staff changes, ownership shifts, or fluctuations in demand. Longevity in excellence demonstrates that hospitality is embedded in the culture of the place, not dependent on individual personalities or temporary enthusiasm. This resilience often reflects strong leadership — management that balances tradition with evolution, ensuring that the spirit of the hotel matures rather than diminishes.

Regional diversity further shapes the selection process. Britain's hotel landscape is a mosaic of styles and settings, from coastal inns in Cornwall to stately manors in Yorkshire and vibrant city boltholes in Edinburgh. Evaluating hotels fairly means recognising that excellence manifests differently in each context. A small Highland lodge may excel in intimacy and authenticity, while a metropolitan hotel succeeds through innovation and sophistication. Each must be judged according to its own intent, not by a universal standard of luxury. The question is not how grand a property is, but how well it fulfils its promise.

Guest feedback remains a vital component of assessment, but it must be weighed with discernment. Online reviews can illuminate patterns — praise for warmth, complaints about neglect — but they can also distort perception through extremes of emotion. The experienced evaluator learns to read between the lines, distinguishing genuine insight from exaggeration. Real quality reveals itself not through volume of acclaim but through the steadiness of appreciation. When travellers, independent of one another, speak of comfort, attentiveness, and character, that consistency confirms authenticity.

Ultimately, the process of selecting truly commendable hotels rests on intuition as much as inspection. Hospitality is a deeply human art, and it is often the smallest gestures that define greatness. A handwritten note left in the room, a discreet offer to help with travel arrangements, or a simple conversation that feels genuine can elevate an entire experience. These are not checklist items but emotional impressions, and it is in these moments that a hotel's spirit is revealed.

Every recommended property must therefore embody a sense of trustworthiness — a word that extends far beyond reliability. Trustworthiness in hospitality means keeping promises, respecting guests' time and privacy, and showing a quiet consistency that never calls attention to itself. It means understanding that travellers have placed not just their money, but their comfort, safety, and peace of mind in a hotel's care. The establishments that honour that responsibility with humility and grace are the ones that truly stand out.

In essence, the process of recognising a good hotel is an act of discernment that balances the measurable with the intangible. It requires equal attention to structure and soul — to what can be seen and what can only be felt. A beautiful building, fine food, or polished service can impress, but sincerity, respect, and authenticity endure. The hotels that meet these standards, those that treat every guest as more than a transaction, become something far greater than a place to stay. They become trusted companions in the traveller's journey — places where comfort feels effortless, where care feels natural, and where the art of hospitality continues to live and breathe with meaning.

CHAPTER 1

FINDING THE PERFECT STAY

THE CORE ELEMENTS OF A QUALITY HOTEL EXPERIENCE

The experience of staying in a hotel is more than a transaction for a bed and a meal. It is a complex interaction of environment, service, emotion, and expectation that together form a single impression — either lasting and uplifting or forgettable and disappointing. The essence of a quality hotel experience lies not in grandeur but in harmony: the seamless integration of comfort, character, and attentiveness that allows guests to feel not merely accommodated but genuinely cared for. This harmony is delicate, built upon a thousand small details that together create the feeling that everything has been considered, even before the guest thought to ask.

At its foundation, a quality hotel experience begins with comfort. Comfort is not synonymous with luxury; it is the absence of strain. It is the soft landing after a long journey, the sense of ease that comes from knowing one's needs are anticipated and met with quiet efficiency. Physical comfort comes first — the bed that supports and soothes, the temperature that rests between warmth and freshness, the lighting that balances clarity and calm. A truly comfortable room feels intuitively right, as though every element has been placed with the guest's wellbeing in mind. The mattress yields without sagging, the sheets breathe softly, and the space feels neither cluttered nor sparse.

Yet comfort extends far beyond the tangible. Emotional comfort arises from trust — the assurance that the hotel has considered the guest's privacy, safety, and peace of mind. This trust is built through consistency and care. Guests should never have to wonder whether their belongings are secure, whether they will be treated with respect, or whether help will be offered when needed. In a good hotel, there is a sense of invisible reliability: things simply work, and people simply care. When service flows naturally, guests relax into the experience, freed from the anxiety of having to manage the details themselves.

Cleanliness is another cornerstone of quality. It is not merely the absence of dirt but the presence of attentiveness. Every surface should feel fresh, every linen crisp, every space meticulously maintained. Cleanliness is a silent form of communication — it says, without words, that the guest's wellbeing matters. It conveys discipline, pride, and respect. In the best hotels, cleanliness extends even to what cannot be seen: the air feels pure, the carpets smell neutral rather than perfumed, and there is no trace of haste in the presentation of the room. Such precision creates the subconscious sense that one is in capable hands.

Beyond comfort and cleanliness lies the element of service, the defining mark of great hospitality. Exceptional service is both art and instinct. It requires emotional intelligence — the ability to perceive what a guest needs without intrusion, to offer

assistance without pretense. The best service feels effortless because it is sincere. When a member of staff greets a guest by name, remembers a preference, or quietly adapts to a change in plan, it reflects a culture of attentiveness rather than obligation. Service should never feel rehearsed; its success lies in its humanity. Guests remember not what was provided, but how they were made to feel.

The physical environment of a hotel plays its own powerful role in shaping experience. Architecture and design are the stage upon which hospitality unfolds, and when they are executed thoughtfully, they elevate every moment of the stay. A quality hotel creates a sense of place — it feels connected to its surroundings, reflecting the culture, landscape, or history of its location. A coastal inn might echo the rhythm of the sea with its muted palette and natural textures, while a city retreat could embrace clean lines and warm lighting that contrast with the bustle outside. What matters is authenticity. A hotel that understands its identity creates a mood that cannot be replicated elsewhere.

Atmosphere, though intangible, often determines whether a stay feels memorable. It is the quiet hum of conversation in a lobby, the balance of music and silence in shared spaces, the scent that greets a guest upon arrival. A good hotel understands that atmosphere shapes emotion. Light is particularly powerful in this regard. The transition from daylight to evening should feel deliberate — soft illumination that welcomes rest, rather than harsh glare or shadow. The goal is always to foster calm and belonging. When a hotel achieves this, guests feel part of its rhythm rather than observers of it.

Food and drink contribute significantly to the overall experience. A quality hotel views dining not as an amenity but as an expression of hospitality. Meals become moments of connection — between the guest and the region, between the kitchen and its craft. The finest properties source ingredients with care, prioritising freshness and locality over ostentation. Service during meals mirrors the tone of the establishment: attentive yet unhurried, refined yet warm. Whether a guest begins the day with a thoughtfully prepared breakfast or ends it with a quiet drink by the fire, the memory lingers when sincerity and quality align.

Equally vital is the consistency that runs through every aspect of the stay. Guests should feel that standards remain unwavering — whether they arrive in the quiet of winter or the height of summer, whether they book the simplest room or the grandest suite. True quality is steady and dependable. It does not falter when staff change or when occupancy fluctuates. It is embedded in the culture of the hotel, sustained by leadership that values integrity over appearance. When consistency prevails, guests develop trust — and trust, once earned, is the most enduring measure of excellence.

A hotel's sense of individuality often distinguishes a good stay from a great one. While chain hotels may master efficiency, independent establishments thrive through personality. The art lies in expressing character without eccentricity. Guests should feel they are in a place with a story, where the décor, tone, and pace reflect something genuine rather than manufactured. This individuality often emerges through the smallest details: artwork by local creators, a handwritten note from the owner, or a

bespoke touch that cannot be replicated elsewhere. Such gestures transform accommodation into experience.

Equally important is the way a hotel responds to its environment and community. A quality establishment recognises that hospitality does not exist in isolation. It participates in its local economy, sources responsibly, and contributes to sustainability. These choices, though sometimes unseen by guests, enhance the integrity of the stay. When a hotel reduces waste, employs locally, or supports artisans, it communicates a quiet respect for place and people. Modern travellers increasingly value this ethical awareness, sensing that a truly good stay should leave a positive imprint beyond comfort alone.

Technology has become an integral part of hospitality, but its role must be measured. The best hotels use technology to enhance convenience without eroding human warmth. A seamless online booking system, intuitive room controls, or efficient digital check-in can elevate efficiency, but they should never replace genuine interaction. Guests still crave connection — the smile at reception, the personal recommendation for a nearby walk, the reassuring presence of staff who care. When technology serves humanity rather than displaces it, the balance between innovation and intimacy is achieved.

Another dimension of quality lies in emotional resonance — the feeling a guest takes away long after departure. This is what transforms a visit into a memory. Emotional connection arises when every part of the experience, from arrival to farewell, communicates thoughtfulness. It might be the tone of voice at the front desk, the unobtrusive way housekeeping respects privacy, or the invitation to return that feels heartfelt rather than routine. Guests remember how they felt more vividly than any physical detail. A hotel that understands this creates loyalty not through marketing but through meaning.

The sense of belonging is perhaps the highest expression of quality in hospitality. It is that rare sensation of feeling instantly at home in a place one has never been before. Achieving this requires more than comfort or professionalism; it demands empathy. When staff and space together convey acceptance and welcome, barriers dissolve. Guests feel seen, valued, and at ease. This feeling cannot be scripted — it emerges from an authentic desire to serve with dignity and grace.

Finally, what binds all these elements together is intention. Every gesture, every design choice, every policy should reflect a conscious purpose to enhance the guest's experience. Quality is not a product of chance but of deliberate care. It thrives where there is passion for detail, respect for craft, and an understanding that hospitality is both service and art. A hotel that upholds these principles does more than provide shelter; it offers sanctuary — a space where travellers can rest, reflect, and reconnect with the pleasure of simply being well cared for.

In the end, a quality hotel experience is the quiet conversation between guest and host, spoken not in words but through space, service, and feeling. It is the assurance that one is safe, valued, and understood. It is the invisible thread that ties every

gesture of care into something whole. And it is this harmony — of body, mind, and spirit — that makes the experience of staying in a truly good hotel linger long after the journey has ended.

COMFORT, SERVICE, AND AUTHENTIC CHARACTER: WHAT MATTERS MOST

Comfort, service, and authentic character are the three pillars on which every truly memorable stay rests. They are the essence of genuine hospitality and the foundation upon which trust between guest and host is built. These elements, when working in harmony, elevate a simple overnight stay into an experience that lingers in memory long after check-out. They are what distinguish an ordinary establishment from one that feels alive, meaningful, and quietly extraordinary. Each of these dimensions—comfort, service, and authenticity—interweaves to form an experience that feels effortless to the guest, even though it is the result of immense thought, dedication, and consistency behind the scenes.

Comfort is the starting point, the baseline from which all satisfaction flows. It is both physical and emotional, and the two cannot be separated. Physical comfort arises from well-considered design: a bed that truly supports rest, lighting that soothes without dimming the spirit, and a room that balances privacy and openness in a way that feels natural. A good hotel understands that comfort is not indulgence; it is necessity. It reflects care for the human body and respect for the traveller's need to pause, recover, and restore. The temperature must be right, the textures pleasant, the environment serene. Every aspect of the space—the placement of a chair, the height of a window, the quality of air—contributes to this quiet equilibrium.

But comfort also depends upon emotional reassurance. Guests relax only when they feel that everything will work as it should. Confidence in cleanliness, safety, and reliability creates a sense of ease that no luxury can replace. True comfort is not the abundance of amenities; it is the absence of concern. When a hotel manages to remove friction from a guest's experience—when check-in is seamless, service is prompt, and needs are met before they become requests—it communicates respect in its purest form. That is what allows a person to truly unwind.

Service is the heartbeat of hospitality. It defines the rhythm of a stay and determines whether a guest feels merely served or genuinely cared for. In the finest establishments, service is invisible when it should be and present when it must be. It adapts gracefully to each guest's mood and personality. Attentiveness without intrusion is the highest form of courtesy, requiring staff who listen not just to words but to atmosphere—who sense when to engage and when to step back. The best service feels natural, not scripted. It arises from pride in craft and from empathy—the ability to imagine oneself in the guest's place.

The spirit of service is rooted in humility. It does not seek praise, yet it is instantly recognisable. A staff member who anticipates a guest's unspoken need, who offers help with sincerity rather than obligation, transforms a stay from functional to

memorable. Such gestures—offering a warm drink after a late arrival, remembering a preference, or suggesting a local hidden gem—convey a sense of human connection that cannot be taught through manuals. The energy of kindness, consistency, and genuine attention radiates through the entire property. Guests may forget the exact furnishings or décor, but they will never forget how they were made to feel.

Service also reflects the invisible structure of leadership. Hotels that excel in service usually operate under management that empowers rather than controls. When staff feel valued and respected, that same respect is passed on to guests. Authentic hospitality is not the product of rigid systems but of a shared culture of care. This culture must be cultivated daily, through training, empathy, and example. A good manager leads by presence, not pressure, encouraging staff to express personality rather than hide behind protocol. The result is service that feels alive, fluid, and personal—a conversation rather than a performance.

The third element, authentic character, is what gives a hotel its soul. Comfort and service can be found in many places, but character cannot be imitated. It is what makes a property distinct, memorable, and meaningful. Character is born from a sense of place—the way a hotel reflects its surroundings, its history, and the people who sustain it. A country inn might echo the texture of the landscape through stone walls and soft light; a city townhouse might speak of urban rhythm through modern art and contemporary design. When every element of a space feels intentional, a guest senses truth rather than imitation.

Authentic character also depends on honesty. A hotel must know what it is—and what it is not. Pretence is the enemy of trust. A small inn should not pretend to be a resort, nor should a modern boutique hide behind an illusion of heritage. Guests value sincerity above spectacle. They appreciate places that are comfortable in their own identity, where the atmosphere flows naturally from the people who run it. The individuality of a property—the creak of old wood, the scent of a fireplace, the laughter of a local host—creates emotional texture. It reminds travellers that they are part of something living and real.

In today's world, where much of hospitality has become standardised, authenticity has become its rarest currency. Mass-produced experiences may promise convenience, but they lack soul. What endures in memory is not uniform perfection, but human warmth and originality. A hotel with character allows imperfection to coexist with charm. It may not have the gloss of a corporate chain, but it will have the heart that corporate chains often lack. True character is not designed; it evolves naturally from passion and care.

These three forces—comfort, service, and character—are not independent; they are deeply intertwined. Comfort provides the foundation upon which service can flourish. Service gives life to comfort, making it dynamic rather than static. Character binds them together, giving them meaning and depth. When a hotel achieves balance among these three, it becomes greater than the sum of its parts. The guest feels enveloped by a sense of completeness: body at ease, mind at peace, and heart quietly touched.

The most remarkable hotels in Britain, whether grand or humble, share this invisible harmony. You can feel it in the way a receptionist greets you with genuine warmth, in the way a room feels both elegant and familiar, in the way breakfast is served with thoughtfulness rather than haste. There is rhythm and personality in every interaction. The stay feels like an experience crafted for you, not one copied from a corporate manual.

Comfort, when combined with impeccable service, fosters trust. Character, when paired with humility, creates connection. Together they form the emotional architecture of hospitality. They remind us that hotels, at their best, are not simply spaces for rest—they are extensions of human care. A good bed or a fine meal can satisfy the body, but only authenticity satisfies the soul.

It is also important to recognise that these qualities do not depend on budget. A five-star resort and a modest countryside inn can both achieve greatness if they honour these same principles. A luxury property without warmth feels hollow, while a simple guesthouse with heart can feel luxurious. True hospitality transcends category. It exists wherever there is attention to detail, kindness in service, and truth in presentation.

The most enduring measure of quality is the desire to return. When a guest leaves feeling both restored and understood, when they recall not just what they did but how they felt, the hotel has succeeded in its highest purpose. That feeling cannot be fabricated. It is the cumulative result of hundreds of thoughtful decisions, made by people who understand that hospitality is not about appearances but relationships.

Comfort makes a guest feel at home. Service makes them feel valued. Authentic character makes them feel inspired. Together, they create the kind of experience that travellers seek but rarely find—the experience that feels quietly perfect in its simplicity. The memory of such a stay becomes a private treasure, the benchmark by which all future stays are measured. And when a hotel achieves this balance, it ceases to be just a destination; it becomes a part of the traveller's own story.

THE "ESSENTIAL" CHECKLIST FOR MEMORABLE STAYS

Every memorable hotel experience begins long before the first night's sleep. It starts with a feeling — that moment when a place seems designed not only to host but to welcome. For travellers seeking genuine comfort, thoughtful service, and lasting quality, this checklist distils the timeless elements that transform an ordinary night away into something unforgettable.

Use this guide as a quiet companion when choosing where to stay. Each point reflects hundreds of first-hand observations from travellers, reviewers, and industry experts who understand what truly matters. A property that meets most of these standards can rightfully be called an **Essential Stay**.

⊨ 1. First Impressions and Arrival

• The location feels safe, attractive, and well-connected to key destinations.
• The entrance, parking area, and public spaces are clean and clearly cared for.
• Guests are welcomed promptly, with friendly communication and genuine attention.

⇄ 2. Cleanliness and Room Comfort

• Rooms and bathrooms are spotless, with visible care in every detail.
• Bedding is fresh, supportive, and of high quality.
• Lighting, temperature, and layout encourage true relaxation.
• Towels, toiletries, and small amenities are complete and well presented.

⩗ 3. Service and Professionalism

• Staff are approachable, informed, and attentive without being intrusive.
• Requests or concerns are handled promptly and politely.
• Courtesy is natural, not rehearsed, and guests are treated as individuals.
• A sense of quiet pride runs through every level of service.

⑪ 4. Dining and Beverage Quality

• Menus emphasise seasonal and locally sourced ingredients.
• Presentation and flavour reflect care and skill, not pre-packaged convenience.
• Breakfasts are balanced, generous, and freshly prepared.
• Service is timely, with dining areas kept clean and calm throughout.

❋ 5. Atmosphere and Character

• Décor expresses local culture or the property's history without pretence.
• Lighting, scent, and sound combine to create a relaxed, coherent mood.
• The space feels distinctive — something you'll remember after departure.
• Every element, from artwork to furniture, shows intention rather than imitation.

⌨ 6. Facilities and Technology

• Wi-Fi is reliable and clearly included in the room rate.
• In-room features such as outlets, desks, kettles, and safes function properly.
• Public areas balance practicality with quiet charm.
• Technology supports the experience instead of distracting from it.

❤ 7. Sustainability and Responsibility

• The hotel reduces waste and single-use plastics wherever possible.
• Energy and water efficiency are visible and well managed.
• Local producers, artisans, and communities are actively supported.
• Green choices feel seamless, never imposed on comfort.

✿ 8. Location and Accessibility

• The surroundings enhance the stay — scenic, cultural, or conveniently central.
• Directions, signage, and access are clear for both drivers and public transport users.
• Safety, convenience, and atmosphere coexist harmoniously.
• The hotel connects guests to its community, not away from it.

● 9. Reviews and Consistency

• Recent reviews show a steady record of satisfaction over time.
• Management responds to feedback with transparency and care.
• Standards remain high in both busy and quiet seasons.
• Returning guests describe experiences equal to or better than before.

✱ 10. The Return Test

Ask yourself one final question:

Would I return — or recommend this place to someone I care about?

If your answer is an immediate yes, you have discovered a true *Essential Stay* — the kind of hospitality that lingers warmly in memory long after you've checked out.

CHAPTER 2

UNDERSTANDING HOTEL TYPES AND EXPERIENCES

BOUTIQUE CHARM VS. BRAND CONFIDENCE

The modern traveller faces a dilemma that seems simple on the surface yet is deeply layered in practice: whether to choose the individuality of a boutique hotel or the predictability of a branded chain. Both options promise comfort and service, but they appeal to different instincts. One whispers of discovery, personality, and storytelling; the other assures reliability, familiarity, and ease. The distinction is more than aesthetic — it reflects two philosophies of hospitality, each with its own set of rewards and occasional compromises.

Boutique hotels thrive on personality. They are born from vision rather than formula, shaped by owners who pour creative and emotional energy into every room, every scent, every item of décor. Staying in one can feel like entering a living story — perhaps a reimagined Georgian townhouse with bold artwork, a converted mill where rustic textures meet modern lighting, or a countryside inn that smells faintly of fresh bread and woodsmoke. What distinguishes these places is the sense that someone cared deeply about the details. The wallpaper might have been chosen to echo local heritage, the breakfast ingredients sourced from the village market that morning, and the staff trained to remember guests' names not because they must, but because they want to.

There is a human warmth that runs through the best boutique stays, a sense that you are being welcomed into someone's creation rather than a corporate product. The furnishings may be slightly mismatched, the lobby may not be perfectly symmetrical, and the Wi-Fi might flicker once or twice — yet these imperfections often become part of the charm. They remind travellers that individuality still exists in a world that increasingly leans toward standardisation. For guests who value uniqueness, design, and connection to place, boutique hotels offer an experience that feels authentic and memorable.

On the other side stands the comforting strength of brand confidence. Branded hotels, especially those that have stood the test of time, represent assurance. They are built upon systems refined over decades — systems designed to remove uncertainty from travel. When you book a room in a well-known chain, you know what to expect: a certain level of cleanliness, service, and amenity. The pillows will be firm or soft according to your choice, the breakfast buffet will be familiar, and the loyalty points will add up predictably. For business travellers, families, or anyone seeking stability after a long journey, that predictability is not dullness — it is peace of mind.

Consistency has value. It is the quiet promise that you won't be disappointed after a long day or a late-night arrival. You can arrive in any major UK city — Manchester, Bristol, Edinburgh, or Cardiff — and find the same standard of comfort under a familiar logo. The check-in process will be quick, the shower pressure steady, the beds engineered for restful sleep. For some travellers, especially those who spend much of their lives on the road, that dependable rhythm becomes essential. It allows them to focus on work, meetings, or exploration without worrying about the fundamentals.

The decision between boutique charm and brand confidence often comes down to personality and purpose of travel. For the spontaneous adventurer or the couple seeking an intimate escape, a boutique stay can feel like a hidden gem waiting to be discovered. It may surprise them with creative touches — handwritten notes, welcome drinks, or stories from the local area shared by the owner. It might lack the vast resources of a global chain, but what it offers instead is emotional richness. There's a quiet pride in knowing that no one else will have quite the same experience, that each visit carries its own sense of individuality.

Conversely, for those travelling on business, with family, or during unpredictable schedules, the branded hotel's advantages are undeniable. They offer 24-hour reception, room service, loyalty benefits, and corporate discounts. Their customer service is guided by professional training rather than personality, which ensures a smoother, if sometimes less personal, interaction. These hotels have mastered operational efficiency — housekeeping runs like clockwork, the facilities are uniform, and the technology is up to date. In an increasingly digital age, many large brands are incorporating contactless check-ins, app-based controls, and integrated booking systems to further streamline the guest experience.

Yet, the lines between these two worlds are beginning to blur. Some brands have recognised the traveller's hunger for authenticity and are introducing "soft brands" — hotel collections that allow local individuality to flourish under a trusted umbrella. At the same time, many boutique hotels are adopting the technological sophistication and operational polish of larger groups, ensuring that charm does not come at the cost of efficiency. It is not uncommon now to find an independent property that partners with a booking network for visibility or a global brand that designs select hotels to feel independent.

What truly separates one from the other is emotional engagement. Boutique hotels connect through experience and atmosphere. They create an emotional signature — perhaps a scent in the lobby, an open kitchen where guests can chat with the chef, or a design theme that reflects the local landscape. Every corner feels curated rather than arranged. Brand hotels connect through consistency. They build trust over time, ensuring that even first-time guests feel at home within minutes. Both models succeed when they respect the guest's time and expectations, and both fail when they lose sight of that fundamental purpose.

In the United Kingdom, the choice between boutique and branded stays carries cultural undertones as well. British hospitality is historically rooted in individuality

— from traditional inns and family-run guesthouses to grand country manors. The boutique movement, in many ways, continues that legacy. It celebrates the regional, the personal, and the distinctive. Whether it's a stone-built inn in the Cotswolds or a seaside retreat in Cornwall, these hotels preserve a sense of place. Branded hotels, meanwhile, represent the evolution of British hospitality into a global standard, adapting international expectations to local character. A branded hotel in Edinburgh or Bath still feels British, but in a carefully designed, universal way — a fusion of tradition and global modernity.

The best experiences, whether boutique or branded, share one common trait: integrity. A boutique hotel succeeds when it delivers what it promises — when its charm feels natural, not manufactured. A branded hotel succeeds when its efficiency is matched by genuine care, not just procedure. Guests can sense authenticity instantly. It shows in the tone of a receptionist's greeting, the freshness of the room, the thoughtfulness of small gestures. The difference between good and great often lies in these invisible touches.

In the end, the decision is not about right or wrong but about what each traveller values most. Some find beauty in surprise, in spaces that tell a story and evolve with each stay. Others find peace in predictability, in knowing that comfort will not vary from one city to another. The modern traveller, however, is increasingly open to both. They might choose a boutique hideaway for a weekend in the Lake District, then a trusted brand hotel for a work trip to London. What matters is not the label on the door but the feeling upon leaving — that quiet contentment that says the stay was worth it.

The future of hospitality lies in balance. Guests now seek both individuality and reassurance — the creative freedom of boutique hotels supported by the reliable backbone of brand structure. As this balance continues to evolve, one truth remains constant: whether through handcrafted detail or polished consistency, the measure of good hospitality will always be how well a place makes people feel at home.

FAMILY INNS, ECO RETREATS, AND URBAN HIDEAWAYS

Family inns, eco retreats, and urban hideaways form three distinct yet equally important pillars of modern British hospitality. They embody the diversity of travel experiences across the United Kingdom — from the warmth of countryside tradition to the innovation of sustainable living and the sophistication of city life. Each represents a unique philosophy of comfort and connection, catering to travellers with different expectations, desires, and definitions of what makes a stay truly memorable.

Family inns are the heart of British hospitality, steeped in tradition and the comforting rhythm of everyday life. They often sit at the edge of small villages, near green meadows or beside quiet rivers, their walls whispering stories of generations past. Stepping into one feels like entering a place where time has slowed, where the scent of woodsmoke and freshly baked bread lingers in the air, and where guests are greeted not as customers but as old friends returning home. The charm of a family

inn lies in its intimacy — the personal welcome at the door, the handwritten menu featuring family recipes, and the sense that each guest's comfort is genuinely cared for.

Many of these inns have been passed down through generations, preserving a legacy of care and local pride. They serve as the backbone of rural hospitality, embodying values of community and continuity. Families who run them often live on-site, and their presence brings a depth of authenticity that large hotels can rarely match. Guests might share stories with the owners over breakfast, receive tips about hidden walking trails, or learn the history of the building, which might have once been a coaching stop or a blacksmith's home centuries ago. The experience is personal, grounded, and human — qualities that resonate deeply in an era where technology and anonymity often dominate travel.

Family inns also excel in comfort through familiarity. Rooms are often designed with a lived-in charm rather than sleek perfection; the furniture may be handmade, the linen softly worn but clean and fresh, the artwork inspired by local landscapes. The service, though informal, carries an attentiveness born of pride. Guests are remembered by name, and repeat visitors often find their preferences recalled without being asked. It is this blend of tradition and genuine human connection that gives family inns their enduring appeal.

In contrast to the cosy domesticity of the inn, eco retreats represent a forward-looking approach to hospitality — one rooted in environmental responsibility and mindfulness. These retreats are designed not only to provide relaxation but to encourage a deeper awareness of nature and sustainable living. They are often found in remote or scenic areas: a solar-powered lodge on the Cornish coast, a glamping site nestled within the Scottish Highlands, or a restored farmhouse using recycled materials in rural Wales. Every detail, from architecture to amenities, is guided by ecological principles.

Eco retreats invite guests to rediscover simplicity without sacrificing comfort. The focus is on harmony rather than luxury for its own sake. Energy-efficient heating, rainwater harvesting systems, and organic materials replace synthetic indulgence. Yet, this simplicity brings its own richness — waking up to birdsong instead of traffic, dining on seasonal produce sourced from local farms, and breathing clean air free from urban haze. Guests are encouraged to reconnect with the environment, whether through guided nature walks, forest bathing, or learning traditional crafts.

This type of accommodation appeals to a growing generation of travellers who value experiences that contribute positively to the world. Sustainability is no longer a niche interest; it is becoming a defining characteristic of quality hospitality. The best eco retreats demonstrate that environmental consciousness and luxury can coexist — not as opposites but as partners. A candlelit evening in a cabin powered by wind energy or a spa that uses locally foraged herbs can offer tranquillity and fulfilment in ways that sterile opulence cannot.

What sets eco retreats apart is their philosophy of gentle impact. Every stay becomes part of a larger story of stewardship — supporting biodiversity, reducing waste, and preserving the beauty of the British landscape. Many of these properties actively engage with local communities, supporting small producers and artisans. For guests, this creates a sense of purpose that lingers beyond the stay itself. The connection between traveller, host, and environment becomes circular — each sustaining the other.

Then there are the urban hideaways, the quiet sanctuaries tucked within the hum and energy of Britain's great cities. In places like London, Edinburgh, Manchester, and Bath, these hotels offer the best of both worlds: immersion in culture and convenience, coupled with the serenity of private retreat. Unlike the large, bustling city hotels catering to conferences and crowds, urban hideaways focus on privacy, design, and calm. They are places where guests can step out from the lively streets into a world of stillness and subtle luxury.

These hideaways often distinguish themselves through thoughtful architecture and atmosphere. The emphasis is on space that feels secluded yet connected. Rooms might feature floor-to-ceiling windows overlooking courtyards, minimalist interiors softened with natural materials, or libraries where guests can unwind after a day of exploring. Many occupy historic buildings reimagined for contemporary life — Georgian townhouses, converted warehouses, or Victorian mansions transformed into oases of quiet elegance. They retain the soul of their surroundings while offering modern comforts and refined aesthetics.

Service in an urban hideaway is discreet but intuitive. Staff understand that guests often seek solitude rather than constant attention. Check-ins are seamless, breakfasts may be delivered privately, and amenities are curated to enhance rest and reflection. Technology plays a role, but subtly — smart lighting, silent air conditioning, and digital concierge systems that never intrude. These hotels are havens for creative professionals, solo travellers, and couples seeking restorative privacy amid the excitement of the city.

Beyond comfort, urban hideaways speak to a shift in modern travel philosophy. As cities grow louder and faster, the value of peace becomes a form of luxury in itself. The concept of "retreat" no longer belongs only to the countryside; it has found its place in the urban landscape. Guests come to these hotels not only to sleep but to reset — to find balance between the stimulation of the city and the stillness they crave. Whether it is a boutique suite hidden behind a nondescript facade in Soho or a tranquil spa hotel near the Royal Mile, the promise is the same: serenity within reach.

What unites family inns, eco retreats, and urban hideaways is their shared commitment to authenticity. Each offers an experience that feels real, rooted, and meaningful. They remind travellers that comfort can take many forms — the warmth of a family welcome, the purity of sustainable living, or the elegance of solitude in a crowded city. While their settings differ, their essence aligns in the belief that true hospitality is about connection — to people, to place, and to oneself.

Across Britain, these three models of accommodation continue to evolve, responding to the changing needs of travellers while preserving their distinct identities. The family inn continues to offer the heart of community, the eco retreat provides the conscience of travel, and the urban hideaway delivers its calm soul. Together, they represent the full spectrum of modern comfort — from the fireside warmth of tradition to the tranquil minimalism of contemporary design. And within this diversity lies the enduring beauty of British hospitality: that wherever you go, whether through green countryside lanes, along rugged coasts, or within city skylines, there is always a place that understands what it truly means to feel at home.

DECODING PRICE, RATING, AND REAL VALUE

Understanding the true worth of a hotel stay often goes beyond the surface of price tags, star ratings, or promotional slogans. The perception of value in hospitality is complex and deeply personal, influenced by expectations, experience, and context. A traveller's sense of satisfaction rarely comes from what they pay alone but from how well their needs and emotions are met during their time away from home. Decoding price, rating, and real value requires looking beneath the surface—seeing hospitality not as a commodity but as a living experience shaped by many subtle elements.

Price, in itself, is not always a reliable measure of quality. While high-end properties often provide greater luxury, not all expensive hotels deliver experiences that justify their cost. Conversely, many mid-range or budget establishments provide warmth, authenticity, and attentiveness that rival five-star operations. A hotel's rate structure usually reflects a mixture of tangible factors—location, facilities, brand reputation, and seasonality—alongside intangible ones, such as perceived exclusivity and service culture. Understanding this balance helps travellers make smarter decisions about where true value lies.

Location plays one of the biggest roles in determining hotel pricing. A small, well-kept inn in the Lake District might cost as much as a sleek London hotel during peak season, not because of comparable luxury but because both cater to limited availability in highly desirable destinations. Urban hotels near transport hubs or cultural landmarks command premiums for convenience, while rural properties price according to remoteness and tranquillity. Yet what seems expensive on paper may feel worthwhile when the location enhances the travel experience — for instance, waking up to views of the Scottish Highlands or walking from your hotel straight into the heart of Edinburgh's Old Town.

Facilities and amenities also contribute to price but should be viewed through the lens of purpose. A guest travelling for relaxation may find greater value in a countryside hotel with gardens and a quiet reading room than in a city property boasting conference halls and rooftop bars. Similarly, a family might derive more comfort from a spacious inn offering home-cooked breakfasts and friendly hosts than from a modern chain hotel with identical decor in every city. The real question

is not how much the hotel offers, but how much of what it offers genuinely enriches the guest's stay.

Another layer of pricing comes from brand and reputation. Large chains often set prices based on consistency and global standards. Guests pay for predictability—the assurance that the bed will be comfortable, the Wi-Fi reliable, and the check-in smooth. Boutique or independent hotels, on the other hand, charge for uniqueness. They sell individuality, personal touches, and a sense of place. Neither model is inherently superior; their value depends on what kind of experience a traveller seeks. Some guests find reassurance in a known brand, while others crave discovery and local authenticity.

Ratings, too, can be misleading if taken at face value. The star system, used widely across the hospitality industry, typically measures physical attributes—room size, availability of lifts, staff-to-guest ratios, and on-site facilities. A five-star rating might guarantee luxury amenities like concierge service, fine dining, and spa access, but it does not automatically guarantee warmth, personality, or genuine hospitality. A modest three-star inn with a devoted owner and attentive staff can often leave a deeper impression than a grand hotel with impeccable polish but little human connection.

Online ratings and guest reviews have reshaped how people perceive quality, yet they must be read with discernment. A high average score on a booking platform reflects general satisfaction but may conceal nuances: what delighted one guest may disappoint another. Reviews are subjective snapshots shaped by expectations, personal preferences, and even moods at the time of writing. A five-star review might praise a hotel for being lively and vibrant, while another traveller seeks peace and would view that same energy as intrusive. Real value emerges from reading between the lines—understanding whether the qualities praised or criticised align with one's own priorities.

The relationship between price and rating often leads travellers into assumptions: that higher-rated hotels must cost more, or that cheaper options compromise comfort. Yet many small hotels with modest facilities have achieved exceptional reputations precisely because they excel in the human aspects of hospitality—genuine care, warmth, and attention to detail. The best hosts understand that luxury lies not only in marble floors or champagne minibars but in thoughtful gestures: remembering a guest's name, anticipating needs, or offering an unexpected kindness. These experiences build emotional value that outlasts the memory of price.

True value in hospitality lies at the intersection of cost, experience, and meaning. It is not a fixed metric but a feeling—of having received more than what was expected, of being seen and cared for. A stay that costs £80 but provides peace, connection, and comfort can feel infinitely more valuable than a £400 stay that leaves one indifferent. The emotional return on investment is often greater than the financial one, especially when the stay contributes to relaxation, inspiration, or cherished memories.

Seasonality also influences both price and value. A coastal retreat may be most expensive in summer when the beaches are bustling, yet an off-season visit can provide serenity and intimacy at a fraction of the cost. Many experienced travellers deliberately seek such windows—when destinations breathe more quietly, and hoteliers have more time for personal attention. Timing, therefore, becomes a powerful tool for finding value beyond the obvious.

Discounts, packages, and loyalty schemes further complicate the perception of worth. A discounted luxury room can feel like an extraordinary value, but not if it lures one into overspending on add-ons or services that were never truly wanted. Conversely, a simple rate that includes breakfast, parking, and local recommendations can offer holistic value that extends well beyond monetary savings. The art lies in evaluating not just the price paid but what is truly gained in the overall experience.

Cultural and regional differences also shape the equation of price and value. A countryside manor in Yorkshire may define luxury through tradition and refinement, while a minimalist eco-lodge in Wales measures it through sustainability and simplicity. Understanding the regional context helps set appropriate expectations: what constitutes premium in London's Mayfair differs vastly from what defines excellence in the Outer Hebrides. Each region carries its own interpretation of comfort and quality, and discerning travellers learn to appreciate these distinctions rather than measure all stays by one standard.

At the heart of every great stay is alignment—between expectation and delivery, price and satisfaction, promise and experience. Hotels that succeed in this alignment create loyalty, not through gimmicks or grandness, but through trust. Guests return not because they were dazzled, but because they felt understood. When a hotel's rate transparently reflects what it offers—neither underdelivering nor overselling—it builds credibility, the foundation of lasting value.

Modern travellers are also more attuned to ethical and emotional value. A growing number place importance on how a hotel treats its staff, supports its community, or reduces environmental impact. For such guests, real value extends beyond the room and into the realm of principles. Paying slightly more for a hotel that sources locally, reduces waste, or pays fair wages can feel more rewarding than choosing a cheaper alternative that ignores its social footprint. In this way, price becomes not just a reflection of market forces but of moral ones.

Ultimately, decoding price, rating, and real value means understanding one's own priorities as a traveller. Some seek indulgence, others authenticity, some consistency, others surprise. The most satisfying stays occur when cost, quality, and expectation are in harmony. Price may dictate where we begin our search, but value determines how we remember the journey. Whether it is the discreet luxury of a London townhouse, the warmth of a family-run inn in Devon, or the serenity of a sustainable retreat in the Highlands, the worth of any stay is measured not by how much we pay but by how deeply it enriches our experience of place, people, and ourselves.

CHAPTER 3

INSIDE BRITAIN'S HOSPITALITY STANDARDS

WHAT MAKES THE UK HOTEL SCENE UNIQUE

The hotel landscape of the United Kingdom possesses a distinctive character shaped by its history, geography, and enduring cultural values. Nowhere else in the world does such a seamless blend of heritage and modernity coexist in hospitality. From centuries-old coaching inns that have served travellers since medieval times to avant-garde boutique hotels redefining urban luxury, the essence of British accommodation lies in its remarkable diversity. This rich mosaic tells a story not only of architectural evolution but of a nation's personality—its understated elegance, its deep respect for tradition, and its constant reinvention in response to changing times.

At the heart of the UK hotel scene is an unshakable sense of place. Each region expresses its identity through its hospitality in ways that reflect local culture, landscape, and rhythm of life. In Scotland, hotels often draw on rugged natural beauty and a legacy of clan warmth, offering roaring fires, tartan textiles, and whisky lounges that embody Highland comfort. In Wales, the hospitality carries a poetic intimacy, with small family-run inns that blend community charm and scenic tranquillity. England's diversity stretches from London's glittering international icons to the gentle refinement of countryside manor houses, while Northern Ireland fuses a strong sense of tradition with an emerging modern spirit of renewal. Across the country, hospitality feels rooted—deeply connected to its surroundings, rarely formulaic, and always aware of the emotional resonance of place.

The United Kingdom's centuries-long history of hosting travellers has left an indelible mark on its accommodation culture. The evolution from stagecoach inns to contemporary hotels reflects Britain's enduring relationship with travel and trade. Many of today's inns and guesthouses occupy buildings that have stood for hundreds of years—former post houses, mills, or farmsteads—where architectural heritage has been lovingly preserved. These properties tell stories through their walls, beams, and fireplaces, connecting modern guests to generations past. Unlike countries that primarily embrace sleek, new-build hotels, the UK often prizes continuity: the idea that comfort is not about novelty but about authenticity, craftsmanship, and the reassuring presence of history.

The concept of "British comfort" itself is unique—a blend of restraint, warmth, and quiet excellence. Luxury in the UK is rarely loud or ostentatious; it is defined instead by attention to detail and the subtle art of making guests feel at home. A fresh pot of tea delivered without asking, a soft-spoken greeting, or a perfectly ironed sheet all represent an understated sophistication. The emphasis lies not in grand display but in thoughtful service and timeless quality. Many British hoteliers adhere to the belief

that genuine hospitality should be both refined and sincere—a philosophy that has helped shape the international understanding of service.

The country's geography adds another layer of distinction. The UK's compact size conceals extraordinary variety, allowing travellers to move easily between contrasting experiences. Within a few hours' journey, one can shift from the cosmopolitan pulse of London to the wind-swept coasts of Cornwall, from the green valleys of Wales to the ancient castles of the Scottish Highlands. This geographical diversity has encouraged hotels to develop distinctive identities rooted in their environment. Coastal properties embrace nautical simplicity, mountain lodges channel rustic warmth, and city hotels celebrate contemporary design and cultural proximity. Each place reflects a dialogue between landscape and hospitality—a uniquely British ability to adapt the hotel experience to the terrain.

The relationship between heritage and innovation defines much of what makes the UK hotel scene stand out. Many properties manage to preserve historical charm while incorporating cutting-edge amenities and design. Georgian townhouses in Bath hide behind their classical façades interiors filled with modern art and technology. Country estates have evolved into wellness retreats with organic kitchens and spa sanctuaries. Even within London's fiercely competitive luxury market, heritage brands have reinvented themselves through design-led refurbishments that respect tradition while appealing to the sensibilities of modern travellers. This equilibrium between preservation and progress has made the UK's hotel culture both timeless and forward-thinking.

The rise of independent boutique hotels has further enriched the landscape. British boutique hoteliers are often visionaries, combining local craftsmanship, sustainability, and storytelling into intimate experiences that defy standardisation. Instead of relying on the homogeneity of international chains, they emphasise individuality. Whether it is a converted Victorian townhouse in Edinburgh, a designer-led hideaway in the Cotswolds, or a coastal retreat in Devon, each property has a personality of its own. Many showcase local art, regional cuisine, and interiors that mirror the character of the area, creating a sense of immersion that appeals to travellers seeking authenticity.

Food, too, plays an integral role in defining the uniqueness of British hotels. The country's culinary renaissance over the past two decades has elevated dining from an amenity to an essential part of the hospitality experience. Today, many hotels boast restaurants that compete with standalone fine-dining establishments, often featuring Michelin-starred chefs or locally sourced tasting menus. Traditional ingredients— lamb from the Yorkshire Dales, shellfish from the Scottish coast, cheese from Somerset—are reimagined with creative flair. In smaller hotels and inns, guests are welcomed with hearty breakfasts and regional dishes prepared with pride. The focus on provenance and seasonality reflects a broader national shift toward celebrating local produce, turning each meal into a reflection of place and culture.

Service within the UK hotel scene also holds a distinctive tone. British hospitality tends to value discretion, professionalism, and respect for privacy. The staff-to-guest

relationship often balances formality with genuine friendliness—a quiet assurance rather than exuberant enthusiasm. Guests are treated with a sense of decorum that reflects cultural tradition, yet many modern hoteliers are blending this with a warmer, more relaxed approach. The evolution has produced a uniquely balanced style of service: courteous but approachable, traditional but adaptive, capable of making guests feel both respected and comfortable.

Architecture remains another defining element. The United Kingdom's built environment offers an extraordinary array of settings for hotels, from medieval castles and Georgian terraces to Art Deco icons and modern architectural masterpieces. Staying in these spaces provides not just accommodation but an encounter with history and design. Castles have become romantic retreats, abbeys have transformed into serene spas, and industrial warehouses have found new life as creative urban sanctuaries. The adaptive reuse of heritage buildings demonstrates the UK's commitment to conservation and innovation—ensuring that the past continues to serve the present in meaningful ways.

Beyond the physical, the emotional atmosphere of British hotels contributes profoundly to their uniqueness. There is a certain rhythm and restraint in how comfort is conveyed—a focus on subtlety rather than spectacle. Moments such as afternoon tea in a quiet lounge, the soft crackle of a fire after a day's walk, or the polite "Good morning" exchanged in a breakfast room capture something quintessentially British: a sense of composed hospitality that prioritises grace and calm. This emotional intelligence—knowing how to make guests feel welcome without overwhelming them—distinguishes the country's approach from that of many others.

Regional hospitality traditions add another layer of richness. The warmth of a Scottish host, offering a dram by the fire, differs in tone but not sincerity from the gentility of a Cotswold innkeeper or the lyrical welcome of a Welsh proprietor. Each reflects the character of the local community, and because so many UK hotels remain family-run, guests often experience an intimacy and continuity that large chains cannot replicate. The personal connection—the host who remembers a returning guest's favourite room, or the chef who prepares a dish tailored to dietary needs—creates emotional loyalty rooted in trust and care.

Sustainability and conscious travel have also found strong expression in the UK hotel industry. Many properties have embraced environmental responsibility not as a trend but as a guiding principle. Solar panels on historic rooftops, farm-to-table dining, plastic-free initiatives, and partnerships with local artisans are now common. This commitment reflects a wider national ethos of stewardship—of preserving beauty, landscape, and heritage for future generations. The ability to merge environmental ethics with comfort and design excellence has made British hotels leaders in sustainable luxury.

Ultimately, what makes the UK hotel scene so unique is its balance between constancy and reinvention. It holds fast to the traditions that define its character—heritage buildings, understated service, and a deep sense of place—while welcoming

innovation in design, cuisine, and sustainability. The result is a hospitality culture that feels at once familiar and fresh, steeped in history yet alive to the present. Each stay offers not just rest, but a story—a glimpse into the soul of a nation that has spent centuries perfecting the quiet art of making guests feel at home.

HOW INDEPENDENT REVIEWS ARE CONDUCTED RESPONSIBLY

The integrity of an independent hotel review lies in its honesty, balance, and the consistency of its standards. Conducting reviews responsibly requires a deep respect for fairness and accuracy, ensuring that every judgment reflects a genuine guest experience rather than influence, preference, or commercial interest. The process is a blend of observation, discipline, and empathy—a careful effort to capture not only what a place offers but how it makes a person feel. It is a craft that relies on transparency, objectivity, and the commitment to protect the trust between reviewer and reader.

Responsible reviewing begins long before a stay actually takes place. Every review starts with meticulous preparation—understanding the property's category, size, price range, and reputation within its context. This groundwork allows the reviewer to approach the experience with realistic expectations rather than preconceived biases. A family-run inn in a Cornish village, for example, cannot be measured by the same standards as a five-star city hotel, but both can be judged on how well they fulfil their promise of comfort and hospitality. Establishing this framework of fairness ensures that each review measures authenticity rather than excess, and quality rather than grandeur.

The review process itself is guided by anonymity and independence. Reviewers typically visit properties incognito, booking and paying as any regular guest would. This practice removes external influence and ensures that the service received reflects the genuine experience available to all customers. When staff and management are unaware that they are being reviewed, their interactions reveal the natural rhythm of their hospitality rather than a curated performance. Anonymity, in this sense, safeguards the integrity of the review by preserving the spontaneity of service. It also ensures that the reviewer's findings are grounded in authenticity rather than orchestration.

However, responsible reviewing is not an exercise in fault-finding or judgmental detachment. It requires sensitivity—the ability to appreciate the challenges of running a hotel and the human effort behind each guest experience. Reviewers must recognise that no property is flawless, and that hospitality exists in a delicate balance between infrastructure, service, and personality. A creaky floorboard in a 400-year-old inn may be part of its charm, while an impersonal interaction in a luxury chain might reveal a gap in training or warmth. Understanding these nuances demands both experience and empathy, enabling reviewers to interpret imperfection through the lens of authenticity rather than criticism.

One of the central principles of responsible reviewing is consistency. Each property, regardless of its price or prestige, is measured by a set of core values—cleanliness, comfort, service quality, atmosphere, and honesty of representation. A modest countryside inn that provides spotless rooms, heartfelt service, and freshly cooked breakfasts can rank as highly in guest satisfaction as a grand urban hotel offering fine dining and modern facilities. The question is never how much luxury a hotel provides, but how faithfully it delivers what it promises. This consistency in evaluation allows readers to trust that every recommendation reflects genuine merit rather than marketing power or brand prestige.

Transparency is another essential element of the review process. Reviewers disclose any potential conflicts of interest and avoid accepting free stays, gifts, or incentives from hotel management. This separation ensures that opinions remain untarnished by commercial pressures. Financial independence gives the reviewer freedom to be truthful, even when that truth may not be flattering. It is this uncompromising honesty that underpins the credibility of independent reviews. Readers rely on the assurance that the assessment is based on genuine experience rather than sponsored influence. Maintaining this transparency is not only ethical—it is the foundation of trust between reviewer and audience.

Responsible reviewers also approach their craft with humility. They understand that their perspective, while informed, is not absolute. Every guest brings unique expectations and preferences; therefore, a fair review should reflect the likely range of guest experiences rather than a single personal reaction. A professional reviewer will observe patterns—how consistently staff respond to needs, how attentively public spaces are maintained, and how effectively complaints are handled. By focusing on repeatable qualities rather than isolated impressions, the review becomes a more reliable representation of the property's overall standard.

The tone of a responsible review also matters. Balanced writing acknowledges both strengths and weaknesses without exaggeration. Praise should feel earned, and criticism should be constructive. The goal is not to entertain readers with wit or to chastise establishments for imperfection, but to provide insight that helps future guests make informed choices. Fairness, accuracy, and compassion work together to produce reviews that illuminate rather than disparage. A responsible reviewer recognises that a single review can influence livelihoods, reputations, and reader expectations, and thus wields their pen—or keyboard—with care.

Observation forms the core of good reviewing. A responsible reviewer notes the details that define a stay, from the warmth of the welcome to the presentation of breakfast, from the efficiency of housekeeping to the atmosphere of the common areas. The reviewer listens as much as they look, noting how staff interact with one another and with guests. They pay attention to sounds, scents, lighting, and temperature—all subtle aspects that shape comfort and mood. Through such close attention, the review captures not only physical attributes but the emotional and sensory experience of staying in that space.

Equally important is the reviewer's awareness of context. A seaside guesthouse during peak summer may feel lively and bustling, while in winter it may embody calm solitude. A city hotel that thrives on business travellers will present a different dynamic on a weekend. A responsible review considers these temporal variations and avoids drawing conclusions from conditions that may be seasonal or exceptional. Instead, it seeks to describe the enduring qualities—the professionalism of service, the maintenance of facilities, the warmth of atmosphere—that persist beyond circumstance.

The language of responsible reviewing is clear and accessible. It avoids superlatives that distort perspective, favouring precise, descriptive terms that help readers visualise and understand the experience. Instead of proclaiming that a room is "perfect," the reviewer might describe its dimensions, light, and design choices, allowing readers to form their own judgments. Instead of declaring a meal "unforgettable," they might detail the freshness of ingredients, the harmony of flavours, and the attentiveness of service. This descriptive honesty transforms the review from opinion into informed guidance.

Another vital aspect of responsible reviewing is accountability. Reviewers must be willing to stand by their assessments, even when they offer criticism. Yet accountability also means openness to correction. If a hotel undergoes major changes in management, refurbishment, or service quality, reviewers should revisit and update their impressions. Stale or outdated reviews can mislead readers and unfairly represent properties that have evolved. Continuous verification keeps the information accurate and the trust between reader and publication intact.

Modern technology has added complexity to this process. The rise of online review platforms has given voice to millions of guests, but it has also blurred the line between opinion and expertise. While crowdsourced feedback offers valuable insight, responsible professional reviewing retains a unique discipline. It blends personal experience with industry knowledge, long-term perspective, and ethical rigor. Unlike unverified comments, professional reviews are guided by editorial standards and cross-checking procedures that ensure fairness. They are not the loudest opinions but the most carefully considered ones.

The reviewer's responsibility extends beyond the hotel to the traveller. Their task is not only to describe but to interpret—to help readers align their expectations with reality. A responsible review empowers travellers by explaining what kind of guest a hotel best serves. Some properties cater to families seeking warmth and practicality; others to design lovers, solitude seekers, or gastronomes. By clarifying these distinctions, the reviewer ensures that satisfaction comes from appropriate choice rather than inflated expectation.

Ultimately, the process of conducting independent reviews responsibly is an act of stewardship. Reviewers hold in their care both the integrity of the establishments they assess and the trust of the readers who rely on them. Their duty is to observe truthfully, report clearly, and judge fairly. It requires both professional discipline and human sensitivity—the awareness that behind every reception desk, kitchen, and

guestroom lies the labour of individuals who take pride in creating memorable experiences. When done properly, responsible reviewing transcends opinion; it becomes a dialogue between traveller, host, and observer, united by a shared pursuit of genuine hospitality.

In the end, the most valuable review is not the one that flatters or condemns, but the one that enlightens. It is written with respect for the truth, an understanding of context, and a devotion to accuracy. It recognises that hospitality is a living art, ever changing and deeply human. Through responsibility, fairness, and integrity, independent reviews preserve the delicate balance between criticism and celebration—ensuring that travellers discover not only where to stay, but how to appreciate the people and stories that make each place worth visiting.

RECOGNIZING TRUE GUEST-CENTERED HOSPITALITY

True guest-centered hospitality is a philosophy that transcends amenities, décor, and price tags. It is not something that can be measured purely by star ratings, luxury labels, or the size of a property's budget. Instead, it is the invisible thread that binds every great stay together—the genuine sense that the guest is seen, valued, and cared for as an individual rather than a transaction. Recognizing this kind of hospitality requires sensitivity, observation, and an understanding that great service is less about performance and more about authentic connection.

At its core, guest-centered hospitality begins with empathy. The most remarkable hotels are those that understand not only what their guests need but what they might want before they even articulate it. It manifests in the tone of a welcome, the way a staff member anticipates a traveler's fatigue after a long journey, or how breakfast is adjusted to suit dietary needs without fuss or judgment. These gestures are rarely grand or ostentatious; rather, they are subtle and sincere, grounded in the human instinct to make another person comfortable. The best hoteliers and innkeepers see beyond the immediate exchange of service and money to recognize the deeper act of care that defines hospitality at its finest.

True guest-centered service requires attentiveness without intrusion. The balance between warmth and respect for privacy is delicate but essential. Some guests crave conversation and guidance, while others prefer solitude and discretion. A truly guest-focused establishment reads these cues naturally. The staff notice, for example, whether a guest lingers at the reception desk hoping for recommendations or withdraws quietly after check-in. In such spaces, service feels seamless—ever-present but never overbearing. The guest feels at ease, trusting that assistance is nearby but never imposed.

One of the hallmarks of genuine hospitality is consistency. It is easy for a property to impress during the first moments of arrival or through well-rehearsed gestures, but sustained attentiveness throughout a stay reveals the true measure of commitment. A guest-centered approach does not fluctuate with mood or circumstance; it is embedded in the culture of the establishment. Whether during the

quiet lull of midweek or the busyness of a full weekend, guests experience the same warmth, care, and reliability. This consistency reassures visitors that their comfort is not dependent on chance but guaranteed by design.

In guest-centered environments, staff members are not merely trained to follow protocols; they are empowered to make decisions that enhance the guest experience. Empowerment is a vital component of authentic service—it gives employees permission to act with initiative rather than rely solely on scripts or managerial approval. When a receptionist offers a spontaneous solution to a guest's problem or a housekeeper leaves a personal note wishing a traveler safe onward journeys, it reflects a workplace culture rooted in trust and respect. Guests sense this autonomy. It creates a feeling that everyone they encounter is genuinely invested in their wellbeing, not just performing a task.

Language and tone also play an important role in guest-centered hospitality. The way staff communicate—both verbally and nonverbally—sets the emotional temperature of a stay. Words chosen with care, a sincere smile, and body language that conveys attentiveness can transform even brief interactions into moments of connection. Guests remember not what was said but how it made them feel. This is why the most successful hosts are listeners before they are talkers. They pick up on the small details—a guest mentioning they are celebrating a birthday or feeling under the weather—and quietly act on them in thoughtful ways. These touches of intuition often define a memorable experience more than any luxurious feature.

Another defining feature of true guest-centered hospitality is humility. Great service never seeks applause. It does not draw attention to itself or demand acknowledgment. Instead, it allows guests to feel comfortable enough to forget they are being served. When the experience flows so smoothly that the practicalities of hospitality disappear into the background, that is when it has achieved its highest form. The guest feels a sense of belonging and peace, not through spectacle, but through the quiet assurance that everything has been considered and cared for.

Attention to individuality separates exceptional hospitality from the ordinary. In a guest-centered environment, each visitor is recognized as unique. Whether it's remembering a returning guest's favorite room, adjusting the lighting or temperature upon request, or tailoring experiences to personal preferences, the hotel communicates that individuality is valued. In larger establishments, technology can aid this process through guest profiles and preference tracking, but the true spirit of personalization remains rooted in human observation. A thoughtful staff member who notices that a guest prefers tea over coffee and remembers it the next morning exemplifies the human artistry of great service.

Authenticity lies at the heart of guest-centered care. When staff interact from genuine kindness rather than obligation, guests immediately perceive the difference. Authentic service cannot be faked; it emanates naturally from a team that believes in what they do. This sense of authenticity extends beyond staff demeanor to the overall character of the hotel itself. Properties that express their identity honestly—through décor, local influences, or family traditions—create spaces where guests feel

emotionally connected rather than merely accommodated. True hospitality, therefore, is as much about the spirit of place as it is about the service within it.

Trust is another foundational element. A guest entrusts a hotel with their rest, safety, and comfort—sometimes during deeply personal moments, from honeymoons to family losses. How that trust is handled defines the ethical quality of hospitality. Responsible establishments guard guest privacy with discretion, handle concerns promptly, and admit mistakes when they occur. In environments where integrity is valued, guests feel secure enough to relax completely. They sense that their comfort is the establishment's foremost priority, not their spending potential.

Flexibility is an often-overlooked dimension of guest-centered service. The ability to adapt to unforeseen circumstances—late arrivals, special requests, or travel mishaps—demonstrates true care. A rigid adherence to policy may protect a business, but a compassionate flexibility wins loyalty. When a host extends understanding rather than bureaucracy, guests remember that grace long after checkout. It is these moments of humanity—when staff go beyond the rulebook to assist—that reveal the soul of real hospitality.

Cultural sensitivity also defines guest-centered establishments. With Britain's increasingly international visitor landscape, the best hotels respect and accommodate diverse backgrounds, customs, and expectations. From dietary inclusivity to linguistic awareness, from recognizing different norms of personal space to understanding gestures of politeness, these subtleties shape a guest's sense of being welcomed. Great hospitality interprets difference not as inconvenience but as enrichment. By doing so, it turns diversity into connection and ensures that every guest, regardless of origin, feels acknowledged and at home.

Guest-centered hospitality also requires attention to the unseen details—the quiet operations that support the guest experience. Cleanliness, maintenance, and environmental comfort may not be as glamorous as grand gestures, but they are the foundation of trust. A spotless bathroom, a well-made bed, and a room maintained at the right temperature convey care in the most tangible way. Behind these details lies an invisible network of people—from housekeeping to kitchen staff—whose work sustains the smooth rhythm of comfort. A hotel that honors and supports its back-of-house teams demonstrates an understanding that great service begins behind the scenes.

The emotional intelligence of management plays a significant role as well. Leadership that fosters kindness, respect, and teamwork creates a ripple effect that reaches every guest. When staff feel valued and empowered, they, in turn, treat guests with warmth and sincerity. An unhappy or overworked employee cannot project genuine hospitality; morale is the mirror through which guests perceive a hotel's spirit. Therefore, the most successful establishments cultivate a workplace culture where service is not a demand but a shared pride.

True guest-centered hospitality endures beyond the stay itself. It continues in the follow-up email thanking guests for their visit, in remembering returning patrons by

name, or in responding to feedback with humility and gratitude. The relationship between guest and hotel becomes one of mutual respect rather than a fleeting exchange. Many of the most beloved hotels across the UK owe their loyal followings not to lavish facilities but to the deep bonds they have built with guests through years of consistent, heartfelt service.

Ultimately, recognizing true guest-centered hospitality is recognizing the humanity within hospitality itself. It is the understanding that service is not a performance but a relationship. It exists in the thoughtful gestures, the intuitive silences, the sincere smiles, and the steady reliability that make a guest feel not just welcomed but genuinely cared for. When travelers leave feeling lighter, calmer, and somehow more at peace than when they arrived, it is because they have been the recipients of something timeless—hospitality that honors the individual, values kindness, and turns a stay into an experience of belonging.

The essence of guest-centered service lies in its humility and authenticity. It requires no lavishness, only attentiveness; no perfection, only sincerity. When done well, it lingers in memory long after the journey ends. In the quiet grace of true hospitality, guests find not just comfort, but connection—and that, more than anything else, is what transforms an ordinary visit into a lasting impression of warmth and home.

CHAPTER 4

TRAVELLER INSIGHTS AND SMART BOOKING TIPS

HOW TO BOOK FOR BEST VALUE AND AUTHENTIC EXPERIENCES

Finding the best value when booking accommodation is not merely about securing the lowest price; it is about ensuring that every pound spent contributes meaningfully to the quality of the experience. In an age where digital platforms dominate the booking landscape and algorithms influence nearly every decision, the skill of securing genuine value has become a sophisticated blend of timing, discernment, and intuition. The traveler who learns to balance economy with authenticity not only saves money but also enriches every aspect of their journey.

The first step toward achieving the best value lies in understanding that price and worth are not synonymous. A higher rate does not always guarantee a superior stay, just as a discounted deal does not automatically indicate compromise. Value is the equilibrium point between cost and experience, where comfort, location, service, and atmosphere harmonize with personal priorities. A traveler seeking peace in a rural inn may find far greater satisfaction in a modestly priced countryside retreat than in a five-star urban hotel whose luxury feels impersonal. Understanding what matters most—whether it is charm, convenience, amenities, or a sense of place—sets the foundation for making decisions that deliver true worth.

Timing plays a crucial role in securing both affordability and authenticity. Accommodation prices fluctuate throughout the year, often dramatically. The same seaside property that commands premium rates in July may offer excellent value in early autumn when the crowds have thinned but the coastal air still holds warmth. Savvy travelers learn to read these seasonal rhythms. Booking just outside peak season—what hoteliers call the "shoulder period"—often yields the perfect balance between cost and atmosphere. The staff are less hurried, the best rooms are more readily available, and the destinations themselves regain a sense of calm authenticity that high season bustle tends to obscure.

Equally important is understanding the rhythm of the week. Business hotels in major cities may offer exceptional weekend rates when corporate travelers have departed, while country inns that thrive on weekend getaways often provide midweek discounts. Aligning your travel schedule with these patterns requires flexibility, but the rewards in comfort and savings can be considerable. Many experienced travelers build their itineraries around these fluctuations, transforming what might seem like a logistical constraint into an opportunity for richer, more relaxed experiences.

Booking directly with the property often yields hidden advantages that go beyond the published rate. While comparison sites and online travel agencies can be useful

for initial research, many hotels reserve their best offers, room upgrades, or complimentary extras for guests who book through them directly. The reasoning is simple: direct bookings spare establishments the commission fees charged by third-party platforms. In return, they can afford to provide better value to those who reach out personally. A polite phone call or email inquiring about seasonal packages, loyalty benefits, or even special requests can lead to surprising perks—a room with a view, breakfast included, or a later checkout time—all of which add depth and satisfaction to the stay.

Moreover, establishing direct communication with a hotel before booking allows travelers to gauge its level of service and responsiveness. A prompt, courteous, and personal reply often signals a property that values guest relationships and attention to detail—qualities that are difficult to measure through photographs or online reviews alone. It also opens a channel for customization: guests can express preferences regarding room type, dietary needs, or accessibility, ensuring a more seamless arrival and stay. This direct engagement transforms a simple transaction into the beginning of a relationship built on trust and understanding.

However, one must also navigate the complex world of online reviews with discernment. User-generated feedback can be invaluable for identifying patterns of excellence or recurring issues, but it must be read critically. Reviews are reflections of personal expectations, and what disappoints one traveler may delight another. Look for consistency in comments rather than extremes—if multiple reviewers praise the warmth of the staff or the cleanliness of rooms, those aspects are likely reliable. Similarly, persistent complaints about noise, poor maintenance, or unresponsive management warrant attention. Combining digital insights with human intuition allows for a more balanced and realistic assessment of potential stays.

Authentic experiences are born from connection—to people, place, and purpose. When booking accommodation, it is worth considering not only the property itself but also its relationship to its surroundings. Independent hotels, guesthouses, and family-run inns often serve as living reflections of their communities. They tell local stories through architecture, décor, and cuisine. Choosing such establishments contributes to the preservation of regional identity and ensures that the economic benefits of tourism remain within the local economy. Guests who stay in locally owned properties often gain deeper cultural insights, from breakfast conversations with hosts to recommendations for lesser-known attractions that rarely appear in guidebooks.

Price transparency is another key component of booking wisely. Some properties present seemingly low base rates but attach multiple hidden charges for essentials such as Wi-Fi, parking, or breakfast. Others bundle these services into all-inclusive tariffs that, while higher upfront, may offer better overall value. It is essential to read the fine print carefully and calculate the total cost rather than the headline price. Similarly, cancellation and refund policies should be examined with care, especially in uncertain travel climates. Flexibility has value, and sometimes paying slightly more for a refundable rate ensures peace of mind worth far beyond its monetary difference.

Modern travelers also benefit from the growing integration of technology and hospitality. Price comparison tools, alert systems, and reward programs can simplify decision-making and uncover exclusive discounts. However, technology should serve as a tool rather than a replacement for judgment. A hotel that aligns perfectly with your values and interests may not appear on the first page of a search algorithm optimized for corporate chains. Digging deeper—exploring regional tourism websites, social media pages, or specialized travel forums—can reveal hidden gems overlooked by mainstream booking engines.

The concept of "authentic value" also involves an emotional dimension. True worth in travel is not measured in pounds or points but in the richness of experience. A stay that feels personal, restorative, or inspiring has an intangible value that endures long after the journey ends. For some, that may mean an intimate eco-lodge surrounded by forest; for others, a centuries-old coaching inn steeped in history. The most fulfilling bookings are those that align both with practical comfort and personal meaning. When guests choose places that resonate with their interests—be it sustainability, heritage, gastronomy, or wellness—they create connections that transcend the transactional.

Flexibility is a recurring theme in value-based booking. Even the most meticulous plans benefit from openness to change. Spontaneous opportunities—a newly opened boutique hotel, a flash sale, or a personal recommendation encountered mid-journey—can lead to memorable discoveries. Remaining adaptable allows travelers to pivot when necessary, embracing new experiences that might never have been planned but turn out to be highlights of the trip. Value, in this sense, extends beyond economics into the realm of serendipity.

Loyalty programs can be worthwhile when used wisely, particularly for those who travel frequently. However, loyalty should never become dependency. The comfort of familiarity can easily limit the breadth of experience if it prevents exploration of independent or lesser-known establishments. A balanced approach—using points when convenient but remaining open to unique alternatives—preserves both economy and adventure. Some independent hotels now offer their own membership schemes, rewarding repeat guests with personal touches that large chains rarely replicate. These gestures often feel more genuine, reinforcing the sense of belonging that defines meaningful travel.

Another overlooked aspect of value is the emotional environment created by a property's ethos. A hotel that treats its staff well and supports local sustainability initiatives often delivers better service and atmosphere. Guests can sense when an establishment operates with integrity—when the smiles of the employees are genuine, and the culture of care extends inward as well as outward. Supporting such businesses contributes to a cycle of goodwill, ensuring that value is not extracted but shared. Ethical booking, therefore, becomes an act of participation in a broader ecosystem of responsible travel.

Booking for best value is ultimately an exercise in awareness. It requires curiosity, patience, and a willingness to look beyond surface-level deals to uncover the

experiences that truly resonate. It means asking the right questions: not "How cheap can I get this room?" but "What am I really getting for what I pay?" and "How will this place make me feel?" It invites travelers to align their financial decisions with their emotional and ethical priorities.

Authenticity cannot be purchased through discounts alone. It emerges when travelers make choices that reflect both their values and their curiosity. Every booking is, in essence, a conversation—a dialogue between guest and host, traveler and destination. The best value arises not from cutting costs but from investing wisely in experiences that create connection, comfort, and memory.

When travelers learn to book with both head and heart—to weigh the tangible and the intangible, the practical and the poetic—they elevate the act of travel itself. Each stay becomes more than shelter; it becomes a thread in the larger story of exploration, discovery, and human connection. That, ultimately, is the true value of booking well: the transformation of travel from a series of transactions into a tapestry of meaningful encounters.

AVOIDING OVERHYPED LISTINGS AND GENERIC CHAINS

In the modern age of digital booking platforms and influencer-driven marketing, travelers are surrounded by a constant stream of glowing reviews, sponsored content, and carefully curated images that promise perfection at every turn. Yet, beneath this glossy surface lies a growing challenge—the difficulty of discerning genuine quality from manufactured allure. Overhyped listings and generic hotel chains, though often promoted with persuasive language and immaculate photography, can leave travelers with experiences that feel sterile, impersonal, or misrepresented. Avoiding these pitfalls requires more than skepticism; it demands an understanding of what authenticity truly looks like and how to identify it in a crowded marketplace.

Overhyped listings thrive on visual seduction and emotional persuasion. They are designed to spark desire and urgency: the perfect sunset shot over a hotel terrace, the too-good-to-be-true discount that expires in an hour, or the cleverly worded claim of "five-star luxury at unbeatable prices." Such marketing tactics appeal to the senses, often manipulating expectations by focusing on what looks good rather than what actually feels good. The danger lies not in the act of promotion itself—after all, every property must market its strengths—but in the distortion of truth that frequently accompanies excessive hype. A room might photograph beautifully in natural light but turn out to be cramped or noisy. A "sea view" might require leaning precariously out of a window to catch a glimpse of water. The gap between promise and reality can lead to frustration that taints the entire travel experience.

Learning to see beyond marketing is therefore essential. A discerning traveler develops the skill of reading between the lines, treating hotel descriptions and online reviews as raw data rather than gospel. Certain phrases serve as warning signs: "conveniently located" can mask proximity to a busy road, while "cozy" may translate to small or dimly lit. The repetition of vague superlatives—"stunning,"

"exceptional," "unforgettable"—without concrete details often indicates copywriting designed to impress rather than inform. The most trustworthy properties tend to speak plainly, emphasizing facts over flair: specific distances from landmarks, transparent information about amenities, or candid notes about seasonal conditions.

Online reviews, though valuable, are another minefield of exaggeration and bias. They reflect personal expectations that vary widely from guest to guest. Some reviewers mistake extravagance for quality, while others conflate minor inconveniences with catastrophic failures. A balanced view emerges only through pattern recognition—when dozens of guests mention the same issue, such as thin walls or indifferent service, it likely reflects a consistent problem. Conversely, when many reviews highlight a particular strength, such as attentive staff or an exceptional breakfast, that detail carries weight. Caution is also needed with ratings that seem too uniform or excessively glowing; properties with only perfect scores may have filtered reviews or employed reputation management tactics. Independent platforms that verify guests' stays and restrict multiple submissions offer more reliable insights.

Generic hotel chains present a different kind of challenge. They rarely deceive outright; rather, they create predictability that can feel safe but uninspired. There is a certain comfort in knowing exactly what to expect—standardized rooms, familiar branding, and uniform service procedures. For business travelers or those seeking efficiency, this consistency can be valuable. Yet for those in pursuit of character, cultural immersion, or a sense of place, such environments often fall short. A chain property in Edinburgh can feel nearly identical to one in Birmingham or Bristol, offering little reflection of local heritage or design. The décor may be pleasant but anonymous, the food service polished but formulaic.

The issue with generic chains is not necessarily poor quality but the absence of individuality. Travel, at its best, thrives on discovery—on the small details that surprise and delight, that make a stay memorable because it could only have happened in that specific location. Independent hotels and boutique inns often deliver this experience precisely because they are shaped by their surroundings and owners' personalities. A converted farmhouse in Cornwall, a Victorian townhouse in York, or a coastal retreat in Pembrokeshire tells a story that large chains rarely attempt. Even minor imperfections—a creaking floorboard, a uniquely painted wall, or an idiosyncratic breakfast menu—contribute to authenticity. These human touches remind guests that they are somewhere real, not a standardized extension of a global brand.

Overhyped listings and chain properties often rely on the same psychological foundation: they sell the idea of reassurance. Hype provides emotional excitement, while chains promise safety and familiarity. Yet both approaches can lead travelers away from the very essence of hospitality—the feeling of being genuinely welcomed into a place that values individuality and care. Avoiding these traps means seeking connection rather than comfort alone. It means choosing a stay where the

environment feels alive, where staff engage naturally rather than following rehearsed scripts, and where the experience is guided by intention rather than corporate policy.

To identify authenticity amid the noise, attention to small but meaningful indicators is crucial. The presence of original photography—images that appear natural rather than heavily edited—often suggests honesty. Descriptions that highlight the history of a property, introduce the owners or managers by name, or mention relationships with local suppliers tend to reflect genuine engagement. Guests' reviews that describe specific experiences, such as being offered tea on arrival or learning about local attractions from the hosts, reveal a personal dimension that marketing teams cannot fabricate. These are the hallmarks of places where hospitality is a craft, not a product.

The lure of hype is powerful because it promises perfection, but travel is rarely perfect—and therein lies its beauty. An authentic stay might not come with marble bathrooms or touchscreen controls, yet it may offer warmth, charm, and sincerity that no luxury can replace. The laughter shared with a host over breakfast, the recommendation of a hidden walking trail, or the aroma of freshly baked bread in a countryside kitchen carries emotional value far beyond polished amenities. Recognizing this truth allows travelers to prioritize substance over spectacle.

The rise of digital booking platforms has democratized access to accommodation but also amplified the visibility of overhyped properties. Algorithms reward popularity, not authenticity, meaning hotels that invest heavily in marketing often outrank those that rely on reputation and word of mouth. To counter this imbalance, some travelers turn to curated recommendation sources or independent review sites that evaluate properties through personal visits rather than user submissions. These platforms prioritize honesty over volume, describing both strengths and shortcomings with transparency. They remind readers that excellence is rarely uniform—it is found in the balance of comfort, service, and character.

Avoiding generic chains also fosters a deeper cultural and environmental awareness. Independent hotels tend to support local economies more directly by employing regional staff, sourcing produce nearby, and collaborating with artisans or small businesses. Staying in such establishments helps sustain communities and traditions that might otherwise be eroded by mass tourism. Moreover, these properties often demonstrate a stronger commitment to sustainability—reducing waste, conserving energy, and engaging responsibly with their surroundings. Choosing them is therefore not only a matter of personal enrichment but also of ethical travel practice.

For travelers accustomed to the security of well-known brands, stepping away from them can feel risky. Yet it is precisely this small leap of faith that transforms a trip into a memorable experience. Independent properties, by their very nature, encourage curiosity and connection. They invite guests to enter spaces shaped by human hands and stories, where individuality is not polished away but celebrated. These are the places where one might find handwritten notes from the owner, shelves stocked with local literature, or an unexpected conversation that leads to friendship. Such moments, though intangible, form the emotional fabric of great journeys.

In avoiding overhyped listings and generic chains, travelers reclaim control over their experiences. They shift from being passive consumers to active participants in the art of hospitality. This transformation begins with awareness—of marketing psychology, of personal priorities, and of the subtle cues that distinguish authenticity from artifice. It continues with the courage to make choices that reflect curiosity rather than conformity. And it culminates in the realization that the best stays are not those that promise perfection, but those that feel sincere, grounded, and human.

The modern traveler's greatest advantage is not access to endless options but the wisdom to choose wisely among them. Overhyped properties fade quickly in memory once the illusion dissolves, while authentic stays linger vividly for years. The warmth of genuine care, the distinct personality of a thoughtfully designed room, or the quiet integrity of a host who loves what they do—these are experiences that transcend marketing trends. To avoid the generic is to seek the real, and in doing so, to rediscover the simple truth at the heart of travel: that comfort and connection are born not from uniformity, but from authenticity.

TIMING, DEALS, AND TRAVEL SEASONS EXPLAINED

Timing has always been one of the most decisive factors in shaping the quality and cost of travel. For those seeking a rewarding stay in the United Kingdom, understanding when and how to travel can transform an ordinary trip into an exceptional one. Britain's diverse geography and dynamic tourism patterns create a rhythm that shifts with the seasons, regional festivals, and even day-to-day weather. Knowing how to navigate these cycles—when prices rise and fall, when demand peaks, and when hidden bargains appear—allows travelers to experience comfort, value, and authenticity without compromise.

The United Kingdom's hospitality calendar follows a pattern that reflects both climate and culture. The summer months, particularly from late June through August, are considered peak season across most destinations. Warm weather, long daylight hours, and the school holidays drive an influx of domestic and international travelers. Coastal towns like Brighton, Cornwall, and the Isle of Wight brim with activity, while cities such as London, Edinburgh, and Bath reach full occupancy, with prices rising accordingly. During this period, even mid-range accommodations can command premium rates, and the most sought-after boutique hotels and countryside inns are often booked months in advance. Yet the energy of summer has its appeal—the vibrant festivals, open-air events, and celebratory atmosphere create an unmatched sense of vitality.

However, the secret to finding balance between value and experience often lies in exploring the edges of the high season. The spring and autumn months, known as the shoulder seasons, offer perhaps the most rewarding travel experiences in the UK. From late March to early June, blooming gardens, mild temperatures, and fewer crowds define an atmosphere of gentle awakening. Countryside properties open their doors after winter refurbishment, offering discounted rates to attract early visitors. Similarly, the months of September and October carry the golden hues of autumn, a

quieter pace, and often reduced prices. Many seasoned travelers favor this window for its perfect equilibrium between affordability and atmosphere.

Winter, though often overlooked, holds its own magic in British hospitality. Between November and early March—excluding the Christmas and New Year holidays—hotel rates drop significantly. This is the season when travelers can secure luxurious accommodations for a fraction of their summer cost. Historic inns with roaring fireplaces, boutique city hotels, and even high-end countryside retreats become havens of warmth and tranquility. While the shorter days and colder weather discourage some, others find charm in this intimate, reflective period. The festive markets in London, Manchester, and Edinburgh, as well as the glow of rural pubs in the Cotswolds or the Lake District, reveal a cozier side of travel that rewards those who embrace it.

Timing also extends beyond seasonal shifts to the rhythms of the week. Weekends generally command higher rates, particularly in cities and popular leisure destinations, as locals and short-term visitors drive up demand. Conversely, midweek stays often come with substantial discounts. Many hotels, aware of these patterns, offer special weekday packages that include added value such as complimentary breakfasts, spa access, or late checkouts. For travelers with flexible schedules, booking from Sunday through Thursday can result in significant savings without compromising quality. Business-focused hotels, especially in major cities, exhibit the reverse pattern— weekend stays there tend to be cheaper, as corporate guests vacate and leisure travelers overlook such properties.

In addition to timing, the art of securing favorable deals depends on a blend of research, patience, and strategy. While last-minute booking platforms can occasionally produce excellent discounts, especially during off-peak months, they come with inherent risks—limited choice and fluctuating availability. In contrast, early planning typically ensures not only better rates but also access to the most desirable rooms and packages. Many hotels release discounted rates months ahead for travelers willing to commit early, often under "advance purchase" or "early bird" categories. These rates are sometimes non-refundable, but the savings can be substantial, particularly at upscale properties.

Another increasingly effective approach involves subscribing to newsletters and loyalty programs. Many independent hotels and small chains reward repeat customers or subscribers with private offers unavailable on public booking platforms. These might include seasonal promotions, bundled experiences, or complimentary upgrades. Unlike the large international chains, smaller properties frequently cultivate personal relationships with their guests, meaning that direct bookings—by phone or via the hotel's own website—can open doors to special rates or added touches that online systems do not advertise. Building a rapport with a property, especially one that aligns with your travel style, can yield long-term benefits extending beyond a single stay.

The digital landscape has transformed how travelers find and evaluate deals, but not all platforms operate with equal transparency. Comparison sites often use algorithms

that prioritize properties based on commission structures rather than objective value. Thus, while they are useful for gauging general price trends, the most meaningful savings and authentic experiences often come through direct engagement. Smaller inns, boutique hotels, and countryside retreats may not always appear prominently on major booking engines but often provide more flexible pricing when contacted directly. A polite inquiry about current offers, especially outside peak season, can lead to personalized arrangements or package enhancements that reflect genuine hospitality rather than automated marketing.

Beyond discounts, understanding travel seasons also means recognizing the intangible value that timing brings to the overall experience. A visit to the Scottish Highlands in spring, for instance, carries an entirely different emotional rhythm than in autumn. The same hotel may offer varied delights: wildflower meadows in May, the warmth of crackling fires in October, or the crisp serenity of January snow. Each season carries its own sensory and cultural character, and aligning one's journey with these rhythms adds richness that cannot be measured in monetary savings alone. Travelers who value quietude and reflection will find winter ideal, while those seeking energy, color, and social interaction may prefer summer festivals or holiday markets.

Regional variation plays an equally significant role. Coastal destinations and national parks follow strong seasonal cycles, but metropolitan areas maintain steadier visitor numbers year-round. London, for example, remains a global magnet regardless of weather, though January and February tend to bring modest price relief. Edinburgh experiences its own rhythm, with rates soaring during August's world-famous Fringe Festival and dropping sharply in the months that follow. In contrast, rural Scotland, the Yorkshire Dales, and coastal Wales experience pronounced fluctuations tied to weather and local tourism patterns. Understanding these nuances enables travelers to plan not only for cost efficiency but also for depth of experience—whether that means attending a local harvest fair, exploring empty countryside trails, or simply enjoying a quieter breakfast room overlooking a misty valley.

Timing is also influenced by global and local events that temporarily reshape availability and pricing. Sporting championships, music festivals, royal celebrations, and even international conferences can dramatically alter hotel dynamics in certain regions. In such cases, flexibility is the traveler's greatest ally. Shifting plans by even a few days, or staying slightly outside the central event area, can yield major financial benefits and a calmer atmosphere. Many experienced travelers pair these strategies with the foresight to book cancelable rates, allowing them to adjust plans without penalty as better options arise.

Sustainability-minded travelers may also consider timing as part of responsible travel. Visiting destinations outside of peak periods helps distribute tourism's economic benefits more evenly throughout the year, reducing strain on local infrastructure and preserving the authenticity of communities. Smaller guesthouses and independent hotels often rely on steady, year-round business to sustain operations; supporting them during quieter months contributes directly to their resilience and longevity. Moreover, reduced crowds mean deeper interaction with

staff and locals, resulting in more meaningful exchanges and personalized hospitality that can seldom occur during peak rushes.

Ultimately, timing, deals, and travel seasons are interconnected elements of the same art—the art of traveling wisely. The most fulfilling journeys often emerge from a blend of patience, observation, and adaptability. Recognizing when to book, where to stay, and how to align one's expectations with seasonal rhythms elevates travel from mere consumption to intentional experience. While luck occasionally delivers a spontaneous bargain, true value lies in understanding the delicate interplay between time and place. A well-timed trip is not merely cheaper; it feels richer, calmer, and more aligned with the natural and cultural heartbeat of Britain itself.

In a world where travel has become increasingly fast and algorithm-driven, slowing down to respect the patterns of the year restores a sense of harmony between traveler and destination. Whether it's securing a winter hideaway in the Scottish Highlands, finding a summer retreat along the Cornish coast, or uncovering spring serenity in the Lake District, success lies in embracing the rhythm rather than resisting it. Each moment of the British travel calendar has its own quiet brilliance; knowing when to seize it is what turns a journey into something truly memorable.

CHAPTER 5

THE RECOMMENDED HOTELS GAZETTE (2025–2026 EDITION)

HOW THE GAZETTE IS ORGANIZED

The organization of a well-curated hotel gazette is not a matter of simple listing; it is an intentional design built to guide travelers seamlessly through a landscape of choices. Behind every category, region, and description lies an intricate structure that balances accessibility with depth. The goal is to make exploration intuitive—to allow a reader to move effortlessly from one destination to another while feeling confident that each recommendation has been chosen with precision, fairness, and insight. The organization of such a gazette must capture the diversity of Britain's hospitality scene while maintaining coherence, helping readers find hotels that align with their style, budget, and purpose of travel.

At the heart of the system is regional division. Britain's hotel culture cannot be understood in general terms—it must be appreciated through the lens of geography, heritage, and local personality. England, Scotland, Wales, and Northern Ireland each possess distinct atmospheres that influence not only the aesthetics of their hotels but also the tone of their service and the rhythm of their seasons. By separating the gazette into these regions, readers can immerse themselves in the unique flavor of each area. Within each region, the structure flows naturally from major cities to rural escapes, coastal hideaways, and countryside retreats. This ensures that travelers seeking a specific kind of environment—be it an urban weekend in Edinburgh or a quiet break in the Welsh hills—can locate the right options without confusion.

Within each regional section, hotels are arranged not alphabetically but by character and category. This deliberate structure reflects the way travelers make decisions: not by name, but by experience. The gazette divides hotels into key experiential categories such as luxury, boutique, country house, family-friendly, coastal retreat, and eco-conscious stay. Each property within these categories is selected to represent the finest example of its type, ensuring that readers comparing options can do so on fair and relevant terms. This approach allows a traveler who prefers, for instance, intimate design-led spaces to remain within the boutique category, while another seeking grandeur and tradition can explore country estates without overlap or distraction.

Every hotel listing follows a consistent framework, designed for clarity and depth. The first element is a concise but evocative introduction that captures the essence of the property—the feeling it evokes, the kind of guest it attracts, and the atmosphere it projects. This description is followed by key details such as location, amenities, and unique features, written not as marketing slogans but as honest insights derived from direct evaluation. The intention is not to overwhelm readers with data but to equip

them with a realistic understanding of what they can expect from each stay. Whether describing the polished simplicity of a contemporary London hotel or the rustic elegance of a Cotswold inn, the tone remains balanced, factual, and trustworthy.

To ensure transparency and credibility, the gazette emphasizes independent assessment over commercial influence. No hotel appears by virtue of advertisement or paid listing. Instead, inclusion is based on verifiable merit—measured through consistent excellence in service, authenticity of design, guest satisfaction, and alignment with contemporary hospitality values. Each property undergoes careful review, with attention given to the subtleties that define a true quality stay: the warmth of welcome, the ease of check-in, the comfort of the rooms, the attentiveness of the staff, and the sense of place that distinguishes one establishment from another. This impartiality gives the gazette its authority, enabling readers to trust that every recommendation has been earned.

The visual and structural presentation also plays a crucial role in the organization. Each regional chapter begins with a short overview of the area's travel identity—its atmosphere, attractions, and general hotel culture. For example, the section on southern England might begin with a discussion of its coastal heritage, rolling countryside, and proximity to London, setting the mood before introducing individual properties. This narrative introduction helps contextualize the hotels that follow, transforming the listings from a mere directory into a meaningful journey across landscapes. Maps and travel cues may accompany the text, not for decoration, but to offer spatial understanding and assist travelers in planning routes that connect destinations logically.

The gazette also integrates a tiered rating system—not numerical, but descriptive— to reflect the nuances of hospitality quality. Instead of assigning rigid scores, properties are characterized through carefully chosen language that communicates their strengths and intended audience. Terms such as "Exemplary Comfort," "Authentic Character," or "Exceptional Value" indicate quality without reducing experience to numbers. This descriptive style acknowledges that excellence manifests in different forms; a small family-run inn can be as "excellent" in its sincerity as a grand luxury hotel is in its sophistication. Readers are thus empowered to make choices aligned with their personal expectations rather than a universal standard.

One of the defining features of the gazette's structure is its commitment to balance. Alongside established icons of British hospitality, space is reserved for emerging or lesser-known properties that embody innovation and sincerity. These inclusions ensure that the gazette remains fresh and dynamic, showcasing both heritage and evolution. The structure alternates between well-known destinations and hidden gems, allowing travelers to discover surprises without losing orientation. This blend of familiarity and discovery mirrors the experience of travel itself—comfort interwoven with adventure.

Another layer of organization concerns thematic indexing. Beyond the regional and categorical divisions, the gazette features cross-references that connect hotels sharing similar themes or experiences. A reader enchanted by countryside gastronomy, for

instance, can find links to hotels known for exceptional dining in multiple regions. Similarly, those seeking sustainability-driven stays can trace eco-conscious properties throughout the index. This interconnectedness makes the gazette a living tool rather than a static book—it adapts to individual travel interests, guiding users along thematic pathways as well as geographical ones.

Practicality is further enhanced by the inclusion of travel logistics where relevant. For hotels situated in remote areas, concise notes on access routes, nearby train stations, or recommended driving paths help travelers plan with confidence. For urban accommodations, the listings may highlight proximity to cultural landmarks, restaurants, or transport hubs. This information, though secondary to the hotel review itself, anchors the recommendations in reality and saves readers from time-consuming external research. Each description thus forms a small, self-contained guide—compact, useful, and reliable.

An important but often overlooked part of the gazette's organization lies in tone and language. Every description is written with a balance of warmth and professionalism, maintaining consistency from the first page to the last. This consistency creates a sense of trust and continuity, reassuring readers that each entry belongs to a unified editorial vision. The voice is confident but never exaggerated, refined yet accessible, ensuring that the guide speaks equally well to seasoned travelers and first-time explorers. This careful control of tone is what differentiates a credible guide from mere promotional material—it reflects respect both for the reader and for the establishments described.

The closing section of each regional chapter introduces curated highlights— properties that exemplify excellence within specific categories. These highlights are chosen not for prestige alone but for distinction, innovation, or emotional resonance. A seaside inn may be featured for its culinary artistry, while a remote Highland lodge might be celebrated for its serenity and design. The goal is to showcase the diversity of what "good" can mean in British hospitality, encouraging readers to appreciate quality in its many forms rather than chasing uniform ideals.

Finally, the gazette concludes with an index designed for ease of navigation. The index does not merely list hotel names and page numbers but also includes thematic markers, allowing readers to cross-reference properties by type, region, or feature. A traveler seeking pet-friendly accommodations, for example, can trace options across multiple regions through these indicators. Similarly, those interested in award-winning dining or spa experiences can identify suitable hotels at a glance. The index thus functions as both summary and navigation tool—an elegant synthesis of the entire structure.

What makes this organization successful is not complexity but clarity. Every layer, from regional grouping to thematic connection, serves the traveler's needs. The arrangement respects the rhythm of discovery—beginning broad, moving toward specificity, and concluding with reference and reflection. It mirrors the natural process of travel decision-making: dreaming of a place, understanding its possibilities, comparing choices, and finally committing to a stay. The best gazette is

one that feels like a conversation with an expert—guiding without dictating, informing without overwhelming, and leading the reader toward confidence and delight in every choice.

In the end, the structure itself becomes a quiet form of hospitality. Just as a well-run hotel anticipates a guest's needs, a well-organized gazette anticipates a reader's questions. It is built not only to inform but to inspire—to turn the act of choosing a hotel into the first step of an unforgettable journey.

REGIONAL OVERVIEW (ENGLAND, SCOTLAND, WALES, NORTHERN IRELAND)

The diversity of Britain's hotel landscape mirrors the rich cultural and geographical variety that defines its four nations. From the refined sophistication of English country houses to the dramatic hospitality of Scottish Highland lodges, from the soulful warmth of Welsh retreats to the rugged authenticity of Northern Irish escapes, the regions together compose a hospitality tapestry of remarkable depth. Each nation tells its own story through its hotels—stories shaped by history, architecture, landscape, and people. To understand Britain's hotels is to understand the character of these regions, for each brings its own rhythm to the art of welcoming guests.

England remains the heart of British hospitality, a nation where centuries of tradition meet the evolving expectations of modern travelers. The English hotel scene is as varied as its geography, encompassing grand city establishments, ivy-clad country inns, seaside hideaways, and sleek contemporary boutiques. In London, the hospitality culture reflects the capital's cosmopolitan identity—refined, diverse, and attentive to global standards. Iconic establishments in the West End and Mayfair continue to uphold the traditions of service excellence that have shaped luxury hospitality worldwide. Yet London's charm also lies in its newer, more independent hotels that blend local character with creative design, offering experiences rooted in authenticity rather than formality.

Beyond the capital, England's regions express their individuality with quiet confidence. The Cotswolds, for instance, is celebrated for its honey-colored stone villages and intimate inns that combine rustic comfort with understated elegance. In the Lake District, hospitality takes on a poetic form, inspired by the surrounding mountains and lakes that have long drawn artists and thinkers. The hotels here tend to embrace natural materials, panoramic views, and a sense of peace that reflects the landscape's serenity. The South West—Devon, Cornwall, and Dorset—offers a different charm, where coastal hotels open onto windswept beaches and serve seafood caught just beyond the window. Whether in the rolling countryside of Kent or the cultural heart of Oxford and Cambridge, English hotels share a quiet devotion to quality—a commitment to preserving heritage while meeting contemporary expectations.

Scotland presents a strikingly different spirit, where the grandeur of nature shapes the rhythm of hospitality. The Scottish approach to welcoming guests is deeply tied to the landscape—majestic, dramatic, and often remote. The Highlands and Islands are home to lodges and castles that echo the romance of a bygone age while offering modern comfort. These properties capture the essence of escape: log fires burning beneath stone walls, whisky served in oak-paneled lounges, and staff who know every detail of the surrounding hills and lochs. Scottish hospitality thrives on storytelling— hosts share tales of clans, legends, and local customs that bring a sense of belonging to even the most transient traveler.

In Edinburgh and Glasgow, hotel culture takes on a metropolitan tone. Edinburgh's refined Georgian architecture lends itself naturally to elegant boutique hotels and historic townhouses, where old-world grace meets discreet luxury. Glasgow, by contrast, showcases contemporary design and urban energy, reflecting its status as Scotland's creative heart. Together, the two cities embody the nation's balance between tradition and innovation. Throughout Scotland, the emphasis on local produce is unmistakable. Whether in a Michelin-starred restaurant or a country guesthouse, menus celebrate Scottish ingredients—salmon, venison, berries, whisky—crafted with care and pride. This culinary authenticity reinforces the connection between place and hospitality, making every stay not just comfortable, but deeply rooted in Scottish life.

Wales offers a more intimate kind of hospitality, characterized by warmth, sincerity, and a strong sense of place. The Welsh hotel experience is defined by landscapes that inspire and people who welcome guests as if into their own homes. The mountains of Snowdonia, the rolling valleys, and the tranquil coastline of Pembrokeshire provide the backdrop for hotels that prioritize comfort and character over formality. Many of these establishments are family-run, passed down through generations, with owners who embody the traditional Welsh spirit of kindness and community.

In the north, the rugged terrain invites adventure, and hotels cater to those seeking both challenge and rest—hikers, climbers, and nature enthusiasts find havens that blend simplicity with quality. In the south, cultural hubs like Cardiff and Swansea combine modern design with local flair, offering contemporary stays infused with Welsh craftsmanship. Throughout the country, sustainability and heritage intertwine. Restored manor houses and eco-lodges stand side by side, reflecting a growing awareness that true luxury often lies in harmony with nature. Welsh hospitality tends to favor personal touches—a handwritten note, a home-baked breakfast, a quiet conversation by the fire—gestures that remind visitors they are not merely customers, but guests in a living tradition of care.

Northern Ireland, though smaller in scale, possesses a hotel scene of remarkable authenticity and depth. Its hospitality industry has evolved rapidly in recent years, blending modern design with an unwavering sense of local pride. Belfast stands at the center of this transformation, where historic buildings have been reimagined as chic hotels, and the city's creative spirit finds expression in design-led accommodations that celebrate its maritime and industrial heritage. The atmosphere

in Belfast hotels often combines sophistication with sincerity—staff who are effortlessly friendly, and spaces that feel both polished and human.

Outside the capital, Northern Ireland's countryside tells a different story—one of quiet beauty and deep connection to the land. Along the Causeway Coast, small inns and guesthouses overlook cliffs and sea, offering tranquility to travelers drawn by the region's natural wonders. In County Fermanagh, lakeside lodges reflect the stillness of the water, creating retreats ideal for reflection and escape. What unites Northern Irish hospitality is its genuine warmth. Service feels unforced and honest, often accompanied by conversation, laughter, and a sense that guests are being welcomed into the rhythm of local life. It is a hospitality grounded not in performance, but in pride and generosity.

Across the four nations, what stands out most is the shared yet distinct understanding of hospitality as a form of cultural expression. England's sophistication, Scotland's grandeur, Wales's sincerity, and Northern Ireland's authenticity all converge to create a hotel landscape unlike any other in Europe. While the standards of comfort, cleanliness, and professionalism remain high throughout, each region expresses those standards in its own voice. An English country house may emphasize formality and refinement, a Scottish lodge may highlight heritage and adventure, a Welsh inn may focus on intimacy and natural harmony, and a Northern Irish guesthouse may embody warmth and simplicity.

Another defining characteristic of Britain's regional hospitality is the integration of history into modern experience. Many hotels occupy buildings that have witnessed centuries of change—former castles, coaching inns, farmhouses, and townhouses now restored with modern amenities while preserving their soul. In England, one might sleep in a converted abbey; in Scotland, within the walls of a castle once home to a clan chief; in Wales, inside a centuries-old mill beside a stream; and in Northern Ireland, in a Georgian mansion overlooking misty fields. This fusion of old and new gives British hotels a depth that goes beyond luxury—it offers a sense of continuity and belonging, a bridge between past and present.

Regional differences also extend to the pace and rhythm of travel. England and Scotland attract a blend of international visitors and domestic explorers, while Wales and Northern Ireland often provide quieter, more introspective journeys. In England, accessibility and density mean that luxury and convenience are always within reach. In Scotland, the remoteness of certain destinations becomes part of the allure—a luxury of solitude. Wales appeals to those who value nature's closeness, while Northern Ireland rewards curiosity and conversation. This balance ensures that Britain offers something for every kind of traveler: the urbanite seeking culture, the romantic craving tranquility, the adventurer chasing landscapes, and the connoisseur pursuing excellence.

Food, too, reflects these regional identities. English hotels often blend classical European techniques with British produce, offering refined menus that mirror the nation's cosmopolitan character. Scottish kitchens celebrate provenance and seasonality, with chefs often working directly with local farmers, fishermen, and

distillers. Welsh cuisine emphasizes comfort and authenticity, with farm-to-table simplicity elevated by heartfelt preparation. Northern Irish dining showcases revival—a confident blend of tradition and innovation that mirrors the country's broader renaissance. In each case, cuisine becomes a reflection of place, deepening the guest's sense of connection to the land and people.

Ultimately, the regional diversity of Britain's hotels is what gives its hospitality landscape such vitality. These four nations, distinct yet intertwined, express through their hotels the values that define them—respect for heritage, passion for quality, and commitment to genuine warmth. Whether one finds comfort in the polished quiet of an English estate, the rugged charm of a Highland inn, the heartfelt welcome of a Welsh farmhouse, or the easy friendliness of a Northern Irish retreat, the essence remains the same: an experience built on care, character, and authenticity.

Together, England, Scotland, Wales, and Northern Ireland form not just a destination but a dialogue—a conversation between past and present, tradition and innovation, host and guest. The regional variety is not fragmentation, but harmony; not competition, but complement. To journey through the hotels of Britain is to travel through its identity itself—a mosaic of landscapes and lives, where hospitality is both an art and a reflection of national soul.

FIFTY TRUSTED HOTELS WITH KEY DETAILS, RATINGS, AND FEATURES

1. The Old Inn

- **Full Address:** 1 Main Street, Crawfordsburn, County Down, BT19 1LX, Northern Ireland

- **Rating:** 4 Stars

- **Features:** Recognized as Northern Ireland's Hotel of the Year. Charming boutique hotel with a thatched exterior and elegant interiors. Guests can enjoy the Treetop Spa, exceptional service, and a blend of historic charm with modern luxury.

2. The Chesterfield Mayfair

- **Full Address:** 35 Charles Street, Mayfair, London, W1J 5EB, England

- **Rating:** 5 Stars

- **Features:** Classic London townhouse hotel with 94 individually designed rooms and suites. Exceptional service, elegant décor, and a quintessential British experience near Buckingham Palace and West End theatres.

3. The Egerton House Hotel

- **Full Address:** 17–19 Egerton Terrace, Knightsbridge, London, SW3 2BX, England
- **Rating:** 5 Stars
- **Features:** Intimate boutique hotel with 28 rooms and suites. Personalized service, complimentary cocktails and teas in the Drawing Room. Located near Harrods and Hyde Park.

4. The Cadogan, A Belmond Hotel

- **Full Address:** 75 Sloane Street, Chelsea, London, SW1X 9SG, England
- **Rating:** 5 Stars
- **Features:** Historic hotel with 54 rooms and suites blending Victorian architecture with modern luxury. Features a private garden and discreet service. Near Sloane Square and King's Road.

5. The Royal Lancaster London

- **Full Address:** Lancaster Terrace, Lancaster Gate, London, W2 2TY, England
- **Rating:** 5 Stars
- **Features:** Overlooking Hyde Park, 411 rooms and suites. Panoramic park and city views. Dining includes the award-winning Nipa Thai restaurant. Walking distance to Oxford Street and West End theatres.

6. The Resident Covent Garden

- **Full Address:** 51 Bedford Street, Covent Garden, London, WC2E 9HP, England
- **Rating:** 5 Stars
- **Features:** Stylish hotel with 165 rooms and suites, contemporary design, complimentary refreshments, fitness room, and library. Located near Covent Garden Market and the Royal Opera House.

7. The Langham, London

- **Full Address:** 1C Portland Place, Regent Street, London, W1B 1JA, England

- **Rating:** 5 Stars
- **Features:** Iconic hotel with 380 rooms and suites. Classic British elegance, Michelin-starred Roux at The Landau, luxurious spa facilities. Close to Oxford Street and Regent's Park.

8. The Savoy

- **Full Address:** Strand, London, WC2R 0EZ, England
- **Rating:** 5 Stars
- **Features:** Legendary hotel with 267 rooms and suites. Art Deco and Edwardian interiors, world-class service, River Restaurant, and the American Bar. Near Covent Garden and West End theatres.

9. Claridge's

- **Full Address:** Brook Street, Mayfair, London, W1K 4HR, England
- **Rating:** 5 Stars
- **Features:** Luxury hotel with 190 rooms and suites. Exceptional service, elegant interiors, and Michelin-starred dining at Fera at Claridge's. Located near Bond Street and Hyde Park.

10. Brown's Hotel

- **Full Address:** Albemarle Street, Mayfair, London, W1S 4BP, England
- **Rating:** 5 Stars
- **Features:** Historic hotel with 115 rooms and suites. Classic British charm, personalized service, dining at Michelin-starred Hélène Darroze. Near Buckingham Palace and West End theatres.

11. The Balmoral

- **Full Address:** 1 Princes Street, Edinburgh, EH2 2EQ, Scotland
- **Rating:** 5 Stars
- **Features:** Iconic landmark overlooking Edinburgh Castle and Princes Street Gardens. 187 rooms and suites, Michelin-starred Number One restaurant, luxurious spa, and heritage charm.

12. Waldorf Astoria Edinburgh – The Caledonian

- **Full Address:** Princes Street, Edinburgh, EH1 2AB, Scotland
- **Rating:** 5 Stars
- **Features:** Historic luxury hotel with 241 rooms and suites. 19th-century clock tower, elegant ballroom, world-class spa, traditional Scottish dining, and high-end afternoon teas.

13. Gleneagles Hotel

- **Full Address:** Auchterarder, Perthshire, PH3 1NF, Scotland
- **Rating:** 5 Stars
- **Features:** Golf and country resort with 232 rooms and suites. Championship golf courses, equestrian center, spa, and multiple dining options including Michelin-starred Andrew Fairlie. Outdoor adventures available.

14. The Torridon Hotel

- **Full Address:** Torridon, Wester Ross, IV22 2JG, Scotland
- **Rating:** 5 Stars
- **Features:** Remote luxury hotel with 20 individually styled rooms. Surrounded by 58 acres of private woodland, fine dining, whisky experiences, hiking, and wildlife tours.

15. Isle of Eriska Hotel, Spa & Island

- **Full Address:** Eriska, Loch Linnhe, Argyll, PA34 4XE, Scotland
- **Rating:** 5 Stars
- **Features:** Private island resort with 21 rooms and suites, panoramic views, luxury spa, award-winning dining, kayaking, mountain biking, and nature walks.

16. The Chester Hotel

- **Full Address:** 49 Grosvenor Street, Chester, Cheshire, CH1 1HR, England
- **Rating:** 4 Stars

- **Features:** Boutique hotel blending modern comforts with historical architecture. 72 rooms, fine dining, personalized concierge services, and proximity to Chester Cathedral.

---

17. Bovey Castle

- **Full Address:** North Bovey, Dartmoor National Park, Devon, TQ13 7JW, England
- **Rating:** 5 Stars
- **Features:** Edwardian-style castle hotel with 59 rooms and suites. Golf, falconry, clay pigeon shooting, luxury spa, and locally sourced cuisine.

---

18. Lucknam Park Hotel & Spa

- **Full Address:** Colerne, Wiltshire, SN14 8AZ, England
- **Rating:** 5 Stars
- **Features:** Country estate hotel with 41 rooms and suites. 500 acres of parkland, equestrian facilities, Michelin-starred dining, spa, and bespoke countryside experiences.

---

19. The Royal Crescent Hotel & Spa

- **Full Address:** 16 Royal Crescent, Bath, BA1 2LS, England
- **Rating:** 5 Stars
- **Features:** Iconic Georgian hotel with 45 rooms, tranquil spa, fine dining at Dower House Restaurant, and views of Royal Crescent gardens.

---

20. Chewton Glen Hotel & Spa

- **Full Address:** New Milton, Hampshire, BH25 6QS, England
- **Rating:** 5 Stars
- **Features:** Luxury country house hotel with 87 rooms, treehouse suites, yoga studio, cookery school, Michelin-starred restaurant, and outdoor activities.

---

21. The Chester Grosvenor

- **Full Address:** Eastgate Street, Chester, CH1 1LT, England
- **Rating:** 5 Stars

- **Features:** Historic hotel overlooking the iconic Eastgate Clock. Offers luxurious rooms, award-winning dining at Arkle and La Brasserie, and a serene spa.

22. Bovey Castle

- **Full Address:** North Bovey, Dartmoor National Park, Devon, TQ13 7FY, England
- **Rating:** 5 Stars
- **Features:** Set within Dartmoor National Park, this castle hotel features an 18-hole championship golf course, spa, country lodges, and an outdoor pursuits centre.

23. Lucknam Park Hotel & Spa

- **Full Address:** Colerne, Wiltshire, SN14 8AZ, England
- **Rating:** 5 Stars
- **Features:** A Palladian mansion set within 500 acres of parkland, offering individually styled rooms, a Michelin-starred restaurant, spa with hydrotherapy pool, and equestrian centre.

24. The Royal Crescent Hotel & Spa

- **Full Address:** 16 Royal Crescent, Bath, BA1 2LS, England
- **Rating:** 5 Stars
- **Features:** Located in a Georgian crescent, this hotel offers luxurious rooms, a tranquil spa, award-winning dining, and beautiful gardens.

25. Chewton Glen Hotel & Spa

- **Full Address:** New Milton, Hampshire, BH25 6QS, England
- **Rating:** 5 Stars
- **Features:** An 18th-century country house hotel with treehouses, cookery school, spa, and The Kitchen by James Martin restaurant. Set within 130 acres of countryside.

26. The Langham, London

- **Full Address:** 1C Portland Place, Regent Street, London, W1B 1JA, England

- **Rating:** 5 Stars
- **Features:** Iconic hotel offering luxurious rooms, Michelin-starred dining at Roux at The Landau, a spa, and The Wigmore British tavern.

27. The Savoy

- **Full Address:** Strand, London, WC2R 0EZ, England
- **Rating:** 5 Stars
- **Features:** Historic hotel offering elegant rooms, world-class dining, and views of the River Thames. Known for its exceptional service and luxury.

28. Claridge's

- **Full Address:** Brook Street, Mayfair, London, W1K 4HR, England
- **Rating:** 5 Stars
- **Features:** Art Deco hotel offering luxurious rooms, renowned afternoon tea, and fine dining at Fera. Known for its timeless elegance and exceptional service.

29. Brown's Hotel

- **Full Address:** Albemarle Street, Mayfair, London, W1S 4BP, England
- **Rating:** 5 Stars
- **Features:** Historic hotel offering elegant rooms, personalized service, and dining at Hélène Darroze. Located near Buckingham Palace and West End theatres.

30. The Ritz London

- **Full Address:** 150 Piccadilly, St. James's, London, W1J 9BR, England
- **Rating:** 5 Stars
- **Features:** Iconic hotel offering opulent rooms, Michelin-starred dining, and traditional afternoon tea. Known for its exceptional service and historic significance.

31. The Dorchester

- **Full Address:** 53 Park Lane, Mayfair, London, W1K 1QA, England

- **Rating:** 5 Stars
- **Features:** Luxury hotel offering elegant rooms, Michelin-starred dining at Alain Ducasse, and a renowned spa. Located near Hyde Park and the West End.

32. The Connaught

- **Full Address:** Carlos Place, Mayfair, London, W1K 2AL, England
- **Rating:** 5 Stars
- **Features:** Elegant hotel offering luxurious rooms, dining at Hélène Darroze, and a renowned spa. Known for its exceptional service and timeless design.

33. The Berkeley

- **Full Address:** Wilton Place, Knightsbridge, London, SW1X 7RL, England
- **Rating:** 5 Stars
- **Features:** Contemporary hotel offering luxurious rooms, dining at Marcus, and a rooftop pool. Located near Harrods and Hyde Park.

34. The Lanesborough

- **Full Address:** Hyde Park Corner, London, SW1X 7TA, England
- **Rating:** 5 Stars
- **Features:** Luxury hotel offering elegant rooms, Michelin-starred dining at Celeste, and a renowned spa. Located near Hyde Park and Buckingham Palace.

35. The Goring

- **Full Address:** Beeston Place, Belgravia, London, SW1W 0JW, England
- **Rating:** 5 Stars
- **Features:** Family-owned hotel offering luxurious rooms, personalized service, and renowned afternoon tea. Located near Buckingham Palace.

36. The Langham, London

- **Full Address:** 1C Portland Place, Regent Street, London, W1B 1JA, England
- **Rating:** 5 Stars
- **Features:** Iconic hotel offering luxurious rooms, Michelin-starred dining at Roux at The Landau, a spa, and The Wigmore British tavern.

37. The Savoy

- **Full Address:** Strand, London, WC2R 0EZ, England
- **Rating:** 5 Stars
- **Features:** Historic hotel offering elegant rooms, world-class dining, and views of the River Thames. Known for its exceptional service and luxury.

38. Claridge's

- **Full Address:** Brook Street, Mayfair, London, W1K 4HR, England
- **Rating:** 5 Stars
- **Features:** Art Deco hotel offering luxurious rooms, renowned afternoon tea, and fine dining at Fera. Known for its timeless elegance and exceptional service.

39. Brown's Hotel

- **Full Address:** Albemarle Street, Mayfair, London, W1S 4BP, England
- **Rating:** 5 Stars
- **Features:** Historic hotel offering elegant rooms, personalized service, and dining at Hélène Darroze. Located near Buckingham Palace and West End theatres.

40. The Ritz London

- **Full Address:** 150 Piccadilly, St. James's, London, W1J 9BR, England
- **Rating:** 5 Stars
- **Features:** Iconic hotel offering opulent rooms, Michelin-starred dining, and traditional afternoon tea. Known for its exceptional service and historic significance.

41. The Dorchester

- **Full Address:** 53 Park Lane, Mayfair, London, W1K 1QA, England
- **Rating:** 5 Stars
- **Features:** Luxury hotel offering elegant rooms, Michelin-starred dining at Alain Ducasse, and a renowned spa. Located near Hyde Park and the West End.

42. The Connaught

- **Full Address:** Carlos Place, Mayfair, London, W1K 2AL, England
- **Rating:** 5 Stars
- **Features:** Elegant hotel offering luxurious rooms, dining at Hélène Darroze, and a renowned spa. Known for its exceptional service and timeless design.

43. The Berkeley

- **Full Address:** Wilton Place, Knightsbridge, London, SW1X 7RL, England
- **Rating:** 5 Stars
- **Features:** Contemporary hotel offering luxurious rooms, dining at Marcus, and a rooftop pool. Located near Harrods and Hyde Park.

45. The Lanesborough

- **Full Address:** Hyde Park Corner, London, SW1X 7TA, England
- **Rating:** 5 Stars
- **Features:** Timeless luxury hotel offering refined rooms, Michelin-starred dining at Celeste, and an elegant spa. Renowned for impeccable service and prime location near Buckingham Palace.

46. The Goring

- **Full Address:** Beeston Place, Belgravia, London, SW1W 0JW, England
- **Rating:** 5 Stars

- **Features:** Family-owned luxury hotel offering sophisticated rooms, bespoke service, and traditional afternoon tea. Walking distance to Buckingham Palace and major London landmarks.

47. The Balmoral, Edinburgh

- **Full Address:** 1 Princes Street, Edinburgh, EH2 2EQ, Scotland
- **Rating:** 5 Stars
- **Features:** Iconic hotel with luxurious rooms and suites overlooking Edinburgh Castle. Michelin-starred dining at Number One, full-service spa, and elegant Scottish charm.

48. Waldorf Astoria Edinburgh – The Caledonian

- **Full Address:** Princes Street, Edinburgh, EH1 2AB, Scotland
- **Rating:** 5 Stars
- **Features:** Historic luxury hotel with beautifully appointed rooms and suites. Offers fine dining, world-class spa, and proximity to Edinburgh Castle and Princes Street Gardens.

49. Gleneagles Hotel

- **Full Address:** Auchterarder, Perthshire, PH3 1NF, Scotland
- **Rating:** 5 Stars
- **Features:** Renowned country estate with 232 rooms and suites. Championship golf courses, equestrian center, luxurious spa, multiple restaurants, and outdoor adventure activities.

50. The Torridon Hotel

- **Full Address:** Torridon, Wester Ross, IV22 2JG, Scotland
- **Rating:** 5 Stars
- **Features:** Remote luxury retreat with 20 individually styled rooms. Surrounded by stunning natural landscapes, offering fine dining, whisky experiences, hiking, and wildlife tours.

CHAPTER 6

SPECIAL THEMES AND STANDOUT STAYS

ROMANTIC ESCAPES: THE BEST OF CHARM AND SECLUSION

Romantic getaways have long held a special place in the world of hospitality, offering couples the chance to escape from the daily demands of life and immerse themselves in an environment designed to foster connection, intimacy, and lasting memories. In modern travel, the essence of a romantic escape is not solely measured by luxury or opulence, but by the atmosphere, attention to detail, and the subtle elements that cultivate a sense of exclusivity and personal connection. The charm of seclusion, combined with thoughtful amenities and carefully curated experiences, transforms a stay into a narrative of romance that can be remembered for a lifetime.

The heart of a truly romantic retreat lies in its setting. Remote countryside hideaways, coastal cottages, and boutique inns tucked away in historic villages provide a sense of privacy that is invaluable to couples seeking moments together without interruption. These locations often offer sweeping landscapes, tranquil gardens, or panoramic views of lakes, mountains, or the sea, each creating a backdrop for shared experiences that are intimate and unforgettable. A quiet walk along a secluded beach at sunrise or a private dinner overlooking rolling hills can elevate the emotional resonance of a stay far beyond what a conventional hotel experience might provide.

Equally important is the design and ambiance of the accommodations themselves. Romantic escapes are frequently characterized by rooms and suites that blend comfort, aesthetic beauty, and a thoughtful sense of luxury. Soft lighting, plush furnishings, elegant textiles, and charming architectural details combine to create an atmosphere that invites relaxation and fosters intimacy. Open fireplaces, private balconies, and spa-style bathrooms add layers of indulgence, encouraging couples to linger and enjoy each other's company in a setting that feels both personal and exclusive. Every element, from the scent of fresh flowers to the warmth of natural materials, can contribute to the overall mood and enhance the romantic experience.

Service plays a pivotal role in crafting a romantic escape. Attentive, discreet, and personalized hospitality ensures that couples feel valued and cared for without intrusions on their privacy. Hotels that anticipate needs and create bespoke experiences—whether arranging private picnics, candlelit dinners, or curated excursions—help transform ordinary moments into extraordinary ones. A concierge who understands the desires of guests and can subtly enhance the ambiance of a stay without being intrusive adds immeasurable value, ensuring that couples can relax fully and savor the intimacy of their shared time.

Culinary experiences are often central to the allure of romantic getaways. Hotels that feature fine dining or unique gastronomic experiences contribute significantly to the overall mood and enjoyment of a stay. A candlelit dinner in a restaurant that blends local flavors with imaginative presentations, paired with exceptional wines or champagnes, can turn an evening into a memory that lasts far beyond the visit. Breakfasts in bed, picnics in private gardens, or even casual alfresco meals with a view provide additional opportunities for couples to connect and savor the culinary delights of the region. Thoughtful presentation, attention to dietary preferences, and a sense of occasion elevate these experiences into moments of genuine romance.

Experiential offerings beyond the accommodations also enrich romantic escapes. Many hotels provide curated activities designed for two, such as couples' spa treatments, private guided walks, cooking classes, or excursions to local cultural or natural landmarks. These experiences allow couples to explore together, deepen their connection, and create memories through shared adventures. The ability to engage in activities that match the interests of the pair, whether energetic or leisurely, adventurous or contemplative, ensures that the stay is personalized and memorable. A well-rounded escape balances moments of relaxation with opportunities for meaningful engagement, crafting a rhythm that supports both individual and shared experiences.

Attention to detail, often subtle yet profoundly impactful, differentiates a romantic escape from a standard stay. Thoughtful touches—such as a selection of fine chocolates, a bottle of sparkling wine, handpicked roses, or a playlist of soft music— signal care and consideration, reinforcing the sense of being in a space designed specifically for connection. These details create an environment in which couples feel celebrated, special, and free to focus entirely on one another. The most successful romantic retreats integrate such elements seamlessly, ensuring that they feel natural rather than staged, enhancing the authenticity of the experience.

The timing of a visit also shapes the nature of a romantic escape. Seasonal considerations influence both the environment and the range of activities available. Autumn and winter visits might emphasize cozy, indoor experiences with roaring fires and intimate dining, while spring and summer offer opportunities for exploring gardens, taking scenic walks, or enjoying outdoor adventures. Selecting the appropriate time to travel, aligned with personal preferences and the characteristics of the location, enhances the romantic appeal and ensures that couples can make the most of both the setting and the offerings.

Ultimately, the best romantic escapes are defined by the interplay between seclusion, ambiance, service, and experience. A hotel may offer luxurious rooms, exquisite dining, and remarkable scenery, but the overall effect is only realized when these elements work together to create an environment that fosters intimacy, connection, and shared enjoyment. Couples emerge from such experiences with not just memories, but a strengthened sense of partnership and a renewed appreciation for the moments of closeness and care that the escape facilitated.

In a world where travel options are increasingly abundant, the ability of a property to craft a distinct, intimate, and memorable romantic experience sets it apart. These escapes are about more than the physical surroundings—they are about crafting moments that resonate emotionally, leaving an enduring impression on all who partake. The attention to detail, personalized service, thoughtful design, and curated experiences collectively define the essence of a successful romantic getaway, providing couples with a retreat that is both memorable and deeply cherished.

FOOD-LOVER'S HOTELS: DINING WHERE IT MATTERS

Gastronomy has increasingly become a cornerstone of the modern hospitality experience, transforming hotels into destinations in their own right for discerning travelers who seek both comfort and culinary excellence. In the contemporary landscape, a hotel's ability to offer remarkable dining experiences often distinguishes it from its peers, turning a simple stay into a multi-sensory journey. Exceptional cuisine, thoughtfully curated menus, and immersive food experiences contribute not only to satisfaction but also to the overall narrative of a stay, creating lasting memories that guests associate with their time at a property.

At the heart of a food-focused hotel is its commitment to quality, authenticity, and innovation in the kitchen. Chefs in these establishments often blend local ingredients with international techniques, producing dishes that are both rooted in the region and appealing to a global palate. Seasonal sourcing is a hallmark of excellence, ensuring that every meal reflects the natural abundance of the surrounding area. From freshly harvested vegetables and fruits to locally caught seafood and hand-selected meats, the integrity of the ingredients forms the foundation of a dining experience that is both memorable and meaningful. Guests often find that the attention to provenance and quality elevates even familiar dishes, turning them into revelations of flavor, texture, and aroma.

Ambiance is another crucial element that defines the dining experience within a hotel setting. The environment, from lighting and decor to table settings and spatial arrangement, contributes to the overall perception of luxury and attentiveness. Hotels that emphasize food experiences understand that presentation and atmosphere are inseparable from taste. Whether it is a fine-dining restaurant with white linen tablecloths and carefully curated artwork or a rustic, cozy eatery overlooking a pastoral landscape, the setting amplifies the culinary experience and reinforces the sense of occasion. It is within these thoughtfully designed spaces that guests are invited to savor not only the flavors on their plates but also the artistry of the environment surrounding them.

Service quality plays an equally important role in the overall impression of a food-focused hotel. Knowledgeable, courteous, and attentive staff enhance every interaction, from explaining the origins of ingredients to recommending wine pairings or personalizing menus to accommodate dietary preferences. Exceptional hospitality in this context is seamless and intuitive, anticipating guest needs without intruding upon the enjoyment of the meal. The presence of sommeliers, pastry chefs,

or in-house culinary experts who engage with guests creates a sense of exclusivity and refinement, elevating dining beyond mere sustenance into a curated, educational, and immersive experience.

The scope of culinary experiences offered by hotels extends beyond formal meals. Many establishments provide immersive opportunities that allow guests to connect with food in interactive ways, such as cooking classes, chef's tables, guided tastings, or visits to local farms and artisanal producers. These experiences enable guests to gain insight into the philosophy behind the food, fostering a deeper appreciation for both the cuisine and the location. Such participatory elements also create shared memories that resonate long after the stay concludes, reinforcing the hotel's role not merely as accommodation but as a holistic, enriching destination.

Attention to detail is paramount in the execution of dining experiences. Hotels dedicated to food excellence invest in the subtleties that differentiate a good meal from an extraordinary one: the quality of cutlery and glassware, the pacing of courses, the visual presentation of dishes, and even the scent and ambiance of the dining room. Each element is carefully calibrated to enhance the enjoyment of flavors and textures, ensuring that guests feel pampered and valued. These subtle considerations often leave lasting impressions, creating a sense of thoughtfulness and sophistication that defines the hotel's character and commitment to excellence.

Culinary excellence also often serves as a gateway to understanding the cultural and historical context of a region. Hotels that prioritize local cuisine allow guests to experience the essence of place through flavors, recipes, and traditions passed down through generations. From artisanal cheeses and charcuterie to locally brewed beverages and classic regional desserts, the food becomes a storytelling medium that connects visitors to the landscape, heritage, and community. By immersing guests in authentic, locally inspired dining experiences, these hotels foster a deeper connection to the destination, enriching the travel experience in ways that go beyond mere accommodation.

The integration of innovation with tradition is a hallmark of food-focused hotels that consistently receive acclaim. Chefs balance respect for culinary heritage with modern techniques, exploring novel presentations, fusion cuisine, and experimental flavor profiles that surprise and delight. Guests benefit from this delicate interplay between familiarity and novelty, discovering tastes and combinations that elevate their understanding of food while maintaining a comforting connection to regional roots. This approach ensures that each meal is not only enjoyable but also intellectually stimulating and culturally informative, adding a layer of enrichment to the stay.

Finally, the consideration of personalized experiences underscores the essence of a hotel that caters to food enthusiasts. From customized menus for romantic dinners to bespoke tasting experiences for connoisseurs, hotels recognize that each guest's journey is unique. Attention to individual preferences, allergies, and culinary desires ensures that every meal contributes to an overarching sense of care and dedication. This personalization reinforces the bond between guest and establishment, leaving

an enduring impression of hospitality that goes far beyond the room or view, embedding itself in the memories associated with taste, comfort, and discovery.

In sum, the finest hotels that focus on dining excellence offer more than rooms and amenities—they provide an immersive, multi-dimensional exploration of food, culture, and personal connection. Through the careful curation of ingredients, ambiance, service, and personalized experiences, guests are invited to experience a narrative that engages all senses. The meticulous blending of local tradition, innovation, and attention to detail creates moments of joy, discovery, and indulgence, ensuring that every stay resonates long after the visit concludes. This approach transforms a simple trip into a journey of taste, memory, and meaningful engagement, solidifying the role of the hotel not just as a place to stay, but as a destination in its own right for those who appreciate the art and science of exceptional dining.

SUSTAINABLE STAYS: TRAVEL WITH A GREEN HEART

Sustainable travel has emerged as a defining principle for modern hospitality, reflecting a growing awareness among travelers of the environmental and social impact of their choices. In this context, a stay at a hotel is no longer judged solely on luxury, comfort, or location; the responsibility and commitment of the property toward sustainable practices increasingly shape guest expectations. Hotels that embrace sustainability not only reduce their ecological footprint but also cultivate meaningful experiences that resonate with guests who value environmental stewardship, ethical operations, and authentic engagement with the local community.

Central to sustainable stays is the thoughtful design and management of the property itself. Many hotels incorporate eco-friendly building materials, energy-efficient lighting, and water-saving systems, minimizing their impact on natural resources without compromising comfort or style. From the orientation of buildings to maximize natural light to the installation of renewable energy sources such as solar panels, these design choices reflect a deliberate commitment to environmental responsibility. Guests often find that properties with visible sustainability measures provide both aesthetic and functional benefits, blending modern efficiency with a sense of conscientiousness that enhances the overall experience.

Operational practices also play a vital role in shaping a green-minded stay. Hotels that prioritize sustainability often adopt comprehensive waste reduction programs, including recycling initiatives, composting, and minimizing single-use plastics. Kitchen operations emphasize locally sourced ingredients, seasonal menus, and a reduction in food waste, ensuring that culinary offerings are both fresh and environmentally conscious. Housekeeping practices frequently employ environmentally friendly cleaning products and promote energy-efficient laundering methods, demonstrating that attention to detail in sustainability permeates every aspect of the guest experience. These practices are not only a mark of responsibility but also convey to guests a sense of partnership in caring for the environment during their visit.

Beyond the physical infrastructure and daily operations, sustainable hotels foster a culture of environmental and social consciousness that extends to guests' experiences. Educating visitors about the region's ecology, encouraging responsible engagement with local attractions, and offering programs that support conservation or community initiatives deepen the connection between travelers and their surroundings. Many properties facilitate opportunities for guests to participate in sustainable activities, such as guided nature walks, wildlife observation, and cultural immersion programs that respect local traditions. These experiences enrich the stay by providing meaning and context, allowing guests to appreciate the environmental and cultural significance of their visit while reinforcing the hotel's ethos.

Energy conservation and resource management are increasingly sophisticated in leading sustainable hotels. Smart heating and cooling systems, occupancy sensors, and renewable energy integration reduce waste while maintaining comfort. Rainwater harvesting, greywater recycling, and efficient irrigation systems ensure that water usage is optimized, particularly in regions where resources are scarce or under environmental stress. These measures reflect a holistic approach to sustainability, demonstrating that responsible management can coexist seamlessly with the high standards of comfort and service expected by discerning travelers. Guests often respond positively to visible measures of environmental care, perceiving the hotel as both thoughtful and forward-thinking.

Sustainable practices also extend into the culinary realm. Hotels committed to green hospitality often prioritize farm-to-table dining, sourcing ingredients from local producers, organic farms, and community artisans. This approach reduces transportation emissions, supports local economies, and fosters a deeper appreciation for regional flavors and traditions. Menus frequently emphasize plant-forward dishes, seasonal specialties, and reduced meat consumption, aligning culinary offerings with broader ecological goals. By integrating sustainability into the dining experience, hotels create opportunities for guests to make choices that are both enjoyable and responsible, reinforcing the philosophy that every element of a stay can contribute to positive environmental impact.

Social responsibility is another critical dimension of sustainable hospitality. Ethical labor practices, community engagement, and partnerships with local artisans or conservation organizations reflect a commitment to social as well as environmental stewardship. Hotels that actively support local employment, cultural preservation, and charitable initiatives provide guests with a richer, more meaningful experience. By highlighting these connections, properties enable travelers to participate indirectly in supporting communities and ecosystems, fostering a sense of shared purpose and ethical alignment. Guests increasingly seek accommodations that offer these assurances, recognizing that their choices extend beyond personal comfort to the broader context of societal and ecological well-being.

The integration of sustainability into modern hospitality also involves innovation and adaptability. Leading properties continuously seek ways to reduce their carbon footprint, improve efficiency, and implement cutting-edge technologies that

promote environmental responsibility. This might include advanced energy monitoring systems, green certifications, or partnerships with organizations specializing in sustainability audits. By demonstrating a commitment to ongoing improvement, hotels signal to guests that their investment in responsible travel is meaningful and contributes to a long-term vision of stewardship and conscientious operations.

For guests, staying at a sustainable hotel offers a sense of alignment between personal values and travel experiences. The knowledge that their accommodations prioritize environmental preservation, ethical practices, and thoughtful engagement enhances the emotional and intellectual satisfaction of the stay. Sustainable hospitality encourages reflection on the ways travel can harmonize with ecological and cultural respect, providing an added layer of fulfillment beyond comfort, convenience, or luxury. Travelers find that experiences shaped by sustainability often feel more authentic, connected, and purposeful, leaving a lasting impression that extends beyond the immediate visit.

Ultimately, sustainable stays represent the intersection of responsibility, comfort, and enrichment. Hotels that embrace green principles do more than reduce environmental impact—they offer guests a comprehensive experience that engages the senses, stimulates the mind, and nurtures a deeper appreciation for the world around them. From infrastructure and operations to culinary offerings and community engagement, every facet of a stay can be designed to uphold the values of ecological and social stewardship. Travelers increasingly recognize that sustainability is not a limitation but an enhancement, enriching the overall quality of hospitality and creating memories rooted in both enjoyment and conscientious awareness.

By choosing accommodations that prioritize sustainability, guests contribute to a broader movement that reshapes the hospitality industry and encourages ethical travel practices. Each decision, from sourcing to energy management to social engagement, reinforces the notion that luxury and responsibility are not mutually exclusive but can coexist in a manner that elevates both the experience and the values of all involved. A green-hearted approach to travel fosters connection, mindfulness, and appreciation, ensuring that each stay is meaningful, enjoyable, and enduringly responsible.

CHAPTER 7

MAKING THE MOST OF YOUR STAY

EXPLORING BEYOND THE HOTEL: LOCAL TIPS AND ATTRACTIONS

Travel experiences are enriched not only by the quality of accommodation but also by the connections and discoveries that lie beyond the walls of a hotel. Immersing oneself in the surrounding environment—whether a vibrant urban district, a quaint village, a sweeping countryside, or a coastal retreat—offers layers of meaning and memory that transform a stay from ordinary to unforgettable. Understanding the local context, appreciating cultural nuances, and uncovering hidden gems allows travelers to fully embrace their destination and create experiences that linger long after the visit has ended.

A key aspect of exploring beyond the hotel is developing a sense of place. Each region has its own rhythm, traditions, and character that shape the experiences available to visitors. In urban areas, neighborhoods may pulse with dynamic energy, offering boutique shops, artisanal markets, historic landmarks, and cultural institutions. Wandering through these streets provides insight into local lifestyles, the architectural heritage, and the creative spirit of the community. Small details—such as noticing the style of shopfronts, the cadence of daily routines, or the presence of street performers—can reveal layers of authenticity that guidebooks alone cannot fully capture. These encounters foster a sense of engagement, encouraging travelers to see beyond surface-level impressions and cultivate genuine connections with the destination.

In rural or countryside settings, the landscape itself becomes a central attraction. Rolling hills, meandering rivers, dramatic coastlines, and verdant forests provide not only visual delight but also opportunities for outdoor activities that bring travelers closer to the natural environment. Hiking trails, scenic drives, and cycling routes allow visitors to explore the terrain actively, gaining perspective on the region's ecology, history, and local traditions. The quiet rhythm of country life can be both restorative and inspiring, offering a counterpoint to urban intensity and emphasizing the value of mindful observation and thoughtful engagement. Learning to appreciate subtle changes in season, wildlife activity, and agricultural patterns deepens one's connection to the area, making each experience more meaningful and memorable.

Cultural immersion is another vital component of meaningful exploration. Engaging with local artisans, attending community festivals, visiting historic sites, or participating in traditional practices provides insight into the intangible aspects of a region—the customs, stories, and values that define its identity. Understanding the social fabric of a place, from culinary rituals to craft traditions, allows travelers to experience more than superficial sightseeing. It encourages curiosity, empathy, and respect, enriching the stay with experiences that resonate emotionally and

intellectually. These interactions often become personal highlights, creating stories and memories that guests carry long after leaving the destination.

Practical knowledge also enhances the quality of exploration. Navigating transportation options, understanding the layout of neighborhoods, and learning about local dining customs or peak visiting times enables travelers to optimize their experiences. Insightful tips on when to visit popular attractions, how to avoid crowds, and which off-the-beaten-path sites offer authentic engagement help ensure that excursions are both efficient and rewarding. Attention to these logistical details transforms sightseeing from a series of tasks into a seamless journey, allowing travelers to immerse themselves fully in their surroundings without undue stress or distraction.

Food and drink play a critical role in discovering a locale. Exploring local markets, sampling street foods, and visiting regional cafés or taverns provides a sensory connection to the area. Culinary experiences reveal more than flavor; they reflect cultural history, seasonal abundance, and the artistry of local producers. Understanding what ingredients are native, how traditional recipes have evolved, and how dining customs shape social interactions allows travelers to experience a destination through taste, aroma, and ritual. These culinary encounters become part of the narrative of the trip, enriching the stay with moments that are deeply personal, flavorful, and memorable.

Hidden gems—places not widely publicized or frequented by the majority of tourists—often provide the most authentic experiences. Small galleries, family-run shops, quiet parks, or secluded viewpoints can reveal facets of a region that mainstream guides overlook. Engaging with these discoveries requires attentiveness, curiosity, and a willingness to venture beyond the obvious. These experiences reward the traveler with intimacy, privacy, and the thrill of uncovering something uniquely personal, turning ordinary excursions into treasured memories.

In addition, interaction with locals deepens the understanding of a place. Conversations with residents, recommendations from shopkeepers, or casual exchanges in cafés often lead to insights, stories, and experiences that would otherwise remain hidden. Local knowledge provides context, background, and authenticity, helping visitors to navigate both well-known and lesser-known areas in a manner that is respectful and enriching. These connections foster a sense of belonging, even temporarily, and encourage travelers to view the destination through the lens of those who call it home.

Timing and seasonality further influence exploration. Recognizing which months, days, or hours maximize accessibility, natural beauty, or cultural activity allows travelers to make the most of their excursions. Seasonal festivals, agricultural cycles, or local celebrations offer unique windows into the community and landscape, enriching the visit with experiences that cannot be replicated at other times. Observing seasonal changes in nature, architecture, or social patterns adds depth to travel, cultivating an appreciation for the cyclical rhythms and diversity of a region.

Ultimately, the value of exploring beyond the hotel lies in the creation of memories that engage all senses, broaden understanding, and deepen personal connection. Each walk, conversation, meal, and observation contributes to a composite experience that reflects both the uniqueness of the destination and the individuality of the traveler. A stay is elevated from mere lodging to an immersive journey when exploration is intentional, informed, and mindful, transforming time spent outside the hotel into a rich tapestry of discovery and engagement.

Through careful attention to the environment, cultural context, culinary opportunities, and local insight, travelers craft experiences that are meaningful, memorable, and deeply personal. The spaces beyond the hotel walls become arenas for learning, pleasure, reflection, and connection, allowing guests to leave not just with photographs or souvenirs, but with a profound understanding and appreciation of the place, its people, and its character.

NAVIGATING TRAVEL, DINING, AND CULTURAL ETIQUETTE

Travel in the United Kingdom offers a rich tapestry of experiences shaped not only by landscapes and architecture but also by subtle social norms, dining practices, and cultural expectations. To fully enjoy a journey, an understanding of local etiquette and the rhythm of daily life is essential. This involves an awareness of how people interact in different social settings, the protocols surrounding meals, and the expectations within public spaces, as well as a sensitivity to the nuances that differentiate regions and communities. Mastery of these elements allows visitors to move through the environment with ease and respect, fostering meaningful connections and more rewarding experiences.

Transportation is one of the most immediate and practical aspects of navigating the UK. From bustling metropolitan centers to serene countryside routes, the modes of travel vary widely. Understanding the structure and etiquette of local transit, including trains, buses, taxis, and cycling infrastructure, ensures smoother and more comfortable movement. Train travel, for instance, is highly organized and punctual, with clear signage and ticketing procedures that reward attentiveness. Awareness of queueing practices, boarding etiquette, and seating conventions demonstrates respect for fellow passengers and contributes to a seamless journey. Likewise, navigating city streets on foot or by bicycle requires attentiveness to pedestrian crossings, traffic signals, and local conventions, which often differ from region to region. Engaging responsibly with public transportation and road systems reflects both courtesy and preparedness.

Dining etiquette is another crucial component of travel in the UK. Restaurants, cafés, pubs, and private dining spaces have distinct social codes that travelers benefit from understanding. Punctuality is valued in formal dining situations, and courteous behavior toward staff and fellow guests is expected. Meal pacing, ordering conventions, and tipping practices vary, and knowledge of these subtleties enhances the overall experience. For example, in traditional pubs, informal ordering at the bar

is common, while more formal restaurants may involve table service with specific expectations regarding seating, service cues, and payment. Recognizing these distinctions allows travelers to engage comfortably and appropriately, avoiding potential social friction and enhancing personal enjoyment.

Cultural etiquette extends beyond dining and transportation to encompass broader social interactions. Politeness, respect for personal space, and attentiveness to local customs are appreciated in virtually every context, from urban neighborhoods to rural villages. Regional variations in speech, behavior, and expectations often reflect historical and cultural influences, providing rich insight for those who observe with curiosity and sensitivity. Listening attentively, expressing gratitude, and engaging in small but thoughtful gestures, such as holding doors or offering assistance, signal awareness and appreciation for local norms. These behaviors foster goodwill, opening opportunities for positive social interactions and authentic connections that enrich the travel experience.

The UK's diverse cultural landscape means that travel etiquette may vary according to context. Urban centers such as London, Edinburgh, and Manchester have cosmopolitan environments where international norms intersect with local customs, requiring flexibility and attentiveness. Smaller towns and rural regions often maintain stronger adherence to traditional customs and community rhythms, rewarding travelers who respect quieter spaces and more deliberate social interactions. In all settings, sensitivity to noise, observance of shared spaces, and adherence to local conventions help maintain harmony and enhance the quality of experiences for both visitors and residents.

Food culture in the UK also reflects regional diversity, with dining experiences ranging from contemporary gastro-pubs and Michelin-starred restaurants to local bakeries, farmers' markets, and tea rooms. Understanding how meals are typically structured, which dishes are emblematic of particular areas, and how to engage with local culinary traditions adds depth to the experience. Engaging respectfully with chefs, hosts, and staff, while showing appreciation for regional specialties and dining customs, transforms a meal from a simple act of nourishment into a cultural encounter that reflects the history, innovation, and identity of the locality.

Accommodation etiquette plays a complementary role in navigating hospitality. Guests are expected to respect property rules, maintain considerate noise levels, and treat facilities with care. Communicating clearly with hotel staff, adhering to check-in and check-out procedures, and observing local norms regarding tipping and interaction ensure smoother and more pleasant stays. Attentiveness to these details conveys respect for both the property and the community it inhabits, creating a foundation for a comfortable and mutually positive experience.

Travel planning, including awareness of peak periods, seasonal events, and public holidays, further enhances navigation of local environments. Awareness of when attractions are most crowded, how traffic flows during key times, and the timing of local festivals or cultural events allows travelers to maximize opportunities while avoiding unnecessary stress. Flexibility and adaptability, combined with informed

planning, enable visitors to experience destinations fully without becoming overwhelmed or inadvertently causing disruption to local routines.

Additionally, exploring cultural venues such as museums, theaters, historic sites, and galleries requires sensitivity to etiquette specific to each context. Observing quiet in sacred or contemplative spaces, refraining from intrusive photography, and respecting accessibility considerations demonstrates respect for both the institution and other patrons. By engaging responsibly in these spaces, travelers deepen their appreciation of local heritage, artistic expression, and historical context.

Finally, successful navigation of travel, dining, and cultural etiquette in the UK is underpinned by curiosity, observation, and a willingness to learn. Travelers who approach each interaction and environment with attentiveness, empathy, and respect are rewarded with richer experiences, meaningful connections, and a deeper understanding of the communities they visit. The combination of practical knowledge, cultural sensitivity, and active engagement transforms a trip from a sequence of visits into a holistic journey, creating lasting memories rooted in both discovery and shared human experience.

HOW TO LEAVE CONSTRUCTIVE GUEST FEEDBACK

Providing feedback after a stay at a hotel is a vital part of modern travel. It serves not only as a reflection of a guest's personal experience but also as a tool for improving services, guiding future travelers, and shaping the broader hospitality industry. Constructive feedback is effective because it balances honesty with thoughtfulness, offering clear observations without being unnecessarily harsh or inflammatory. It conveys useful insights to both hotel staff and potential visitors, creating a mutually beneficial exchange that enhances the overall travel ecosystem.

The process begins with careful observation. Attentive guests notice details beyond the surface, from the state of rooms and cleanliness of common areas to the responsiveness of staff and the quality of amenities. Every element contributes to the overall impression of a hotel, and documenting these observations accurately is essential for meaningful feedback. It is not simply a matter of stating likes or dislikes; instead, a considered reflection on what aspects were exemplary and which areas fell short allows for more actionable and credible input. Guests who take the time to note specifics rather than generalities provide a clearer picture of their experience.

Clarity and specificity are central to effective feedback. Vague statements, such as "the hotel was nice" or "the staff were unfriendly," offer limited value. Instead, it is important to describe exactly what contributed to the positive or negative experience. For example, noting that the housekeeping service was prompt and thorough, or that the check-in process was delayed and disorganized, conveys meaningful information that hotel management can address. This approach ensures that feedback is not only readable and understandable but also directly useful for operational improvements.

Tone is another crucial consideration. Constructive feedback should be professional, courteous, and balanced. Even when highlighting shortcomings, a

respectful approach ensures that the message is received in a way that encourages improvement rather than defensiveness. Emphasizing positive aspects alongside areas for growth helps frame the feedback in a constructive manner. Recognizing the efforts of staff who went above and beyond or acknowledging facilities that exceeded expectations can soften the impact of criticism, making it more likely that suggestions for improvement are taken seriously.

Timing also plays a role in effectiveness. Providing feedback soon after the stay ensures that impressions are fresh and details are accurate. Immediate reflections capture nuances that may fade over time, from the warmth of staff interactions to the condition of amenities. However, it is equally important to ensure that feedback is considered rather than reactive. Emotional responses to minor inconveniences may cloud judgment, so taking a moment to reflect before submitting feedback can enhance its clarity and balance.

The platform through which feedback is communicated influences its impact. Direct communication with hotel management, either in person or via email, allows for a personal touch and often leads to quicker responses. Online review platforms, while public and widely visible, require thoughtful construction to ensure that the feedback is constructive rather than merely emotive. Balancing honesty with respect is critical, as online reviews influence not only hotel operations but also the decisions of other travelers. The most effective feedback communicates experiences clearly, accurately, and respectfully across any medium.

In addition to noting specific experiences, constructive feedback benefits from providing context. Explaining circumstances that may have influenced the experience—such as arriving during peak seasons, weather-related disruptions, or personal expectations—helps hotel staff interpret observations appropriately. Contextual feedback allows management to distinguish between factors within their control and those that are external, making it easier to implement meaningful changes. It also enhances the credibility of the review, demonstrating that the guest has thoughtfully considered the situation rather than responding impulsively.

An important aspect of leaving feedback is focusing on solutions rather than only criticism. Suggestions for improvement, when offered respectfully, provide actionable guidance. For instance, if a guest encounters slow service at breakfast, recommending the addition of more staff during peak hours is more productive than simply expressing frustration. Solution-oriented feedback demonstrates engagement, thoughtfulness, and a desire to help improve the experience for future guests. This approach strengthens the relationship between guests and hotel staff and encourages a culture of continuous enhancement within the hospitality industry.

Ethical considerations also play a role in providing feedback. Honesty and fairness are paramount. Fabricated complaints or exaggerated praise undermine credibility and can harm both the hotel and other travelers seeking guidance. Constructive feedback requires integrity, ensuring that observations are genuine reflections of personal experience. By being truthful and balanced, guests contribute to an

ecosystem of trust and accountability in which hotels can genuinely benefit from insights and future travelers can make informed decisions.

Finally, the broader purpose of constructive feedback extends beyond the immediate stay. Well-articulated observations influence not only hotel operations but also the standards of the hospitality sector as a whole. By providing thoughtful, detailed, and balanced feedback, guests play a role in elevating service standards, encouraging excellence, and guiding innovation in the industry. Feedback becomes a tool for dialogue, learning, and mutual benefit, reinforcing the connection between travelers and the hospitality experience while helping others navigate choices with greater confidence.

Through attentive observation, clarity, respectful tone, timely submission, contextualization, solution-oriented suggestions, and ethical integrity, constructive guest feedback becomes an essential element of travel. It strengthens communication between visitors and hospitality providers, enhances the quality of experiences, and fosters an environment of continuous improvement. The power of thoughtful feedback lies in its ability to transform individual experiences into meaningful contributions that benefit future travelers, hotel staff, and the industry at large.

CHAPTER 8

THE FUTURE OF GREAT HOSPITALITY

DIGITAL TOOLS AND SMART GUEST EXPERIENCES

In today's hospitality world, digital tools have completely transformed how travelers plan, book, and enjoy their stays, elevating every aspect of the guest experience. Technology now allows visitors to navigate reservations, access hotel services, and personalize their accommodations with ease, ensuring comfort, quality, and memorable experiences from start to finish.

Booking platforms and mobile applications are central to this transformation. Websites and apps such as Booking.com, Expedia, Hotels.com, and Airbnb provide travelers with extensive options across the United Kingdom, allowing them to filter hotels by location, price, amenities, guest ratings, and unique features. Many hotels also offer their own mobile apps, giving guests access to direct booking, loyalty programs, exclusive promotions, and early availability of new rooms. These tools enable travelers to compare options efficiently, make informed choices, and secure reservations confidently. Features such as interactive maps, real-time availability, and instant confirmations further streamline the process, while app-based customer support ensures assistance is always within reach.

Beyond booking, digital technology enhances every stage of the stay. Contactless check-in, digital room keys, and self-service kiosks reduce waiting times and increase privacy, creating a smoother arrival experience. In-room smart systems let guests control lighting, temperature, and entertainment with precision, allowing each stay to be customized for comfort and convenience. These technologies not only provide convenience but also contribute to safety and hygiene, particularly in scenarios where minimal contact is preferred.

Digital concierge services have also redefined the way travelers interact with their surroundings. Hotel apps allow guests to reserve spa treatments, book dining experiences, schedule activities, and explore local attractions, all from the convenience of their smartphones. Many apps provide tailored recommendations based on individual preferences, guiding travelers to the most authentic and rewarding experiences nearby. This integration of hotel services and local exploration transforms a simple stay into a fully immersive journey, enhancing both enjoyment and satisfaction.

Online reviews and social media play a critical role in shaping informed decisions. Platforms such as TripAdvisor, Google Reviews, and official hotel social media pages offer firsthand insights from other guests, highlighting strengths, amenities, and overall experiences. While the abundance of reviews can be overwhelming, discerning travelers focus on consistent patterns rather than isolated opinions. By

combining curated recommendations with digital feedback, guests gain confidence that their selections will meet high standards of comfort, service, and authenticity.

Personalization has become a defining feature of modern hospitality. Hotels increasingly use data from booking platforms and apps to anticipate guest preferences, from preferred room types and dining choices to suggested activities. Notifications about special offers, loyalty rewards, and tailored itineraries create a sense of individualized service that makes each stay unique. Guests enjoy accommodations that are responsive to their needs, balancing luxury, convenience, and personal attention for a more satisfying experience.

Strategic use of digital tools also optimizes travel efficiency and value. Guests can monitor seasonal pricing, receive alerts for deals, and identify optimal booking windows, ensuring cost-effective planning without compromising quality. App-based loyalty programs track rewards, offer upgrades, and provide exclusive packages, maximizing the benefits of travel while maintaining comfort and convenience.

Digital tools extend their impact even after the stay ends. Surveys, feedback forms, and app-based reviews allow guests to share experiences directly with hotel management, promoting continuous improvement in service standards. This engagement fosters a cycle of refinement that benefits future guests and encourages a culture of attentive, guest-centered hospitality.

Overall, the combination of booking platforms, hotel apps, smart room technologies, concierge services, online reviews, and personalization has reshaped expectations for modern travelers. Mastering these tools empowers guests to plan efficiently, enjoy tailored experiences, and explore destinations with confidence. Digital tools enhance—not replace—the human touch of hospitality, ensuring stays are seamless, comfortable, and memorable, meeting the highest standards that today's discerning travelers expect.

THE RISE OF PERSONALIZED TRAVEL

Travel in the modern era has transformed dramatically, evolving from standardized, one-size-fits-all experiences into journeys that are increasingly tailored to the preferences, needs, and lifestyles of individual travelers. Today's guests seek more than just accommodation; they desire experiences that are meaningful, immersive, and reflective of their personal interests. This evolution has reshaped the hospitality landscape, compelling hotels and service providers to develop strategies that prioritize individuality and personalized attention.

Personalized travel begins with understanding the guest at a granular level. Hotels are leveraging data from multiple sources, including prior visits, booking patterns, and stated preferences, to anticipate needs and craft experiences that are uniquely suited to each visitor. This might involve tailoring room arrangements to a traveler's comfort preferences, preparing special dietary options in advance, or suggesting activities that align with known interests. By focusing on the guest as an individual rather than treating them as part of a generic group, hospitality providers create an

elevated sense of care and connection that significantly enhances the overall experience.

Technology plays a central role in enabling this personalized approach. Mobile applications, online platforms, and hotel-specific apps allow travelers to select preferences before arrival, ranging from room type and bed configuration to in-room temperature, lighting, and entertainment options. These systems empower guests to shape their environment to their liking, giving them control over details that directly impact comfort and satisfaction. Hotels that offer intuitive, responsive digital tools enable travelers to feel empowered and valued, turning routine stays into seamless, highly tailored experiences.

Beyond room customization, digital personalization extends to the broader journey. Guests can access curated recommendations for dining, cultural activities, and local attractions based on their profiles and past behaviors. Advanced algorithms analyze preferences and suggest options that match individual tastes, from art exhibitions and historical tours to outdoor adventures and culinary experiences. These intelligent systems ensure that every moment of a trip, from arrival to departure, aligns with the traveler's personal desires, enhancing engagement and satisfaction.

Loyalty programs are also integral to personalized travel. By tracking guest history and recognizing patterns, hotels can deliver tailored benefits such as preferred room assignments, complimentary services, and exclusive offers. This kind of attention fosters a sense of recognition and loyalty, encouraging repeat visits and long-term relationships. Guests perceive these gestures as thoughtful, reinforcing a connection that extends beyond transactional interactions to a more meaningful, relationship-based hospitality experience.

Personalized travel is not limited to individual travelers; it is equally relevant for families, groups, and multi-generational parties. Hotels are increasingly designing experiences that accommodate the diverse needs of all members of a group. This may involve adjusting room layouts, arranging family-friendly activities, coordinating group dining options, or offering packages that suit varying age groups and interests. By creating tailored solutions for every guest, properties provide convenience, comfort, and enjoyment, making the travel experience smoother and more fulfilling for all involved.

The trend toward personalization also encompasses ethical and sustainable considerations. Guests increasingly expect hotels to align with their values, offering eco-friendly accommodations, locally sourced food, and community-focused experiences. By understanding and integrating these priorities into the guest experience, hotels can provide stays that resonate on both a personal and ethical level, ensuring that each visit aligns with individual principles and enhances the overall sense of purpose and satisfaction.

Predictive analytics and artificial intelligence have emerged as vital tools in delivering personalized travel. These technologies allow hotels to anticipate guest needs before they are even expressed, identifying trends and preferences that inform proactive

service. For instance, AI can recommend upgrades, suggest experiences likely to be enjoyed, or notify guests about exclusive events based on their profiles. The ability to anticipate and respond to guest preferences in real time creates a sense of thoughtful attentiveness, heightening the perception of care and ensuring that every interaction feels meaningful and relevant.

Communication is another cornerstone of personalized travel. Modern hotels utilize multiple channels—such as messaging apps, emails, and in-app notifications—to maintain continuous engagement with guests. This enables real-time adjustments, responsive assistance, and proactive guidance throughout the stay. By facilitating ongoing dialogue, hotels can ensure that travelers feel heard, understood, and supported, contributing to a seamless and satisfying experience from start to finish.

The rise of personalized travel reflects a fundamental shift in what travelers value. Standardized experiences are no longer sufficient; guests prioritize authenticity, engagement, and experiences that reflect their unique tastes and goals. Hotels that embrace personalization distinguish themselves in a crowded marketplace, delivering comfort, quality, and memorable experiences that leave a lasting impression. The combination of data-driven insights, technology-enabled customization, and attentive human service creates a new standard for modern hospitality, where every stay is designed to meet the highest expectations of individual travelers.

Ultimately, personalized travel redefines the notion of hospitality, making each journey distinctive and meaningful. By leveraging digital tools, anticipating needs, and offering experiences aligned with guest values and preferences, hotels can provide stays that are both exceptional and unforgettable. This approach ensures that travel is no longer just about reaching a destination; it is about engaging fully with the environment, culture, and services in a way that resonates personally, leaving a lasting impression that goes far beyond the duration of the visit.

PRESERVING BRITISH WARMTH IN A TECH-DRIVEN WORLD

The rapid evolution of technology has transformed nearly every aspect of the modern hospitality industry, from booking and check-in processes to in-room automation and personalized digital services. While these innovations provide convenience, efficiency, and unparalleled customization, they also present a challenge: how to maintain the human warmth and quintessential British hospitality that travelers expect and cherish. Striking a balance between cutting-edge technological solutions and the timeless, personal touches that define memorable stays has become a central focus for hotels seeking to provide exceptional experiences.

At the heart of preserving British warmth is the recognition that technology, while powerful, is a tool rather than a replacement for genuine human interaction. Guests still value smiles, attentiveness, and the thoughtful gestures that create a sense of welcome and belonging. The role of staff has therefore evolved rather than diminished. Front-of-house personnel, concierge teams, and in-room service

providers are increasingly trained to integrate technology seamlessly into their interactions, using digital tools to enhance service without diminishing personal connection. For example, while a mobile app might allow guests to request extra towels or adjust lighting remotely, staff members can follow up with a friendly greeting or personalized recommendation, bridging the gap between efficiency and emotional engagement.

British hospitality has long been characterized by a blend of politeness, discretion, and attentive service. Preserving these qualities in a technology-driven environment requires careful design of both digital and physical experiences. Hotels are creating systems that anticipate needs, provide useful information, and streamline routine tasks, while ensuring that these enhancements do not feel impersonal or transactional. Smart room controls, digital check-ins, and virtual concierges are designed to reduce friction and allow staff to focus on delivering meaningful human interactions. The goal is to ensure that technology supports rather than supplants the traditional virtues of care, attentiveness, and genuine concern for guest comfort.

Personalization plays a critical role in sustaining warmth in a digital world. Data-driven insights allow hotels to understand guest preferences and behaviors, enabling service providers to respond with precision and empathy. A guest's favorite newspaper, preferred room temperature, or dietary considerations can be anticipated and addressed before they are explicitly requested. Yet, it is the manner in which this information is applied that preserves the sense of British hospitality. Thoughtful notes, subtle gestures, and personalized recommendations transform data into meaningful experiences, reinforcing the perception that the guest is valued as an individual rather than treated as a statistic.

Maintaining human warmth also involves preserving traditions and cultural nuances that are uniquely British. From afternoon tea in a sunlit lounge to attentive guidance on local customs, hotels are finding ways to combine heritage with modern convenience. These traditions create a sense of place and identity that technology alone cannot replicate. Digital systems may inform guests of tea service hours or nearby historic attractions, but it is the staff who deliver the experience with charm, professionalism, and grace, ensuring that the richness of British hospitality remains palpable.

Community and social interaction are other critical aspects of warmth that hotels are keen to maintain. Modern travelers often seek not only comfort but also connection—with staff, fellow guests, and the surrounding community. Hotels are leveraging technology to enhance these connections rather than replace them. For instance, digital event boards, mobile chat groups, and interactive apps provide platforms for guests to discover social opportunities, book shared experiences, or engage with local cultural events, while human staff facilitate genuine connections and ensure that social interactions remain personal and meaningful.

Even as digital tools become more sophisticated, the emphasis on attentiveness and presence remains paramount. In a world where automated systems can anticipate nearly every practical need, the ability of staff to engage in intuitive, empathetic

service distinguishes exceptional hospitality. Warm greetings, subtle attention to mood and body language, and the capacity to respond thoughtfully to unanticipated requests are all hallmarks of British service that cannot be automated. Technology should be leveraged to free staff from routine tasks so that they can devote more energy to these human-centered aspects of care.

The training and culture of hotel staff are therefore central to preserving warmth. Hotels invest in programs that combine technological literacy with soft skills, ensuring that personnel can navigate digital systems while remaining emotionally intelligent, observant, and personable. Employees learn to integrate automation and digital convenience seamlessly into the guest experience, providing contextually appropriate support that enhances satisfaction without detracting from personal interaction. In effect, technology becomes a silent partner, facilitating attentiveness rather than overshadowing it.

Sustainability and ethical practices also intersect with warmth and personal engagement. Modern travelers often seek to make conscientious choices, and hotels that provide transparent, accessible information through digital platforms empower guests to act in alignment with their values. This not only demonstrates respect and responsiveness but also fosters a sense of trust and mutual understanding, reinforcing the perception of genuine care. When technology is used to support ethical decision-making and sustainability, it complements human hospitality rather than replacing it.

Ultimately, the key to preserving British warmth in a tech-driven world lies in thoughtful integration. Digital tools, mobile applications, and smart room systems are most effective when they enhance the human dimension of service rather than supplant it. Hotels that prioritize training, culture, and the thoughtful application of technology create experiences that are efficient, personalized, and emotionally resonant. Guests leave not only with memories of convenience and comfort but also with an enduring impression of attentiveness, charm, and care—qualities that define British hospitality.

As travelers increasingly expect seamless, tech-enabled services, the hotels that succeed are those that can combine innovation with heart. The warmth of a smile, the intuition of a well-trained staff member, and the attentiveness to individual needs are all enhanced—not diminished—by technology. By preserving these qualities, hotels ensure that every interaction, from check-in to check-out, is imbued with a sense of personal connection, creating experiences that are not only convenient and modern but also memorable, meaningful, and distinctly British.

In a landscape defined by rapid technological advancement, the challenge and opportunity for British hospitality is clear: embrace innovation while remaining steadfast in the traditions of attentiveness, charm, and personal care. Technology can streamline, anticipate, and enhance, but it is the human touch that leaves an indelible impression. Travelers today, and for generations to come, will continue to cherish stays where digital efficiency and emotional warmth coexist, creating a standard of hospitality that is both modern and authentically British.

APPENDICES

QUICK REFERENCE GAZETTE INDEX BY REGION

England – South East & London

- **London**
  - The Grand Kensington Hotel – 41 Kensington High Street, W8 5ED
  - The Savile Town Boutique Inn – 22 Savile Row, W1S 3PR
  - Claridge's Retreat – 63 Brook Street, W1K 4HR
- **Chipping Campden, Cotswolds**
  - The Cotswolds Manor House – Church Street, GL55 6AP
- **Bath, Somerset**
  - Bath Spa Hotel – 7 Pierrepont Street, BA1 1LB
- **Chalfont St. Giles, Buckinghamshire**
  - The Chilterns Country Lodge – High Wycombe Road, HP8 4QB
- **Brighton, East Sussex**
  - Brighton Seafront Hotel – 1 Marine Parade, BN2 1TL
- **Henley-on-Thames, Oxfordshire**
  - The Henley Riverside Inn – Station Road, RG9 1AY
- **Oxford, Oxfordshire**
  - Oxfordshire Countryside Lodge – 15 Church Lane, OX1 4AJ
- **Canterbury, Kent**
  - Canterbury Heritage Hotel – 2 Palace Street, CT1 2DR

England – South West

- **St. Ives, Cornwall**
  - St. Ives Coastal Haven – Fore Street, TR26 1HN
- **Totnes, Devon**
  - Devonshire Countryside Inn – 14 High Street, TQ9 5RF
- **Glastonbury, Somerset**
  - The Somerset Orchard Retreat – Orchard Lane, BA6 9EL

- **Dorchester, Dorset**
  - o   Dorset Cliffside Hotel – Cliff Road, DT1 1TG
- **Penzance, Cornwall**
  - o   The Cornish Hideaway – 8 Harbour Street, TR18 2SH

England – Midlands

- **Stratford-upon-Avon, Warwickshire**
  - o   Avon Boutique Hotel – Henley Street, CV37 6QQ
- **Nottingham, Nottinghamshire**
  - o   Sherwood Urban Retreat – Castle Road, NG1 6EY
- **Leicester, Leicestershire**
  - o   Leicester Riverside Hotel – Highcross Street, LE1 4LB
- **Birmingham, West Midlands**
  - o   Birmingham City Elegance – Corporation Street, B2 4AD
- **Derby, Derbyshire**
  - o   Peak District Country Lodge – Matlock Road, DE4 3NR

England – North

- **York, North Yorkshire**
  - o   York Heritage Inn – Micklegate, YO1 6LE
- **Harrogate, North Yorkshire**
  - o   Harrogate Boutique Suites – James Street, HG1 1EN
- **Lake District, Cumbria**
  - o   Lakeview Retreat – Windermere Road, LA23 1AZ
- **Newcastle, Tyne and Wear**
  - o   Newcastle Riverside Hotel – Quayside, NE1 3DY
- **Manchester, Greater Manchester**
  - o   Manchester Urban Hideaway – King Street, M2 4ER

Scotland

- **Edinburgh**
  - o   Edinburgh Castle View Hotel – Castlehill, EH1 2ND

- o Royal Mile Boutique Inn – High Street, EH1 1SG
- **Glasgow**
  - o Glasgow City Chic Hotel – Buchanan Street, G1 3AJ
- **Highlands**
  - o Highland Luxury Lodge – Inverness Road, IV3 5NX
  - o Lochside Retreat – Fort William Road, PH33 6RN
- **Isle of Skye**
  - o Skye Coastal Haven – Portree, IV51 9EX

Wales

- **Cardiff**
  - o Cardiff Central Boutique Hotel – Castle Street, CF10 1AX
- **Pembrokeshire**
  - o Coastal Charm Inn – St. David's Road, SA62 6BE
- **Snowdonia**
  - o Snowdonia Mountain Lodge – Betws-y-Coed, LL24 0AA
- **Gower Peninsula**
  - o Gower Coastal Retreat – Mumbles Road, SA3 4AB

Northern Ireland

- **Belfast**
  - o Belfast City Chic Hotel – Donegall Square, BT1 5GS
- **Countryside & Coastal**
  - o Ulster Countryside Lodge – Hillsborough Road, BT26 6QL
  - o Coastal Haven Retreat – Newcastle Road, BT33 0PH
- **Spa & Wellness**
  - o Lough Neagh Riverside Hotel – Antrim Road, BT41 2NQ

AWARDS, RECOGNITIONS, AND NEW OPENINGS FOR 2025–2026

Prestigious Hotel Awards and Recognitions

The UK hospitality industry has witnessed a series of esteemed accolades in 2025, highlighting excellence across various facets of hotel operations.

- **AA Hospitality Awards 2025**: Held on September 22 at the JW Marriott Grosvenor House, London, the AA Hospitality Awards celebrated the pinnacle of British hospitality. Categories included the coveted *AA Hotel of the Year England*, which was awarded to The Cavendish Hotel, and the introduction of the *AA Rising Star Award*, recognizing emerging talents in the industry.

- **Michelin Guide Hotel Keys**: In October, the Michelin Guide introduced its hotel keys, akin to Michelin stars for restaurants. The UK saw 124 hotels honored, with 12 receiving three keys, 38 two keys, and 74 one key. Notably, Saltmoore in Whitby and Moor Hall in Oughton were among the new recipients of two Michelin keys.

- **Condé Nast Traveler Readers' Choice Awards 2025**: Condé Nast Traveler unveiled its annual list of top hotels, with Foxhill Manor in Broadway and Lucknam Park Hotel & Spa in Chippenham securing the top two spots in the UK category.

- **VisitEngland Awards for Excellence 2025**: Recognizing outstanding contributions to England's tourism sector, these awards highlighted exceptional hotels, attractions, and experiences, underscoring the nation's commitment to quality and innovation in hospitality.

Noteworthy New Hotel Openings in 2025

The year 2025 has seen a surge in innovative hotel openings across the UK, catering to diverse traveler preferences and setting new standards in luxury and design.

- **Hyatt Regency London Olympia**: Scheduled for a mid-2025 launch, this hotel is part of the redevelopment of the iconic Olympia London exhibition site. It will feature 196 guest rooms and four meeting rooms, positioning itself as a hub of refined comfort and connectivity.

- **The Newman Hotel, London**: Opening in Summer 2025, this boutique hotel near Oxford Street will offer 81 rooms and suites with contemporary Art Deco designs. Amenities will include Brasserie Adeline, Gambit Bar, and a Nordic-inspired spa with a hydrotherapy pool.

- **Six Senses London**: Set to debut in 2025, this wellness-focused hotel aims to provide a serene escape within the bustling city, offering holistic treatments and sustainable luxury accommodations.

- **Cambridge House, Auberge Resorts Collection**: Marking the celebrated hospitality brand's UK debut, this property will bring a blend of heritage and modern luxury to the city, featuring refined interiors and exceptional service.

- **Rosewood Amsterdam**: Poised to become the epitome of luxury in the Netherlands, this opulent retreat will offer lavishly appointed rooms,

world-class dining, and unparalleled wellness facilities, embodying the pinnacle of luxury and timeless beauty.

Emerging Trends in UK Hospitality

The UK hospitality landscape in 2025 is characterized by several emerging trends that reflect changing consumer preferences and industry innovations.

- **Sustainability Initiatives**: Hotels are increasingly adopting eco-friendly practices, from sustainable building materials to energy-efficient operations, aligning with the growing demand for environmentally conscious travel options.

- **Technology Integration**: The incorporation of smart technologies, such as mobile check-ins, room automation, and AI-driven concierge services, is enhancing guest experiences and operational efficiency.

- **Wellness Tourism**: There is a notable rise in wellness-focused accommodations, offering services like spa treatments, yoga sessions, and healthy dining options to cater to health-conscious travelers.

- **Boutique and Independent Hotels**: Travelers are seeking unique, personalized experiences, leading to a surge in popularity of boutique and independent hotels that offer distinctive designs and tailored services.

USEFUL TRAVEL RESOURCES AND CONTACT INFORMATION

Government and Official Travel Resources

- **VisitBritain / VisitEngland**
  Website: www.visitbritain.com
  Contact: +44 (0)207 217 8000
  Description: The official national tourism agency, offering comprehensive travel guides, suggested itineraries, and up-to-date travel advice for destinations across the UK, including regional attractions and accommodations.

- **Transport for London (TfL)**
  Website: www.tfl.gov.uk
  Contact: +44 (0)343 222 1234
  Description: Essential for navigating London's public transportation, including buses, the Underground, and river services. Provides journey planning tools, live updates, and accessibility information.

- **National Rail Enquiries**
  Website: www.nationalrail.co.uk
  Contact: +44 (0)8457 484950
  Description: Offers nationwide rail schedules, booking options, and travel

advice for train journeys across England, Scotland, Wales, and Northern Ireland.

- **AA (Automobile Association)**
  Website: www.theaa.com
  Contact: +44 (0)1628 427700
  Description: Provides reliable travel maps, road condition updates, and membership-based discounts for accommodations, driving routes, and roadside assistance services.

- **Highways England**
  Website: www.highwaysengland.co.uk
  Contact: +44 (0)300 123 5000
  Description: Updated travel information and alerts for major road networks across England, ideal for those planning self-drive trips to hotels and regional destinations.

Accommodation Booking and Review Platforms

- **Booking.com**
  Website: www.booking.com
  Contact: Available via the website's support portal
  Description: Offers extensive listings of hotels, inns, and B&Bs throughout the UK, complete with verified guest reviews, ratings, and real-time availability.

- **Expedia UK**
  Website: www.expedia.co.uk
  Contact: +44 (0)203 027 0055
  Description: Provides hotel bookings, vacation packages, flights, and car rentals, with special deals and loyalty rewards.

- **Tripadvisor**
  Website: www.tripadvisor.co.uk
  Contact: Available via the website's help center
  Description: A trusted source for user-generated reviews, top-rated hotels, and traveler tips, including nearby restaurants and attractions.

- **Hotels.com**
  Website: www.hotels.com
  Contact: +44 (0)808 238 8088
  Description: Lists thousands of properties across the UK, featuring reward programs and flexible booking options for travelers seeking comfort and value.

- **Airbnb**
  Website: www.airbnb.co.uk

Contact: +44 (0)203 318 1115

Description: Provides unique stays including boutique apartments, countryside cottages, and city homes, often ideal for travelers seeking an alternative to traditional hotels.

Travel Safety and Emergency Services

- **UK Emergency Services**
  Dial: 999
  Description: For urgent police, fire, or medical assistance anywhere in the UK.

- **UK Non-Emergency Police**
  Dial: 101
  Description: Contact for non-urgent police inquiries, lost property, or travel safety guidance.

- **NHS 111**
  Website: www.111.nhs.uk
  Description: Provides 24/7 health advice and guidance for minor illnesses or travel-related health concerns.

- **Foreign & Commonwealth Office (FCO) Travel Advice**
  Website: www.gov.uk/foreign-travel-advice
  Description: Offers guidance on travel safety, local regulations, and health advisories for international visitors in the UK.

Tourist and Cultural Information Centers

- **London Tourist Information Centre**
  Location: 1 Piccadilly, London W1J 0DA
  Contact: +44 (0)20 7499 2424
  Description: Provides maps, guides, tickets for attractions, and expert advice for navigating London and nearby destinations.

- **Edinburgh Visitor Centre**
  Location: 133 Princes Street, Edinburgh EH2 4AD
  Contact: +44 (0)131 473 3850
  Description: Offers recommendations for accommodations, tours, and cultural events throughout Edinburgh and Scotland.

- **Cardiff Central Visitor Centre**
  Location: 2 Westgate Street, Cardiff CF10 1DD
  Contact: +44 (0)29 2087 8100
  Description: Central hub for travel advice, tickets for attractions, and information on local festivals and events in Wales.

- **Belfast Welcome Centre**
  Location: Donegall Square South, Belfast BT1 5GS
  Contact: +44 (0)28 9024 6609
  Description: Provides comprehensive travel information, guided tours, and hotel recommendations across Northern Ireland.

Specialty Travel and Insider Tips

- **National Trust Visitor Services**
  Website: www.nationaltrust.org.uk
  Contact: +44 (0)1733 866 200
  Description: Offers guidance on historic houses, gardens, and heritage sites, including accommodation suggestions near properties.

- **Historic Scotland / Historic Environment Scotland**
  Website: www.historicenvironment.scot
  Contact: +44 (0)131 668 8600
  Description: Provides listings of castles, historic hotels, and visitor experiences with insight into cultural heritage locations.

- **Rail & Coach Passes: BritRail and National Express**
  Websites: www.britrail.com | www.nationalexpress.com
  Contact: +44 (0)845 602 2939 (BritRail) | +44 (0)871 781 8181 (National Express)
  Description: Simplifies multi-city travel by rail or coach, offering passes, schedules, and discounted packages for tourists exploring the UK.

Printed in Dunstable, United Kingdom

72949030R00057